DRAMA
Play, Performance, Perception

Thelma Altshuler
Paula Milton

Miami-Dade Community College

KENDALL/HUNT PUBLISHING COMPANY
2460 Kerper Boulevard,
Dubuque, Iowa 52001

This book has been prepared by Miami-Dade Community College to accompany visual materials produced by the British Broadcasting Company—British Open University.

This book is not considered as a requirement of BOU Course A307.

Copyright © 1979 by Miami-Dade Community College

Library of Congress Catalog Card Number: 78-71649

ISBN 0-8403-1989-4

All rights reserved. No part of this publication may be reproduced, stored in a retrieval system, or transmitted, in any form or by any means, electronic, mechanical, photocopying, recording, or otherwise, without the prior written permission of the copyright owner.

Printed in the United States of America

B 401989 01

Contents

Illustrations, **p. iv**
Introduction, **p. v**

MODULE 1. Introduction to Critical Appreciation, p. 1

Miss Julie, **p. 6**
Peer Gynt, **p. 44**

MODULE 2. Playwrights and Plotting, p. 61

The Wild Duck, **p. 66**
The Three Sisters, **p. 82**
The Ghost Sonata, **p. 100**

MODULE 3. Dramatis Personae, p. 115

Oedipus Tyrannus, **p. 119**
Macbeth, **p. 137**
Woyzeck, **p. 178**
St. Joan, **p. 191**
The Venetian Twins, **p. 210**

MODULE 4. The Conventions of Theatre, p. 227

The Way of the World, **p. 231**
Ubu Roi, **p. 259**
Sizwe Bansi Is Dead, **p. 275**
Six Characters in Search of an Author, **p. 283**

Illustrations

Diagram of Changing Theater Conventions, **p. viii**

Scenes from *Peer Gynt*, **pp. 55–57**

Diagram of Plot Structures, **p. 62**

Scenes from *The Wild Duck*, **pp. 75–77**

Scenes from *The Three Sisters*, **pp. 90–92**

Scenes from *The Ghost Sonata*, **pp. 108–110**

Diagram of Greek Theater, **p. 123**

Scenes from *Macbeth*, **pp. 172–174**

Scenes from *Woyzeck*, **pp. 185–187**

Scenes from *St. Joan*, **pp. 206–208**

Sketch of Harlequin, **p. 212**

Scenes from *Way of the World*, **pp. 253–255**

Scenes from *Ubu Roi*, **pp. 270–272**

Introduction

The Prologue: How to Prepare for the Theatre Experience, p. vi
- I. Overview or Syllabus of Material to be Studied, p. vi
- II. On the Differences in Reading and Viewing a Play, p. vii
- III. The Least Demanding Plays: A Word on Melodrama, p. vii
- IV. Looking Below the Surface, p. ix
- V. Plays in Chronological Order, p. xi
- VI. Characters: Remembering Names, p. xi
- VII. The Basic Structure of the Play: Five Questions to Ask Yourself, p. xii
- VIII. Cultural Context: How to Consider the Relationship of History to the Theatre, p. xiv
- IX. Plays in Translation: What Is to Be Considered, p. xv

PROLOGUE

Why people go to a theatre, what they expect from a theatre experience, and how they evaluate this theatre experience are questions which require answers for anyone interested in art. Why play writing is considered both craft and art, what distinguishes drama from theatre, playscript from stageplay, and how story, plot, and dramatic composition relate are questions basic to anyone interested in dramatic literature. Why heroes, heroines, rogues, and villains attract attention and interest, what contribution character makes within the total action of a playscript, and how a playwright creates and reveals character are questions basic to anyone interested in the dynamics of drama. Why understanding conventions[1] directly affects the viewer's ability to appreciate a play, playreader or a playgoer; what constitutes these conventions, and how playwrights use familiar conventions, yet sometimes startle us with new conventions, are questions basic to anyone interested in becoming a spirited, active member of an audience. Why the creative artists of the theatre intrigue us, what comprises the work and creative activity of a team of talented collaborators, and how this collaboration moves from study through rehearsal to performance are questions basic to anyone who seeks to increase his understanding and appreciation of theatre art and playgoing.

With these questions in mind, this course *DRAMA: PLAY, PERFORMANCE, PERCEPTION,* has been designed with four major modules of study: "Introduction to Critical Appreciation"; "Playwrights and Plotting"; "Dramatis Personae: Heroes, Heroines, Rogues, Villains"; and "The Conventions of Theatre."

Module 1 *Introduction to Critical Appreciation* serves as an introduction to the theatre condition and to the theatre experience. A look at *Miss Julie* (Strindberg) in rehearsal enables the viewer to understand more fully the amount of thought and work that goes into a final production. An excerpt from *Peer Gynt* (Ibsen) further illustrates the theatre event.

Module 2 *Playwrights and Plotting* studies the art of arranging dramatic events. It helps the student to differentiate between the classical plot, the geometric plot, the modern episodic plot, and even the plotless plot. Excerpts illustrating the craft and art of dramatic composition are from *The Wild Duck* (Ibsen), *The Three Sisters* (Chekhov), and *The Ghost Sonata* (Strindberg).

Module 3 *Dramatis Personae* continues the process of separating the art of drama into its major components. Here attention is focused on the central characters in a drama. Supporting the concept of character in context are excerpts from *Oedipus Tyrannus* (Sophocles), *Macbeth* (Shakespeare), *Woyzeck* (Buchner), *St. Joan* (Shaw), and *The Venetian Twins* (Goldoni).

Module 4 *The Conventions of Theatre* reminds us that the illusion which is drama uses symbols and takes liberties with reality in order to work its enchantment. Illustrating the variety and the changing nature of conventions are excerpts from *The Way of the World* (Congreve), *Ubu Roi* (Jarry), *Sizwe Bansi Is Dead* (Fugard), and *Six Characters in Search of an Author* (Pirandello).

The title *Drama: Play, Performance, Perception* suggests the format for the text. The opening section, "On Reading and Viewing," serves as an introduction to *drama*. The four module divisions follow, with an introductory essay for each module of study. Emphasis is placed on each *play* within the module. Material on the play, a plot summary, and an article of criticism or a critical review of the play's production are included. To emphasize the performance a list of objectives,

---

1. See page 58 "Stage and Terms" for a definition of "conventions."

program notes, production information, director's notes, and a "Focus in Viewing" section are also included for most of the plays.

Drama: Play, Performance, Perception aims at breaking down the act of viewing into its many facets and then reconstructing the viewing experience so that it is more rewarding and ultimately more entertaining. The text is a supplement to the television broadcasts of fourteen plays that range from classical (B.C.) to revolutionary (1970's).

ON READING AND VIEWING

Some theatre people may argue that plays should be seen, not read. Because most plays were written to be shown to audiences, an individual reader cannot understand a play as he would in the company of others looking at a production. The play in print, according to this argument, is just words waiting for actors, lights, costumes, movement, and audience response. The viewer, who might have laughed at a well-delivered comic line, may smile when he reads the same line, but it is more likely that he will show no outward sign of pleasure. Other viewers affect us, encourage us to show emotions. The reader is usually alone, trying to bring to life characters and dialogue.

Still, there are arguments for reading a play instead of (or in addition to) seeing it performed. One reason is *variety*. The reader has an almost unlimited number of plays from which to choose. Instead of writing for a production of the play at a particular time, he can read what and when he likes. Another reason for reading a play is *timing*. The play reader can read at whatever speed is comfortable, rather than at the pace set by actors. The reader is in control, able to adjust speed according to familiarity and interest. Difficult or particularly enjoyable parts can be reread. In a sense the reader is like the owner of a film projector and a private collection of films with the power to rewind, speed up, or run in slow motion. Reading a play, rather than seeing one, puts the emphasis on *literary* values rather than visual ones. The reader is more conscious of words than is the member of an audience. The reader can savor a line of dialogue for its cleverness, its wisdom, its individual application to life, without outside distractions.

Reading a play is like reading any other work of fiction; the reader can give free rein to imagination. The characters can look and sound almost as the reader wishes—tall, short, fair, dark, graceful, or clumsy. The reader becomes the director of each play, with a perfect cast of imaginary actors.

Watching a play production reduces the range of imagination, but there is the advantage of being able to benefit from the creative imaginations of directors, actors, scene designers, etc. Ideally, one should have the opportunity to view and to read and review.

THE LEAST DEMANDING PLAYS

But *which* play? The easiest plays to read and understand are those which are already familiar because the reader has seen so many like them on stage or screen or television. A private-eye mystery would be easy to read because the reader could fill in details to go with the names of the detective, the victim, the suspects, the police. Backgrounds would be simple, too: an office, a bank, a shopping center, or a hospital room perhaps. Such plays set in modern times, with

viii　Introduction

CONVENTION CHANGES WITH ACTOR-AUDIENCE RELATIONSHIP

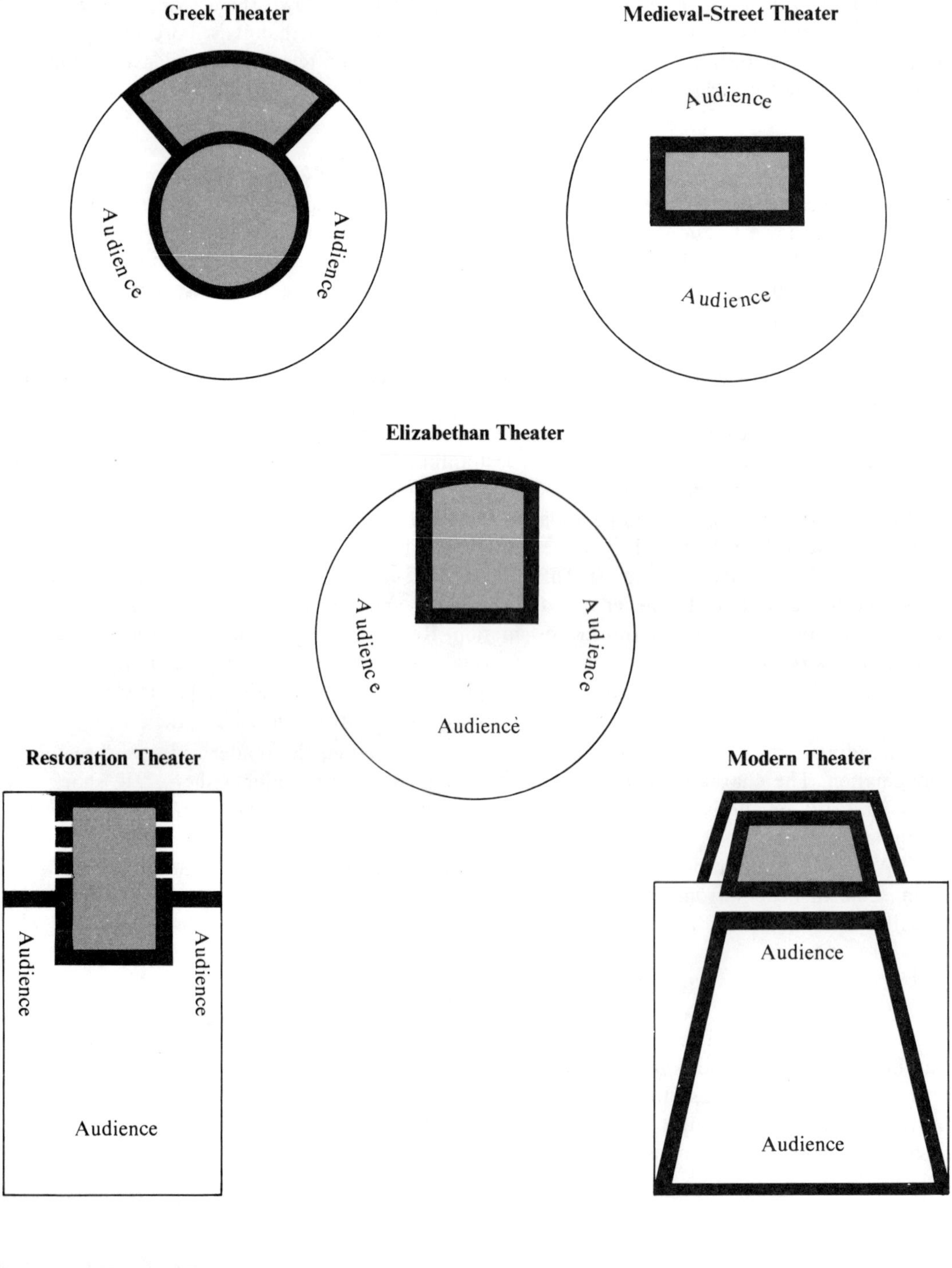

Greek Theater

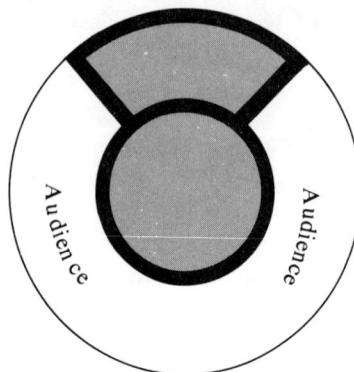

Medieval-Street Theater

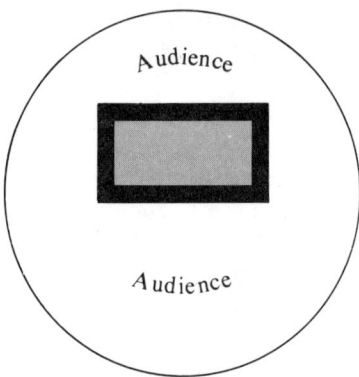

Elizabethan Theater

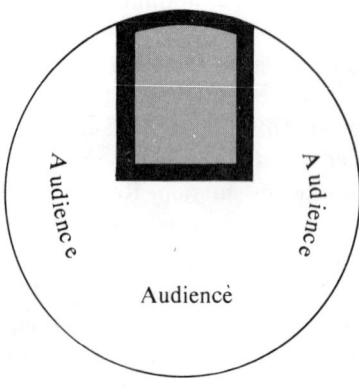

Restoration Theater

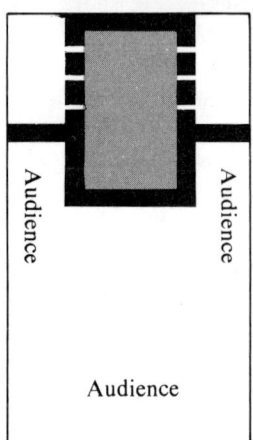

Modern Theater

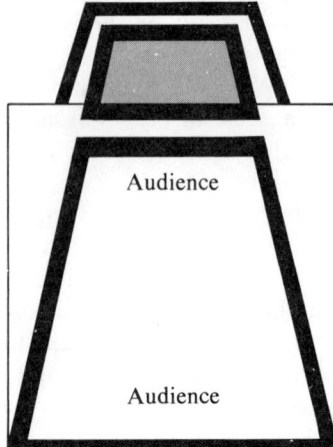

familiar, one-dimensional characters, and with emphasis on action are pleasant diversion. They present little challenge to viewers familiar with the offerings of commercial television.

In many respects the melodramatic play of action is like a comic book. There is no need to linger over dialogue, because it is kept to a minimum: "There's the body . . ." "Let's go . . ." "You can't prove nothin' . . ." "Your one big mistake . . ." "Take that!" Such dialogue would fit easily into the balloons indicating speech of a comic book character. The emphasis is on things—weapons, missing documents, broken glass, etc. The characters are like stick figures who kill or are killed amidst the guns and glass.

Another kind of play emphasizes persons whose words need more careful examination because they are meant to reveal character. These are people, rather than stick figures. They are not "The Boss," "The Hen-pecked Husband," The Hardened Criminal," or "The Hippie." Rather, like real people, they don't fit just one category. In plays emphasizing character, the reader must be on guard against making quick assumptions about what such people would do. He must read, watch, and listen as if waiting to learn more about someone he had recently met. And just as it is impossible to learn about real, live people by making snap judgments, so too in reading a play it would be wrong to decide that all was known on the basis of a page or two. But the playwright gives more clues to character than the real-life counterpart shows.

LOOKING BELOW THE SURFACE

If the reader is uncertain about how much attention should be paid to character, he should try to discover if the speakers are meant to be "real" or stock characters. If a short play is obviously funny, with joke-filled lines, the emphasis should be on the lines themselves, not on the speakers, who are merely there to deliver the laughs. After a few minutes, the reader can recognize the relationship and the fact that it isn't really going anywhere in the sense of character development. If the scene is an office, and the boss is middle-aged and predatory, while the secretary is pretty and flirtatious, the reader can be almost sure that no further attention is needed to the characters as people. They are stock characters who would fit as well on the comic page as in a play. Such characters are fun because they are so exaggerated, but there would be no point in trying to look beneath the surface to analyze them.

Sometimes the playwright deliberately wants to create a stereotype in order to make a serious commentary, as in some of the modern plays: Alfred Jarry's *Ubu Roi* or Luigi Pirandello's *Six Characters in Search of an Author*. Types are used to evoke the universal in a way that more specific identification would not do. The parents could be *any* mother and father in *Six Characters* and the setting could be anywhere. In *Ubu Roi* Ma and Pa are deliberate distortions, obviously unreal. Even the "Kingdom of Poland," as described, is a deliberately fantastic kingdom of cartoon devices with a deliberately undefined king and usurper. These presentations work as long as they are not confused with the "real."

Lengthy explanations of individual lines and scenes are unnecessary for those readers with less than scholarly interest in a play. Still, for most plays—particularly those not written for mass audiences—some explanation is necessary. Excessive background material may be pedantic, but no background material at all can be chaotic; purposes and methods of presentation that are unfamiliar may cause misunderstanding. Much depends upon the nature of the play, the ease or difficulty with which it can be read, and what the reader is expected to do about it later.

Though their devotees may argue otherwise, murder mysteries or romantic comedies written for Broadway can be read with no prior introduction. They can be analyzed and compared by experts who find significance even in a confection designed to be consumed and forgotten—the heroine chose the happy-go-lucky journalist over the rich but stuffy banker, for instance, or the butler did it. Most plays in anthologies of drama, however, are either more serious in content or more difficult for modern readers because customs have changed so much during the intervening years.

Reading such plays with no preparation at all has the appeal of spontaneity and freedom, and all the risk of future blunder—unless one is willing to talk about a play entirely in terms of himself. "I would never have done what that character did" tells that the reader identifies with the character, but one must wonder if that reader really understood the character in context. Still, there is pleasure in reading plays as a pastime. It is the sort of pleasure experienced at an amusement park, where it is enough to enjoy the sights and the sounds without knowing who built the roller coaster or how it works or how long it will probably last. In reading a play designed primarily for amusement, it is possible to go along just for the ride; when it is over, it is then enough to express pleasure or pain with no further discussion beyond "Exciting," "I liked it," "I liked that part where. . ." and so on. Some people leave a restaurant with similar expressions, or a boat show with vague impression of a lot of gleaming metal. People who argue against prior knowledge and analysis are perhaps remembering the uncluttered appreciation of a walk in the country, where there can be delight in the cool air, the sight of a bird, a leaf falling, without knowledge of terms and names. The argument against excessive analysis has been carried to its extreme by those who say that meaning does not exist, that analysis destroys beauty, even that thinking is unnecessary complication.

Such a position is unscholarly, perhaps anarchic. A few "rules" may clarify a work of art. Perhaps one more analogy may be appropriate. While it would be possible for someone who knew no Japanese to enjoy a walk down a street in Tokyo, it would be even more fascinating to be able to understand the meaning of those flashing signs. It would be entertaining to understand how things worked, what went on behind the facade. A visitor entering a temple would be comfortable with some former knowledge. He would know to remove his shoes, cover his head, stand, or kneel as was expected. He would not offend the natives. Those, on the other hand, who do only what is familiar exclude themselves from many of the joys of life.

Considering the theatre, the inflexible person would then be limited to the very familiar plays of popular culture—a musical comedy, a contrived farce, a horror story. He would be limited to his century, or decade, and would hear nothing but some worn-out ideas which would make him wonder why anyone ever considered drama to be an important art form. The more daring reader (who knows to remove his shoes in the temple) would "try out" another century, a demanding playwright with fresh ideas, or a powerful, experimental way of telling a story (if, indeed, the play consists of any story at all).

In this course the student will read excerpts and view varied plays from different periods in theatrical history. The five major historical periods, from which the plays are taken, are Classical, Elizabethan, Neo-classical, 19th Century Realistic, and Modern. Each had its own methods of staging, subject matter, type of dialogue, and audience expectations. But before going into period differences, the student of drama should examine some of the characteristics which all plays have in common: characters, plot, and cultural context.

PLAYS IN CHRONOLOGICAL ORDER

Play	Author	Date of Play	Nationality
Oedipus	Sophocles	430 B.C.	Greek
Macbeth	Shakespeare	1606	English
The Way of the World	Congreve	1700	English
The Venetian Twins	Goldoni	1748	Italian
Woyzeck	Buchner	1837	German
Peer Gynt	Ibsen	1867	Norwegian
The Wild Duck	Ibsen	1884	Norwegian
Miss Julie	Strindberg	1886	Swedish
Ubu Roi	Jarry	1896	French
The Three Sisters	Chekhov	1901	Russian
The Ghost Sonata	Strindberg	1906	Swedish
Six Characters in Search of an Author	Pirandello	1921	Italian
Saint Joan	Shaw	1923	Irish
Sizwe Bansi Is Dead	Fugard	1972	South African

CHARACTERS: REMEMBERING NAMES

In "real" (off-stage) life, meeting people involves a name and a face. We spend about a second hearing the name and a longer time with the person himself. The opposite is true of plays. Most printed plays have a list of characters with some identification next to each name. We must learn to match the identification and the name when reading, to keep the characters straight. The amount of identification depends on the playwright and the customs in effect when the play was written. The identification varies from simply the occupation (king, soldier, servant, etc.) to a fairly long description, as in the plays of George Bernard Shaw, which include appearance, income, and interests. But no matter how much identification there is on the first page, the reader is left with just the name preceding each speech after the page is turned. We are expected to remember who the people are by their names alone. This is difficult for many of us because we are used to seeing a person without a name tag. Playwrights and teachers expect playreaders to link the name with the person. The task is easy when the cast is small and the names have a familiar sound with origins in the reader's own culture. The easiest play to read would have a list of characters with names clearly revealing who they were like "Mr." and "Mrs." followed by a couple of names easily recognized by age and sex. David Rabe's play *Sticks and Bones* went even further. In order to characterize the way the "average" American family greeted a returned veteran, he names his characters "Ozzie," "Harriet," "David," and "Ricky." The major difficulty comes from long lists, foreign-sounding names, and abbreviations.

When reading a play with a long list of names, the student might find it helpful to copy the list and keep it handy while reading. This sounds tedious, but it is even more tedious to keep flipping back to the opening page. This is particularly helpful if the characters change roles from time to time. Writers of comedy have had masters dressed as slaves, men dressed as women, and implausible revelations about who was really someone's long-lost son (with a fortune which now allows him to marry the heroine). Russian names, often have nicknames, which, to English-speaking readers, bear little relationship to the actual name. Trying to learn a whole system of names can distract the reader from the content.

Names can be important clues. "Foible," "Lady Wishfort," and "Fainall" are characters whose names provide a clue that the playwright does not intend for them to be taken very seriously, as a viewing of Congreve's *The Way of the World* will prove. For a Tennessee Williams play, names are often a clue to character: Alma, Stella, Rosa, Brick, and Chance suggest the qualities of the characters themselves. For example, Alma, which means soul, is the name of the minister's daughter in *Summer and Smoke,* and the drama contrasts her spiritual concerns with the more physical son of the doctor who is her neighbor.

The card with names completely spelled out is also useful for those editions of plays which save space by using abbreviations. The reader of a Shakespearean play may find that Northumberland, Hotspur, Brabantio, and Nerissa have become "North," "Hots," "Brab," and "Ner," which further confuses the sex, rank, and relationships of each character. When the problem is compounded by having to keep straight a complicated plot and verse dialogue, the whole enterprise appears overwhelming.

The reason for remembering names is for purposes of communication. In discussing a play or writing about it, whether the form be free-wheeling or short-answer recall, it is simply more useful to remember the name of a character than to try to identify him (her) in another way. The abuse of memory is foolish recall of insignificant detail. But the alternative is vacant staring and grabbing at air in an effort to communicate. The happy medium is to learn the names as the people are introduced and then to go on to learn some important things about them and the play.

BASIC STRUCTURE

Five questions to help you understand how a play is structured:

1. *Where does it take place?* This is called setting. The setting for the first scene is usually found just under the opening, as "the house of Hjalmar Ekda." The setting may include no more than that, or there may be movement from one room to another.
2. *Who will be the important characters?* Sometimes a play opens with dialogue by the main characters. More often, in traditional plays, the lesser characters talk about others who will appear. In a theatre the audience may greet the arrival of major characters with applause. The reader, on his own, can merely note that the introductory pages contain the talk and action of lesser characters, perhaps servants, who prepare the way for the principal characters.

3. *What are the circumstances when the play begins?* Usually the action in the beginning of the play tells us, but we can also learn from explanatory dialogue. As two servants talk in *The Ghost Sonata,* we learn about the regular entertainment provided by the colonel and his silent friends, the ghosts. The servant explains this to the other servant, but is instructing the reader or viewer as well. Exposition is important because it tells what the play will be about. The play doesn't really get going until the exposition is over. Exposition is necessary for both serious and comic plays. In classical plays the exposition quickly introduces characters and situation. In plays aiming for realism there may be the sort of extra conversation in which characters (like people off-stage) digress from a main point.
4. *What is the basic conflict?* Once exposition is over, there comes a point at which people are engaged in a struggle or a quest. Someone wants something, someone stands in the way. The reader must recognize the goal or lose interest in the whole enterprise. In Shaw's *St. Joan* the conflict is soon made clear: the belief of the heroine vs. that of the spokesmen for the major social institutions that oppose her. To have action in the play, there must be this conflict. If Joan had managed to convince military, royal, and church leaders to believe in her voices, there would be no play. Recognizing the conflict is important to understanding the ideas in the play.
5. *What must happen?* At the end of even the first few pages of a traditional plot, the reader should recognize what must happen. There will be either a physical struggle or knowledge, where previously there had been ignorance, or a spiritual victory of one character over another. This is particularly true of the structure of plays written before the 20th Century. For example: Oedipus has promised to help the people of Thebes by solving the murder of his predecessor, King Laius. He must do as he has promised, and the audience waits to see him learn the truth that he is the criminal he seeks. Macbeth is tempted to pursue his own ambitions (and his wife's) through murder. We await the outcome of the witches' prophecies as he tries to outwit them.

The young lovers in *The Way of the World* are prevented from marrying by the old lady who controls the heroine's fortune. We watch with confidence (it is, after all, a comedy) as the lovers manage to outwit their opposition and resolve their problems by getting the money and each other.

If, as in absurdist 20th Century drama, the author's point is that life has no point, or that society is disorganized and unjust, the plot will be deliberately episodic, promising a climax that does not come, deliberately unstructured, to underscore the belief that life has no neat rewards for the deserving. The play itself may seem to have no ending in a sense, if many questions remain unanswered or if events are presented in random fashion to reflect the plotlessness of the human condition. In short, a play's structure often parallels its message. The viewer, however, should not settle too quickly for the belief that the play lacks a conventional plot, just because characters may digress from one main theme.

In Anton Chekhov's *The Three Sisters* it may seem that nothing happens, because the main characters do not achieve their stated dreams. The sisters long to return to Moscow. Throughout the play, many events occur—marriage, love affairs, a fire, a duel, the departure of the soldiers—but, at the end, the sisters still talk about their desire to go to Moscow. Their fortunes are even worse than at the beginning of the play, and the audience knows a great deal about each sister. In terms of visible onstage action it would seem that nothing happens, and to the unobservant there would seem to be not enough for a play. But the basic structure is there: the fierce desire to change is what the play is about.

The ability to find basic structure is the ability to understand a play. Answering the preceding five questions is one of the best ways of reaching understanding. Usually, on first reading, one is distracted by individual lines, by a subplot, or a relationship which recalls personal memories. But once one has finished the play and has gone back to the beginning, one will usually be able to answer the questions stated again here:

1. Where does the play take place?
2. Who are the important characters?
3. What is the opening situation?
4. What is the basic conflict?
5. What must happen (where is it heading)?

CULTURAL CONTEXT: THE USE OF HISTORY

Excessive interest in history as preparation for reading can diminish the pleasure of the play itself. A boring slide presentation, the unctuous voice of the narrator talking about the beauties of the past, the picture of the playwright's birthplace, the church he attended, etc. can be deadly to audiences who have not yet learned to care about the writer of plays still unfamiliar.

Shakespeare has suffered most from this excessively historical approach, but there are other victims. The student who gets bogged down in history perhaps has no way of knowing that most playwrights have written in order to entertain audiences. Instead, the learner spends weeks in preparation for what is supposed to be the great event itself—the play. There is hushed expectation as he learns the look of a typical costume of the time, the appearance of a typical house, and the names of the various occupations. Reading with so much attention to detail becomes an exercise in futility. Fortunately, a more enlightened approach to history is found in most play collections.

More important than a knowledge of costume, furniture, and slang phrases is a recognition that certain dated beliefs, which may affect understanding of the entire work, were popular when the play was written.

A play may deal with the revenge which one man takes as a result of an insult to his family. The audience at the time the play was written would understand that such revenge was common. The injured party would not expect to ask the intervention of the law in the form of a sheriff or a policeman. The modern reader, who must take for granted this insistence on individual revenge, is aided by countless movies and television shows about the early West, and there should be no resistance to the notion of revenge for the honor of a kinsman.

A play may deal with insistence on sexual purity. An unmarried girl before the 20th century was expected to be accompanied by a lady-in-waiting or by a female relative acting as chaperone. The belief was, at one time, that any violation of this rule by an impassioned suitor was also a violation of the girl herself. Similarly, the finding of a fan or a handkerchief in the apartment of a bachelor would have been enough to ruin the reputation of not only an unmarried girl but a married woman or a widow as well. It is necessary to remain within the historical context of the time in order to understand such a play.

Other examples of dated beliefs formerly accepted as normal by audiences that might seem strange to us today are the following:

1. Credence in witches, omens, oracles
2. The unquestioned authority of a monarch
3. Oppressive fears about guilt and sin for an act which would now be overlooked or explained in psychological terminology
4. A wife whose only purpose in life is to be subordinate to her husband and who therefore has no desires or goals apart from him
5. The belief in the automatic superiority or inferiority of a group of people

The reader of a play in which any of these roles or situations appear must free himself from the constant desire to assert his own, more modern attitudes. That is basic to an understanding of the play, for otherwise there would be too many intrusions of disbelief. Of course, the pretense of sharing an old belief lasts only during the play. Close the book and you return to your own century.

The recognition of the way history is shown through the play enhances one's understanding of the play. Just as it is possible to take special note of attitudes about court life, snobbishness, or class structure in the speeches of Molière's *The Would-Be Gentleman,* so it is possible to notice assumptions about the role of husband or wife in Shakespeare's *The Taming of the Shrew.* If Kate is a "shrew" throughout the play, in contrast, the viewer or reader can surmise, through reference to speeches by other women in the play and by Kate herself, what the model wife, her opposite, would have been like.

PLAYS IN TRANSLATION

As any speaker of more than one language knows, translation is far more than a matter of "merely" saying something in another language. Many choices are possible to the translator who knows both languages well, and who is therefore able to select the appropriate tone. The translator of a play written more than a generation ago must clarify meaning in a way suitable for each speaker and must also try to keep in mind the beliefs of the time the play was written. Plays receive new translations in order to keep up with the sense of language of each new generation. Critics differ in their opinions on such a practice.

The translator who is too faithful to the original—too literal—risks sounding awkward and pretentious. For example, if, in the original language, it is appropriate to ask "How are you?" then "Comment allez-vous?" should not be translated literally as "How do you go?" However, the translator must be careful to avoid specialized idioms which will date too quickly. If a young person is speaking and would ordinarily use slang terminology, the translator is faced with the choice of words to use: in years to come, "super," "cool," and "dandy" are likely to call attention to themselves and away from the meaning of the play.

Even the director is in a sense a translator as actors are chosen. The trained ear can distinguish among accents, particularly in long scenes between two actors. The characters and their situation will sound different according to the class and level of education of the speaker. In Strindberg's drama *Miss Julie* the servant Jean has made love to Julie, the Count's daughter. As they speak to each other, an actor playing Jean sounds like a possible husband for Miss Julie if both actors use the same accent. If Jean sounds as though he came from a lower class, he sounds wrong no matter what he says. Modern audiences, however democratic, need to understand that society at the end of the 19th Century would have recognized Jean as an absolutely intolerable son-in-law for Miss Julie's father, the Count.

The translator's choice of words must help to set the time as well. In one translation Julie says to Jean, "I couldn't bear the scandal," which in another version of the same line becomes "I couldn't bear the shame and dishonor." *Scandal* seems tame compared to *shame and dishonor,* words closer to the playwright's original language, though they may seem quaint today. In order to emphasize the importance of social inequality at the time, the translator deliberately selected old-fashioned language which modern audiences may accept as bringing them closer to an understanding of the author's intention. The actor playing with a lower-class accent says, "Do you think I've never had a woman before?" The actor sounding more aristocratic, in another translation, puts it more delicately: "Do you think I've never been there before?" Similarly, the first version uses *whore;* the second uses *mistress.* The translator has difficult tasks: to avoid pomposity and slang, to present words faithful to the playwright's meaning, and to communicate current meaning to modern audiences as if the play were being presented in its own time.

Audiences unwilling to make the journey to beliefs of the past will continue to misunderstand. They will be baffled by Miss Julie's distress at her "surrender." Why doesn't she simply marry her father's servant, or run off with him, or seek another lover? No translation can compensate for the provinciality of such questions which would be asked only by persons locked into their own time. For others, it is often illuminating to compare two translations of the same passage. Perhaps the gloom of Ibsen's plays results largely from the stiffness of the best known translations. It may be that plays, like jokes, suffer so much in translation that they can be truly understood only by those familiar with the language of the original.

MODULE 1

Introduction to Critical Appreciation

    I. Introduction, p. 2
   II. Study materials for *Miss Julie*, p. 6
  III. Study materials for *Peer Gynt*, p. 44

You will find a more detailed outline preceding each of the plays.

DRAMATIC VISION: ART OF VIEWING

Within each of us is an instinct for the dramatic, for writing drama, for dressing the part. Who of us does not remember our childhood joy in the world of make-believe as we somewhat clumsily dressed up in the clothes of mother and dad? We allowed our imaginations to take us on flights of fancy. A room could become the lavish ballroom of a great palace; a garbage can lid could become a fancy shield in the hands of a gallant warrior, or a mere box could become a fort or a cave.

It was in this wonderful world of make-believe that our child's mind could raise the magical *IF.* "If I were a king. . ." If I were a queen. . ." "If I were in a jungle or in space. . ." The pretense was limitless. The playing was given over to the imagination, which could carry us as far as we wanted to go, even to the acting out of last Saturday's matinee. Within this spirit of play was planted a sense of imitation and performance, a theatric element in life.

Of course, theatre is not merely a product of adults seeking to continue or to relive their childhood by playing games, dressing up and assuming new identities, or pursuing only diversion. Rather, theatre expresses a part of man's nature as innate as the imaginative play of the child. Other life experiences and events contain elements which unite to form drama and supply stimulus for theatre art. For instance, there is a dramatic element in life which springs from wants, wishes, hopes, and desires that runs into conflict with obstacles thwarting fulfillment. Perhaps we want a job promotion, but are refused; we desire love and recognition, but are denied. These and similiar situations represent the dramatic element of tension and conflict in life.

Another element found in life is the philosophic/psychologic element. Characteristic of human nature is our attempt to find ways in which to understand ourselves and each other, to find meaning, to interpret life, to speculate, to judge, to value, to gain wisdom. These three life elements—theatric, dramatic, and philosophic/psychologic—when united, are the active ingredients found in drama and theatre art. As audience members in the theatre, we can witness human tensions and conflict so imitated and performed as to heighten or reflect the meaning and values of human life.

Theatre art intensifies daily experience. The playwright, director, performers, and technical collaborators focus our attention, thoughts, and feelings to a given space, time, and situation. One writer describes a theatre experience as a moment of vital contact: a life spark leaps from the playwright's soul to the stage and then to the audience. Theatre is the home of illusion; the play is art and exists in the realm of the carefully constructed make-believe. When we enter into this realm, we are asked to become enthusiastic participants in the pretense.

There is an art to viewing a play in performance. Viewing the play for maximum enjoyment is a multilevel process. Viewing in terms of meaning, language, character, message, is called *content viewing.* To observe the play for plotting and for what is technically happening in a play's performance is considered *craft viewing.* Finally, *critical viewing* is perceiving the playwright's purpose, the importance of this purpose, and deciding how well this purpose is realized.

What makes "drama" drama is precisely the element which lies outside and beyond the words, and which has to be acted to give the playwright's concept its full value. As a *playreader,* you come in direct contact with the playwright's mind and you visualize the written drama as a living play in your imagination—your mind's eye. As a *playgoer,* you hear and see a stageplay presented directly by actors who seek your total reaction, including sensory perception, empathetic and affective response, and critical and synthesizing abilities. In trying to get the fullest enjoyment and enrichment from both the drama and the stageplay, the reader/audience must try to understand how the play can contribute to the sum total of human expression and thought. Seeing a play is not a passive pursuit. Rather, it is an active, even a public event to be experienced and shared.

While going to the theatre is important and should be encouraged, one must recognize that some circumstances may make it difficult to attend live theatre. Television, although a different medium from the theatre, gives one the opportunity to view concentrated performances which, it is to be hoped, will exercise and excite our dramatic imagination and increase our enjoyment and appreciation of theatre art. In turn, developing the habit of responding with critical sharpness to the events on a stage will help us to seize the important moments of *real* life as they rush by us.

BACKSTAGE REALITY—ONSTAGE ILLUSION

Many theatregoers find it an intriguing experience to look behind the scenes into the backstage world of theatre art. Perhaps it is a secret longing to participate in the powerful atmosphere of the theatre, to become part of an imaginative world. Perhaps it is curiosity about the methods and materials used by theatre technicians in creating stage reality, or perhaps it is fascination with the techniques and creative processes through which a performer evolves from a person, to an actor, to a character.

Whatever the reason, a sharpened awareness of the craft of theatre artists constitutes the most subtle level of viewing. A major part of *craft viewing* is the ability to disengage the actor from the character, the technical effect from the technical design, and, especially, the hand of the director from the words of the playwright. Above all, it should be remembered that the goal of the actor, the director, and the collaborative artists is to induce the audience into a suspension of disbelief, so that their artistry—like that of the magician—is lost in the total illusion.

Behind the web of illusion spun by the collaborative artists may lie the reality of many hours, days, and weeks of hard work in creating and producing a theatre art event. The artists may be many and varied: producer and assistants, stage director and assistants, art director and technical designer, costume designer and make-up designer, publicity and program designer, and so on. The craft and art of this team of artists and technicians lie in their collected abilities to create from the playscript a stageplay directly performed before a live audience.

The creative activity undergoes three basic phases: (1) the reading, study, and understanding of the playscript; (2) the designing-constructing and the rehearsing-developing of the expressive tools/techniques of the stageplay; and (3) the communication and performance of the product of the creative work before an audience.

The director's responsibility is to blend the dramatic elements, to synthesize the work of the collaborative artists, to create the sense of unity needed for bringing the play to life and raising it to the level of art. Based on his understanding of the story and his study of the playwright's craft, the director interprets the play.

It is his concept which will dominate and unify the production. When directing the actors, a director might take one of three approaches: he may insist that his actors respond specifically and solely to his interpretation; he may allow the actors their own interpretation, or he may impose some of his ideas upon the actors, while encouraging some freedom of interpretation.

The *Miss Julie* director, Richard Callanan, uses the third approach. He guides the principal members of his cast through role analysis and into characterization. He assists their concentration, relaxes them, stimulates memories of their own experiences in order to crystalize behavioral motivation, and encourages them to vocally and physically explore their portrayal of characters, so that the technique and artistry meld into a unified performance.

Actually, the responsibility of the director in today's theatre is relatively new. It is likely that Sophocles, as with all Greek poet-dramatists, directed his own plays. Shakespeare, both playwright and actor, probably offered suggestions and had a hand in directing his fellow actors.

Certainly this was true of Molière, who was playwright, leading actor, and director for his troupe of players. For about two centuries, the manager of a troupe, or stage manager, assumed what we now consider directorial duties. In the *commedia dell' arte* plays the troupe manager selected the scenario and the players directed themselves. The concept of the director as a distinctive theatre artist has developed largely within the last hundred years influenced mainly by Stanislavsky of the Moscow Art Theatre.

The director's responsibility has come to mean more than his principal job of planning and conducting rehearsals and directing productions. In addition, his interpretation or concept serves as a guide for the production in a more comprehensive sense. His concept determines and shapes all the technical production elements: scenery, lights, costumes, and make-up. The director holds conferences and production meetings with the various designers and directors of the technical staff, and after the concept is established, he turns over the designing and its direction to their respective areas of expertise. Consequently, the role of the contemporary director is to work with and coordinate all aspects of a production. He molds the skills and talents of the cast, craftsmen, and crew into an esthetic unity and readies this artistic team to present the final product of all its creative collaboration.

The stage manager assumes the major responsibility of running the show during the final (dress and technical) rehearsals of the production. On opening night (and throughout the play's run) the stage action and the backstage operation are in the stage manager's hands. The director, meanwhile, is seated in the audience observing and assessing the production as it undergoes its ultimate, supreme test. The director is alert to audience reaction because he knows the stimulating effect of mutual communication upon the audience and the actors.

The actor, like the director, is an interpretive artist with skills different from those of the playwright. Mutually dependent, they nevertheless create separate art forms. An actor conveys a characterization that may be somewhere between what the playwright intended and the director, or even the actor, construes it to be. The actor's incarnation of the person imagined by the playwright comes through voice and action. Voice interpretation includes speech pattern, tone, emphasis, and timing. Action interpretation involves gesture, movement, facial expression, or any "business" other than dialogue by which an actor performs a role. The actor is the living agent through which the character becomes a mover of the story. It is not necessarily the technique of the actor we as an audience appreciate, but the product of the actor's technique.

Miss Julie: In Rehearsal offers us a rare opportunity to see individuals at work in their chosen profession as actors. We watch the process whereby these actors evolve into characters. We observe their techniques of developing their characterizations. We witness the actors' manipulation of the tools of expression (vocal treatment, body attitudes). Finally we watch the actors add their accoutrements: the costumes, gestures, and personal properties (perhaps a handkerchief or a flower).

After these few minutes backstage observing the creative process at work, we return to our audience seats to experience the onstage creation of theatre art and artists. Now we can clearly separate the person from the actor and the actor from the character, and if we have either a positive or negative reaction, it is toward the character (the playwright's creation) and not toward the individual actor. Certainly we can disagree with the interpretation. But at least we no longer confuse work with product, worker with mechanics, or reality with illusion.

It may be that this closer inspection backstage will lead to disenchantment: the scenery loses its magic and becomes only painted canvas stretched on a frame lashed to other frames, and the actors without make-up or costume appear ordinary. The pretense is gone. Make-believe no longer exists.

On the other hand, perhaps this closer inspection backstage has heightened our understanding, increased our appreciation, augmented our evaluation of the work involved in the creation of illusion. Now, as we view the cumulative effect of the coalition of playwright, director, actor, and theatre artists, we will respond with critical sensitivity to the total theatre experience. Now through an understanding of the skills gained in critical appreciation, we may become both a responsive and responsible viewer-participant in the art of the theatre.

MISS JULIE

by

August Strindberg
(1849–1912)

A. Play Notes *(Miss Julie)*, p. 7
B. Commentary, p. 9
C. Reviews, p. 9
D. Objectives, p. 10
E. Program Notes, p. 11
F. *Miss Julie*, p. 12
G. A List of BBC Actors and Production Coordinators, p. 39
H. Director's Notes, p. 40
I. Focus in Viewing, p. 41
J. Additional Plays, p. 42
K. Stage Terms, p. 42

Play Notes

However necessary it may be as the starting point for understanding, no summary of plot ever fully reveals a work of art. The summary for the one-act play *Miss Julie* is inadequate; for the action of the play is as much in what the characters say as in what they do. What the two main characters "do," if judged by external movements on the stage, is very little, and would be tiresome to viewers unaccustomed to paying close attention to the interactions of people.

All that happens externally is a conversation and a drink in the kitchen of a grand household. The cook, Christine, is in her own room asleep through part of the play. The valet, Jean, is asked to drink beer with Miss Julie, daughter of the Count who is Jean's employer. They talk for a while, mainly about the childhood of the servant and his early recognition of great social differences between rich and poor. Then, hearing voices from the other servants coming into the house, they exit into Jean's room.

Later, when they come out of the room, after having made love, they talk about the possibility of running away together, possibly setting up a hotel in Switzerland, thus ignoring the alienation caused by class differences that would be inevitable if they stayed in their own country. Christine reappears, reminding them of the difficulties in this attempt to overlook social position. Jean gives up the dream and returns to his duties as a servant. Julie leaves to commit suicide. End of play, end of story for the viewer concerned only with external action. August Strindberg, however, did not write the play for this viewer. He knew that what happened was as much inside as outside of his characters. He provided the more sensitive viewer with the material that could provoke speculation about motives and sexual struggle. Strindberg later used visible, grotesque objects in *The Ghost Sonata* (1907)—the bust of Beethoven, a death screen, a woman who screeched like a parrot, hyacinths, a Buddha, the ghosts themselves, as well as eerie transformations of young and old. But in the earlier play, *Miss Julie* (1888), he depended more on what the people said to each other. The play is rewarding to viewers willing to observe psychological nuance.

The main scene between Jean and Julie begins playfully, each speaking a little French. When the lady compliments him on his gentlemanly appearance and his ability with language, he suggests that she is flattering him, for "gentleman" would not be the word usually applied to one of his station. (Strindberg's own childhood is relevant. As the son of a servant, he remained aware through his lifetime of the humiliations suffered by the servant class.) Still, Julie continues to play, even to flirt dangerously. They have a drink together after she urges him to disregard class distinctions and not allow a lady to drink alone. He refers to the request as an "order," reminding her once again of the disparity in their stations in life. She breaks with convention still further when she asks him to kiss her shoe in a toast to her health.

In the background are sounds of merriment as the many servants on the estate enjoy the music and dancing of Midsummer's Eve. Jean shows awareness of those outside when he remarks, "We can't go on like this. . . .Someone might come in and see us." To the modern viewer the couple's behavior seems innocent rather than alarming. But the remark underscores deeply-held beliefs about class distinctions and the scandal which could—and does contribute to the ruination of a life.

An actress can interpret Miss Julie as high strung, or imperious, or passive. The way the lines are spoken varies from one production to another, depending often on when the actress sees Julie headed for destruction. The details of characterization are worked out in rehearsal. Even with actors using the same translation, the words take on different meanings as accents, laughs, and eye and body movements change.

Some actors portray Jean as a low-bred brute, causing audiences to see him as insensitive. Most viewers believe that a person who speaks "well"—that is, with the accent of upper-class or standard English—has finer sensibilities than the person who has trouble with the language, perhaps saying "dese" instead of "these." The inability to pronounce "th" may be charming in someone born in another country. For the native-born speaker, however, mispronunciations are marks against him, though not perhaps so much today as when George Bernard Shaw wrote *Pygmalion* and gave the world the Cockney girl who was accepted as a lady once she mastered elocution.

The actor lapsing into dialect as he says some of Jean's speeches may earn the sympathy of members of the audience who perhaps remember their own struggles to "sound educated" and are resentful of the powerful people who have, voluntarily or not, made them feel alien to the dominant culture. But for others, a low-class Jean who *sounds* low class becomes an upstart, a menace to his employer's daughter. Julie then becomes much more sympathetic as the genteel lady unable to match the strength of the brutish, experienced predator.

Miss Julie, by laughing or frowning, can change the interpretation of a few words. "Now drink my health," she says. But how should the words be said? The words by Strindberg invite almost infinite stimulus and variety as the power struggle begins. A crucial remark follows each of Jean's rather long reminiscences of childhood. After one impassioned speech revealing his yearning to play with the Count's daughter and his despair at recognizing his lowly status, after all the details of his awe at the chasm separating the ugliness of his life and the beauty of hers, Miss Julie places him in a whole subgroup, rather than as the individual he apparently deserves to be, by asking, "Do all poor children feel like that?" Putting Jean into the class "*all* poor children" diminishes him as an individual. The question might crush a more timid man. He repeats "*All* poor children?," then rallies to reply. In his next speech he gives a long, almost sociological explanation of class differences, even remarking on some of the advantages of being animal rather than human. But he returns to his personal reminiscences.

Julie continues to maintain distance, commenting not on his feelings but on his choice of words and educational background, as if she were an interviewer: "You put things very well. . . ." The scene continues, with quick changes of power; at times, Julie is the lady, amused, mocking, even disdainful. At other times, Jean assumes control, asserting masculine superiority, pointing out wider sexual experience and the truth behind the lady's pose of innocence.

Talk of sex makes them equal for a time. But when he requests permission to leave, she continues the flirtation with the suggestion that they become even more daring, not only drinking but going outside once more to dance where the crowd can see them.

It is Jean who points out the true feelings of servants toward their masters. Trapped, unable to stay in the kitchen where they will be seen by the others or to go outside, they retreat to Jean's room. Later, when they come out, it is as lovers. The balance of power continues to shift throughout the rest of the play, till it ends, in a sense, with disaster for both: death for her, continued servitude for him.

Commentary

On March 5, 1956 *Time* reviewed *Miss Julie*. Five days later another review of the same production appeared in *Saturday Review*.

Saturday Review praised the production as inventive because of the special touches devised by the director. The *Time* review concentrates on the playwright's theme. Both reviews praised the acting of Viveca Lindfors in the title role.

Saturday Review, March 10, 1956

Strindberg Without Tears

. . . In *Miss Julie* Strindberg has written a "Midsummer Night's Nightmare," a turning outward of the physically destructive forces that gnaw at us within. While the author's fascinating introduction, which can be found in "Six Plays by Strindberg" (Anchor Books, $1.25), explains the forces let loose during the play, adapter-director George Tabori has used an approach of his own. His Miss Julie is not so much a man-hater seduced by a sadistic servant as she is a neurotic, aristocratic child who destroys herself by seducing a nineteenth-century Stanley Kowalski. The point of the play now seems to be that once a woman of the upper-class abandons herself to a sexuality that cannot be gratified by the over refined members of her own class she must resign herself to living in dishonor. She can either degenerate to the coarseness of people whose sense of values she does not respect, or she can retain her own sense of dignity through suicide. To this violent duet Strindberg has added a cook who represents what later turned up in Shaw under the name of "middle-class morality."

As Miss Julie, Viveca Lindfors gives a perceptive and sexually charged performance that never loses it sense of innate nobility. However, her portrayal of Miss Julie as a weak woman caught in the forces around her inhibits her use of the more terror-striking emotional responses. She plays almost no notes between the middle of the scale and high C, and doesn't move us as much emotionally as she does intellectually. James Daly contributes a strong performance as Jean, avoiding throughout the temptations to make the character crafty. His "Love is a game to be played after work." "We don't have all day and all night like you" hurls a rugged accusation at the leisure class. Ruth Ford's carryings-on as the cook make an amusing burlesque, and Jamie Smith and Laurinda Barrett are briefly effective in Dionysian rites that both mock and celebrate what is happening in the adjacent bedroom.

Mr. Tabori has shown taste and inventiveness in his direction. Miss Julie's knocking over of the clothes tree that symbolizes Jean's awe of his upper-class master is a nice touch as is the more humorous moment when Jean sloshes some strong-smelling kerosene under his armpits when he should be in the most romantic transport of ecstasy. Alvin Colts's wonderfully simple set with its projected background catches poetically the ripeness of the situation.

The result of this Strindberg double bill is a tasteful and lucid insight into a great modern playwright, whose works are either too seldom presented here or when they are usually become the occasion for some conventional and meaningless overacting.

Henry Hewes

Reprinted with permission from *Saturday Review.* Copyright © 1956 by Saturday Review.

Time, March 5, 1956

Old Play in Manhattan

Miss Julie still asserts, after 68 years, Swedish Playwright August Strindberg's unflinching though unbalanced view of life. During those years, the theatre has seldom offered bolder naturalism than Strindberg's or more psychopathic intensities, and never, certainly, a more implacable war between the sexes. The conflict in *Miss Julie* is as much between classes as sexes. At a Midsummer Eve revel, arrogant, dissatisfied Miss Julie, the neurotic child of parents who hated each other, becomes infatuated with her father's valet and tempts him into an affair. Respectful enough beforehand, he turns sneeringly overbearing. But, however revolted, Miss Julie is also desperate. She steals her father's money to try to run away with her lover, in the end seizes her lover's razor to do away with herself.

Each of them scarred by ugly memories, they enact—as man as woman, as menial and lady—an ugly drama. Their spitting and clawing seems sick, savage, yet never beyond belief. In the current production, the play's power is more spasmodic than sustained; despite George Tabori's playable adaptation too much tends to date. Though Swedish-born Viveca Lindfors succeeds in the title role, James Daly overstresses what is crude in the valet by a crudity of attack. Even so, *Miss Julie* has explosive elements that neither O'Neill, Hellman nor Tennessee Williams has ever surpassed.

Objectives

Actor and Director: *Miss Julie* **in Rehearsal**

You, the student, after studying *Miss Julie* and the related materials should be able to

1. recognize and describe the role of the director in blending dramatic elements and synthesizing the work of the collaborative artists.
2. recognize that an actor's craft requires selecting from various acting approaches in order to interpret and play a character.
3. recognize the director's and actors' creative and interpretive roles in the putting together of a performance.
4. discern what part of a stage production is craft, set apart from the playwright's work.
5. recognize some of the problems that Strindberg saw as part of late 19th Century life.

Reprinted by permission from *TIME*, The Weekly Newsmagazine; Copyright Time Inc., 1956.

Program Notes

Actor and Director: *Miss Julie*

A crucial scene from a seminal work in European drama is enacted in rehearsal, with the director, an actor, and an actress discussing their own lives in relation to interpretation of the roles. The scene selected from the August Strindberg play involves a struggle for power between the daughter of a nobleman and the servant of her father, as they remember the gulf between them as children and the present possibilities for a dangerous sexual alliance. The shifts in power and the variety of interpretation are subtle and fascinating. Patrick Stewart (seen as Oedipus Tyrannus in another play of the series) and Lisa Harrow (the Daughter in *Six Characters in Search of an Author)* are visited backstage, as they work with BBC director Richard Callanan on how to play a powerful scene. The program concludes with a full-dress version of the scene.

MISS JULIE[1]
A Naturalistic Tragedy

CHARACTERS

Miss Julia, aged twenty-five
Jean, a valet, aged thirty
Christine, a cook, aged thirty-five

>   The action takes place on Midsummer Eve[2] in the kitchen of the count's country house.
>   A large kitchen: the ceiling and the side walls are hidden by draperies and hangings. The rear wall runs diagonally across the stage, from the left side and away from the spectators. On this wall, to the left, there are two shelves full of utensils made of copper, iron, and tin. The shelves are trimmed with scalloped paper.
>   A little to the right may be seen three-fourths of the big arched doorway leading to the outside. It has double glass doors, through which are seen a fountain with a cupid, lilac shrubs in bloom, and the tops of some lombardy poplars.
>   On the left side of the stage is seen the corner of a big cookstove built of glazed bricks; also a part of the smokehood above it.
>   From the right protrudes one end of the servants' dining table of white pine, with a few chairs about it.
>   The stove is dressed with bundled branches of birch. Twigs of juniper are scattered on the floor.
>   On the table end stands a big Japanese spice pot full of lilac blossoms.
>   An icebox, a kitchen-table, and a wash-stand.
>   Above the door hangs a big old-fashioned bell on a steel spring, and the mouthpiece of a speaking tube[3] appears at the left of the door.
>   CHRISTINE is standing by the stove, frying something in a pan. She has on a dress of light coloured cotton, which she has covered up with a big kitchen apron.
>   JEAN enters, dressed in livery and carrying a pair of big, spurred riding-boots, which he places on the floor in such manner that they remain visible to the spectators.

JEAN Tonight Miss Julia is crazy again; absolutely crazy.
CHRISTINE So you're back again?
JEAN I took the count to the station, and when I came back by the barn, I went in and had a dance, and there I saw the young lady leading the dance with the gamekeeper. But when she

---

From THREE PLAYS by Strindberg, "Miss Julia," translated by Edwin Bjorkman, 1964. Reprinted by permission of Branden Press, Inc.

1. Translated from the Swedish by Edwin Björkman.
2. Midsummer Eve. In the northern lands of Europe the longest day of the year was popularly celebrated in pagan times by a vigil or wake the preceding night, which became the Christian feast of St. John's Eve on June 23. This summer solstice festival is still in Scandinavian countries a time of all-night merry-making comparable to the Yule celebration of the winter solstice. It is romantically associated with midsummer madness and the appearance of supernatural beings.
3. Speaking tube. In elegant homes of the late Victorian era the family communicated with the servants' quarters by speaking tubes in the walls.

caught sight of me, she rushed right up to me and asked me to dance the ladies' waltz with her. And ever since she's been waltzing like—well, I never saw the like of it. She's crazy!

CHRISTINE And has always been, but never the way it's been this last fortnight, since her engagement was broken.

JEAN Well, what kind of a story was that anyhow? He's a fine fellow, isn't he, although he isn't rich? Ugh, but they're so full of notions. *(Sits down at the end of the table)* It's peculiar anyhow, that a young lady—hm!—would rather stay at home with the servants—don't you think?—than go with her father to their relatives!

CHRISTINE Oh, I guess she feels sort of embarrassed by that rumpus with her fellow.

JEAN Quite likely. But there was some backbone to that man just the same. Do you know how it happened, Christine? I saw it, although I didn't care to let on.

CHRISTINE No, did you?

JEAN Sure, I did. They were in the stable yard one evening, and the young lady was training him, as she called it. Do you know what that meant? She made him leap over her horse-whip the way you teach a dog to jump. Twice he jumped and got a cut each time. The third time he took the whip out of her hand and broke it into a thousand bits. And then he got out.

CHRISTINE So that's the way it happened? You don't say!

JEAN Yes, that's how that thing happened. Well, Christine, what have you got that's tasty?

CHRISTINE *(Serves from the pan and puts the plate before* JEAN*)* Oh, just some kidney which I cut out of the veal roast.

JEAN *(smelling the food)*. Fine! That's a great delicacy. *(feeling the plate)* But you might have warmed the plate.

CHRISTINE Well, if you ain't harder to please than the count himself! *(Pulls his hair playfully.)*

JEAN *(irritated)*. Don't pull my hair! You know how sensitive I am.

CHRISTINE Well, well, it was nothing but a love pull, you know.

*(*JEAN *eats.* CHRISTINE *opens a bottle of beer.)*

JEAN Beer—on Midsummer Eve? No, thank you! Then I have something better myself. *(Opens a table-drawer and takes out a bottle of claret with yellow cap)* Yellow seal, mind you! Give me a glass—and you use those with stems when you drink it pure.

CHRISTINE *(returns to the stove and puts a small pan on the fire)* Heaven preserve her that gets you for a husband, Mr. Finicky!

JEAN Oh, rot! You'd be glad enough to get a smart fellow like me. And I guess it hasn't hurt you that they call me your beau. *(Tasting the wine)* Good! Pretty good! Just a tiny bit too cold. *(He warms the glass with his hands.)* We got this at Dijon. It cost us four francs per litre, not counting the bottle. And there was the duty besides. What is it you're cooking—with that infernal smell?

CHRISTINE Oh, it's some deviltry the young lady is going to give Diana.

JEAN You should choose your words with more care, Christine. But why should you be cooking for a bitch on a holiday eve like this? Is she sick?

CHRISTINE Ye-es, she is sick. She's been running around with the gatekeeper's pug—and now's there's trouble—and the young lady just won't hear of it.

JEAN The young lady is too stuck up in some ways and not proud enough in others—just as was the countess while she lived. She was most at home in the kitchen and among the cows, but she would never drive with only one horse. She wore her cuffs till they were dirty, but she had to have cuff buttons with a coronet on them. And speaking of the young lady, she doesn't take proper care of herself and her person. I might say even that she's lacking in refinement. Just now, when she was dancing in the barn, she pulled the gamekeeper away from Anna and asked him herself to come and dance with her. We wouldn't act in that way. But that's just how it is: when upper-class people want to demean themselves, then they grow mean! But she's splendid! Magnificent! Oh, such shoulders! And. . .and so on!

CHRISTINE Oh, well, don't brag too much! I've heard Clara talking, who tends to her dressing.

JEAN Pooh, Clara! You're always jealous of each other. I, who have been out riding with her— And then the way she dances!

CHRISTINE Say, Jean, won't you dance with me when I'm done?

JEAN Of course I will.

CHRISTINE Do you promise?

JEAN Promise? When I say so, I'll do it. Well, here's thanks for the good food. It tasted fine! (Puts the cork back into the bottle.)

JULIA (appears in the doorway, speaking to somebody on the outside). I'll be back in a minute. You go right on in the meantime.

(JEAN slips the bottle into the table-drawer and rises respectfully.)

JULIA (enters and goes over to CHRISTINE by the wash-stand).Well, is it done yet?

(CHRISTINE signs to her that JEAN is present.)

JEAN (gallantly). The ladies are having secrets, I believe.

JULIE (strikes him in the face with her handkerchief). That's for you, Mr. Pry!

JEAN Oh, what a delicious odor that violet has!

JULIA (with coquetry). Impudent! So you know something about perfumes also? And know pretty well how to dance—Now don't peep! Go away!

JEAN (with polite impudence). Is it some kind of witches' broth the ladies are cooking on Midsummer Eve— something to tell fortunes by and bring out the lucky star of one's future love?

JULIA (sharply). If you can see that, you'll have good eyes, indeed!

(To CHRISTINE) Put it in a pint bottle and cork it well. Come and dance a schottische with me now, Jean.

JEAN (hesitatingly). I don't want to be impolite, but I had promised to dance with Christine this time. . . .

JULIA Well, she can get somebody else—can't you, Christine? Won't you let me borrow Jean from you?

CHRISTINE That isn't for me to say. When Miss Julia is so gracious, it isn't for him to say no. You just go along, and be thankful for the honour, too!

JEAN Frankly speaking, but not wishing to offend in any way, I cannot help wondering if it's wise for Miss Julia to dance twice in succession with the same partner, especially as the people here are not slow in throwing out hints.

JULIA (flaring up). What is that? What kind of hints? What do you mean?

JEAN (submissively). As you don't want to understand, I have to speak more plainly. It don't look well to prefer one servant to all the rest who are expecting to be honoured in the same unusual way. . . .

JULIA Prefer! What ideas! I'm surprised! I, the mistress of the house, deign to honour this dance with my presence, and when it so happens that I actually want to dance, I want to dance with one who knows how to lead, so that I am not made ridiculous.

JEAN As you command, Miss Julia! I am at your service!

JULIA (*softened*). Don't take it as a command. Tonight we should enjoy ourselves as a lot of happy people, and all rank should be forgotten. Now give me your arm. Don't be afraid, Christine! I'll return your beau to you!

(JEAN *offers his arm to Miss Julia and leads her out.*)

Pantomime
Must be acted as if the actress were really alone in the place. When necessary she turns her back to the public. She should not look in the direction of the spectators, and she should not hurry as if fearful that they might become impatient.

CHRISTINE is alone. A tune played on a violin is heard faintly in the distance.

While humming the tune, Christine clears off the table after Jean, washes the plate at the kitchen table, wipes it, and puts it away in the cupboard.

Then she takes off her apron, pulls out a small mirror from one of the table drawers and leans it against the flower jar on the table; lights a tallow candle and heats a hairpin, which she uses to curl her front hair.

Then she goes to the door and stands there listening. Returns to the table. Discovers the handkerchief which Miss Julia has left behind, picks it up, and smells it, spreads it out absent-mindedly and begins to stretch it, smooth it, fold it up, and so forth.

JEAN *(enters alone)* Crazy, that's what she is! The way she dances! And the people stand behind the doors and grin at her. What do you think of it, Christine?

CHRISTINE Oh, she has her time now, and then she is always a little queer like that. But are you going to dance with me now?

JEAN You are not mad at me because I disappointed you?

CHRISTINE No!—Not for a little thing like that, you know! And also, I know my place.

JEAN *(putting his arm around her waist)*. You are a sensible girl, Christine, and I think you'll make a good wife.

JULIA *(enters and is unpleasantly surprised; speaks with forced gayety)* Yes, you are a fine partner—running away from your lady!

JEAN On the contrary, Miss Julia, I have, as you see, looked up the one I deserted.

JULIA *(changing tone)* Do you know, there is nobody that dances like you!—But why do you wear your livery on an evening like this? Take it off at once!

JEAN Then I must ask you to step outside for a moment, as my black coat is hanging right here.

(Points toward the right and goes in that direction.)

JULIA Are you bashful on my account? Just to change a coat? Why don't you go into your own room and come back again? Or, you can stay right here, and I'll turn my back on you.

JEAN With your permission, Miss Julia

(Goes further over to the right; one of his arms can be seen as he changes his coat.)

JULIA *(to* CHRISTINE*)* Are you and Jean engaged, that he's so familiar with you?

CHRISTINE Engaged? Well, in a way. We call it that.
JULIA Call it?
CHRISTINE But it didn't come to anything just the same.

(JEAN *enters, dressed in black frock coat and black derby.*)

JULIA Tres gentil, Monsieur Jean! Tres gentil![4]
JEAN Vous voulez plaisanter, Madame!
JULIA Et vous voulez parler francais! Where did you learn it?
JEAN In Switzerland, while I worked as sommelier[5] in one of the big hotels at Lucerne.
JULIA But you look like a real gentleman in your frock coat! Charming! *(Sits down at the table.)*
JEAN Oh, you flatter me.
JULIA (*offended*) Flatter—you!
JEAN My natural modesty does not allow me to believe that you could be paying genuine compliments to one like me, and so I dare to assume that you are exaggerating, or as we call it, flattering.
JULIA Where did you learn to use your words like that? You must have been to the theatre a great deal?
JEAN That, too. I have been to a lot of places.
JULIA But you were born in this neighbourhood?
JEAN My father was a cotter[6] on the county attorney's property right by here, and I can recall seeing you as a child, although you, of course, didn't notice me.
JULIA No, really!
JEAN Yes, and I remember one time in particular—but of that I can't speak.
JULIA Oh, yes, do! Why—just for once.
JEAN No, really, I cannot do it now. Another time, perhaps.
JULIA Another time is no time. Is it as bad as that?
JEAN It isn't bad, but it comes a little hard. Look at that one! *(Points to* CHRISTINE, *who has fallen asleep on a chair by the stove.)*
JULIA She'll make a pleasant wife. And perhaps she snores, too.
JEAN No, she doesn't, but she talks in her sleep.
JULIA (*cynically*) How do you know?
JEAN (*insolently*) I have heard it.

(Pause during which they study each other.)

JULIA Why don't you sit down?
JEAN It wouldn't be proper in your presence.
JULIA But if I order you to do it?
JEAN Then I obey.

---

4. Tres gentil, etc.
   JULIA. Very fine, Mr. John! Very fine!
   JEAN. You want to joke, madame!
   JULIA. And you want to speak French!
5. sommelier, wine steward.
6. cotter, a cottager or peasant.

JULIA Sit down, then!—But wait a moment! Can you give me something to drink first?
JEAN I don't know what we have got in the icebox. I fear it is nothing but beer.
JULIA And you call that nothing? My taste is so simple that I prefer it to wine.
JEAN *(takes a bottle of beer from the icebox and opens it; gets a glass and a plate from the cupboard, and serves the beer).* Allow me!
JULIA Thank you. Don't you want some yourself?
JEAN I don't care very much for beer, but if it is a command, of course. . . .
JULIA Command?—I should think a polite gentleman might keep his lady company.
JEAN Yes, that's the way it should be. *(Opens another bottle and takes out a glass.)*
JULIA Drink my health now!

(JEAN hesitates.)

JULIA Are you bashful—a big, grown-up man?
JEAN *(kneels with mock solemnity and raises his glass).* To the health of my liege lady!
JULIA Bravo!—And now you must also kiss my shoe in order to get it just right.

(JEAN hesitates a moment; then he takes hold of her foot and touches it lightly with his lips.)

JULIA Excellent! You should have been on the stage.
JEAN *(rising to his feet).* This won't do any longer, Miss Julia. Somebody might see us.
JULIA What would that matter?
JEAN Oh, it would set the people talking—that's all! And if you only knew how their tongues were wagging up there a while ago. . . .
JULIA What did they have to say? Tell me—sit down now!
JEAN *(sits down)* I don't want to hurt you, but they were using expressions—which cast reflections of a kind that—oh, you know it yourself! You are not a child, and when a lady is seen alone with a man, drinking—no matter if he's only a servant—and at night—then. . . .
JULIA Then what? And besides, we are not alone. Isn't Christine with us?
JEAN Yes—asleep!
JULIA Then I'll wake her. *(Rising)* Christine, are you asleep?
CHRISTINE *(in her sleep).* Blub-blub-blub-blub!
JULIA Christine!—Did you ever see such a sleeper.
CHRISTINE *(in her sleep).* The count's boots are polished—put on the coffee—yes, yes, yes—my—my—pooh!
JULIA *(pinches her nose).* Can't you wake up?
JEAN *(sternly).* You shouldn't bother those that sleep.
JULIA *(sharply).* What's that?
JEAN One who has stood by the stove all day has a right to be tired at night. And sleep should be respected.
JULIA *(changing tone).* It is fine to think like that, and it does you honour—I thank you for it. *(Gives JEAN her hand)* Come now and pick some lilacs for me.

(During the following scene CHRISTINE wakes up. She moves as if still asleep and goes out to the right in order to go to bed.)

JEAN, With you, Miss Julia?
JULIA With me!

JEAN But it won't do! Absolutely not!

JULIA I can't understand what you are thinking of. You couldn't possibly imagine. . . .

JEAN No, not I, but the people.

JULIA What? That I am fond of the valet?

JEAN I am not at all conceited, but such things have happened—and to the people nothing is sacred.

JULIA You are an aristocrat, I think.

JEAN Yes, I am.

JULIA And I am stepping down. . . .

JEAN Take my advice, Miss Julia, don't step down. Nobody will believe you did it on purpose. The people will always say that you fell down.

JULIA I think better of the people than you do. Come and see if I am not right. Come along! *(She ogles him.)*

JEAN You're might queer, do you know!

JULIA Perhaps. But so are you. And for that matter, everything is queer. Life, men, everything—just a mush that floats on top of the water until it sinks, sinks down! I have a dream that comes back to me ever so often. And just now I am reminded of it. I have climbed to the top of a column and sit there without being able to tell how to get down again. I get dizzy when I look down, and I must get down, but I haven't the courage to jump off. I cannot hold on, and I am longing to fall, and yet I don't fall. But there will be no rest for me until I get down, no rest until I get down, down on the ground. And if I did reach the ground, I should want to get still further down, into the ground itself—have you ever felt like that?

JEAN No, my dream is that I am lying under a tall tree in a dark wood. I want to get up, up to the top, so that I can look out over the smiling landscape, where the sun is shining, and so that I can rob the nest in which lie the golden eggs. And I climb and climb, but the trunk is so think and smooth, and it is so far to the first branch. But I know that if I could only reach that first branch, then I should go right on to the top as on a ladder. I have not reached it yet, but I am going to, if it only be in my dreams.

JULIA Here I am chattering to you about dreams! Come along! Only into the park!

(She offers her arm to him, and they go toward the door.)

JEAN We must sleep on nine midsummer flowers tonight, Miss Julia—then our dreams will come true.

(They turn around in the doorway, and JEAN *puts one hand up to his eyes.)*

JULIA Let me see what you have got in your eye.

JEAN Oh, nothing—just some dirt—it will soon be gone.

JULIA It was my sleeve that rubbed against it. Sit down and let me help you. (Takes him by the arm and makes him sit down; takes hold of his head and bends it backwards; tries to get out the dirt with a corner of her handkerchief.) Sit still now, absolutely still! *(Slaps him on the hand)* Well, can't you do as I say? I think you are shaking—a big, strong fellow like you! *(Feels his biceps)* And with such arms!

JEAN *(ominously).* Miss Julia!

JULIA Yes, Monsieur Jean.

JEAN   Attention! Je ne suis qu' un homme.[7]
JULIA Can't you sit still! There now! Now it's gone. Kiss my hand now, and thank me.
JEAN   (*rising*)   Miss Julia, listen to me. Christine has gone to bed now. . . . Won't you listen to me?
JULIA Kiss my hand first.
JEAN   Listen to me!
JULIA Kiss my hand first!
JEAN   All right, but blame nobody but yourself!
JULIA For what?
JEAN   For what? Are you still a mere child at twenty-five? Don't you know that it is dangerous to play with fire?
JULIA Not for me. I am insured.
JEAN   (*boldly*)   No you are not. And even if you were, there are inflammable surroundings to be counted with.
JULIA That's you, I suppose?
JEAN   Yes. Not because I am I, but because I am a young man.
JULIA Of handsome appearance—what an incredible conceit! A Don Juan, perhaps. Or a Joseph? On my soul, I think you are a Joseph!
JEAN   Do you?
JULIA I fear it almost.

(*JEAN goes boldy up to her and takes her around the waist in order to kiss her.*)

JULIA (*gives him a cuff on the ear*). Shame!
JEAN   Was that in play or in earnest?
JULIA In earnest.
JEAN   Then you were in earnest a moment ago also. Your playing is too serious, and that's the dangerous thing about it. Now I am tired of playing, and I ask to be excused in order to resume my work. The count wants his boots to be ready for him, and it is after midnight already.
JULIA Put away the boots.
JEAN   No, it's my work, which I am bound to do. But I have not undertaken to be your playmate. It's something I can never become. . . . I hold myself too good for it.
JULIE You're proud!
JEAN   In some ways, and not in others.
JULIA Have you ever been in love?
JEAN   We don't use that word. But I have been fond of a lot of girls, and once I was taken sick because I couln't have the one I wanted: sick, you know, like those princes in the Arabian Nights who cannot eat or drink for sheer love.
JULIA Who was it?

(*Jean remains silent.*)

JULIA Who was it?
JEAN   You cannot make me tell you.
JULIA If I ask you as an equal, ask you as—a friend: who was it?

---

7. Attention! etc. Be careful! I'm only a man.

JEAN It was you.

JULIA *(sits down)*. How funny!

JEAN Yes, as you say—it was ludicrous. That was the story, you see, which I didn't want to tell you a while ago. But now I am going to tell it. Do you know how the world looks from below—no, you don't. No more than do hawks and falcons, of whom we never see the black because they are always floating about high up in the sky. I lived in the cotter's hovel, together with seven other children, and a pig—out there on the grey plain, where there isn't a single tree. But from our windows I could see the wall around the count's park, and apple trees above it. That was the Garden of Eden, and many fierce angels were guarding it with flaming swords. Nevertheless I and some other boys found our way to the Tree of Life—now you despise me?

JULIA Oh, stealing apples is something all boys do.

JEAN You may say so now, but you despise me nevertheless. However—once I got into the Garden of Eden with my mother to weed the onion beds. Near by stood a Turkish pavillion, shaded by trees and covered with honeysuckle. I didn't know what it was used for, but I had never seen a more beautiful building. People went in and came out again, and one day the door was left wide open. I stole up and saw the walls covered with pictures of kings and emperors, and the windows were hung with red, fringed curtains—now you know what I mean. I *(breaks off a lilac sprig and holds it under* MISS JULIA'S *nose)*—I had never been inside the manor, and I had never seen anything but the church—and this was much finer. No matter where my thoughts ran, they returned always—to that place. And gradually a longing arose within me to taste the full pleasure of—enfin!⁸ I sneaked in, looked and admired. Then I heard somebody coming. There was only one way out for fine people, but for me there was another, and I could do nothing else but choose it.

(JULIA, *who has taken the lilac sprig, lets it drop on the table.*)

JEAN Then I started to run, plunged through a hedge of raspberry bushes, chased right across a strawberry plantation, and came out on the terrace where the roses grow. There I caught sight of a pink dress and pair of white stockings—that was you! I crawled under a pile of weeds—right into it, you know—into stinging thistles and wet, ill-smelling dirt. And I saw you walking among the roses, and I thought: if it be possible for a robber to get into heaven and dwell with the angels, then it is strange that a cotter's child, here on God's own earth, cannot get into the park and play with the count's daughter.

JULIA *(sentimentally)*. Do you think all poor children have the same thoughts as you had in this case?

JEAN *(hesitatingly at first; then with conviction)*. If all poor—yes—of course. Of course!

JULIA It must be a dreadful misfortune to be poor.

JEAN *(in a tone of deep distress and with rather exaggerated emphasis)*. Oh, Miss Julia! Oh!—A dog may lie on her ladyship's sofa; a horse may have his nose patted by the young lady's hand, but a servant—*(changing his tone)*—oh well, here and there you meet one made of different stuff, and he makes a way for himself in the world, but how often does it happen? However, do you know what I did? I jumped into the mill brook with my clothes on, and was pulled out, and got a licking. But the next Sunday, when my father and the rest of the people

---

8. Enfin! well!

were going over to my grandmother's, I fixed it so that I could stay at home. And then I washed myself with soap and hot water, and put on my best clothes, and went to church, where I could see you. I did see you, and went home determined to die. But I wanted to die beautifully and pleasantly, without any pain. And then I recalled that it was dangerous to sleep under an elder bush. We had a big one that was in full bloom. I robbed it of all its flowers, and then I put them in the big box where the oats were kept and lay down in them. Did you ever notice the smoothness of oats? Soft to the touch as the skin of the human body! However, I pulled down the lid and closed my eyes—fell asleep and was waked up a very sick boy. But I didn't die, as you can see. What I wanted—that's more than I can tell. Of course, there was not the least hope of winning you—but you symbolised the hopelessness of trying to get out of the class into which I was born.

JULIA You narrate splendidly, do you know! Did you ever go to school?

JEAN A little. But I have read a lot of novels and gone to the theatre a good deal. And besides, I have listened to the talk of better-class people, and from that I have learned most of all.

JULIA Do you stand around and listen to what we are saying?

JEAN Of course! And I have heard a lot, too, when I was on the box of the carriage, or rowing the boat. Once I heard you, Miss Julia, and one of your girl friends. . . .

JULIA Oh!—What was it you heard then?

JEAN Well, it wouldn't be easy to repeat. But I was rather surprised, and I couldn't understand where you had learned all those words. Perhaps, at bottom, there isn't quite so much difference as they think between one kind of people and another.

JULIA You ought to be ashamed of yourself! We don't live as you do when we are engaged.

JEAN (*looking hard at her*). Is it so certain? Well, Miss Julia, it won't pay to make yourself out so very innocent to me. . . .

JULIA The man on whom I bestowed my love was a scoundrel.

JEAN That's what you always say—afterwards.

JULIA Always?

JEAN Always, I believe, for I have heard the same words used several times before, on similar occasions.

JULIA What occasions?

JEAN Like the one of which we were speaking. The last time. . . .

JULIA (*rising*). Stop! I don't want to hear any more!

JEAN Nor did she—curiously enough! Well, then I ask permission to go to bed.

JULIA (*gently*). Go to bed on Midsummer Eve?

JEAN Yes for dancing with that mob out there has really no attraction for me.

JULIA Get the key to the boat and take me out on the lake—I want to watch the sun rise.

JEAN Would that be wise?

JULIA It sounds as if you were afraid of your reputation.

JEAN Why not? I don't care to be made ridiculous, and I don't care to be discharged without a recommendation, for I am trying to get on in the world. And then I feel myself under a certain obligation to Christine.

JULIA So it's Christine now.

JEAN Yes, but it's you also—Take my advice and go to bed!

JULIA Am I to obey you?

JEAN For once—and for your sake! The night is far gone. Sleepiness makes us drunk, and the head grows hot. Go to bed! And besides—if I am not mistaken—I can hear the crowd coming this way to look for me. And if we are found together here, you are lost!

CHORUS (is heard approaching).

> Through the fields come two ladies a-walking,
> Treederee-derallah, treederee derah.
> And one has her shoes full of water,
> Treederee-derallah-lah.
>
> They're talking of hundreds of dollars,
> Treederee-derallah, treederee-derah.
> But have not between them a dollar,
> Treederee-derallah-lah.
>
> This wreath I give you gladly,
> Treederee-derallah, treederee-derah.
> But love another madly,
> Treederee-derallah-lah.

JULIA I know the people, and I love them, just as they love me. Let them come, and you'll see.
JEAN No, Miss Julia, they don't love you. They take your food and spit at your back. Believe me. Listen to me—can't you hear what they are singing?—No, don't pay any attention to it!
JULIA *(listening)*. What is it they are singing?
JEAN Oh, something scurrilous. About you and me.
JULIA How infamous! They ought to be ashamed! And the treachery of it!
JEAN The mob is always cowardly. And in such a fight as this there is nothing to do but to run away.
JULIA Run away? Where to? We cannot get out. And we cannot go into Christine's room.
JEAN Oh, we cannot? Well, into my room, then! Necessity knows no law And you can trust me, for I am your true and frank and respectful friend.
JULIA But think only—think if they should look for you in there!
JEAN I shall bolt the door. And if they try to break it open, I'll shoot! Come! *(Kneeling before her)* Come!
JULIA *(meaningly)*. And you promise me. . . .
JEAN I swear!

(MISS JULIA *goes quickly out to the right.* JEAN *follows her eagerly.*)

Ballet

The peasants enter. They are decked out in their best and carry flowers in their hats. A fiddler leads them. On the table they place a barrel of small-beer and a keg of "brannvin," or white Swedish whiskey, both of them decorated with wreathes woven out of leaves. First they drink. Then they form in ring and sing and dance to the melody heard before:

"Through the fields come two ladies a-walking."

The dance finished, they leave singing.

JULIA *(Enters alone. On seeing the disorder in the kitchen, she claps her hands together. Then she takes out a powder puff and begins to powder her face).*

JEAN *(enters in a state of exaltation).* There you see! And you heard, didn't you? Do you think it possible to stay here?

JULIA No, I don't think so. But what are we to do?

JEAN Run away, travel, far away from here.

JULIA Travel? Yes—but where?

JEAN To Switzerland, the Italian lakes—you have never been there?

JULIA No. Is the country beautiful?

JEAN Oh! Eternal summer! Orange trees! Laurels! Oh!

JULIA But then—what are we to do down there?

JEAN I'll start a hotel, everything first class, including the customers.

JULIA Hotel?

JEAN That's the life, I tell you! Constantly new faces and new languages. Never a minute free for nerves or brooding. No trouble about what to do—for the work is calling to be done: night and day, bells that ring, trains that whistle, 'busses that come and go; and gold pieces raining on the counter all the time. That's the life for you!

JULIA Yes, that is life. And I?

JEAN The mistress of everything, the chief ornament of the house. With your looks—and your manners—oh, success will be assured! Enormous! You'll sit like a queen in the office and keep the slaves going by the touch of an electric button. The guests will pass in review before your throne and timidly deposit their treasures on your table. You cannot imagine how people tremble when a bill is presented to them—I'll salt the items, and you'll sugar them with your sweetest smiles. Oh, let us get away from here *(pulling a time-table from his pocket)*—at once, with the next train! We'll be in Malmo at 6:30; in Hamburg at 8:40 tomorrow morning; in Frankfort and Basel a day later. And to reach Como by way of the St. Gotthard it will take us—let me see—three days. Three days!

JULIA All that is all right. But you must give me some courage—Jean. Tell me that you love me. Come and take me in your arms.

JEAN *(reluctantly).* I should like to —but I don't dare. Not in this house again. I love you—beyond doubt—or, can you doubt it, Miss Julia?

JULIA *(with modesty and true womanly feeling).* Miss?—Call me Julia. Between us there can be no barriers hereafter. Call me Julia!

JEAN *(disturbed).* I cannot! There will be barriers between us as long as we stay in this house—there is the past, and there is the Count—and I have never met another person for whom I felt such respect. If I only catch sight of his gloves on a chair I feel small. If I only hear that bell up there, I jump like a shy horse. And even now, when I see his boots standing there so stiff and perky, it is as if something made my back bend. *(Kicking at the boots)* It's nothing but superstition and tradition hammered into us from childhood—but it can be as easily forgotten again. Let us only get to another country, where they have a republic, and you'll see them bend their backs double before my liveried porter. Backs have to be bent, but not mine. I wasn't born to that kind of thing. There's better stuff in me—character—and if I only get hold of the first branch, you'll see me do some climbing. Today I am a valet, but next year I'll be a hotel owner. In ten years I can live on the money I have made, and then I'll go to Roumania and get myself an order. And I may—note that I say may—end my days as a count.

JULIA Splendid, splendid!
JEAN Yes, in Roumania the title of count can be had for cash, and so you'll be a countess after all. My countess!
JULIA What do I care about all I now cast behind me! Tell me that you love me: otherwise—yes, what am I otherwise?
JEAN I will tell you so a thousand times—later. But not here. And above all, no sentimentality, or everything will be lost. We must look at the matter in cold blood, like sensible people. *(Takes out a cigar, cuts off the point, and lights it)* Sit down there now, and I'll sit here, and then we'll talk as if nothing had happened.
JULIA *(in despair).* Good Lord! Have you then no feelings at all?
JEAN I? No one is more full of feeling than I am. But I know how to control myself.
JULIA A while ago you kissed my shoe—and now!
JEAN *(severely).* Yes, that was then. Now we have other things to think of.
JULIA Don't speak harshly to me!
JEAN No, but sensibly. One folly has been committed—don't let us commit any more! The count may be here at any moment, and before he comes our fate must be settled. What do you think of my plans for the future? Do you approve of them?
JULIA They seem acceptable, on the whole. But there is one question: a big undertaking of that kind will require a big capital—have you got it?
JEAN *(chewing his cigar).* I? Of course! I have my expert knowledge, my vast experience, my familiarity with several languages. That's the very best kind of capital, I should say.
JULIA But it won't buy you a railroad ticket even.
JEAN That's true enough. And that is just why I am looking for a backer to advance the needful cash.
JULIA Where could you get one all of a sudden?
JEAN It's for you to find him if you want to become my partner.
JULIA I cannot do it, and I have nothing myself. *(Pause.)*
JEAN Well, then that's off.
JULIA And. . . .
JEAN Everything remains as before.
JULIA Do you think I am going to stay under this roof as your concubine? Do you think I'll let the people point their fingers at me? Do you think I can look my father in the face after this? No, take me away from here, from all this humiliation and disgrace!—Oh, what have I done? My God, my God! (Breaks into tears)
JEAN So we have got around to that tune now!—What you have done? Nothing but what many others have done before you.
JULIA *(crying hysterically).* And now you're despising me! —I'm falling, I'm falling!
JEAN Fall down to me, and I'll lift you up again afterwards.
JULIA What horrible power drew me to you? Was it the attraction which the strong exercises on the weak—the one who is rising on one who is falling? Or was it love? This—love! Do you know what love is?
JEAN I? Well, I should say so! Don't you think I have been there before?
JULIA Oh, the language you use, the thoughts you think!

JEAN Well, that's the way I was brought up, and that's the way I am. Don't get nerves now and play the exquisite, for now one of us is just as good as the other. Look here, my girl, let me treat you to a glass of something super fine.

(He opens the table-drawer, takes out the wine bottle and fills up two glasses that have already been used.)

JULIA Where did you get that wine?
JEAN In the cellar.
JULIA My father's Burgundy!
JEAN Well, isn't it good enough for the son-in-law?
JULIA And I am drinking beer—I!
JEAN It shows merely that I have better taste than you.
JULIA Thief!
JEAN Do you mean to tell on me?
JULIA Oh, oh! The accomplice of a house thief! Have I been drunk, or have I been dreaming all this night? Midsummer Eve! The feast of innocent games. . . .
JEAN Innocent—hm!
JULIA (*walking back and forth*). Can there be another human being on earth so unhappy as I am at this moment?
JEAN But why should you be? After such a conquest? Think of Christine in there. Don't you think she has feelings also?
JULIA I thought so a while ago, but I don't think so any longer. No, a menial is a menial. . . .
JEAN And a whore a whore!
JULIA (*on her knees, with folded hands*). O God in heaven, make an end of this wretched life! Take me out of the filth into which I am sinking! Save me! Save me!
JEAN I cannot deny that I feel sorry for you. When I was lying among the onions and saw you up there among the roses—I'll tell you now—I had the same nasty thoughts that all boys have.
JULIA And you who wanted to die for my sake!
JEAN Among the oats. That was nothing but talk.
JULIA Lies in other words!
JEAN (*beginning to feel sleepy*). Just about. I think I read the story in a paper, and it was about a chimney-sweep who crawled into a wood-box full of lilacs because a girl had brought suit against him for not supporting her kid.
JULIA So that's the sort you are. . . .
JEAN Well, I had to think of something—for it's the high-faluting stuff that the women bite on.
JULIA Scoundrel!
JEAN Rot!
JULIA And now you have seen the back of the hawk
JEAN Well, I don't know. . . .
JULIA And I was to be the first branch. . . .
JEAN But the branch was rotten. . . .
JULIA I was to be the sign in front of the hotel. . . .
JEAN And I the hotel. . . .
JULIA Sit at your counter, and lure your customers, and doctor your bills. . . .

JEAN No, that I should have done myself.
JULIA That a human soul can be so steeped in dirt!
JEAN Well, wash it off!
JULIA You lackey-love, you menial, stand up when I talk to you!
JEAN You lackey-love, you mistress of a menial—shut up and get out of here! You're the right one to come and tell me that I am vulgar. People of my kind would never in their lives act as vulgarly as you have acted tonight. Do you think any servant girl would go for a man as you did? Did you ever see a girl of my class throw herself at anybody in that way? I have never seen the like of it except among beasts and prostitutes.
JULIA (*crushed*). That's right: strike me, step on me—I haven't deserved any better! I am a wretched creature. But help me! Help me out of this, if there be any way to do so!
JEAN (*in a milder tone*). I don't want to lower myself by a denial of my share in the honour of seducing. But do you think a person in my place would have dared to raise his eyes to you, if the invitation to do so had not come from yourself? I am still sitting here in a state of utter surprise.
JULIA And pride. . . .
JEAN Yes, why not? Although I must confess that the victory was too easy to bring with it any real intoxication.
JULIA Strike me some more!
JEAN (*rising*). No! Forgive me instead what I have been saying. I don't want to strike one who is disarmed, and least of all a lady. On one hand I cannot deny that it has given me pleasure to discover that what has dazzled us below is nothing but cat-gold; that the hawk is simply grey on the back also; that there is powder on the tender cheek; that there may be black borders on the polished nails; and that the handkerchief may be dirty, although it smells of perfume. But on the other hand it hurts me to have discovered that what I was striving to reach is neither better nor more genuine. It hurts me to see you sinking so low that you are far beneath your own cook—it hurts me as it hurts to see the fall flowers beaten down by the rain and turned into mud.
JULIA You speak as if you were already above me?
JEAN Well, so I am. Don't you see: I could have made a countess of you, but you could never make me a count.
JULIA But I am born of a count, and that's more than you can ever achieve.
JEAN That's true. But I might be the father of counts—if. . . .
JULIA But you are a thief—and I am not.
JEAN Thief is not the worst. There are other kinds still farther down. And then, when I serve in a house, I regard myself in a sense as a member of the family, as a child of the house, and you don't call it theft when children pick a few of the berries that load down the vines. (*His passion is aroused once more.*) Miss Julia, you are a magnificent woman, and far too good for one like me. You were swept along by a spell of intoxication, and now you want to cover up your mistake by making yourself believe that you are in love with me. Well, you are not, unless possibly my looks might tempt you—in which case your love is no better than mine. I could never rest satisfied with having you care for nothing in me but the mere animal, and your love I can never win.

JULIA Are you so sure of that?

JEAN You mean to say that it might be possible? That I might love you: yes, without doubt—for you are beautiful, refined (*goes up to her and takes hold of her hand*), educated, charming when you want to be so, and it is not likely that the flame will ever burn out in a man who has once been set on fire by you. *(Puts his arm around her waist)* You are like burnt wine with strong spices in it, and one of your kisses. . . .

(He tries to lead her away, but she frees herself gently from his hold.)

JULIA Leave me alone! In that way you cannot win me.

JEAN How then?—Not in that way! Not by caresses and sweet words! Not by thought for the future, by escape from disgrace! How then?

JULIA How? How? I don't know— Not at all! I hate you as I hate rats, but I cannot escape from you!

JEAN Escape with me!

JULIA (*straightening up*). Escape? Yes, we must escape!—But I am so tired. Give me a glass of wine.

(JEAN *pours out wine.*)

JULIA (*looks at her watch*). But we must have a talk first. We have still some time left. (Empties her glass and holds it out for more.)

JEAN Don't drink so much. It will go to your head.

JULIA What difference would that make?

JEAN What difference would it make? It's vulgar to get drunk—What was it you wanted to tell me?

JULIA We must get away. But first we must have a talk—that is, I must talk, for so far you have done all the talking. You have told me about your life. Now I must tell you about mine, so that we know each other right to the bottom before we begin our journey together.

JEAN One moment, pardon me! Think first, so that you don't regret it afterwards, when you have already given up the secrets of your life.

JULIA Are you not my friend?

JEAN Yes, at times—but don't rely on me.

JULIA You only talk like that—and besides, my secrets are known to everybody. You see, my mother was not of noble birth, but came of quite plain people. She was brought up in the ideas of her time about equality, and woman's independence, and that kind of thing. And she had a decided aversion to marriage. Therefore, when my father proposed to her, she said she wouldn't marry him—and then she did it just the same. I came into the world—against my mother's wish, I have come to think. Then my mother wanted to bring me up in a perfectly natural state, and at the same time I was to learn everything that a boy is taught, so that I might prove that a woman is just as good as a man. I was dressed as a boy, and was taught how to handle a horse, but could have nothing to do with the cows. I had to groom and harness and go hunting on horseback. I was even forced to learn something about agriculture. And all over the estate men were set to do women's work, and women to do men's—with the result that everything went to pieces and we became the laughingstock of the whole neighbourhood. At last my father must have recovered from the spell cast over him, for he rebelled, and everything was changed to suit his own ideas. My mother was taken sick—what kind of sickness it was I don't know, but she fell often into convulsions, and she used to hide herself in the garret or in the garden, and sometimes she stayed out all night. Then came the big fire, of which you have heard. The house, the stable, and the barn were burned down and this under circumstances which made it look as if the fire had been set on purpose. For the disaster occurred the day after our insurance expired, and the money sent for renewal of the policy had been delayed by the messenger's carelessness, so that it came too late. *(She fills her glass again and drinks.)*

JEAN Don't drink any more.

JULIA Oh, what does it matter!—We were without a roof over our heads and had to sleep in the carriages. My father didn't know where to get money for the rebuilding of the house. Then my mother suggested that he try to borrow from a childhood friend of hers, a brick manufacturer living not far from here. My father got the loan, but was not permitted to pay any interest, which astonished him. And so the house was built up again. *(Drinks again)* Do you know who set fire to the house?

JEAN Her ladyship, your mother!

JULIA Do you know who the brick manufacturer was?

JEAN Your mother's lover?

JULIA Do you know to whom the money belonged?

JEAN Wait a minute—no, that I don't know.

JULIA To my mother.

JEAN In other words, to the Count, if there was no settlement.

JULIA There was no settlement. My mother possessed a small fortune of her own which she did not want to leave in my father's control, so she invested it with—her friend.

JEAN Who copped it.

JULIA Exactly! He kept it. All this came to my father's knowledge. He couldn't bring suit; he couldn't pay his wife's lover; he couldn't prove that it was his wife's money. That was my mother's revenge because he had made himself master in his own house. At that time he came near shooting himself— it was even rumoured that he had tried and failed. But he took a new lease of life, and my mother had to pay for what she had done. I can tell you that those were five years I'll never forget! My sympathies were with my father, but I took my mother's side because I was not aware of the true circumstances. From her I learned to suspect and hate men—for she hated the whole sex, as you have probably heard—and I promised her on my oath that I would never become a man's slave.

JEAN And so you became engaged to the County Attorney.

JULIA Yes, in order that he should be my slave.

JEAN And he didn't want to?

JULIA Oh, he wanted, but I wouldn't let him. I got tired of him.

JEAN Yes, I saw it—in the stable-yard.

JULIA What did you see?

JEAN Just that—how he broke the engagement.

JULIA That's a lie! It was I who broke it. Did he say he did it, the scoundrel?

JEAN Oh, he was no scoundrel, I guess. So you hate men, Miss Julia?

JULIA Yes! Most of the time. But now and then—when the weakness comes over me—oh, what shame!

JEAN And you hate me too?

JULIA Beyond measure! I should like to kill you like a wild beast.
JEAN As you make haste to shoot a mad dog. Is that right?
JULIA That's right!
JEAN But now there is nothing to shoot with—and there is no dog. What are we to do then?
JULIA Go abroad.
JEAN In order to plague each other to death?
JULIA No—in order to enjoy ourselves: a couple of days, a week, as long as enjoyment is possible. And then—die!
JEAN Die? How silly! Then I think it's much better to start a hotel.
JULIA *(without listening to* JEAN*)*.—At Lake Como, where the sun is always shining, and the laurels stand green at Christmas, and the oranges are glowing.
JEAN Lake Como is a rainy hole, and I could see no oranges except in the groceries. But it is a good place for tourists, as it has a lot of villas that can be rented to loving couples, and that's a profitable business—do you know why? Because they take a lease for six months—and then they leave after three weeks.
JULIA *(naively).* Why after three weeks?
JEAN Because they quarrel, of course. But the rent has to be paid just the same. And then you can rent the house again. And that way it goes on all the time, for there is plenty of love—even if it doesn't last long.
JULIA You don't want to die with me?
JEAN I don't want to die at all. Both because I am fond of living, and because I regard suicide as a crime against the Providence which has bestowed life on us.
JULIA Do you mean to say that you believe in God?
JEAN Of course, I do. And I go to church every other Sunday. Frankly speaking, now I am tired of all this, and now I am going to bed.
JULIA So! And you think that will be enough for me? Do you know what you owe a woman that you have spoiled?
JEAN *(takes out his purse and throws a silver coin on the table).* You're welcome! I don't want to be in anybody's debt.
JULIA *(pretending not to notice the insult)* Do you know what the law provides?
JEAN Unfortunately the law provides no punishment for a woman who seduces a man.
JULIA *(as before)* Can you think of any escape except by our going abroad and getting married, and then getting a divorce?
JEAN Suppose I refuse to enter into this mésalliance?
JULIA Mésalliance. . . .
JEAN Yes, for me. You see I have better ancestry than you, for nobody in my family was ever guilty of arson.
JULIA How do you know?
JEAN Well, nothing is known to the contrary, for we keep no pedigrees—except in the police bureau. But I have read about your pedigree in a book that was lying on the drawing room table. Do you know who was your first ancestor? A miller who let his wife sleep with the king on one night during the war with Denmark. I have no such ancestry. I have none at all, but I can become an ancestor myself.

JULIA That's what I get for unburdening my heart to one not worthy of it; for sacrificing my family's honour. .. .
JEAN Dishonour! Well, what was it I told you? You shouldn't drink, for then you talk. And you must not talk!
JULIA Oh, how I regret what I have done! How I regret it! If at least you loved me!
JEAN For the last time: what do you mean? Am I to weep? Am I to jump over your whip? Am I to kiss you, and lure you down to Lake Como for three weeks, and so on? What am I to do? What do you expect? This is getting to be rather painful! But that's what comes from getting mixed up with women. Miss Julia! I see that you are unhappy; I know that you are suffering; but I cannot understand you. We never carry on like that. There is never any hatred between us. Love is to us a play, and we play at it when our work leaves us time to do so. But we have not the time to do so all day and all night, as you have. I believe you are sick—I am sure you are sick.
JULIA You should be good to me—and now you speak like a human being.
JEAN All right, but be human yourself. You spit on me, and then you won't let me wipe myself—on you!
JULIA Help me, help me! Tell me only what I am to do—where am I to turn?
JEAN O Lord, if I only knew that myself!
JULIA I have been exasperated, I have been mad, but there ought to be some way of saving myself.
JEAN Stay right here and keep quiet. Nobody knows anything.
JULIA Impossible! The people know, and Christine knows.
JEAN They don't know, and they would never believe it possible.
JULIA *(hesitating)*. But—it might happen again.
JEAN That's true.
JULIA And the results?
JEAN *(frightened)*. The results! Where was my head when I didn't think of that! Well, then there is only one thing to do—you must leave. At once! I can't go with you, for then everything would be lost, so you must go alone—abroad—anywhere!
JULIA Alone? Where?—I can't do it.
JEAN You must! And before the Count gets back. If you stay, then you know what will happen. Once on the wrong path, one wants to keep on, as the harm is done anyhow. Then one grows more and more reckless—and at last it all comes out. So you must get away! Then you can write the count and tell him everything, except that it was me. And he would never guess it. Nor do I think he would be very anxious to find out.
JULIA I'll go if you come with me.
JEAN Are you stark mad, woman? Miss Julia to run away with her valet? It would be in the papers in another day, and the count could never survive it.
JULIA I can't leave! I can't stay! Help me! I am so tired, so fearfully tired. Give me orders! Set me going, for I can no longer think, no longer act.
JEAN Do you see now what good-for-nothings you are! Why do you strut and turn up your noses as if you were the lords of creation? Well, I am going to give you orders. Go up and dress. Get some travelling money, and then come back again.
JULIA (in an undertone). Come up with me!

JEAN To your room? Now you're crazy again! (Hesitates a moment) No, you must go at once! *(Takes her by the hand and leads her out.)*

JULIA *(on her way out).* Can't you speak kindly to me, Jean?

JEAN An order must always sound unkind. Now you can find out how it feels!

(JULIA *goes out.* JEAN, *alone, draws a sigh of relief; sits down at the table; takes out a notebook and a pencil; figures aloud from time to time; dumb play until* CHRISTINE *enters dressed for church; she has a false shirt front and a white tie in one of her hands.)*

CHRISTINE Goodness gracious, how the place looks! What have you been up to anyhow?

JEAN Oh, it was Miss Julia who dragged in the people. Have you been sleeping so hard that you didn't hear anything at all?

CHRISTINE I have been sleeping like a log.

JEAN And dressed for church already?

CHRISTINE Yes, didn't you promise to come with me to communion today?

JEAN Oh, yes, I remember now. And there you've got the finery. Well, come on with it. *(Sits down;* CHRISTINE *helps him to put on the shirt front and the white tie. Pause.)*

JEAN *(sleepily).* What's the text today?

CHRISTINE Oh, about John the Baptist beheaded, I guess.

JEAN That's going to be a long story, I'm sure. My, but you choke me! Oh, I'm so sleepy, so sleepy!

CHRISTINE Well, what has been keeping you up all night? Why, man, you're just green in the face!

JEAN I have been sitting here talking with Miss Julia.

CHRISTINE She hasn't an idea of what's proper, that creature! *(Pause).*

JEAN Say, Christine.

CHRISTINE Well?

JEAN Is't it funny anyhow, when you come to think of it? Her!

CHRISTINE What is it that's funny?

JEAN Everything! *(Pause.)*

CHRISTINE *(Seeing the glasses on the table that are only half emptied).* So you've been drinking together also?

JEAN Yes.

CHRISTINE Shame on you! Look me in the eye!

JEAN Yes.

CHRISTINE Is it possible? Is it possible?

JEAN *(after a moment's thought).* Yes, it is!

CHRISTINE Ugh! That's worse than I could ever have believed. It's awful.

JEAN You are not jealous of her, are you?

CHRISTINE No, not of her. Had it been Clara or Sophie, then I'd have scratched your eyes out. Yes, that's the way I feel about it, and I can't tell why. Oh my, but that was nasty!

JEAN Are you mad at her then?

CHRISTINE No, but at you! It was wrong of you, very wrong! Poor girl! No, I tell you, I don't want to stay in this house any longer, with people who don't act decently, would you? It's to lower oneself, I think.

JEAN Yes, but it ought to be a consolation to us that they are not a bit better than we.
CHRISTINE No, I don't think so. For if they're no better, then it's no use trying to get up to them. And just think of the count! Think of him who has had so much sorrow in his day! No, I don't want to stay any longer in this house. And with a fellow like you, too. If it had been the County Attorney—if it had only been someone of her own sort. . . .
JEAN Now look here!
CHRISTINE Yes, yes! You're all right in your way, but there's after all some difference between one kind of people and another—No, but this is something I'll never get over!—And the young lady who was so proud, and so tart to the men, that you couldn't believe she would ever let one come near her—and such a one at that! And she who wanted to have poor Diana shot because she had been running around with the gatekeeper's pug!—Well, I declare!—But I won't stay here any longer, and next October I get out of here.
JEAN And then?
CHRISTINE Well, as we've come to talk of that now, perhaps it would be just as well if you looked for something, seeing that we're going to get married after all.
JEAN Well, what could I look for? As a married man I couldn't get a place like this.
CHRISTINE No, I understand that. But you could get a job as a janitor, or maybe as a messenger in some government bureau. Of course, the public loaf is always short in weight, but it comes steady, and then there is a pension the widow and the children.
JEAN *(making a face)*. That's good and well, but it isn't my style to think of dying all at once for the sake of wife and children. I must say that my plans have been looking toward something better than that kind of thing.
CHRISTINE Your plans, yes—but you've got obligations also, and those you had better keep in mind!
JEAN Now don't you get my dander up by talking of obligations! I know what I've got to do anyhow. *(Listening for some sound on the outside)* However, we've plenty of time to think of all this. Go in now and get ready, and then we'll go to church.
CHRISTINE Who is walking around up there?
JEAN I don't know, unless it be Clara.
CHRISTINE *(going out)*. It can't be the Count, do you think, who's come home without anybody hearing him?
JEAN *(scared)*. The Count? No, that isn't possible, for then he would have rung for me.
CHRISTINE *(as she goes out)*. Well, God help us all! Never have I seen the like of it!

(The sun has risen and is shining on the tree tops in the park. The light changes gradually until it comes slantingly in through the windows. JEAN *goes to the door and gives a signal.)*

JULIA *(enters in traveling dress and carrying a small bird cage covered up with a towel; this she places on a chair)*. Now I am ready.
JEAN Hush! Christine is awake.
JULIA *(showing extreme nervousness during the following scene)*. Did she suspect anything?
JEAN She knows nothing at all. But, my heavens, how you look!
JULIA How do I look?
JEAN You're as pale as a corpse, and—pardon me, but your face is dirty.
JULIA Let me wash it then—Now! *(She goes over to the washstand and washes her face and hands.)* Give me a towel—Oh!—That's the sun rising!

JEAN And then the ogre bursts.
JULIA Yes, ogres and trolls were abroad last night!—But listen, Jean. Come with me, for now I have the money.
JEAN (*doubtfully*). Enough?
JULIA Enough to start with. Come with me, for I cannot travel alone today. Think of it—Midsummer Day, on a stuffy train, jammed with people who stare at you—and standing still at stations when you want to fly. No, I cannot! I cannot! And then the memories will come: childhood memories of Midsummer Days, when the inside of the church was turned into a green forest—birches and lilacs; the dinner at the festive table with relatives and friends; the afternoon in the park, with dancing and music, flowers and games! Oh, you may run and run, but your memories are in the baggage car, and with them remorse and repentance!
JEAN I'll go with you—but at once, before it's too late. This very moment!
JULIA Well, get dressed then. (*Picks up the cage.*)
JEAN But no baggage! That would only give us away.
JULIA No, nothing at all! Only what we can take with us in the car.
JEAN (*has taken down his hat*). What have you got there? What is it?
JULIA It's only my finch. I can't leave it behind.
JEAN Did you ever! Dragging a bird cage along with us! You must be raving mad! Drop the cage!
JULIA The only thing I take with me from my home! The only living creature that loves me since Diana deserted me! Don't be cruel! Let me take it along!
JEAN Drop the cage, I tell you! And don't talk so loud—Christine can hear us.
JULIA No, I won't let it fall into strange hands. I'd rather have you kill it!
JEAN Well, give it to me, and I'll wring its neck.
JULIA Yes, but don't hurt it. Don't—no, I cannot!
JEAN Let me—I can!
JULIA (*takes the bird out of the cage and kisses it*). Oh, my little birdie, must it die and go away from its mistress!
JEAN Don't make a scene, please. Don't you know it's a question of your life, of your future? Come, Quick! (*Snatches the bird away from her, carries it to the chopping block and picks up an axe.* Miss Julia *turns away.*)
JEAN You should have learned how to kill chickens instead of shooting with a revolver—(*brings down the axe*) —then you wouldn't have fainted for a drop of blood.
JULIA (*screaming*). Kill me too! Kill me! You who can take the life of an innocent creature without turning a hair! Oh, I hate and despise you! There is blood between us! Cursed by the hour when I first met you! Cursed be the hour when I came to life in my mother's womb!
JEAN Well, what's the use of all that cursing? Come on!
JULIA (*approaching the chopping block as if drawn to it against her will*). No, I don't want to go yet. I cannot—I must see—Hush! There's a carriage coming up the road. (*Listening without taking her eyes off the block and the axe*) You think I cannot stand the sight of blood. You think I am as weak as that—oh, I should like to see your blood, your brains, on that block there. I should like to see your whole sex swimming in blood like that thing there. I think I could drink out of your skull, and bathe my feet in your open breast, and eat your heart from the spit!—You think I am weak; you think I love you because the fruit of my womb was

yearning for your seed; you think I want to carry your offspring under my heart and nourish it with my blood—bear your children and take your name! Tell me, you, what are you called anyhow? I have never heard your family name—and maybe you haven't any. I should become Mrs. "Hovel," or Mrs. "Backyard"—you dog there, that's wearing my collar; you lackey with my coat of arms on your buttons—and I should share with my cook, and be the rival of my own servant. Oh! Oh! Oh!—You think I am a coward and want to run away! No, now I'll stay—and let the lightning strike! My father will come home—will find his chiffonier opened—the money gone! Then he'll ring—twice for the valet—and then he'll send for the sheriff—and then I shall tell everything! Everything! Oh, but it will be good to get an end to it—if it only be the end! And then his heart will break, and he dies!—So there will be an end to all of us—and all will be quiet—peace—eternal rest!—And then the coat of arms will be shattered on the coffin—and the count's line will be wiped out—but the lackey's line goes on in the orphan asylum—wins laurels in the gutter, and ends in jail.

JEAN There spoke the royal blood! Bravo, Miss Julia! Now you put the miller back in his sack!

(CHRISTINE *enters dressed for church and carrying a hymn book in her hand*)

JULIA *(hurries up to her and throws herself into her arms as if seeking protection).* Help me, Christine! Help me against this man!

CHRISTINE *(unmoved and cold).* What kind of performance is this on the Sabbath morning? *(Catches sight of the chopping block)* My, what a mess you have made!—What's the meaning of all this? And the way you shout and carry on!

JULIA You are a woman, Christine, and you are my friend. Beware of that scoundrel!

JEAN *(a little shy and embarrassed).* While the ladies are discussing I'll get myself a shave. *(Slinks out to the right.)*

JULIA You must understand me, and you must listen to me.

CHRISTINE No, really, I don't understand this kind of trolloping. Where are you going in your travelling dress—and he with his hat on—what?—What?

JULIA Listen, Christine, listen, and I'll tell you everything. . . .

CHRISTINE I don't want to know anything. . . .

JULIA You must listen to me. . . .

CHRISTINE What is it about? Is it about this nonsense with Jean? Well, I don't care about it at all, for it's none of my business. But if you're planning to get him away with you, we'll put a stop to that!

JULIA *(extremely nervous).* Please try to be quiet, Christine, and listen to me. I cannot stay here, and Jean cannot stay here—and so we must leave. . . .

CHRISTINE Hm, hm!

JULIA *(brightening up).* But now I have got an idea, you know. Suppose all three of us should leave—go abroad—go to Switzerland and start a hotel together—I have money, you know—and Jean and I could run the whole thing—and you, I thought, could take care of the kitchen—Wouldn't that be fine!—Say yes, now! And come along with us! Then everything is fixed!—Oh, say yes! *(She puts her arms around* CHRISTINE *and pats her.)*

CHRISTINE *(coldly and thoughtfully).* Hm, Hm!

JULIA *(presto tempo).* You have never travelled, Christine—you must get out and have a look at the world. You cannot imagine what fun it is to travel on a train—constantly new people—new countries—and then we get to Hamburg and take in the Zoological Gardens in passing—

that's what you like—and then we go to the theatres and to the opera—and when we get to Munich, there, you know, we have a lot of museums, where they keep Rubens and Raphael and all those big painters, you know—Haven't you heard of Munich, where King Louis[9] used to live—the king, you know, that went mad—And then we'll have a look at his castle— he has still some castles that are furnished just as in a fairy tale—and from there it isn't very far to Switzerland—and the Alps, you know—just think of the Alps, with snow on top of them in the middle of the summer—and there you have orange trees and laurels that are green all the year around

(JEAN *is seen in the right wing, sharpening his razor on a strop which he holds between his teeth and his left hand; he listens to the talk with a pleased mien and nods approval now and then.*)

JULIA (*tempo prestissimo*). And then we get a hotel—and I sit in the office, while Jean is outside receiving tourists—and goes out marketing—and writes letters—That's a life for you—Then the train whistles, and the 'bus drives up, and it rings upstairs, and it rings in the restaurant —and then I make out the bills—and I am going to salt them,[10] too—You can never imagine how timid tourists are when they come to pay their bills! And you—you will sit like a queen in the kitchen. Of course, you are not going to stand at the stove yourself. And you'll have to dress neatly and nicely in order to show yourself to people—and with your looks—yes, I am not flattering you—you'll catch a husband some fine day—some rich Englishman, you know— for those fellows are so easy (*slowing down*) to catch—and then we grow rich—and we build us a villa at Lake Como—of course, it is raining a little in that place now and then— but (*limply*) the sun must be shining sometimes—although it looks dark—and—then—or else we can go home again—and come back—here—or some other place. . . .

CHRISTINE Tell me, Miss Julia, do you believe in all that yourself?

JULIA (*crushed*). Do I believe in it myself?

CHRISTINE Yes.

JULIA (*exhausted*). I don't know: I believe no longer in anything. *(She sinks down on the bench and drops her head between her arms on the table.)* Nothing! Nothing at all!

CHRISTINE(*turns to the right, where* JEAN *is standing*). So you were going to run away!

JEAN (*abashed, puts the razor on the table*). Run away? Well, that's putting it rather strong. You have heard what the young lady proposes, and though she is tired out now by being up all night, it's a proposition that can be put through all right.

CHRISTINE Now you tell me: did you mean me to act as cook for the one there—?

JEAN (*sharply*). Will you please use decent language in speaking to your mistress! Do you understand?

CHRISTINE Mistress!

JEAN Yes!

CHRISTINE Well, well! Listen to him!

JEAN Yes, it would be better for you to listen a little more and talk a little less. Miss Julia is your mistress, and what makes you disrespectful to her now should make you feel the same way about yourself.

---

9. King Louis. Ludwig II (1845–1886), the passionate friend and patron of Wagner, built the fantastic castle of Neuschwanstein high in the Bavarian Alps and decorated it with romantic pictures of Lohengrin, Tannhauser, and Tristram and Iseult inspired by Wagner's operas.

10. salt them, pad them with charges.

CHRISTINE Oh, I have always had enough respect for myself. . . .
JEAN To have none for others!
CHRISTINE —not to go below my own station. You can't say that the count's cook has had anything to do with the groom or the swineherd. You can't say anything of the kind!
JEAN Yes, it's your luck that you have had to do with a gentleman.
CHRISTINE Yes, a gentleman who sells the oats out of the count's stable!
JEAN What's that to you who gets a commission on the groceries and bribes from the butcher?
CHRISTINE What's that?
JEAN And so you can't respect your master and mistress any longer! You—you!
CHRISTINE Are you coming with me to church? I think you need a good sermon on top of such a deed.
JEAN No, I am not going to church today. You can go by yourself and confess your own deeds.
CHRISTINE Yes, I'll do that, and I'll bring back enough forgiveness to cover you also. The Saviour suffered and died on the cross for all our sins, and if we go to him with a believing heart and a repentant mind, he'll take all our guilt on himself.
JULIA Do you believe that, Christine?
CHRISTINE It is my living belief, as sure as I stand here, and the faith of my childhood which I have kept since I was young, Miss Julia. And where sin abounds, grace abounds too.
JULIA Oh, if I had your faith! Oh, if . . . .
CHRISTINE Yes, but you don't get it without the special grace of God, and that is not bestowed on everybody.
JULIA On whom is it bestowed then?
CHRISTINE That's just the great secret of the work of grace, Miss Julia, and the Lord has no regard for persons, but there those that are last shall be the foremost. . . .
JULIA Yes, but that means hs has regard for those that are last.
CHRISTINE *(going right on).* —and it is easier for a camel to go through a needle's eye than for a rich man to get into heaven. That's the way it is, Miss Julia. Now I am going, however—alone—and as I pass by, I'll tell the stableman not to let out the horses if anybody should like to get away before the count comes home. Good-bye! *(Goes out.)*
JEAN Well, ain't she a devil!—And all this for the sake of a finch!
JULIA *(apathetically).* Never mind the finch!—Can you see any way out of this, any way to end it?
JEAN *(ponders).* No!
JULIA What would you do in my place?
JEAN In your place? Let me see. As one of gentle birth, as a woman, as one who has—fallen. I don't know—yes, I do know!
JULIA *(picking up the razor with a significant gesture).* Like this?
JEAN Yes!—But please observe that I myself wouldn't do it, for there is a difference between us.
JULIA Because you are a man and I a woman? What is the difference?
JEAN It is the same as that between man and woman.
JULIA *(with the razor in her hand).* I want to, but I cannot!—My father couldn't either, that time he should have done it.
JEAN No, he should not have done it, for he had to get his revenge first.
JULIA And now it is my mother's turn to revenge herself again, through me.

JEAN Have you not loved your father, Miss Julia?

JULIA Yes, immensely, but I must have hated him, too. I think I must have been doing so without being aware of it. But he was the one who reared me in contempt for my own sex—half woman and half man! Whose fault is it, this that has happened? My father's—my mother's—my own? My own? Why, I have nothing that is my own. I haven't a thought that didn't come from my mother; and now this last—this about all human creatures being equal—I got that from him, my fiance—whom I call a scoundrel for that reason! How can it be my own fault? To put the blame on Jesus, as Christine does—no, I am too proud for that, and know too much—thanks to my father's teachings—And that about a rich person not getting into heaven, it's just a lie, and Christine, who has money in the savings bank, would't get in anyhow. Whose is the fault?—What does it matter whose it is? For just the same I am the one who must bear the guilt and the results. . . .

JEAN Yes, but. . . .

(Two sharp strokes are rung on the bell. MISS JULIA *leaps to her feet.* JEAN *changes his coat.)*

JEAN The count is back. Think if Christine. . . .*(Goes to the speaking tube, knocks on it, and listens.)*

JULIA Now he has been to the chiffonier!

JEAN It is Jean, your lordship! *(Listening again, the spectators being unable to hear what the Count says)* Yes, your lordship! *(Listening)* Yes, your lordship! At once! *(Listening)* In a minute, your lordship! *(Listening)* Yes, yes! In half an hour!

JULIA *(with intense concern).* What did he say? Lord Jesus, what did he say?

JEAN He called for his boots and wanted his coffee in half an hour.

JULIA In half an hour then! Oh, I am so tired. I can't do anything; can't repent, can't run away, can't stay, can't live—can't die! Help me now! Command me, and I'll obey you like a dog! Do me this last favour—save my honour, and save his name! You know what my will ought to do, and what it cannot do—now give me your will, and make me do it!

JEAN I don't know why—but now I can't either—I don't understand—It is just as if this coat here made a—I cannot command you—and now, since I've heard the Count's voice—now—I can't quite explain it—but—Oh, that damned menial is back in my spine again. I believe if the Count should come down here, and if he should tell me to cut my own throat—I'd do it on the spot!

JULIA Make believe that you are he, and that I am you!—You did some fine acting when you were on your knees before me—then you were the nobleman—or—have you ever been to a show and seen one who could hypnotize people?

(JEAN *makes a sign of assent.)*

JULIA He says to his subject: get the broom. And the man gets it. He says: sweep. And the man sweeps.

JEAN But then the other person must be asleep.

JULIA *(ecstatically).* I am asleep already—there is nothing in the whole room but a lot of smoke—and you look like a stove—that looks like a man in black clothes and a high hat—and your eyes glow like coals when the fire is going out—and your face is a lump of white ashes. *(The sunlight has reached the floor and is now falling on* JEAN. *)* How warm and nice it is! *(She rubs her hands as if warming them before a fire.)* And so light—and so peaceful!

JEAN *(takes the razor and puts it in her hand).* There's the broom! Go now while it is light—to the barn—and *(Whispers something in her ear.)*

JULIA *(awake).* Thank you! Now I shall have rest! But tell me first—that the foremost also receive the gift of grace. Say it, even if you don't believe it.

JEAN The foremost? No, I can't do that!—But wait—Miss Julia—I know! You are no longer among the foremost—now when you are among the last!

JULIA That's right. I am among the last of all: I am the very last. Oh!—But now I cannot go—Tell me once more that I must go!

JEAN No, now I can't do it either. I cannot!

JULIA And those that are foremost shall be the last.

JEAN Don't think, don't think! Why, you are taking away my strength, too, so that I become a coward—What? I thought I saw the bell moving!—To be that scared of a bell! Yes, but it isn't only the bell—there is somebody behind it—a hand that makes it move—and something else that makes the hand move—but if you cover up your ears—just cover up your ears! Then it rings worse than ever! Rings and rings, until you answer it—and then it's too late—then comes the sheriff—and then—

(Two quick rings from the bell.)

JEAN *(shrinks together; then he straightens himself up).* It's horrid! But there's no other end to it!—Go!

(JULIA *goes firmly out through the door.)*

CURTAIN

A Listing of BBC Actors and Production Coordinators

MISS JULIE

by

August Strindberg

CAST

JEAN	PATRICK STEWART
MISS JULIE	LISA HARROW

PRODUCTION

DESIGNER	GEORGE WISNER
MAKE-UP SUPERVISOR	MAGGIE WEBB
PRODUCED/STUDIO DIRECTOR	RICHARD CALLANAN

Director's Notes

RICHARD   For five days I rehearsed a scene from Strindberg's MISS JULIE with Lisa Harrow and Patrick Stewart. Our aim was to find the ways in which the text could be made to live. Some of the work was textual discussion, some had to do with television technique, but most was concerned with simple trial and error, working through the scenes to find the rightness or truth of the characterization and action. A text moves towards performance as the actors embody it physically through imagination and emotion, and this is particularly true of a play like MISS JULIE, a personal and sexual encounter between a mistress and her servant on Midsummer Eve. We edited this program from recordings made over the five days of rehearsal; rehearsals seldom make steady progress. Blind alleys and sudden insights are more usual. To begin with here's an exchange followed through from first reading to final performance. The servant Jean has claimed he had a secret childhood love.

PATRICK   As this very early state of rehearsal, the actor's work is based on two things, his analysis and study of the text done in isolation plus his instinctive feel towards the character as he first reaches out to him from the text.

LISA   Ideas change during rehearsal because actors are attempting to marry decisions based on textual analysis, and those coming from personal and emotional experience. In other words I can't be Strindberg's Miss Julie except through my own person.

RICHARD   The complexity of the characters, and the speed with which the mood of the scene changes were our major challenges: they arise directly from Strindberg's vivid form of naturalism. We can see this as again we follow a short section through different stages of rehearsal.

RICHARD   The fourth day of rehearsal and we are not happy with what we have achieved, not even sure that we have the right approach.

RICHARD   It's day five of rehearsal, the day before the studio performance and we try again to run the scene through from the beginning.

PATRICK   I chose that moment to end the run-through, but in fact the scene had broken down long before that because I was not engaging myself with the character because of the shortness of time. I was attempting to create a tension, create an atmosphere and a character too, that it was a series of beautiful lies but nothing was true or real.

LISA   That's right, and I know that I didn't have any of the inner rhythm of Miss Julie at all. I mean, I was still remembering moves and how we went from one section to the other and meant intellectual connections rather than actually letting them go and just finding a life underneath the actual fabric of the scene.

RICHARD   That was our last attempt at a run-through of the scene; the next day we performed it in the studio.

PATRICK   On the morning that we recorded this scene I was still convinced that we'd be unable to get through it. I think that was because I had underestimated the actor's intuitive response to a performance situation and so we did the scene. Curiously enough we did the scene for the very first time without forgetting the lines.

LISA   That's right. It was very heady because when we drove down the road afterwards we thought "My goodness, we actually did it, we did it." But then, when seeing it, I mean the sense of excitement that we had while doing it, I didn't see that. When I saw, what I saw, watching it with all the gaps and sort of areas of questioning that I still wanted to ask about the scene, that it wasn't complete yet. It wasn't nearly where we wanted to have been.

PATRICK There were areas that were left untouched that we skated over because of the studio and performance situation. I had to dominate my own nerves, my own terror, and therefore I appear much too confident, much too bold and brave in the scene when I should have been afraid, weak, insecure.

LISA I thought I was too vulnerable, too young really. I mean, I'd imagined her in my head as being someone sophisticated in a way and much more of a woman than I came across. I mean, I came across as a wide-eyed eighteen-year-old, I thought. Very vulnerable and that was for me quite a shock.

PATRICK What was interesting about the performance though was that we were still in a fluid state. . . .

LISA (*interrupting*) That's right.

PATRICK . . .in the studio. We were making new choices, new selections there and then at that moment—choices that we had never made, that had never been offered to us when we were in rehearsal.

LISA Mm.

PATRICK And that's where the actor's mystery, intuitive mystery, comes into play. Something you cannot prepare for in rehearsal.

LISA That's right.

Focus in Viewing

This presentation is unique to all of those in the series. The emphasis is not on the finished product, but rather on *how* the product is finished. Watching the artists develop their characterizations, we become aware of the creative process at work, and, it is hoped, come to a greater understanding and appreciation of theatre artists. The playscript of MISS JULIE has been included in order to facilitate evaluation of the interpretations presented and to guide personal interpretations of the characters.

Content Viewing

1. Julie and Jean compare dreams. Julie explains that in her dream she is stuck in a tree and wants to jump down but is afraid. Jean, on the other hand, explains that he is on the ground looking up at the branches of a tree. He cannot, however, reach the first branch. He jumps and jumps to no avail. The tree dreams are metaphors (symbols) for their situations in life. Explain.
2. Jean tells Julie how beautiful life can be; Julie says that "everything is a scum that floats across the water until it sinks." Consider their respective lives and the irony of their viewpoints and explain that irony.
3. Is Jean infatuated, do you think, with Julie or her "position?" Explain.
4. What does Jean's survival and Julie's demise suggest about aristocracy and the masses throughout the ages?
5. Jean explains to Julie that as a child he slept under an elder tree (reputed to exude poisonous fumes) to kill himself because he had no hope of ever winning Julie. Julie, in turn, kills herself because she feels she has "no hope." Was there ever hope for either of them that they failed to understand? Explain.

Craft Viewing

1. Lisa Harrow and Patrick Stewart rehearse this particular exchange a number of times:

   JULIE Who was she? ("she" refers to someone with whom Jean said he was once in love)
   JEAN You cannot order me to tell you that.
   JULIE Who was she?
   JEAN You.
   JULIE How absurd!

   You will note that Lisa and Patrick vary their interpretations of these lines. Lisa plays Julie as proud, as flirtatious, as confused, and as touched in different readings of these lines. Patrick plays Jean as embarrassed, as floundering, as confused and as indignant when delivering the above lines at different times. In the finished performance both actors have a note of curious hopefulness in their voices when delivering this dialog. Of all the ways that Lisa and Patrick interpret these lines, which do you think is the most accurate and effective? Why?
2. The director, Richard Callanan, explains to Lisa that "Julie's actions are not premeditated. Julie is floundering and clutching." Do you think Lisa plays Julie as such? Should she? Explain.
3. Lisa says that she sees Julie's suicide as positive because Julie finally acts. How might Lisa's understanding of Julie's death affect her portrayal of Julie?
4. When Lisa as Julie says "kiss my hand" to Jean, the director sees Lisa's interpretation as a parody of her social position. He explains to Lisa that she should deliver the line as a flirtation. How else might Lisa deliver this line?
5. Does watching *Miss Julie* in rehearsal detract from or enhance the final product? Explain.
6. Do you think a play is better if the viewer is unaware of the production as a collaborative work? Explain.

Critical Viewing: Overview

1. Now that this play is part of your experience, what significance does *Miss Julie* hold for you?

Additional Plays that Demostrate Similar Concepts

The Father-Strindberg
Desire Under the Elms-Eugene O'Neill
Dark at the Top of the Stairs-William Inge
The Philanthropist-Christopher Hampton
Look Back in Anger-John Osborne

Stage Terms

Above—Farther up stage.
Bearing—The use of the actor's body to indicate character.
Down Stage—The part of the stage closest to the audience.

Green Room—Actor's off-stage waiting area.
Open Up—Play more directly to the audience.
Play In —To play to the center.
Play Out—To play to the outside.
Proscenium—The picture frame that surrounds the stage.
Sides—Typed copies of an actor's part that give cues and his own part only.
Up Stage—The part of the stage farthest from the audience.

PEER GYNT

by

Henrik Ibsen
(1828–1906)

A. Play Notes: Fact and Fancy in *Peer Gynt*, p. 45

B. Peer: Hero and Anti-hero, p. 45

C. Peer Gynt: Story and Plot Summary, p. 46

D. Commentary: Peer Gynt and the Critics, p. 49

E. Comic Essay, p. 51

F. Background Material for *Peer Gynt*,
   1. The Norwegian Folktale, p. 52
   2. *Peer Gynt* as an Epic, p. 52

G. Objectives, p. 53

H. A List of BBC Actors and Production Coordinators, p. 54

I. Focus in Viewing, p. 58

J. Stage Terms, p. 58

K. Additional Plays, p. 59

Play Notes: Fact and Fancy in *Peer Gynt*

Peer Gynt was not written for the stage. On the rare occasions when it is performed, it requires imagination and often patience from performers and audiences alike. In *Peer Gynt*, a fanciful poem and play, Threadballs speak; Death is personified by a Tall Man and a Button Molder. Trolls have tails and live in a fanciful kingdom where the rules are "Troll Rules." Peer physically ages before us. We are asked to believe we are watching not an evening in a man's life but his whole life from youth to old age. Peer makes great leaps of imagination and so must we, the audience. And perhaps because *Peer Gynt* was written to be read, sometimes a theatre audience may find it impossible to "suspend disbelief" and accept Ibsen's fanciful dreams. Enigmatic Byorgs and Sphinxes speaking from out of nowhere require from the audience great leaps of faith, trust, and imagination.

Ibsen, like Peer, may occasionally go too far. Like Peer's mother, Aase, we may wish to throw up our hands and say, "Enough! Don't expect me to go along with this."

As an audience, we must stretch our imagination, fill in gaps and believe in a larger-than-life world. Because it requires more of us as an audience, *Peer Gynt* is often categorized as a forerunner of the expressionism of August Strindberg, and the absurdity of Luigi Pirandello and Eugene Ionesco.

If we remember that *Peer Gynt* is a folk tale, we may be willing to accept its absurdity. Peer, the Trolls, the reindeer ride, and much more in *Peer Gynt* come directly from Norwegian folklore. For the 19th Century Norwegian audience, these allusions were familiar and easy to accept. This is not the case for a 20th Century audience. An appreciation of *Peer Gynt* as a folk or epic drama takes work, imagination, and perhaps a little love.

Peer Gynt, a stylized nonrealistic story of Norway's search for identity and more important of Everyman's search for identity, was originally written as an epic poem and is very much within that tradition. There is an epic hero, Peer, whose characteristics and deeds represent the characteristics and myths of his homeland. Peer, as a character, comes straight out of Norwegian folklore. His story, long and episodic, tells of Peer's weaknesses, strengths, and the possible fate of Norway. As a poem and as a play, *Peer Gynt* is more epic than dramatic. In an epic, the character of a hero is static, not significantly changing throughout. In drama, the hr characters usually grow up as we watch them. *Peer Gynt,* despite aging in the play, is the same person from beginning to end. He is a 19th Century Norwegian man who cannot face the facts of life: rejection, poverty, limited opportunity, age, and death. Yet these fears make him different from other epic heroes, such as Achilles or Odysseus who are above such human emotion. He is, in fact, one of the first heroes in literature who is cut from ordinary cloth. Peer in not the king; he is, instead, one of the crowd who would line the street to see the king. Peer is not even admirable but a dreamer whose only connection with reality is Solveig's love for him and his meetings with the Button Molder (Death).

Peer: Hero and Anti-Hero

Peer is an anti-hero because we do not wish to emulate him. In this sense he may be one of the first anti-heros of modern dramatic literature. Peer is a selfish boy who never grows up; at the end of his travels, at the end of the play, he is still a selfish boy, always dreaming and thinking of himself. The Troll King's motto, "Troll to thyself be enough," is precisely the motto that Peer adopts. It may sound something like "to thine own self be true" but, in fact, it lacks the integrity of that motto. "Troll, to thyself—be enough" is, rather, a selfish approach to living. The "enough" part gives it away. Self-love may be primary, but Ibsen seems to be questioning whether it is enough without concern and love for others. The world outside Peer does not matter. Because Solveig loves, she is the only character in *Peer Gynt* who is a realized human being. A girl at the beginning of the play, she has developed into a woman by the end.

Peer remains a Troll. The Troll King tells him, "You took away my motto graven on my heart." Worst of all, Peer *could* have been more. " *You* were meant to be a gleaming button on the world's waistcoat, but your loop was missing," says the Button Molder. Peer defied his destiny. Peer's failure is that he did not grow into the man, given his gifts, he could have been. So he must be melted down.

Through Peer's narrow-minded approach to life, Ibsen satirizes not only individual selfishness but the narrow-minded nationalism of the Norwegian people who, when *Peer Gynt* was written, were in the midst of a political and social movement that threatened to separate and isolate the Norwegians from their fellow Scandinavians. Ibsen was telling his countrymen that, like Peer, they too might end up with nothing.

After Norway became independent of Denmark, there were attempts to purify the Norwegian language. Ibsen saw these attempts as excessive. There were also attempts to rewrite Norwegian history and to give Norway a romantic tradition. *Peer Gynt* is a symbol of those attempts to impose patriotism and an excessively romantic view of life on a people who were not ready to accept it.

Story and Plot Summary

Act I. Scene 1. The play opens with Peer telling his mother a "tall tale," a lie about catching a reindeer. His mother, Aase, yells at him for lying. She tells him he will come to no good. He says he will be Emperor! She tells him that he has missed his chance to make a good marriage and that there is a wedding the next day. Peer decides that they will both go to the wedding.

Scene 2. At the wedding, Peer overhears peasants gossiping about his drunken father. Peer daydreams of being the Kaiser. A blacksmith friend stops Peer and invites him to join the wedding party.

Scene 3. The wedding guests snub Peer. He sees Solveig and invites her to dance. At first she accepts and then refuses. Ingrid, the bride, has locked herself in her room, and the bridegroom asks Peer's help in getting her out. Peer asks Solveig again to dance, and he makes up stories of what he will do if she again refuses. There is confusion, and a drunken crowd scene ends with Peer carrying the bride over the hill while her father watches in rage.

Act II. Scene 1. Peer sends back Ingrid, the bride. He explains that because he was wretched, he took her, but that, in fact, she is not for him. Ingrid goes down the hill, leaving him and returning to her home.

Scene 2. It is storming. Aase searches in every direction but cannot find Peer. Solveig follows Aase and expresses an interest in Peer.

Scene 3. Three cowherd girls invite Peer into their hut. They dance away over the hill with Peer between them.

Scene 4. Peer, among the mountains, imagines that he sees his father feasting. He leaps forward and runs his nose against a rock, falls, and remains lying on the ground.

Scene 5. Peer is on a mountainside, following a Woman in Green. They exchange fantasies: she is the daughter of a king, and he is the son of Queen Aase. A gigantic pig comes running in. They mount and gallop away on their "noble charger."

Scene 6. In the Royal Hall of the King of Trolls, Peer stands before the Troll King. The Troll King promises Peer his daughter and a future kingship, but he must answer the riddle: What is the difference between Trolls and Men? The answer that the king gives is, "Man says: To thyself be true." Trolls say: "Troll, to thyself be enough." Peer must also accept the habit of the Trolls. He must cast off his breeches. He must drink of their goblet, and he must have a tail. Peer refuses, then consents. The Troll King says he must scratch Peer's eye so that his vision will be oblique and he will then see everything as perfect. Peer refuses and wishes to leave. He explains that he must have his freedom. The Troll King gets angry. Peer tries to get away and is attacked by the Trolls. Chruch bells are heard and the Trolls disperse. The Royal Hall falls to pieces. Everything disappears.

Scene 7. Peer flails around in the dark. Peer hears a voice in the darkness. It is the Boyg. Peer invites the voice in the blackness to fight with him. Birds are heard overhead. The Boyg shrinks to nothing.

Scene 8. Outside a hut in Aase's pasture, Peer wakes up and sees Helga, Solveig's younger sister. She explains that she and Solveig rang the church-bells. Peer frightens her, and she runs away.

Act III. *Scene 1.* Peer is in the woods, felling timber. He is an outlaw. He daydreams and says he must stop daydreaming. He sees a boy cut off his finger. He understands the desire to cut off a finger to avoid military service, but to really *do* it horrifies him.

Scene 2. Aase and Kari talk of Peer. They find a casting ladle he once used to mould buttons.

Scene 3. Peer bolts the door to his hut so no one can come in. Solveig appears and tells Peer that she has come home to him and that she has left her parents. He is joyous and invites her to share his hut. Solveig goes inside the hut. A woman appears with a boy behind her. The daughter of the Troll King, now an ugly hag, introduces the boy as Peer's son. She leaves and Solveig appears at the door of the hut, but Peer, feeling it would be a sacrilege to be with Solveig, goes off. Solveig says she will wait.

Scene 4. Aase is dying. Peer visits her, and there is a scene at her bedside with Peer telling her a "lie" about taking her to a party at a castle. Aase lies back, imagining the castle and the ride to it, and dies. Peer escapes to the sea coast.

Act IV. *Scene 1.* Peer, now middle-aged, is on the southwest coast of Morocco. He has, by now, traveled all over the world, selling slaves, rum, and Bibles. After a group of tourists hear him tell about his treasures, they plan to take his ship from him.

Scene 2. Peer runs along the shore and watches his confiscated ship moving out to sea. The ship goes up in smoke and sinks. He hears a growl in the bushes and climbs a tree for safety.

Scene 3. A group of women are resting. One announces that he is the Emperor's charger and his secret clothes have been stolen.

Scene 4. Peer is is in the tree defending himself against a group of apes.

Scene 5. Peer is in the desert where thieves have left a stolen horse and clothes. Peer decides to build a kingdom in the desert. He sees the horse and robes, then gallops off across the desert.

Scene 6. Peer is now a prophet in oriental robes, surrounded by Anitra and a troupe of dancing girls. He is attracted to Anitra, who asks him for a jewel from his turban, which he gives to her.

Scene 7. Anitra and Peer talk.

Scene 8. Peer rides into the desert with Anitra. He stops and shows off his physical strength to Anitra. She steals his money and rides off.

Scene 9. Peer takes off his Turkish robes and is in European clothes once more. Peer blames his misguided attachment to Anitra on the prophet's life. He sets out again to seek a new, ennobling venture.

Scene 10. Solveig, now middle-aged, is still waiting at the hut for Peer.

Scene 11. Peer, in Egypt, plans to travel to Greece and Italy.

Scene 12. Peer is near Cairo before a sphinx. He addresses it as Boyg. Professor Begriffenfelt, speaking German, comes from behind the Sphinx. He asks Peer who the sphinx is. Peer says, "He is himself." Begriffenfelt, impressed with that answer, greets Peer as the Messiah, the Emperor of Exegesis, and invites him to come to Cairo.

Scene 13. Begriffenfelt shows Peer into a cage, locks it, and explains he is now in a lunatic asylum. It is here, he explains, that men are most themselves, full of themselves and nothing else. The scene ends with Peer lying in the mud and Begriffenfelt on top of him, crowing, "Peer, the Emperor of Self."

Act V. Scene 1. Peer, now an old man, is on his way back to Norway. He sees a shipwreck from the deck where he is standing as the scene begins. A Stranger appears on the deck and asks Peer for a corpse. Peer angrily refuses. The Stranger goes into the cabin. The ship is then wrecked.

Scene 2. Peer, in the water, clings to an overturned boat. The ship's cook tries to hold on to the boat, too, but it will hold only one man and Peer pushes the cook into the water. The Stranger appears in the water, holding on to the boat. He asks again for Peer's corpse. Peer again refuses. The Stranger disappears.

Scene 3. In a churchyard, Peer listens to a Priest give a eulogy over a man who has four fingers on his right hand.

Scene 4. Peer observes an auction near a ruined mill. It is an auction of Peer's belongings. His things go cheaply. Peer listens to people discuss him, as if he were dead.

Scene 5. Peer is in a clearing, his hut behind him. He is on all fours, grubbing for wild onions. He peels one onion, layer by layer. Each layer seems to represent an aspect of himself. There is no kernel, Peer discovers. There are only smaller and smaller layers. Solveig's voice is heard from the hut. She is singing.

Scene 6. Peer is on the moor. The patches of threadballs at his feet speak to him.

Scene 7. On another part of the moor, Peer meets the Button Molder, who tells Peer that he is to go into his ladle, to be melted down because he is neither sinner enough for suffering nor virtuous enough for another fate. Peer tries to bargain with him. He asks the Button Molder to give him a chance to prove that in his life he has been himself. The Button Molder agrees to meet him at the next crossroads.

Scene 8. On still another part of the moor, Peer meets the Old Man, who announces himself as the Troll King, now a beggar. Peer asks him to testify that he has been virtuous because he refused to become a Troll. The Old Man tells Peer that he has lived like a Troll, like an egoist.

Scene 9. At the crossroads, Peer again meets the Button Molder. If Peer cannot prove he was not a great sinner, the Button Molder tells him that he will meet him at the next crossroads.

Scene 10. Peer meets the Thin Person. Peer recognizes him as the King, himself. The Thin Person tells Peer that he, Peer, has not sinned enough to avoid being melted down. The Thin Person announces that he is looking for Peer Gynt. Peer tries to mislead him, sending him away to the Cape of Good Hope.

Scene 11. At the crossroads, the Button Molder tells Peer that his time is up. They come to Solveig's hut. Day is dawning. Solveig is nearly blind. The Button Molder tells Peer he will meet Peer at the third crossroads, and then disappears. Peer throws himself before Solveig. She welcomes him home, to her arms, like a mother welcoming a child. The Button Molder's voice is heard, saying that he will meet Peer. Solveig sings and rocks Peer in her arms.

Commentary: *Peer Gynt* and the Critics

Critical reviews of a production of *Peer Gynt* tend to begin with a reminder that the play is, after all, a closet play, rarely performed, and that the staging continues to be difficult. If the play is brought up to date through costumes, modern slang, method acting, or contemporary props, the director may be blamed for lacking respect for a play which is part of theatre history. If the play is not brought up to date, the production may be accused of being worthwhile but tiresome; in that case, those involved are applauded for their noble but uncommercial effort. It is difficult to attract an audience with a play that is "worthwhile" but not entertaining. Of course, all productions of classical plays face similar difficulties. Some are therefore confined to college campuses. There they can be subsidized to provide acting experience for undergraduates and extra credit for students writing reports on them.

Despite its difficulties—perhaps even because of its challenge—*Peer Gynt* has been presented in notable commercial productions, which have been reviewed by demanding critics. In a 1945 production with Ralph Richardson as Peer, Sybil Thorndike as Aase, and Laurence Olivier as the Button Molder, directed by Tyrone Guthrie at London's Old Vic, the hero was called "vacillating and unstable," the play "unactable," and the production "a striking success." A review of the play in 1951 commented that the hero, more of an idea than an actual character, was a generalized warning against selfishness. The play, so said the review, appears to offer a range of roles, as the "hero" goes from one episode to another; yet it risks being dull as a theatrical venture because too little is known about Peer in the beginning for audiences to care what happens to him throughout the play. Even the symbolism is murky.

New Republic, Feb. 1, 1960

Another Critic of *Peer Gynt:*
What's Wrong With the Phoenix

The intentions of the Phoenix Company, which aspires to create a repertory of "time-honored and modern classics," are lofty and honorable, but their productions this year have overwhelmed me with fatigue, impatience, and gloom. My anguished imagination is now subject to a fearful hallucination in which I see the finest works of the greatest dramatists strewn about the Phoenix stage like so many violated corpses, while a chorus of newspaper reviewers (*Peer Gynt* by Henrik Ibsen, Phoenix Theatre) gleefully sings dirges in the wings. Perhaps it is unfair to blame anyone

Reprinted from *New Republic* by permission of the author.

but the reviewers themselves for the absurdities they write about Aristophanes and Ibsen; certainly, journalists—occupied with exalting the present—have always been inclined to knock the past. Yet, it cannot be denied that the Phoenix has provided a generous supply of corks for this popgun fusillade.

For it seems to me that the Phoenix, while outwardly more deferential towards the past than the reviewers, is inwardly just as indifferent to it. Instead of letting these plays stand on their own legs, the company's policy is to hale them into the 20th Century by the nearest available appendages. In *Lysistrata* this resulted in an extremely painful attempt at topicality. (A collection of pneumatic females chanted "Sex Almighty, Aphrodite, rah, rah, rah!") In *Peer Gynt,* the effort is less clumsy but no less obfuscating—a varnish of "theatrical values" is spread thickly over the surface of the play. The Phoenix production never betrays the slightest hint that *Peer Gynt* has an intellectual content, a consistent theme, or, for that matter, any interest at all beyond a histrionic sweep. Stuart Vaughan, the director, has staged the mad scene, for example, as a frenetic phantasmagoria which is quite chilling in its effect, but one has not the vaguest idea what such a scene is doing in the play. With directorial emphasis on stage effects, crowd scenes, and occasional "Method" touches in the relations between characters, what was conceived as a masterful play of ideas emerges as just another stage piece, and a pretty boring one at that.

But *Peer Gynt's* claim to "classical" stature does not rest on the fact that it provides fat parts for actors, compelling scenes, or the opportunity for designers, directors, and technicians to display their wares; nor is the play particularly distinguished by any profound psychological insights. Considered strictly as *theatre* (a word which is coming to mean the very opposite of *drama),* the play undoubtedly has severe defects, especially in form. But like all great works, *Peer Gynt* survives it because it is larger than its *personae* or its effects, and because what it has to say about the nature of existence remains both wide and deep.

In fact, *Peer Gynt,* written almost a hundred years ago, tells us more about our own condition than almost anything written in America in recent years, for Peer's concern with Self is one of the central problems of our national life. A fanciful storyteller with a prancing imagination, Peer might have developed into a great man, but he is too absorbed in appearances to become anything more than a great illusionist. As rapist, as honorary troll, as slave trader, as entrepreneur, as prophet, he is the incarnation of compromise, the spirit of accomodation, the apotheosis of the middle way. He whirls giddily around the globe, justifying his absolute lack of conviction and principle with the protest that he is being true to himself. The inevitable conclusion to this maniacal egotism is insanity, and it is in the madhouse that Peer is crowned Emperor. Neither saint nor sinner, Peer finally learns he has been a worthless nonentity who existed only in the love of a faithful wife, and at the end of the play he is waiting to be melted down, like all useless things, by the Button Molder. "He who forfeits his calling, forfeits his right to live, "wrote Kierkegaard, who believed—like Ibsen—that careerist self-absorption and mindless self-seeking are the most monstrous waste of life. Or, to put it as the Button Molder puts it to Peer: "To be yourself, you must slay yourself."

"To be yourself is to kill the worst and therefore to bring out the best in yourself," is the way the passage reads in the Phoenix production, which will give you some idea how easily a profundity can become a copy book maxim. But although Norman Ginsbury's doggerel, inaccurate rendering makes William Archer's Victorian bromides seem sublime and precise, the adaptor is not exclusively to blame for the general amorphousness of the evening. Stuart Vaughan's cutting seems almost designed to make the work incomprehensible, and the central roles are all pretty well miscast. If the Phoenix were a true repertory company, Fritz Weaver would have been ideally placed in the part of the Button Molder; since it is not, he plays the leading role. A heroic actor with a fine gift for irony, Weaver begins to make some sense when Peer gets older; but his heavy style is inappropriate to the younger, quicksilver Peer who is turned into an earthbound swain with a clumsy pair of hooves.

In brief, we must be grateful to the Phoenix for wanting to mount this play, at the same time wondering what the animating impulse was to do so. In the past, the Phoenix had no policy other than to survive; today, its brochure speaks of creating a "new tradition in the theatre." But since the Phoenix has developed no new methods of staging, no new methods of playing, no new interpretative approach, I am puzzled about what this new tradition will be There seems to be an authentic desire, as yet unrealized, to create a "working, professional group that can grow as a unit," but we have yet to see any sign that the "time-honored and modern classics" will function as anything more than showcases for the company. Alas, the trouble with the Phoenix is the trouble with the American theatre at large; isolated within its theatre walls, it shows no willingness to abandon itself to any purpose higher than its own existence. In this regard, Ibsen's play remains a cogent lesson; for if the American theatre is ever to be a place for art, it must learn to slay itself.

Robert Brustein

The following introductory article to *Peer Gynt* written by Howard Moss gives the reader an inkling of the usual reaction of audiences to the play:

A Comic Essay on Henrik Ibsen

A spasmodic of prefilthied snow plummeted past the window. The frozen fishnet of Oslo, diamonded by stars, lay before his studio, a study in deadness. Only the fire provided any sense of movement; and for that, he was grateful. The studio was on a height near the port but the usual sound of the fishermen, the occasional foghorn, the shouts and songs that roared from the water all the summer long were absent. All was frozen into a frightening silence. Only the leaping fire stimulated his imagination. And that, it seemed, was not enough. Something dreadful was happening to the most preeminent playwright in Europe.

"What, what, what is wrong?" he asked himself, as if he were a stutterer. Should he take out the letter from Shaw again, those pages of praise that might restore his self-confidence? Or the note, somewhat ambiguous, from Wagner? Of course, he knew Chekhov despised his work. So what? What did the merely melancholy Russians know of the Northern sickness, the Northern anguish, the Northern poison? True, they were snow-blue, too, but what a vast gulf separated their vodka and samovars and violins from the icy gaieties and cold depths of the Scandinavians? He must forget Chekhov's comment; he must remember Shaw's. That was the pass he had come to.

From INSTANT LIVES by Howard Moss. Copyright © 1974 by Howard Moss. Reprinted by permission of the publishers, E.P. Dutton & Co., Inc.

He had used them all up, the themes. He had done women's rights, and syphilis, and waterworks and power. He had done the neurotic woman feeding herself on the artist, destroying them both in the process. (He must not, today of all days, think of H. . . . Whereever she was, he hoped she was suffering horribly, suffering the way she had made half of Oslo suffer. What a fool he had been to write *A Doll's House!* It had only given her an excuse to walk out on him!)

He thought of topics, but they slipped from his mind almost as soon as they formulated themselves. Bear-baiting? No, no, that was in another country, and besides, the bear . . . Alcoholism? He reached for the beer that, it seemed, had become his one solace. It was 5:00 a.m. and he'd already gone through eight cases! The misuse of lumber? The smuggling in of wigs? If he could only think of something that would capture the imagination of the young! They were the ones who went to the theatre these days. Vanity presses?

He sat up with a start. The suffering of audiences! That was it! And he began *Peer Gynt* at once.

Examples of Norwegian Folktale in *Peer Gynt*

1. Weak persons with supernatural qualities
2. Hat as a common symbol
3. The process of making a person invisible
4. Ability to take the shape of an animal (The bear, particularly, a traditional Norwegian symbol of strength and the devil, and the dog is another familiar symbol)
5. Messenger of Death in much Norwegian folklore
6. Boasting, exaggerating, and generally telling tall tales
7. A tail as a common symbol (The Trolls are recognizable by their tails. Reference to this ornament as belonging to a subhuman group is very common in Norwegian folklore. As a rule the possessors are not proud of it.)
8. Character of Peer Gynt derived from Norwegian folklore but used only as a starting point
9. Reindeer ride
10. The crossroads, often a symbol for choice of death in Norwegian folklore

Peer Gynt as an Epic

I. Characteristics of the Epic Poem
   A. A long narrative poem reflecting heroic deeds of national heroes
   B. Oral or written, but originally oral
   C. Usually deals with deeds of kings and warriors
   D. Transmits national traditions
   E. Common subjects: myths, heroic legends, histories, religious tales, animal stories, philosophical, or moral theories
II. Function of Epic
   A. To stir up a feeling of nationalism and pride in the traditions of a nation
   B. To supply models of heroic behavior

III. Development of Epic
   A. Earliest known epic poetry: Sumerian, before 3000 B.C.
   B. Greek epics, such as Hesiod's *Theogony* (c. 700 B.C.), influenced by Sumerian and Babylonian poetry
   C. *Odyssey* and *Iliad* derived from same Near Eastern influences
   D. First Roman national epic: *Aeneid* of Virgil (70-19 B.C.) based on epics of Homer
   E. Germanic epic *Beowulf,* written in 8th Century A.D.
   F. French epic poem in form of *chanson de geste* (best known: *Chanson de Roland,* written around end of 11th Century)
   G. Arthurian Romance derived from Celtic mythology
   H. *Divine Comedy* of Dante (1265–1321)

Objectives

You, the student, after studying *Peer Gynt* should be able to

1. recognize what Ibsen is suggesting about human nature through *Peer Gynt.*
2. identify examples of Norwegian folklore in *Peer Gynt.*
3. identify elements of the epic in *Peer Gynt.*
4. be able to discuss why, despite difficulties in production, *Peer Gynt* continues to be staged.

The play has not only been criticized for being confusing, but also static, over dramatic, and inconsistent. Yet, as Donald Malcolm said, "one must recognize a single theme, an inner logic, that binds together the disparate elements of this dramatic poem. Peer Gynt is Ibsen's incarnation of the romantic idea of 'self-realization,' and every passage of the play reveals another aspect of this ingenious kind of selfishness, together with a glimpse of its paradoxical result—the destruction of the self. And this is the note that must be persistently struck if the play is to cohere on the stage."

A Listing of BBC Actors and Production Cooodinators

PEER GYNT

by

Henrik Ibsen

Translated by
Michael Meyer

CAST

PEER GYNT	PATRICK MOWER
SOLVEIG	LORNA HEILBRON
AASE	BETTY HARDY
STRANGE PASSENGER THIN PERSON	PETER COPLEY
BUTTON MOLDER	KENNETH CRANHAM
CAPTAIN	JOHN WENTWORTH
BOATSWAIN	ERIC MASON
PRIEST	BASIL CLARKE
TROLL KING	ESMOND KNIGHT
COOK	BILLY HAMON
STEERSMAN	DAVID NEILSON
MAN IN GRAY	ROY SPENCER
VILLAGER	GILLIAN BAILEY

PRODUCTION

SET DESIGN	GEORGE WISNER
COSTUME DESIGNER	BARBARA KIDD
MAKE-UP SUPERVISOR	MAGGIE WEBB
ORIGINAL MUSIC	DUDLEY SIMPSON
DIRECTOR	JOHN SELWYN GILBERT

Peer

Thin Person

Button Molder and Peer

Focus in Viewing

Unlike most of today's television programs, *Peer Gynt* is not realistically depicted. Some of the stage properties (spinning wheel, coffin, onion, ladle) and sets (boat deck, boat hull, house) lend themselves to a highly stylized production.

Content Viewing

1. If one were to describe Peer Gynt as "caught between two worlds," what would the two worlds be?
2. What elements in Peer Gynt are drawn from Norwegian folktales?
3. Peer's pilgrimage is a metaphor for what?
4. Which characters intrigued you? Why?
5. How would you describe Peer's character? What is his philosophy, his view of himself? Does his attitude change?
6. What in *Peer Gynt* makes it an "epic play?"

Craft Viewing

1. What conventions do you need to accept before you can enter into the spirit of this production?
2. In what way, if at all, would you have directed the production differently?
3. Do you agree, or disagree, with the actors' characterizations or interpretations? Were they consistent, honest, convincing, clear? Discuss.
4. Does the play lend itself to a television production? Explain.
5. Is there one moment or scene which stands out in your memory (as either good or bad)? Tell about it.

Critical Viewing: Overview

1. Now that this play and its production are part of your experience, what is the major significance that *Peer Gynt* holds for you?
    I. Some 19th Century epic poets: Alfred Tennyson, Walter Scott, Lord Byron, and William Morris
    J. 20th Century epic poets: Walt Whitman and Stephen Vincent Benêt

Stage Terms

Ad Lib—(From Ad Libitum meaning "at pleasure") Lines not supplied or specified by the script.

Aside—Something that an actor tells the audience while other characters are on stage. The other characters are not aware of the message.

Closet Drama—A play suited primarily for reading rather than production.

Conventions of the Theatre—General agreement about basic principles of drama that are not written but are expected.

Drama Criticism—The analysis, interpretation, and evaluation of drama; it is not limited to derogation. Criticism increases understanding and intelligent enjoyment.

Exposition—The presentation of the background material necessary for an understanding of the action; usually found in the beginning of the play; Exposition should be a compelling way of attracting attention to the characters and situation.

Additional Plays That Demonstrate Similar Concepts

Brand—Ibsen
Everyman—Anonymous (medieval)
Faust—Goethe
The Misanthrope—Molière

MODULE 2

Playwrights and Plotting

I. Introduction, p. 63
  A. Craftsman and Artist: A Brief Explanation of What the Playwright Does, p. 63
  B. The Development of Plot, p. 63
     1. Sophocles, Shakespeare, Scribe, p. 63
     2. Ibsen, p. 64
     3. Chekhov, p. 64
     4. Strindberg, p. 65
II. Study materials for *The Wild Duck,* p. 66
III. Study materials for *The Three Sisters,* p. 82
IV. Study materials for *The Ghost Sonata,* p. 100

You will find a more detailed outline preceding the introduction and each of the plays.

PLOT STRUCTURES

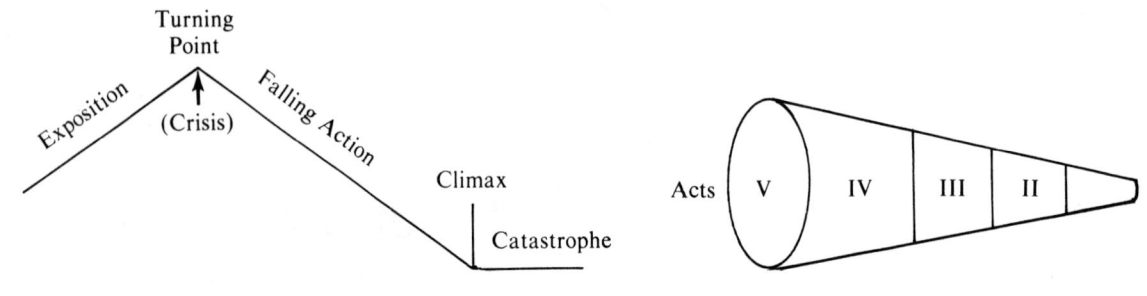

Greek Play (No Act Divisions)

Exposition — Turning Point (Crisis) — Falling Action — Climax — Catastrophe

Elizabethan Five-Act Division—Funnel Action

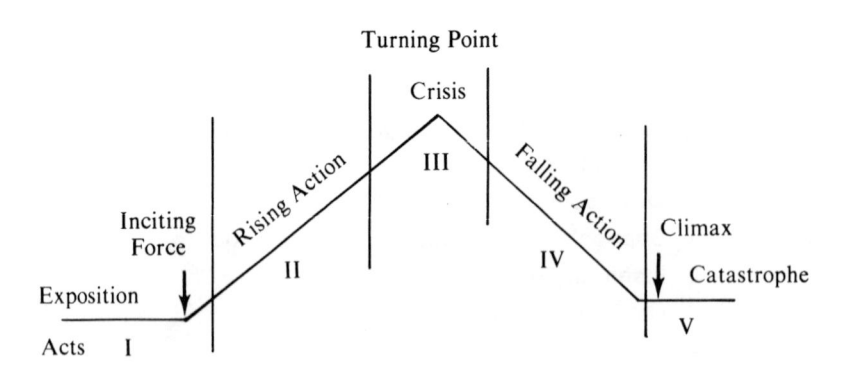

Acts V, IV, III, II

Elizabethan Five-Act Play

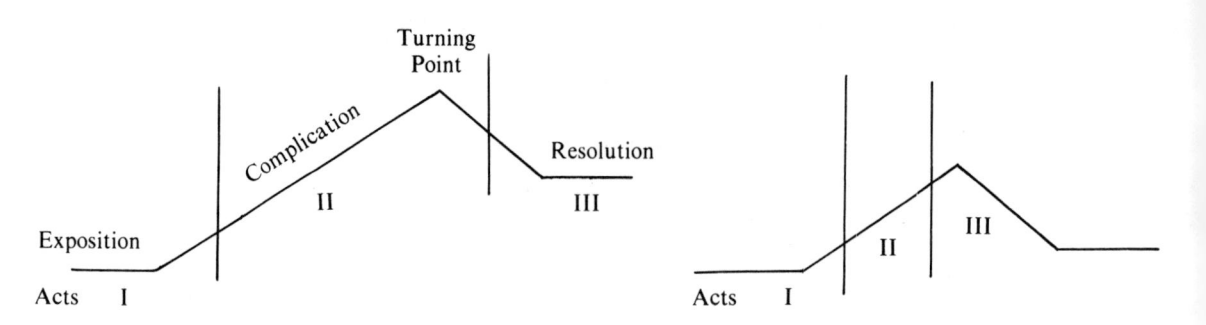

Acts I: Exposition — Inciting Force — II: Rising Action — III: Turning Point / Crisis — IV: Falling Action — V: Climax / Catastrophe

Modern Three-Act Play

Acts I: Exposition — II: Complication — Turning Point — III: Resolution

Modern Three-Act Play

Acts I — II — III

PLAYWRIGHT: CRAFTSMAN AND ARTIST

In the theatre a written script is performed, which has been creatively conceived, carefully organized, and controlled by the playwright. A playwright uses a form of reality without copying it. He gives us an abbreviation of reality by distilling from the world of reality the exact events which suit his dramatic purpose. Then, he intensifies the life experience and raises it to its highest imaginative power. He takes a life reality, which is perhaps full of anticlimaxes, and he works by extracting, combining, sifting these anticlimactic events into a highly intensified moment of decisive action. He constructs the play's climactic moment. He is not unlike a musician who composes a symphony or an architect who designs a building. The playwright becomes a master craftsman, an artist, who gives us his point of view of life, human nature, and the human condition. He makes note of the inconsistency of behavior in real life, and from his knowledge of people, along with his theory of personality and his philosophy of life, he shapes individuals into stage characters who matter.

It may well be that real life allows insufficient time for us to step back and take a look at human nature or that we are unwilling to look at ourselves as we really are. The playwright, however, attempts to focus our time and our thoughts on his created characters and their actions in order to heighten our awareness of ourselves and others.

Because life does not interpret itself, this becomes the job of the playwright who must arrange events to communicate meaning or a significant lack of meaning. He can capture a moment, which in real life might have sped past us, freeze that moment, and hold that moment up for our inspection. A truth that might have dissolved before us can, with the playwrights skill, become crystallized.

As a craftsman, the playwright devises and develops a story into a *playscript*. This playscript represents the sum total of his creative energies and craft. It contains the construction of plot, development of character and action, written dialogue, and often stage effects and directions. This same playscript, when moved into theatre art, becomes a *stageplay* which calls for the direct experience between an audience and an actor. A *playscript* can exist without an audience, simply as a work of dramatic literature. A *stageplay* requires the presence of an audience, experiencing the play's performance through the art of theatre. These two separate but related areas of *dramatic literature* and *theatre art* unite in a dynamic way to comprise a definition of *drama*.

The creating of a playscript may be thought of as a process. Of the elements of a playscript, Aristotle believed that *plot* was the single most important. Plot is the structure of a play, the pattern of its action, the design and arrangement of events, rather than the story or the theme of a play.

THE DEVELOPMENT OF PLOT

Sophocles, Shakespeare, Scribe

Plot structures have changed and developed over the years. The Greeks perfected the *pyramid plot structure* in which the possibilities of outcome narrow as the drama progresses until an obligatory moment or climax is reached. *Oedipus Tyrannus* may well possess the ideal classical plot in that, since everything necessary for the outcome has already taken place, nothing can alter the moment of truth the hero is doomed to face. Shakespeare expanded plot structure in the area of "rising action" to accommodate his interest in language and character. Eugéne Scribe, 19th Century French dramatist, specified a formula for plot structure which is known as the *"well-made play."* The pyramid structure, or well-made play, still provides the foundation for dramatic craft.

It should be pointed out that there are advantages and disadvantages to well-made plays and pyramid plot structures. They guide our emotions, create suspense and anticipation, in preparation for the climactic moment, and thus offer the playwright a rich showcase for whatever he may wish to say. But they can be overly predictable, can sacrifice character in the interest of plot movement (characters fitting into situation rather than situation developing out of character), and can send us back to reality with the expectation that life itself moves in an orderly, planned way toward certain climactic moments which may never occur.

Ibsen

Ibsen took Scribe's well-made play and used it for his own purpose. Ibsen's *The Wild Duck* is an example of the well-made play and the classical pyramid structure, in which each line, each gesture sweeps us to an inevitable and inescapable climax. Nothing is wasted in an Ibsen play. For instance, the scene between the hero Gregers and his father is developed with economy and consummate character revelation. *The Wild Duck* builds to a terrifying climax in which an innocent girl is the tragic victim of misguided idealism and selfishness. Ibsen's plays are usually cited as examples of realism.

Chekov

Like Ibsen, Chekhov portrays the reality of life. Unlike Ibsen, who sought to compact issues and personal and social problems into a "well-made" structure, Chekhov released structure. He breathed into it a flow of life which captured and preserved "the moment." Chekhov was the master of the "little moment," as opposed to the one massive climactic scene (e.g., the death of Hedvig in *The Wild Duck,* the entry of Oedipus blinded and wearing a dark red mask). Chekhov perceived life as a series of climaxes, most of which usually go unnoticed, and his art was to make us more perceptive, more intensely aware of life's moment-by-moment unfolding. Especially was he the poet/playwright of silences and what they whisper to us. Thus, Chekhov's plotting was less obvious than Ibsen's.

Whereas Sophocles painted in oil using primary colors, and Ibsen painted his people and issues with bold brush strokes, using multiple nuances and shadings, Chekhov merged his people and places into a glimpse of a moment on a smooth-wash water color canvas.

Checkhov almost never broke his own rule that an author, like a puppeteer, should keep his hands and feet concealed. Gently and subtly he wove his plot into a lush carpet in which the design is sensed rather than analyzed. Chekhov's flow-of-life, or *episodic structure,* has had tremendous influences on the development of dramatic craft in the 20th century. He especially influenced motion pictures, in which the intense focusing on slight incidents of great significance is made even more effective than on a stage. Playwrights identified as absurdists, who reject the well-made play and call our attention to life's irrational structures and anticlimaxes, are Chekov's legacies.

Strindberg

Strindberg's work ruptured realism, the "well-made play," and classicism. *The Ghost Sonata* is an example of Strindberg's departure from dramatic realism, of his freeing himself from literal truth in order to explore the depth and ambiguity of the inner man. Strindberg peoples his stage with bizarre characters and mystifying events that come not from reality but from the shadowy land of the subconscious. *The Ghost Sonata* surprises and puzzles, rather than leading to a geometric resolution; but, even when we are most perplexed by its mystery, we are enthralled by its imagery—as limitless as our dream world.

These three playwrights—Ibsen, Chekhov, Strindberg—are acknowledged as master plot craftsmen whose contributions to dramatic literature justify their high-rank as creative artists.

THE WILD DUCK

by

Henrik Ibsen
(1828–1906)

A. Play Notes: Realism and Symbolism in *The Wild Duck,* p. 67
   1. The Structure of the Play, p. 67
   2. Conventions of 19th Century Realistic Drama (Exemplified in the Wild Duck), p. 67

B. Story and Plot Summary, p. 68
C. Reviews of *The Wild Duck,* p. 69
D. Commentary: A Brief Summary of the Reviews, p. 72
E. Objectives, p. 73
F. Program Notes, p. 73
G. A List of BBC Actors and Production Coordinators, p. 74
H. Director's Notes
   1. Other Plays by Ibsen, p. 78
   2. Themes in *The Wild Duck,* p. 78
   3. Director's Plot Summary, p. 78
   4. Staging *The Wild Duck* for Television, p. 79

I. Focus in Viewing, p. 80
J. Additional Plays That Demonstrate Similar Concepts, p. 81
K. Stage Terms, p. 81

Play Notes

Realism and Symbolism in *The Wild Duck*

Henrik Ibsen was an iconoclast, a smasher of false gods, of cherished beliefs. To the audiences of the 1880's, his plays were shocking, upsetting, and, on occasion, of questionable taste. Ibsen defied the rules of gentility and exposed the hypocrisies of society. Some of the subjects of Ibsen's wrath were corruption in the church and in the business community, the inequality of the sexes, deception in politics, and prudishness and greed, in general. He made audiences look at the very things they spent their lives trying to avoid; he was, therefore, not always popular. In some ways he was like the hero of another of his plays, an "enemy of the people" who forced the townspeople to face the pollution in their own back yards.

In *The Wild Duck,* Ibsen is the enemy of self-styled idealism, (Gregers) and self-centered narrowness (Hjalmar). Ibsen's mouthpiece is Dr. Relling who talks of the major sickness that afflicts these two men and most people: the life lie. Gregers and Hjalmar represent two different extremes of this lie. Gregers deludes himself into believing that all people are strong and virtuous enough to live with the truth; while Hjalmar deludes himself into believing that psychological denial is a solution. Hedwig, of course, is caught between their delusion and denial. The wild duck living in the attic is, in one way or another, a symbol for these three characters because it survives in a perverse present that is eventually destroyed by the past.

The Structure of the Play

Although Ibsen's symbolism was quite complex and involved, his play structure is conventional and easy to understand; his well-made play has a clear beginning, middle, and end. He gave careful attention to the dialogue to make it seem "real"—that is, like everyday speech—but no line in his well-made plays is extraneous. An Ibsen character never speaks out of character. The play is constructed so that each line has a purpose, which the audience will no doubt discover as the play unfolds. *The Wild Duck* has many surprises, as secrets of the past keep emerging in the present, to the shock and embarrassment of characters involved. Nothing happens by accident in Ibsen, and, to a modern audience, his careful craftsmanship can seem contrived or even comic. But to his Victorian audience, the well-made play with its predictable orderliness must have been comforting—more comforting than the explosive ideas contained within the play.

Conventions of 19th Century Realistic Drama

1. Prose dialogue, authentic furniture, costumes—all necessary for verisimilitude.
2. Plays depicting social problems resulting from what the author believes are damaging laws and attitudes. Examples are: *Ghosts* and *The Wild Duck*.
3. Strong psychological motivation.
4. Characteristics of the "well-made play" with clues planted early in the play that are later shown to be important, economy of speech and movement, and a strong, definite climax.
5. Emphasis on the way present events are influenced by the past, usually some error in judgment or belief which has current consequences.
6. Indictment of institutions more than of individuals.

7. Very strong, suspenseful drama with characteristics of melodrama.
8. Themes which middle-class audiences found offensive because they cut into the pretenses of the age and resulted in the exposure of hypocrisy.
9. A belief of the playwright that progress was possible, if the public would recognize false beliefs and relationships.

Story and Plot Summary

Act I. This act takes place in Haakon Werle's home, where a dinner party is being held. Many years ago, Haakon had been involved in an illegal logging venture with Old Ekdal, an associate. Edkal was convicted and imprisoned; Haakon Werle was acquitted. Haakon's son, Gregers, has just returned home after a long absence; he has invited his old friend, Hjalmar, who is Ekdal's son, for the occasion. It is then established that Haakon aided Hjalmar's education and photographic work after Hjalmar had been engaged to his present wife, Gina, Haakon's former employee. Gregers insinuates that Haakon was more than casually interested in Gina and that out of respect for his dead mother's memory, and for all she had to suffer, he will leave home to fulfill his "life's mission." (We later find out how these comments were related to one another.)

Act II. This act and the following three acts take place in Hjalmar Ekdal's studio. Gregers, Haakon's son, comes by to visit and talk with Old Ekdal, renowned as a hunger in his younger days. Old Ekdal shows Gregers his attic—filled with rabbits, poultry, pigeons, and the wild duck, one that Haakon Werle had helped Old Ekdal capture, prior to the scandal that put Old Ekdal in prison. Gregers asks to rent an extra room and, despite Gina's protestations, makes arrangements to do so. Hjalmar proclaims he has a mission in life—to improve his father's lot, and renting a room is a step in the right direction.

Act III. Gregers talks with Hjalmar's daughter, Hedvig[1], who is apparently going blind. She tells Gregers about the attic where she spends much of her time, where the wild duck is the prize of a simulated forest and menagerie. Gregers then talks with Gina and discovers that she is, in fact, the one who runs the photography business. Hjalmar dreams of an amazing invention that will rescue his father by restoring the Ekdal name. Haakon Werle makes an entrance; he tries to change Gregers' mind but he will have nothing to do with his father or his business. Gregers' mission is to open Hjalmar's eyes to the truth (that Hedvig is really the child of Gina and Old Werle, Greger's father).

Act IV. Hjalmar speaks with Gina about his suspicions, and she finally admits to her affair with Haakon Werle. To Hjalmar, everything is lost and Gregers is surprised that the two, instead, do not plan a new life based upon the truth. Dr. Relling, who lives downstairs, warns them to be careful that Hedvig's not harmed. They learn that Hedvig is to receive a deed of gift from Haakon Werle (100 crowns a month to go to Old Ekdal, and then to her). Hjalmar questions whether or not he is Hedvig's real father, when the gift comes. Gina says she doesn't know, and Hjalmar prepares to leave. He snubs Hedvig, and does not even look at her. Gregers maintains throughout that self-sacrifice is of utmost importance. He then persuades Hedvig to kill the wild duck as an act of sacrifice to prove her devotion to her father.

---

1. Hedvig spelled also Hedwig, depending upon the translation.

Act V. Relling argues with Gregers saying that he believes Hjalmar to be an incompetent, with a talent for speaking other people's thoughts. Relling stresses the need for what he calls life illusion values, believing self-delusion to be a necessity for most people. Gregers maintains that one should seek the truth, outside oneself, in a spirit of sacrifice. Hedvig persuades her grandfather to shoot the wild duck. Hjalmar prepares to leave and says that he will take Old Ekdal with him. He refuses to have Hedvig in his presence, for she is an intruder in his life. He tells Gregers that perhaps Hedvig has never honestly loved him. Hedvig then shoots herself. Gregers sees this as an act that ennobles Hjalmar; Relling says it will be forgotten within a year's time.

Three Reviews of *The Wild Duck*
From: *The Moral Impulse* by Morris Freedman

. . . The dim-witted, smug, unrelenting, ugly self-righteousness of Gregers serves the poisonous ends of fanaticism. Yet even Gregers, like Dr. Stockman, is fanatical in a noble cause. We cannot deny the abstract validity of his wishing to have persons live by the truth. It is certainly better to live by truths and ideals than by illusions, for deceptions and hypocrisies to be wiped away, for Nora to be given her due as a person, for Mrs. Alving to be able to break away from her unsavory past, for the townspeople to heed Dr. Stockman.[2] But it is ignorant or stupid to behave as though the truth always will or must have easy, immediate acceptance. There are large truths and small ones, there is the right time to reveal the truth, and the wrong time, the right place and the wrong one. This simple enough distinction, obvious to Relling, to Gina, to the older Werle, is in no way apparent to the high-mindedly dense Gregers. The earthy Relling and the airy Gregers argue the point abstractly, but philosophical matters easily enough become practical ones. Hedvig, the child, grimly acts out Greger's murky symbolic nonsense. . . .

Ibsen's sardonic humor emphasizes the folly of all the busy righteousness and smartness. Look whom Gregers is trying to redeem! Hjalmar is a ninny, a clown, a good-hearted, good-natured, good-looking, self-indulgent, simple-minded lout. He cannot even run away from home like any self-respecting ten year old. Gregers goes about presenting the claim of the ideal to humanity and cannot keep his own room clean. But Ibsen's wryest humor is to be found in some of the pretentious symbolism about the wild duck. Only the weak-minded, the unbalanced, or the young get carried away by the symbolic solemnity, Gregers, Hedvig, Hjalmar, Ekdal. The wild duck is another red herring. We can make so much of it that finally we make nothing. The serious persons in the play never get involved with equating the duck with Hedvig, with Hjalmar, with Ekdal; they impatiently dismiss this kind of poeticizing. Watch the birdie and miss the sleight of hand, miss the study of depravity in the name of morality. As in *An Enemy of the People,* we can get so involved in the mechanics of the events, we neglect the character of the persons involved in them. And, of course, in all of these plays, it is so much easier, intellectually and morally, to study the surface scrupulously.

But the duck does lurk as an obvious enough symbol, and we cannot entirely pretend that it is only a red herring. Even before we learn of the duck, Werle refers to Ekdal in terms of the duck. "There are people in the world," he says to his son, "who dive to the bottom the moment

From THE MORAL IMPULSE: MODERN DRAMA FROM IBSEN TO THE PRESENT by Morris Freedman. Copyright © 1967 by Southern Illinois University Press. Reprinted by permission of Southern Illinois University Press.
2. Here the author refers to characters in other plays by Ibsen.

they get a couple of slugs in their bodies and never come to the surface again." Gregers is taken by the image, for, when he learns of the duck, he promptly equates it with Hjalmar and then calls himself a bird dog who will raise the duck from the depths. This wry, point-by-point working out of the allegorical intent might have remained simple burlesque, an instance of how literary obsession can unsettle the weak mind, were it not for the climax that actually develops Hedvig's self-identity with the duck under Gregers' relentless pressure. The glib symbolism of the duck would remain farcical did it not result in death.

A good deal is made of the freedom, the wildness, of the duck before its capture. These paeans to the untrammeled natural state of the duck are ironic. Man, unlike the duck, does not live in nature. He must always be trapped by the limitations of native capacity, the demands of society, the accidents of fate. Moreover, he must, when necessary, actively, consciously, imprison himself by life illusions, as Relling puts it. The wild duck in its attic prison prospers and gets fat, and it would have continued doing so (as would Hjalmar and Hedvig) if Gregers had not insisted on imposing the ideal on the real, imposing literature on life. . . .

In *The Wild Duck* the social context is irrelevant. But even in the earlier plays, for all of the force exerted by society on lives, individuals are not absolved of their own complicity in their fate. The sins of the fathers may indeed be passed on to the children, but the disaster that ensues is not automatic, and certainly not to be blamed on society; the tragedy is personal. This is made peculiarly explicit in *The Wild Duck,* for Gregers is to be found guilty of Hedvig's death, not Werle for her weak eyes. . . .

Ibsen's heroes, and they are few, are those who can live not only with themselves and with others but in society and with fate. They are, most importantly, concerned with the largest possibility, not with truth alone, but with lies and deceptions and accommodations, with compromises and resignations, with the whole range of human effort to live in the daily, natural, and human world.

Time—The Theatre, January 20, 1967

Integrity Fever

The Wild Duck. Henrik Ibsen asked men and women to be honest with themselves. He saw most human beings as hypocrites of the heart, defilers of the mind, and desiccators of the spirit. In his plays he waged an inexorable assault on the timid frauds, the sick souls, and audaciously exposed social dry rot. Integrity was his dramatic Excalibur. The profound irony of *The Wild Duck* is that it unflinchingly examines the human havoc that can result from so ruthless a devotion to honesty.

Gregers Werle (Clayton Corzatte) is a man with a raging case of "integrity fever" who prates high-mindedly of "the claim of the ideal." His pinched nostrils seem to sniff moral pollution in the air. He abominates his widowed father, a pompous timber merchant, accusing him of real and fancied slights to his dead mother. Taking lodgings in the modest household of a former classmate, Hjalmar Ekdal (Donald Moffat), Gregers uncovers more extensive proof of his father's evil ways. Not only did he bring lifelong disgrace to Hjalmar's father through a crooked timber deal, but

Reprinted by permission from *TIME,* The Weekly Newsmagazine; Copyright Time Inc. 1967.

he also seduced Hjalmar's wife (Betty Miller), a former housekeeper in the Werle household; Gregers' father sired the little daughter that Hjalmar dotes on, believing her to be his own. As an act of expiation, the older Werle all but supports the Ekdal household.

Hjalmar and his wife have built a happy house of illusions. In a constant alcoholic trance, Hjalmar's father stocks the attic with birds and rabbits, at which he takes an occasional potshot when he is in a hunting mood. Hjalmar himself is a dilettantish portrait photographer whose wife manages the business while he nurses the mirage that he is on the threshold of a world-shaking scientific discovery. The little girl (Jennifer Harmon) is content merely to love her supposed father and her pet wild duck.

To Gregers, this happiness is corrupt. These people must purge themseves of illusions, face bruising realities. He bluntly tells them the truth of things, and in one way or another kills the family he hoped to cure. A cynically humane doctor tells him of another cure: "I try to discover the basic lie, the pet illusion, that makes life possible, and then I foster it."

Any duel between appearance and reality is so close to the main artery of drama's heart that it is intrinsically exciting. Nonetheless, the APA production of *The Wild Duck* is cozy when it should be caustic, chucklesome when it should roar with outraged laughter, genteelly aggrieved when it ought to be spurting pain. The APA troupe does its customarily accomplished job of acting and touches off sporadic match flares of understanding throughout the play, but Ibsen had a crueler intention: to drag everything and everyone screaming into unrelenting light.

Saturday Review, January 28, 1967

THE THEATER
"Be Not Too Tame Neither"

The newest APA Repertory Company production takes a fresh look at Ibsen's *The Wild Duck*. Both the translation by Eva Le Gallienne and the staging by Stephen Porter succeed to a considerable extent in finding an intermediate point between the oldfashionedness of the work's moralizing rigidity and pathos and the surprising modernity of Ibsen's strong-minded observations of socio-pathological ironies.

At the outset we are led to empathize with Gregers Werle, an exceedingly honest and moral son who courageously repudiates his wealthy father for having been an adulterer, felon, and dissimulator. But when we move down a class into a household whose members comprise the major victims of his father's sins, we gradually recognize a more interesting confrontation. Like some modern psychiatrist, Gregers interprets the contentment of the Ekdal family as sick, for it depends upon a number of fantasies.

The nominal head of this household, Hjalmar Ekdal, is guilty of small sins that attend the apparently harmless self-indulgences of a mediocre person. He lies about his social accomplishments; he refuses to recognize his come-down-in-the-world father at a fashionable party. He is so preoccupied with his own conceit that he forgets to bring his daughter a promised present; he lets his wife do all the work while he fosters a necessarily vague pride in the notion that he is working on some "invention;" he criticizes his father for having shot himself to assert the family honor,

© Saturday Review, 1967. All rights reserved.

but in the next breath proclaims his own courage in choosing to live on with the burden of his father's disgrace rather than taking his own life; he encourages his wife to confide in him about her past and then admits he wouldn't have married her had he known about it; and, most self-centeredly of all, he has no compunction about cruelly rejecting his child's affection when he suspects that she may not be his daughter.

Thus, instead of seeming to be a play that attacks Gregers Werle for his destruction of one family's happiness, it becomes one that shows the more "innocent" Ekdal as being more despicable than the "guilty" Werle. A pragmatic selfishness tied to a sense of responsibility can be more admirable than a deluded selfishness that is irresponsible.

As Hjalmar, Donald Moffat gives us a mixture of ridiculous vanity, comic slow-wittedness and transparent self-indulgence. With the help of the huge, distorted overcoat Nancy Potts has designed for him, he seems to have been drawn by Ronald Searle. His patently comic facade keeps us from ever becoming sorry for him. On the other hand, Richard Woods's nicely understated portrayal of the elder Werle somehow catches our sympathy.

As Gregers, Clayton Corzatte chooses to serve this concept of the play by making his motivation seem more psychotic than philosophical. Balanced against his compulsion for fantasy dispelling is the family doctor, seedily portrayed by Joseph Bird, whose therapeutic formula is simply to discover the basic lie that makes his patient's life possible and then to foster it.

Betty Miller plays Hjalmar's practical-minded wife with a just barely restrained impatience that makes the role more modern. Jennifer Harmon forestalls the danger of sticky sentimentality by playing the little girl as a kind of simple-minded clod. And Sydney Walker is most entertaining as the bibulous and senile elder Ekdal, whose occasional shrewd asides tell us that he knows the lies of the land.

Indeed, all of the roles are here performed with a greater homogeneity of speech and style than are presently to be found in any other American company which attempts a classical repertoire. Achieving such refined and clear performances as the APA has progressively done in its six years of growth is praiseworthy, of course. But the happy thing about *The Wild Duck* is that it reminds us that the APA can be adventurous at the same time that it practices its more traditional virtues.

Henry Hewes

Commentary on the Reviews

The Moral Impulse

In his essay, Freedman warns against our focusing upon the particular details and symbols in *The Wild Duck* (that have always been emphasized) to the exclusion of equally important points. In an attempt to keep the play in a realistic, meaningful context, he calls our attention to the characters and how they fit into their given society.

Integrity Fever

In this *Time* article, the reviewer first emphasises the importance of the moral controversies in *The Wild Duck,* then criticizes the APA production for watering down these issues, concluding that what should have been a blaze of comedy and tragedy becomes only an erratic spark.

The Theatre

Henry Hewes, *Saturday Review* critic, believes that the character portrayal in the APA production makes the play a happy medium between old fashioned and modern style. Actor nuance balanced the play between nineteenth and twentieth century theatre, maintaining the important conventions, but forsaking the ridiculous melodrama.

Objectives

After viewing the play and reading about *The Wild Duck,* you, the student, should be able to do the following:

1. Identify some of the new conventions developed and expanded by Ibsen that added to the advance of theatrical realism.
2. Recognize how the controversial content of Ibsen's plays mirrored social and personal conflict.
3. Appreciate the blend of melodrama and the "well-made play" structure in *The Wild Duck*.

Program Notes

The Wild Duck

Henrik Ibsen's *The Wild Duck* includes the elements that earned him the title of Father of Modern Drama. The family of Hjalmar Ekdal must face the truth, insistently presented by old friend Gregers Werle. When Ekdal doubts that he is the father of Hedwig, the elements of melodramatic surprise grip audiences in this well-paced play. The small cast of characters includes the innocent, the self-deluded, and the realistic. Many interests are served in this prose drama: family relationships, the nature of truth, the well-made play, the mixture of realism and symbolism, all in a deceptively simple looking play which can be understood on many levels. Accompanying minidocumentary describes Ibsen's place in theatre history, with emphasis on innovations in realistic presentation. The edited television tape consists of the last part of Act IV and the whole of Act V, introduced by a short scene between Gregers and Haakon Werle, culled from Acts I and III.

Playwrights and Plotting

A Listing of BBC Actors and Production Coordinators

THE WILD DUCK

by

Henrik Ibsen

Produced by The British Broadcasting Company

CAST

HJALMAR EKDAL	ANTHONY AINLEY
GREGERS WERLE	MICHAEL BRYANT
GINA EKDAL	JO KENDALL
HEDVIG EKDAL	VERONICA QUILLIGAN
RELLING	RICHARD BEALE
OLD EDKAL	GEOFFREY BAYLDON
HAAKON WERLE	JOHN CITROEN
MOLVIK	TOM DURHAM

PRODUCTION

SET DESIGN	STEVE SCOTT
COSTUME DESIGN	BRIAN COX
MAKE-UP SUPERVISOR	DIANNE MILLAR
DIRECTOR	NICK LEVINSON

The Wild Duck by Henrik Ibsen was written in five acts. In our television version we concentrate on the last forty-five minutes in which the events of the past catch up with the present, and the tragic action unfolds.

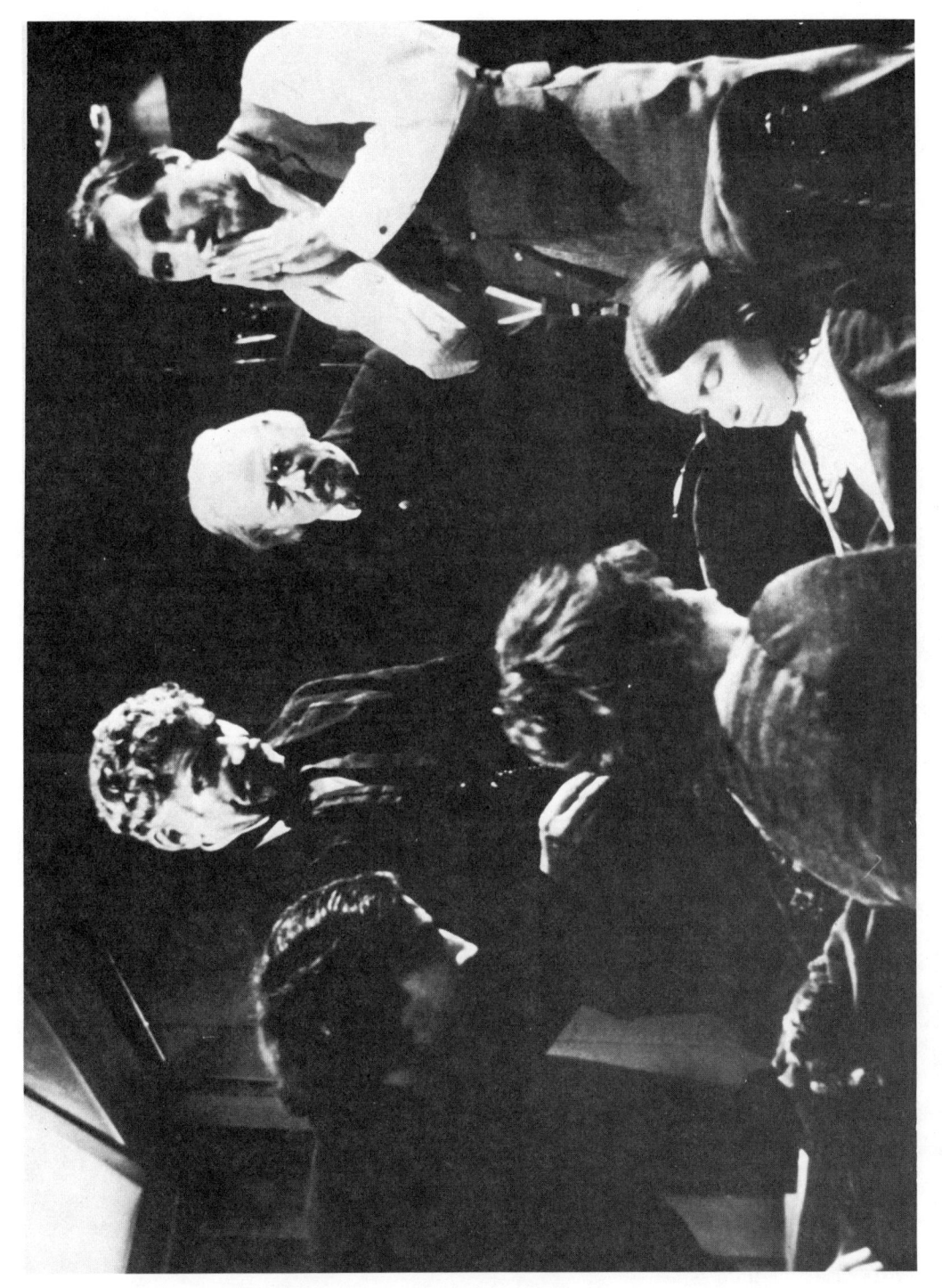

(*Clockwise*) Hedvig, Gina, Molvik, Dr. Relling, Gregers Werle, Hjalmar Ekdal

Old Werle

Hedvig

Director's Notes

Nick Levinson, the Director, writes about Ibsen and the play.

Other Plays by Ibsen

Henrik Johan Ibsen was born in 1828 in Norway and died in Christiana (Oslo) in 1906. He emerged as a major dramatist in his 40's in Norway and then became increasingly influential in Europe from the 1870's onwards with such plays as *Pillars of the Society, A Doll's House, Ghosts, The Enemy of the People, The Wild Duck, Rosmersholm, Hedda Gabler, The Master Builder, John Gabriel Borkman,* and others. During his career Ibsen established a new style of realism, which was expressed in theatrical productions that stunned late nineteenth century audiences by their apparent lifelikeness.

THEMES IN *THE WILD DUCK*

The Wild Duck and subsequent plays were originally criticised as being obscure. In the case of 'The Wild Duck' this was probably because of the rather strong symbolism set in motion by the title. The symbol of the wild duck shot down and kept in captivity certainly pervades the play and can be seen as symbolic of the predicament of most of the characters.

As Bernard Shaw made it clear in the *Quintessence of Ibsenism,* it is wrong to see Ibsen just as a critic of social injustice. His plays certainly rip the lid off 19th century bourgeois society but they go further and deal with more fundamental and timeless human feelings and behavior. But without going into a too detailed analysis of the play, one can say that the play attacks the following: 1. the pretensions of respectability amongst the provincial Norwegian bourgeoisie 2. the role of the idealist who believes he can transform people's lives by facing them into the truth 3. male egoism, especially in man's relation to women.

A Plot Summary by the Director

The play opens with a lavish party at Haakon Werle's house. Werle is a rich old man who has made his money in timber. His son Gregers Werle meets his erstwhile friend Hjalmar Ekdal and learns of his marriage to Haakon Werle's ex-house servant Gina and about the birth of their child, Hedvig, who is suffering from a disease which is causing her to go blind. Hjalmar's father had been a partner of Old Werle but had been disgraced by being sent to prison as the result of a business scandal. It seems that he took the blame and the wily Haakon Werle got cleared. The father appears by accident at the party as a broken old man earning a pittance copying papers in the Werle's office. Hjalmar is embarrassed and leaves the party. Gregers Werle finds out that his father, Old Werle, was responsible for setting up the Ekdal marriage and for paying to train Hjalmar as a photographer after *his* father's scandal. Was this just to make up for Hjalmar's father's disgrace? Another string of motives emerge. Gina, Hjalmar's wife and one-time house servant to Haakon Werle, had been pursued and seduced by the old man. Could Hjalmar's beloved child be his too? This suggestion becomes stronger when we learn that the old man is going blind as well as Hedwig.

But all these shady events have been buried beneath layers of deception. Hjalmar is ignorant of the sordid truth. His appalling egoism helps him hide the truth and create a glowing but false idea of himself as a potentially great poet, artist, inventor, and head of a happy family. Like the wild duck, which Haakon Werle had shot down and retrieved from the sea bed (by means of his dog), Hjalmar had been injured by the old man's egoism. Like the duck, which is now kept in Hjalmar's attic in a make-believe forest populated with rabbits and hens, Hjalmar is kept in a false world of sly deception by the old man's "generosity." Similarly, Hedvig, if she is Haakon Werle's daughter and has been wounded by inheriting his eye disease, is a "wild duck" kept in a false world with no future but impending blindness. The play is full of similar elaborations of the theme of the wild duck symbol and that of sight, light and darkness, falsehood and truth. But despite these falsehoods, all things seem to run smoothly in the Edkal household until Gregers Werle decides to face Hjalmar with the truth.

This is where our version of the play begins. Of course, Hjalmar is unable to take the truth and only retreats into further self-indulgent fantasies, seeing himself as a tragic victim who must reject his daughter and leave the family. Hedvig cannot understand why her father has rejected her and is persuaded by the idealist Gregers to sacrifice the thing she loves most, the wild duck, in order to regain his love. Again Gregers implants this idea in her in an attempt to manipulate other people for their own good. Again it is misguided. Unseen, Hedvig goes into the loft where the wild duck is kept with Hjalmar's gun. Hjalmar is too self-obsessed with his own sorrow to see the danger. While dramatising his plight to Gregers, Hedvig fires a shot in the loft. They think it is Hjalmar's father who makes a habit of going 'hunting' there, shooting rabbits which he believes are bears in the great forest. But Hjalmar's father emerges drunk from his room, accusing Hjalmar of "going shooting alone." Gregers proclaims that it is Hedvig making the sacrifice to regain her father's love. At last Hjalmar realizes the danger. Hjalmar and Gina rush into the loft and find her lying on the floor. Relling, a doctor, who has fallen on ill times, is called and Hedwig is put on the sofa. Relling pronounces her dead. This appalling loss at least brings Hjalmar and Gina together again, but for how long? All leave the room, except Gregers and Relling. Gregers tells Relling that Hedvig's sacrifice has not been in vain but Relling, an anti-idealist, replies that it is common to find nobility in the face of death, but give Hjalmar a few months and he will have turned this tragedy to his own use so that he can sentimentalize about it.

Relling is an important character. He has brushed up against Gregers before and learned how dangerous he can be. He tried earlier to warn Hjalmar of the dangers of listening to Gregers. Relling is a realist who paradoxically sees the need to preserve the make-believe world in which the Ekdals live: he even builds up Hjalmar's 'life'lie' by making him believe that he could be a great inventor.

This tremendous indictment against blind unswerving idealism comes, in Ibsen's career, just after the play, *The Enemy of the People,* which tended to go in the opposite direction, showing the heroic stance of a man who held his ground against superior forces so as not to compromise what he believed was right. This prevents us from accusing Ibsen of cynicism and emphasizes the depth and complexity of his work.

Staging *The Wild Duck* for Television

Ibsen's instructions for the staging of the play are specific: a lavish set for the party scene in Act I, then the attic studio of Hjalmar Ekdal with its door leading into the loft which the rabbits share with the wild duck. Never do we actually see inside the loft; its animals, dead Christmas trees, and contraptions, made by Hjalmar and his father, are the world of their imagination, which is best left to ours. In Ibsen's instructions, the set is made up of three walls with four doors and sliding doors to the loft. For our television production it was necessary to change this very theatrical arrangement. A nearly L-shaped set allows the cameras to get in for close-shooting. We cut down on the number of doors by having two openings in the set leading off to the kitchen and living rooms.

The 'realism' of early Ibsen productions was quite different from the 'realism' we are used to on television or in the cinema; Ibsen's doors had door knobs on them, but they were only painted! Our policy has been to avoid the realism common in contemporary television without making the set seem stagey. To achieve what we wanted was difficult because television is such a close-up medium. The set for Hjalmar's attic studio is not supposed to trick anyone into believing it is a real attic studio, but to symbolize this place as an environment for the play to take place in. With a few exceptions, we have tried to include only furniture and props which are used or referred to in the play. The photographer's back drop and camera are in this case extravagances, but for those who know the play, they are an important symbol.

Nick Levinson

Focus in Viewing

There will almost always be ambiguity over this play's total meaning. The main question about *The Wild Duck,* presumably, is simple to state but not to answer. The question seems to be this: Is it better to know the whole truth about oneself and one's relationships or to be blind to, or content with, things as they are, even if blindness or contentment includes a degree of self-delusion? Hedvig's eye glasses, the photography studio itself, and frequent references to sight suggest the importance of this question.

Content Viewing

1. Why does Gregers insist that the truth be known? Is this really wrong? Why or why not?
2. What is your opinion of Hjalmar? Why?
3. Why do you think Hedvig kills herself?
4. With what philosophy does Ibsen wish us to align ourselves?
5. What in the lives of the characters could the wild duck symbolize?

Craft Viewing

1. How is *The Wild Duck* a well-made play? How does Ibsen prepare us for the climax? Is there a resolution? Explain.
2. Cite examples of realism in the play. What significance could there be in Ibsen's having placed much of the action in a photographic studio with an adjacent attic loft?
3. What are examples in the production of the director's interpretation?
4. Were you sympathetic, unsympathetic, or neutral to Gina, Hedvig, and Relling as portrayed?
5. Do you think the stage set supported the playscript and the stageplay as Ibsen intended? Why or why not?
6. Is there one moment or scene which stands out in your memory? More than one? Which ones, and why?

Critical Viewing: Overview
1. Was the playwright successful in achieving his purpose? Discuss.
2. Was the production successful? Discuss.
3. Now that this play and its production are part of your experience, what significance does *The Wild Duck* hold for you?

Additional Plays That Demonstrate Similar Concepts

Ghosts, A Doll's House, Hedda Gabler—Ibsen

The Glass Menagerie, A Streetcar Named Desire, Summer and Smoke— Tennessee Williams

The Children's Hour, The Little Foxes—Lillian Hellman

Come Back, Little Sheba—William Inge

The Iceman Cometh—Eugene O'Neill

Stage Terms

Well-made play—An overly precise and calculated plot structure, outgrowth of 19th Century melodrama, but employed by Ibsen as the vehicle of thesis drama.

Verisimilitude—The major convention developed during the 19th Century and still a major convention of a drama; the imitation of the surface appearance of reality through authenticity in setting, costume, and presumably language. Examples are *The Wild Duck* and *Miss Julie*.

Meliorism—The philosophy, popular at the end of the last century, that nature and society could improve. It forms the basis of the thesis plays of Ibsen and Shaw.

Melodrama—A play characterized by extravagant theatricality and by the predominance of physical action, character types, and plot.

THE THREE SISTERS

by

Anton Chekhov
(1860–1904)

A. Play Notes: Structure in *The Three Sisters*, p. 83
    1. Chekhov's Innovations, p. 83
    2. A Three Part Structure and Staging, p. 83
    3. How the Staging Compares to Greek Drama, p. 83
B. Differences Between the Approaches of Ibsen and Chekhov, p. 84
C. Story and Plot Summary, p. 84
D. Reviews of *The Three Sisters*, p. 85
E. Commentary: A Brief Summary of the Reviews, p. 88
F. Objectives, p. 88
G. Program Notes for the BBC Production, p. 88
H. A List of BBC Actors and Production Coordinators, p. 89
I. Conclusion to Act I, p. 93
J. Focus in Viewing, p. 98
K. Additional Plays That Demonstrate Similar Concepts, p. 99
L. Stage Terms, p. 99

Play Notes
Structure in *The Three Sisters*

Chekhov's Structural Innovations

Chekhov came to the theatre late in life, after a career as a physician. A background of scientific awareness undoubtedly influenced his revolutionary style of writing drama. He did away with the play of one central figure, in favor of the play of a group of persons, their actions, and interactions. Almost all the characters in a Chekhov drama are at one time or another objects of sympathetic understanding; they are the heroes of a microcosmic drama that has a beginning, a middle, and an end but is not the basis for the total plot. Chekhov's plays are plotless, in contrast with almost every form of drama that precedes them. They reflect the dedicated physician's concern for all of his patients, an insight gained through listening and observing, and an unwillingness to make moral judgment. Checkhov's naturalistic plays resulted in an entirely new system of acting and directing: the Stanislavsky method.[1]

A Three Part Structure and Staging

The basic architecture of *The Three Sisters* is apparently constructed with much attention paid to the number three: three agents, three parts of a triangle, three time orientations (past, present, future), and so on. As the first act begins, so does the last act end. At the beginning, for example, three female agents are downstage, and three male agents are upstage. At the beginning of the play, the three sisters are appropriately introduced. Masha, in a black dress, is seated, reading a book. She is 22 years old and has been married to the school teacher Koolygin for four years. Irena, dressed in white, stands lost in thought. Irena, 20, is unmarried, and the day—the fifth of May—is her Saint's Day. Olga, wearing the dark blue uniform dress of a female teacher, is correcting student exercise books and walking to and fro. Olga, 28, is the oldest and is unmarried.

Separated in space, but at the same time together in the downstage area, the three sisters are balanced by a group of three army officers in the ballroom upstage. The youngest officer, Baron Nikolay Lvovich Toozenbach, is a lieutenant, who is in love with Irena, the youngest sister. Toozenbach is not yet 30 years old. The tall, erect officer with a mustache is Captain Vasily Vasilevich Soliony; he is probably in his early 30's. He, too, is in love with Irena, but he will not tell her until the next act. The oldest officer, Ivan Romanovich Chebutykin, is an army doctor, close to 60 years old.

How the Staging Compares to Greek Drama

From what we see, as well as from what we hear, at the very beginning, we are able to compare the two groups—the sisters downstage and the three army officers upstage—to the chorus of ancient Greek drama. The Greek chorus also was divided into two groups; the first group danced and sang the *strophe,* which literally means an act of turning, after which the second group danced and sang the *antistrophe,* which was composed of an answer to the *strophe.* In a similar way, the

---

1. Konstantin Stanislavsky (1863–1938), founder of the Moscow Art Theatre (1898) is best known for advocating innovations typified in his productions of Chekhov's plays (1898–1940). In these plays the acting was truthful, simple, and without theatricality. Aware of Chekhov's intent to portray psychological internal development, Stanislavsky directed his actors to portray the characters with subtlety and simplicity of external expression.

two groups in *The Three Sisters* dance and sing. We also see a likeness to ancient Greek drama when the messenger arrives on stage to report happenings off-stage.

Another element from ancient Greek drama is that of reversal—the changing of the direction of action. For instance, at the end of the first act, the sisters, their brother, and their officer friends engage in the celebration of Irena's Saint's Day party. It is high noon, sunny and bright outdoors, and it is springtime. The sisters and their brother are secure inside their home. In the last act, the sisters and their brother are outside in the garden. Their home has been sold to pay off the gambling debts of Andrey. It is high noon, with the cooling sun of autumn. The army is leaving, and the time has come to say good-bye forever. The possessors of home, security, and warmth among friends in the first act have become, by the last act, the dispossessed.

Another playwriting technique used by Chekhov to create a feeling of the flow of life, and consequently the appearance of reality, is the consistent pattern of agent's arriving and departing. This technique also contributes to the open-endedness and reality of *The Three Sisters*.

Differences Between the Approaches of Ibsen and Chekhov

Ibsen	Chekhov
The sets, dialogues, and plots of Ibsen's plays reflect his belief in what results when one lives truthfully; a sense of purpose, an order results, which parallels the structure of a "well-made play."	The sets, dialogues, and plots of Chekhov's plays reflect his naturalistic "let-it-unfold-as-it-will" philosophy.
What people say and do is a key to their thoughts. (Because of this belief Ibsen's characters have a great deal of interaction.)	The human mind is so complex that it is difficult to understand the motivation for what people say and do. (Because of this belief, Chekhov's characters are somewhat detached.)
Definite solutions exist for the problems of society.	The world is so complex and illogical that happiness cannot come through legislation or change in attitudes.
Issues, feelings, and ideas have solutions, if one will only have the strength to choose to do "right."	Issues, feelings, and ideas are not absolute or clear-cut. Life is a series of dilemmas.

Story and Plot Summary

The play begins on Irena's Saint's Day with the three sisters recalling the death of their father, exactly a year ago. The sisters, Olga, Masha, and Irena, are joined by the Army doctor Chebutykin and by the Baron Toozenback, an Army lieutenant. On this day they meet the new battery commander for the first time. He is a lieutenant-colonel, Vershinin. Among the guests is another officer, Soliony.

The three sisters and their brother Andrey had once lived in Moscow, a city they remember with great affection. They have hopes of returning to Moscow and of the professorship which they believe Andrey will soon be offered.

Toozenbach and Soliony are in love with Irena. Masha is bored by her marriage to Koolyghin, who seems not to be aware of his wife's feelings or the effect he has on other people.

There are events in the play: the marriage of Andrey to Natasha (who is at first in awe of the family), the affair which develops between Masha and Vershinin, a fire which causes refugees to seek shelter in the home of the family, the unfaithfulness of Natasha, gambling debts, the birth of children, and the firing of servants.

But most of all there is talk, talk in which characters describe their memories and hopes. By the end of the play, there has been change, but it is not possible to describe an ending as being "happy" or "unhappy" without identifying with the aspirations of a central character. Chekhov's plays require a broader, more dispassionate view, even the ability to be amused by the vanities, self-delusions, and limited abilities of most people, onstage or off. The family is deeper in debt than at the beginning. The sister-in-law Natasha has taken over more of the house for her own needs. Work has turned out to be a disappointment. The possible marriage which might have rescued Irena ends with Soliony shooting the Baron in a duel. Masha's lover Vershinin leaves with the other officers, and Masha continues in her loveless marriage to Koolyghin, who might have made a suitable husband for Olga. Moscow remains a hoped-for paradise, now more remote than ever.

*Broadway Postscript,*SR/August 24, 1963

Opening Up the Open Stage
Minneapolis-St. Paul

The ultimate challenge proponents of the open stage will have to meet is how to make modern plays as effective on it as they were on the stages for which they were originally written. The third and fourth productions of this first repertory season run the new Tyrone Guthrie Theatre smack into this problem.

Chekhov's *The Three Sisters* is being played here on a large platform crammed with furniture and viewed on three sides by a mass of spectators who are as aware of audience response to the action before them as they are of the play itself. Director Guthrie has taken his first plunge into open-stage Chekhov with a forthright boldness but with a complete avoidance of the sort of theatrical stunting he sometimes uses to shake up Shakespeare's too familiar works. Sure-handedly, he presents the beautifully constructed symphony of provincial desperations as deeply serious to the participants but somewhat comic to outsiders. Only after we have laughed, do we perhaps realize that their silliness is not without correspondence to our own.

While the style of performance is not yet uniform, the apparent intention is toward a sharply delineated extroversion supported by an inner awareness that the inadequacy of action intensifies each character's dissatisfaction with his ineffectuality. Most memorable is Claude Woolman's embullient Tusenbach, who entertains us enormously as he repeats himself with an enthusiasm that grows in inverse proportion to his diminishing inner conviction. The marvelous, grotesque quality of Mr. Woolman's performance is sustained in his final scene, in which he seems to suggest the rather romantic notion that Tusenbach allowed himself to be killed in a duel in order to release

Reprinted with permission from *Saturday Review.* Copyright © 1963 by Saturday Review.

his fiancée from marriage to a man she liked and respected but with whom she could never be in love. Rita Gam's Masha becomes a touching portrait of an unhappily married woman who falls in love with an unhappily married man. And again the frustrations of this unconsummated affair lead to a romantic final parting. As the object of her love, Robert Pastene achieved one very funny moment when he replies to Tusenbach's gauche over-statement with a telling "Yes."

Sir Tyrone's company must be commended for moving through Chekhov's universe so efficiently and for making *The Three Sisters* entertaining and meaningful to fresh audiences. While one suspects that a more perfectly selected cast might achieve a more "Chekhovian" result on this stage, it might well prove less popular than the present production, which is the finest of the adventurous Minnesota Theatre Company's opening season efforts.

Henry Hewes

Broadway Postscript, SR/July 18, 1964

Russian the Season?

Since a majority of my distinguished colleagues have extravagantly praised the new Actors Studio Theatre production of Chekhov's *The Three Sisters,* this group's brave venture of opening a serious play in June may be a notable and happy triumph of art over show-biz tradition. Such a triumph is appropriate, for the Actors Studio has done more than any other organization to reintroduce the notion that theatre *is* an art, and that, as in other art forms, its talented practitioners should work to satisfy their own rather than a public taste.

For a dozen years or so, the Studio's contribution to the mainstream of American Theatre has been indirect. It has nourished the talents and helped develop the techniques of many performers who have gone on to use what they have acquired at the Studio in Broadway plays and in movies. However, in such media, they usually found themselves collaborating with many actors and directors who did not share their way of working and their objectives, or, even if they did, felt an overriding responsibility to substitute for art pragmatic devices that would lead more surely to public success.

During the last two seasons the Actors Studio has supplemented its training program with a nonprofit producing organization. This move has enabled it to extend fuller exercise of its own taste and values in Broadway playhouses. But, although anyone who takes theatre seriously must support this step as logically desirable, one finds oneself questioning the effectiveness of the new values offered.

What are these values? Director Lee Strasberg has said that he would like this Actors Studio Theatre production of *The Three Sisters* to be like an impressionist painting and mean different things to each viewer. This has been achieved largely by a de-emphasis of theatrical punctuation and conventional climaxes. Thus the play appears as a continuum of life. There is also deliberate disruption of the old-fashioned theatrical idea of focusing on one or two characters for any length of time and a breaking up of mood whenever it starts to accumulate. And to be sure that we see the play as a more total picture of society, there is much use of offstage sounds and intrusions by minstrels and carnival celebrants.

Reprinted with permission from *Saturday Review.* Copyright © 1964 by Saturday Review.

Mr. Strasberg has also said that for him the events of the play are there primarily for the purpose of character revelation. Thus the performers seem less involved with each other than they do with their personal selfish needs and feelings. At the beginning, Geraldine Page's Olga appears almost in a subconscious trance as she senses her own state of being and the climate of life around her. The expository lines about her father's death, her detested job of schoolteaching, and her determination to return to Moscow melt into her physical attunement to a spring day and her general longing for fulfillment. Throughout the play she remains a true but passive character. Shirley Knight's Irena is also passive, a dry portrait of innocence, a pretty decoration, helpless to do anything but serve that purpose.

Emerging most strongly in this production is Kem Stanley's Masha, but hers, too, is a self-generated solo, following her own intuitive inner currents. For instance, her decision to stay for lunch, which in other productions has always seemed the result of the new Colonel's fascinating speech, is here played capriciously as if prompted by a desire for romance rather than by the irresistible attractiveness of the Colonel. But later, Miss Stanley presents us with two truly marvelous manifestations of her libido. The first comes when after forbidding the Colonel to speak love to her, she suddenly feels a rush of desire and tells him he can. And the second emerges at the moment when she heartbreakingly and nakedly confesses her illicit love to her sisters. Miss Stanley also employs a sarcastic sense of humor so penetrating that it occasionally jumps out of the play. Her delivery of "She walks like the one that started the fire" is so funny that we instantly forgive the slight bump of objectivity it injects.

Because of this dramatic emphasis, more psychological than social, the sisters seem less the victims of over-refinement, in an epoch when Russian aristocracy was giving way to a less graceful but more democratic way of life, than they do of their own failings, which they understand almost too well. Thus Barbara Baxley finds herself over-stressing the coarseness of their middleclass sister-in-law, and, compared to them, Gerald Hiken's brother seems for the most part, unnecessarily subdued, and Robert Loggia over-relishes Solyony's villainy.

It is also hard to understand Masha's attachment either to her husband, who is portrayed as a raucous buffoon by Afred Paulsen, or to the Colonel, who is played with a too casual geniality by Kevin McCarthy. The most satisfactory performance is given by Luther Adler as the old doctor. Mr. Adler is adroitly funny as he concentrates on the minor and shallower pleasures of life, as if he knew all along that the seemingly more intense concerns of the others were in the long run as trivial and arbitrary as this production of the play tends to make them appear.

Mr. Strasberg has created some wonderfully vital scenes, such as the one in which Tusenbach and the brother do a spirited Russian dance, or another when the girls are all waltzing around the piano. These help create a feeling that provincial life with its constant visits by officers from the local garrison is not so bad. And Randall Jarrell's new translation is, without being anachronistic, so modern that the play could be taking place in some present-day Midwestern town. Theoni V. Aldredge's costumes are bright and appropriate, and Will Steven Armstrong's settings attractive and poetic.

Indeed, if one is able to regard a play as a montage of acting explorations and artistically conceived supplements, this production is an extraordinary event. But for some of us, who rightfully or wrongfully seek more conventional theatrical fulfillment of our conception of Chekhov and *The Three Sisters,* the presentation fails to harmonize its impressions, or even to leave us with a series of impressions we can mentally synchronize. Partly, this effect may stem from the exigencies of casting, but partly it may also be inherent in the Studio's approach to production.

The great promise in an Actors Studio Theatre Company is that two or more actors stimulating each other within the logic of a scene can bring more genuine excitement and fuller expression to the plays they perform than is ordinarily achieved. But in *The Three Sisters,* too much of the performance seems to have been created by actors working consciously and with widely varying success at the task of character exploration. They have hardly been concerned at all with the play's action and with reactions to the words Chekhov has written for them. While it is true that most of the people in *The Three Sisters* don't really mean what they say, this fact emerges better if they seem to be trying desperately to mean it and are even momentarily persuaded that the other characters mean what they say, too. As it stands, our appreciation of their work is constantly mixed with our exasperation at what these artists and their director have chosen to do.

Henry Hewes

Commentary

The preceding two articles are critical reviews by Henry Hewes, who attended two productions of Chekhov's *The Three Sisters* presented by different acting companies and designed for differing theatre settings. In the first article, he notes the effect of the type of stage on the production and its subsequent audience response. In the second article, he says that a more conventional approach to the play would have suited him and that the actors were still exploring their characters. The production was too modern and too confusing for the audience to determine the purpose of actors and directors.

Over the years, critics have noted that one of the greatest difficulties a director of *The Three Sisters* faces is how to maintain Chekhov's musical, flowing, style while ensuring that the play has enough structure to be coherent.

Objectives

A study of Chekhov's *Three Sisters* should enable you, the student, to do the following:

1. Recognize Chekhov's ability to transform the natural flow of life from moment to moment into a meaningful dramatic experience.
2. Appreciate Chekhov's innovative contributions to theatre as represented in *The Three Sisters.*

Program Notes from the BBC Production

The Three Sisters

Anton Chekhov's drama of a family trapped in the provinces is given sympathetic but detached treatment in these excerpts from Acts III and IV. Each of the sisters is carefully delineated—at first in a scene from Irena's Saint's Day celebration in Act I, then later when the forceful sister-in-law Natasha has rearranged the household to emphasize her values in opposition to theirs. Masha's affair with the colonel, Olga's perennial complaints, Irena's naive hopes for the future, the doctor's self-pity, Koolygin's pedantry—all are presented in this play, which may be seen as either comic or tragic, but inevitably as real. A minidocumentary examines Chekhov's reputation as master of mood and character and urges audience ability to view without judging. The edited television tape consists of the last part of Act I. Act III is nearly complete.

A Listing of BBC Actors and Production Coordinators

THE THREE SISTERS

by

Anton Chekhov

CAST

MASHA	KATHRINE SCHOFIELD
VERSHININ	JEREMY KEMP
OLGA	VIVIEN HEILBRON
IRENA	TESSA WYATT
ANDREY	DAVID STRONG
NATASHA	WENDY ALLNUTT
CHEBUTYKIN	MARK DIGNAM
TOOZENBACH	BEN KINGSLEY
KOOLYGHIN	GEORGE LITTLE
SOLIONY	FRANK VINCENT
FEDOTIK	MIKE SAVAGE
RODE	IAN OLIVER
FERRAPONT	HAROLD BENNETT
ANFISA	MARY BARCLAY

PRODUCTION

SET DESIGN	COLIN BOWLES
COSTUME DESIGN	BARBARA KIDD
MAKE-UP SUPERVISOR	MAGGIE WEBB
DIRECTOR	NICK LEVINSON

Irena

Masha

Olga and Natasha

THE THREE SISTERS

by

Anton Chekhov

Translated by
Elisaveta Fen

Act III of Chekhov's *The Three Sisters* contains the climax of the play when, for the first time, all the main characters face the truth of their situation. But first we introduce them at the end of Act I. The Prozorov family and their friends are celebrating Irena's Saint's Day. It is the occasion when Masha first meets Vershinin, whom we find philosophizing with Toozenbach. This excerpt was taken from the script for the BBC television production.

THE CONCLUSION OF ACT I

(A drawing-room in the Prozorovs' house. ANDREY *has left the room unnoticed.)*

TOOZENBACH You say that in time to come life will be marvelously beautiful. That's probably true. But in order to share in it now, at a distance so to speak, we must prepare for it and work for it.

VERSHININ *(gets up)* Yes. . . . What a lot of flowers you've got there. . . .*(looks around)* And what a marvelous house! I do envy you! All my life I seem to have been pigging it in some quarter, with two chairs and a sofa and a stove which always smokes. It's the flowers that I've missed in my life, flowers like these. . . .*(picks flowers and gives it to* OLGA.*)* Oh, well, never mind!

TOOZENBACH Yes, we must work. I suppose you're thinking I'm a sentimental German. But I assure you I'm not—I'm Russian. I don't speak a word of German. My father was brought up in the Greek Orthodox faith.

(A pause)

VERSHININ *(Walks up and down)* You know, I often wonder what it would be like if you could start your life over again—deliberately, I mean, consciously, I mean . . . suppose you could put aside the part of your life you'd lived already, as though it was just a sort of rough draft, and then start another one like a fair copy. Now I think that if that happened, the thing you'd want most of all would be not to repeat yourself. You'd try at least to create a new environment for yourself, a house like this one, for instance, with some flowers and plenty of light. . . . I have a wife, you know, and two little girls; and my wife's not very well, and all that. . . . Well, if I had to start my life all over again, I wouldn't marry . . . no, no!

(Enter KOOLYGHIN, *in the uniform of a teacher.)*

KOOLYGHIN *(approaches* IRENA*)* Congratulations, dear sister—from the bottom of my heart, congratulations on your Saint's Day. I wish you good health and everything a girl of your age ought to have! And allow me to present you with this little book. . . .

Excerpt from *Three Sisters* from Anton Chekhov: PLAYS, translated by Elisaveta Fen (Penguin Classics, 1959) pp. 263–270. © Elisaveta Fen, 1951. Reprinted by permission of Penguin Books, Ltd.

(Hands her a book)

It's the history of our school covering the whole fifty years of its existence. I wrote it myself. Of course, quite a trifle—I wrote it in my spare time when I had nothing better to do—but I hope you'll read it nevertheless. Good morning to you all!

(to VERSHININ*)*

Allow me to introduce myself. Koolyghin's the name; I'm a master at the secondary school here. And a town councilor.

(to IRENA*)*

You'll find a list in the book of all the pupils who have completed their studies at our school during the last fifty years. *Feci quod potui, faciant meliora potentes.*

(kisses MASHA*)*

IRENA But you gave me this book for Easter!
KOOLYGHIN *(Laughs)* Did I really? In that case, give it back to me—or no, better give it to the Colonel. Please do take it, Colonel. Perhaps you'll read it some time when you've nothing better to do.
VERSHININ Thank you very much. *(prepares to leave)* I'm so very glad to have made your acquaintance. . . .
OGLA But you aren't going, are you? Really . . . you mustn't.
IRENA But you'll stay and have lunch with us! Please do.
OLGA Please do.
VERSHININ *(bows)* I see I've intruded on your Saint's Day party. I didn't know. Please forgive me for not offering you my congratulations.

(Goes into the ballroom with OLGA.*)*

KOOLYGHIN Today is Sunday, my friends, a day of rest; let each of us rest and enjoy it, each according to his age and his position in life! We must remember to roll up the carpets and put them away till the winter. . . . We must remember to put some naphthaline or Persian powder in them. Now the Romans . . . they enjoyed good health because they knew how to work and how to rest. They had *mens sana in corpore sano.* Their life had a definite shape, a form. You know the director of the school says that the most important thing about life is form. . . . A thing that loses its form is finished and that's just as true in our ordinary, everyday lives.

(Takes MASHA *by the waist and laughs.)*

Masha loves me. My wife loves me. You must remember to put the curtains away with the carpets, too. You know, I'm very cheerful today, I'm in unusually good spirits. . . . Masha, the director has invited us round to his house at four o'clock today—this afternoon. A country walk has been arranged for the teachers and their families.

MASHA I'm not coming.
KOOLYGHIN *(distressed)* But, Masha, darling, why not?
MASHA I'll tell you later. . . . *(crossly)* Oh, all right, I'll come, only leave me alone now. . . .

(Walks to piano)

KOOLYGHIN And after the walk we shall spend the evening at the director's house. You know, in spite of weak health, that man is certainly sparing no pains to be sociable. A first-rate, thoroughly intelligent man! A most excellent person! After the conference yesterday he said to me: "Fiodor Ilyich, I'm tired," he said. "I'm tired!"

(Clock chimes—looks at his watch)

Your clock is seven minutes fast. "I'm tired," he said.

(The sound of the violin is heard off stage.)

OLGA Will you come and sit down, please? Lunch is ready. There's pie.

KOOLYGHIN Ah, Olga my dear girl! Last night I worked until eleven o'clock, and I felt tired; but today I'm so happy.

(Goes to the table in the ballroom)

My dear Olga!

CHEBUTYKIN *(puts the newspaper in his pocket and combs his beard.)* A pie? Excellent!

MASHA *(Sternly to* CHEBUTYKIN*)* Remember, you mustn't take anything to drink today. Do you hear? It's bad for you.

CHEBUTYKIN Never mind. I've got over that weakness long ago! I haven't done any serious drinking for two years. *(impatiently)* Anyway, my dear, what does it matter?

MASHA All the same, don't you dare drink anything. Mind you, don't now! *(crossly, but taking care her husband does not hear.)* So now I've got to spend another of these damnable boring evenings at the director's!

TOOZENBACH I wouldn't go if I were you, and that's that.

CHEBUTYKIN Don't you go, my dear.

MASHA Don't go, indeed! Oh, what a damnable life! It's intolerable. . . .

(goes into the ballroom)

CHEBUTYKIN *(follows her)* Well, well. . . .

SOLIONY *(As he passes* TOOZENBACH *on the way to the ballroom)* Cluck, cluck, cluck. . . .

TOOZENBACH: Do stop it, Soliony. I've really had enough of it. . . .

SOLIONY Cluck, cluck, cluck. . . .

KOOLYGHIN *(Gaily)* Your health, Colonel! I'm a schoolmaster . . . and I'm almost one of the family here, as it were. I'm Masha's husband. She's got a sweet nature, such a very sweet nature!

VERSHININ I think I'll have a little of this dark vodka. *(drinks)* Your health!

(To OLGA*)*

I do feel very happy being with you people!

*(*IRENA *and* TOOZENBACH *remain in the drawing-room)*

IRENA I'm afraid Masha's a bit out of humor today. She got married when she was eighteen, you know, and then her husband seemed the cleverest man in the world to her. It's different now. He's the kindest of men, but not the cleverest.

*(*ANFISA *brings soup)*

OLGA *(impatiently)* Andrey, will you please come?
ANDREY *(off stage)* Just coming.

(enters and goes to the table. OLGA *starts serving soup.)*

TOOZENBACH What are you thinking about?
IRENA Oh, nothing special. You know, I'm quite afraid of Soliony. No, really, I'm quite afraid of him. Everytime he opens his mouth he says something silly.
TOOZENBACH He's a strange fellow. I feel sorry for him, even though he irritates me. In fact, I feel more sorry for him than irritated. I think he's shy. When he's alone with me, he can be quite sensible and friendly, but in company he's offensive and bullying. Don't go over there just yet, let them get settled down at the table. Let me stay beside you for a bit. Tell me what you're thinking about.

(pause)

You're twenty . . . and I'm not thirty yet myself. What years and years we still have ahead of us, a whole long succession of years, all full of my love for you. . . .
IRENA Please, don't talk to me about love, Nikolai Lyovich.
TOOZENBACH *(not listening)* Oh, I long so passionately for life, I long to work and strive so much, and all this longing is somehow mingled with my love for you, Irena. And just because you happen to be beautiful, life appears beautiful to me! What are you thinking about?
IRENA You say that life is beautiful. Maybe it is—but what if it only seems to be beautiful? Our lives, I mean the lives of us three sisters, haven't been beautiful up until now. The truth is that life has been stifling us, like weeds in a garden. I'm afraid I'm crying. . . . So unnecessary. . . .

(Quickly dries her eyes and smiles. TOOZENBACH *moves over left of* IRENA.)

We must work, work! The reason we feel depressed and take such a gloomy view of life is that we've never known what it is to make a real effort. We're the children of parents who despised work. . . .

*(*IRENA *and* TOOZENBACH *pause and look at each other as* NATASHA *enters wearing a pink dress with a green belt.)*

NATASHA They've gone into lunch already . . . I'm late. . . . *(Glances at herself in a mirror and adjusts her dress.)* My hair seems to be all right. . . . *(Catches sight of* IRENA.*)* My dear Irena Serghyeevna, congratulations! *(Gives her a vigorous and prolonged kiss.)* You've got such a lot of visitors. . . . I feel quite shy. . . . How do you do Baron?
OLGA *(enters the drawing-room)* Oh, there you are, Natalia Ivanovna. How are you, my dear?

(They kiss)

NATASHA Congratulations! You've such a lot of people here, I feel dreadfully shy. . . .
OLGA Oh, they're all old friends. *(alarmed, dropping her voice.)* You've got a green belt on! My dear, that's surely a mistake!
NATASHA Why, is it a bad omen, or what?
OLGA No, but it just doesn't go with your dress . . . it looks so strange. . . .
NATASHA *(tearfully)* Really? But it isn't really green, you know, it's a sort of dull color. . . .
(follows OLGA *to the ballroom)*

(They ALL stand as NATASHA *enters ballroom. She goes round left to sit. All sit.)*

KOOLYGHIN Irena, you know, you really ought to find yourself a good husband. In my view it's high time you got married.

CHEBUTYKIN Yes, I think it's time you found yourself a nice little husband too, Natalia Ivanovana.

KOOLYGHIN Natalia Ivanovna already has a husband in view.

MASHA *(strikes her plate with her fork)* A glass of wine for me, please! Three cheers for our jolly old life! We keep our end up, we do!

KOOLYGHIN Masha, you won't get more than five out of ten for good conduct!

VERSHININ This is delicious. What is it made of?

SOLIONY Black beetles!

IRENA Ugh! Ugh! How disgusting!

OLGA We're having roast turkey tonight, and then apple tart. Thank goodness, I'll be here all day today . . . this evening, too. You must all come this evening.

(They start eating)

VERSHININ May I come this evening, too?

IRENA Yes, please do.

NATASHA They don't stand on ceremony here.

CHEBUTYKIN "Nature created us for love alone. . . ." *(laughs)*

ANDREY *(crossly)* Will you stop it, please? Aren't you tired of it yet?

*(*FEDOTIK *and* RODE *come in with a large basket of flowers.)*

FEDOTIK Oh look here, they're having lunch already!

RODE *(in a loud voice)* Having their lunch? So they are, they're having lunch already.

(Everyone turns)

FEDOTIK Wait half a minute.

(Takes a snapshot)

One! Just half a minute more. . . !

(Takes another snapshot)

Two! All over now.

(They pick up the basket and go into the ballroom where they are greeted uproariously.)

RODE *(Loudly)* Congratulations, Irena Serghyeevna! I wish you all the best, everything you'd wish for yourself! You look most charming today.

FEDOTIK *(Takes a snapshot)*

(Takes another photo. Then takes a top out of his pocket.)

By the way, look at this top. It's got a wonderful hum.

IRENA What a sweet little thing!

(Pause in conversation)

MASHA "A green oak grows by a curving shore. And round that oak hangs a golden chain. . . . A green chain around that oak. . . ." *(Peevishly)* Why do I keep on saying that? Those lines have been worrying me all day long?

(Slight pause)

KOOLYGHIN Do you know, we're thirteen at table?
RODE *(loudly)* You don't really believe in these old superstitions, do you?

(Laughter)

KOOLYGHIN When thirteen people sit down to table, it means that some of them are in love. Is it you, by any chance, Ivan Romanych?
CHEBUTYKIN Oh, I'm just an old sinner . . . but what I can't make out is why Natalia Ivanovna seems so embarrassed.

(Loud laughter. NATASHA *runs out into the drawing-room, passing* ANDREY, *who follows her.)*

Focus in Viewing

The emphasis in this production is Act III; it is the kernel of the play which contains the climax. Throughout the presentation there is a certain choreographed quality which pervades the movement and the stage pictures. Often the actors are grouped in compositions that have a depth of field; the focus is moved to the foreground in a close-up shot with others in the background, reacting. Notice especially the lighting design in this production, as it creates mood and atmosphere and supports meaning and character.

Content Viewing

1. *The Three Sisters* emphasizes people and atmosphere rather than plot. What characters remain trapped in self-delusion and what characters gain understanding by the play's end? Discuss.
2. Write a brief basic description of Olga, Masha, Irena, and Natasha.
3. Why does Masha prefer Vershinin to Koolyghin? Talk about all three characters.
4. When Olga and Natasha argue about firing or keeping Nanny, the argument represents a conflict between the survival instinct and gentility. Support one or the other and explain why.
5. After having viewed *Miss Julie* answer this: Compare and contrast Olga's argument with Natash (over Nanny) with Jean and Julie's argument over what they should do. What do the arguments say about class difference?

Craft Viewing

1. What props, positioning of characters, and mood nuances are used in the BBC production to show the three sisters and Natasha's change in status after three years have passed?
2. How does the director of the television production make us aware of the tension that exists between the characters?
3. If you were directing what would you have done differently, or what do you think was done well?
4. We sense the somber atmosphere in the house "three years later." Aside from the dialogue, what makes us aware of the hopeless situation?
5. Are there moments or scenes that stand out in your memory? Which ones and why?

Critical Viewing: Overview
1. What signficance does *The Three Sisters* hold for you?

Additional Plays That Demonstrate Similar Concepts

The Cherry Orchard, The Sea Gull, Uncle Vanya—Chekhov
Riders to the Sea—John Millington Synge
Juno and the Paycock—Sean O'Casey
A Long Day's Journey into Night—Eugene O'Neill
Paradise Lost—Clifford Odets

Stage Terms

Up Stage—The part of the stage farthest from the audience.
Down Stage—The part of the stage closest to the audience.
Theatrical Naturalism—A belief underlying most of the drama of the 20th Century that only natural forces prevail. These can be outer (in the form of natural phenomena or society or war) or inner (in the form of drives and passions that man cannot control). The naturalists do not believe that man can make significant changes in his environment. Some naturalists, notably Chekhov, find the world neutral, neither friendly nor actively hostile to man; example is *The Three Sisters*.

THE GHOST SONATA

by

August Strindberg
(1849–1912)

A. Play Notes: The Structure of *The Ghost Sonata,* p. 100
    1. Expressionism, p. 101
    2. Other American Expressionist Playwrights, p. 101
    3. Significant Items in *The Ghost Sonata,* p. 102
    4. Major Themes of Strindberg's, p. 102
B. Story and Plot Summary, p. 102
C. A Review of *The Ghost Sonata,* p. 104
D. Commentary: A Brief Summary of the Review, p. 106
E. Objectives, p. 106
F. Program Notes from the BBC Production, p. 106
G. A List of BBC Actors and Production Coordinators, p. 107
H. Director's Notes, p. 111
I. Focus in Viewing, p. 112
J. Additional Plays That Demonstrate Similar Concepts, p. 113
K. Stage Terms, p. 114

Play Notes
Structure in *The Ghost Sonata*

Expressionism in The Ghost Sonata

The *Ghost Sonata* is a modern play, reflecting major trends in 20th Century art and philosophy. These include the importance of the subconscious, the questioning of external reality, a rejection of traditional solutions to complex problems, and a concentration on the impact of the irrational.

The psychological emphasis of the play is evident from the start. Like characters from a dream recalled on a psychiatrist's couch, the characters in *The Ghost Sonata* obey the rules of the unconscious. They appear and disappear at will, violating the confines of the daytime world. They represent old fears, longings, and the desire for revenge, without the concealment demanded by the conscious waking world. One of the characters, for instance, the Cook in the household of an apparently wealthy man, is accused of starving the family. Yet the accuser, the daughter in the family, is physically normal, not emaciated. The Cook has drained the family in an emotional way, in the sense that we use the term "starved for affection."

There is no strict accounting for time or place. Characters appear and disappear: one of them living in a closet, others going through the motions of host and guests but without either refreshments or conversation, and still another contracting illness, aging and dying within a few minutes of stage time. Characters change identity, the young man becoming transformed into the person of an old enemy of his family, the old woman at times muffled like a mummy, squawking like a parrot, or making lucid and insightful denunciations in clear speech.

Characters are more types than individually developed people: The Old Man, The Student, The Colonel, The Mummy, The Fiancee, The Cook, etc. Some have names, but there is no effort to depict real people, as there was even with such diverse playwrights as Shakespeare and Chekhov, who created believable human beings for the stage. Strindberg's *The Ghost Sonata* is an example of expressionism, the stage counterpart of expressionistic painting. As a Van Gogh painting assaults the emotions with strong, forceful application of paint, reaching beneath the surface with broad, powerful strokes, an expressionistic play is deliberately heavy-handed and shocking, overstated and pessimistic, rejecting compassion in favor of rage.

American Expressionist Playwrights

American expressionists have included Eugene O'Neill and Elmer Rice. In O'Neill's *The Hairy Ape* the main character is an irrational and animal-like stevedore rejected by both polite human society and an ape in the zoo, indicating that we are neither completely human nor animal. In Rice's expressionistic play, *The Adding Machine,* the "people" on the stage were portrayed as extensions of a technological society, with numbers rather than names, the main character being Mr. Zero, a bookkeeper retired after being replaced by an adding machine. The appearance on the contemporary stage of characters in non-human representations has become commonplace in serious theatre, Off Broadway, and on the college campus. Playwrights and audiences alike recognize that a statement about lack of purpose and conventional moral values is not only a matter of what characters in a play say but of the manner in which the play is presented. Chaos as a theme is at odds with a play staged in accordance with an orderly presentation of believable human beings, and a construction dependent upon the unities of time, place, and action. Though the expressionistic play makes exaggerated use of objects and setting, there is no need to attempt a one-for-one symbolic equivalent. The objects are mentioned, and they are visible. They seem to have a meaning beyond the strictly utilitarian.

Significant Items in *The Ghost Sonata*

The Ghost Sonata contains either the appearance or the mention of such diverse significant items as hyacinths, a death screen, the bust of Beethoven, a parrot, soy sauce, the Buddha, and cork put under the leg of a wobbly table—not the ordinary appurtenance of a household. To attempt meaning for each in the sense that one item "stands for" weakness, nourishment, wisdom, or any other attribute would be excessively literal. Instead, all contribute to the overall experience of a play designed to be shown in a small room, or chamber, in the intimate manner of chamber music, as opposed to performances of symphonies or chorales suitable for a large auditorium.

Major Themes of Strindberg's

The play, then, sacrifices normal expectations about plot and character in a manner popular in the early 20th Century. In theme it is like other plays which reject optimistic hope for the future through legislative change, obedience to religious law, or even the good which may arise out of increased awareness of self.

But the play is more than a preoccupation with concerns of the time; it is, in addition, the expression of a particular artist whose mother had been a servant and who was himself preoccupied with the war between the sexes. In *Miss Julie,* Strindberg examines the sexual and social tensions between a man and a woman of different social strata—the servant and the daughter of a nobleman. The play shows a power struggle ending in death for one and submission for the other. In another play, *The Father,* a woman gains mastery over her husband and reduces him to the helplessness of a lunatic in a strait-jacket. Strindberg's concern with domination, nourishment, and destruction comes from his own personal world of nightmare and presented in stage form where they have more universal application. Though *The Ghost Sonata* is not a "well-made" play in the way of most 19th Century drama, it is nevertheless a play with plot, themes, and individual moments; the play communicates to audiences willing to accept the expressionistic vision that goes beyond and beneath the literal.

Story and Plot Summary

Like all great works of art, *The Ghost Sonata* suffers from the attempt to reduce it to a restatement of plot. This summary will not be the recitation of character entrance and exit or an attempt to interpret speech or symbols. It is, rather, a basic outline of a play.

In the opening scene, a Milkmaid (or the apparition of a milkmaid) is approached by a Student, who asks her to wipe his eyes. His hands are not clean. He says he has been helping the wounded in an accident and needs help. An Old Man says news of the accident is in the paper, but the name of the heroic student has not been published, only his picture. The Student says he does not care for publicity or reward. The Old Man says that the Student has a voice like someone he once knew, a merchant name Arkeholtz. The Student says that the merchant was his father.

The Old Man says that the Student's father robbed him of his life's savings; the Student had been told the opposite story—that the Old Man was the robber and the Student's father the victim.

The Old Man, who is crippled, says he needs help. He asks the Student to assist him in getting around. He invites him to the theatre in order to meet the Colonel and his daughter. He hopes the Student and the girl will fall in love and be married. He points to the Colonel's house, to the room with hyacinths, where the girl lives, and to a dead man, a consul, covered with white sheets. The Old Man had not been able to see the Milkmaid. He points to the old woman sitting at the window and says that he and she had once been engaged to be married, that the old woman was once young and beautiful. He asks that the young man take his hand, which is cold. The young man does so but is terrified, claiming that the touch of the hand saps him of strength.

He meets the Colonel's daughter, who looks like the marble statue of her mother. The Old Man says that he is very rich and would like to help the student. He is disappointed in his own son and would like to make the Student his heir. The Old Man's servant, Johansson, appears and wheels the old man around the corner, as the Student watches and the Colonel's daughter waters the flowers at her window.

The Student asks Johansson what the old man wants: Johansson responds that the old man wants power, that he kills his enemies and never forgives. He says that the old man once was a Don Juan but that he lost his women. Now he steals human beings and enslaves them.

The Milkmaid returns, raises her arms, as if she is drowning, and gazes at the Old Man, who is stricken with horror and demands to be taken away. He reminds the Student to be sure to go to the theatre to see a performance of *The Valkyrie*.

Scene II (or the Second Movement of the Chamber Play) is the Colonel's home. The Colonel's servant is instructing Johansson on how to serve the guests tea. Johansson says that he wheels the Old Man in his wheel chair during the daytime but that he works nights as a waiter. Bengtsson, the Colonel's servant, says that this is to be a ghost supper because the same people appear, always saying the same things and that the mistress of the house is a crazy lady who sits in a cupboard, like a mummy. She is the Colonel's wife, making sounds like a parrot, whistling and asking to see Jacob. The statue is of the old woman as she had been when she was a young girl. Bengtsson shows Johansson the screen that is put around people when they are going to die.

The Old Man comes in, even though he is not an invited guest. He asks to be announced as Mr. Hummel. When he hears the Mummy say "Pretty Polly" he thinks the house is haunted. But the Mummy calls him Jacob and speaks to him in a natural voice. She says that the Colonel's daughter is actually "our child," that is, hers and Jacob's.

The Old Man says that he plans revenge on the Colonel for taking the Mummy away from him and marrying her. The Mummy tells him not to do so, or he will die. She asks why the Old Man plans to arrange for the Student to marry the Daughter. She names the guests at the supper—all people who have hurt each other in the past, all people who continue to live but who are awaiting death.

The Old Man talks with the Colonel, who says he is in the power of the Old Man and asks what he must do. The Old Man tells the Colonel to dismiss Bengtsson, the servant. The Old Man has promissory notes signed by the Colonel. Everything in the Colonel's house belongs to the Old Man. He exposes the Colonel as being a fake and a fraud—not really a colonel or a nobleman, not entitled to wear the signet ring. He forces him to take off his wig and false teeth, to shave his mustache and be revealed as the servant he actually is.

Just as the Colonel is being stripped, the Student arrives and is introduced to the Daughter.

The Mummy is invited in to meet the other guests. The Old Man says that talk conceals meaning, that false witnesses can always be found, but that masks eventually will be torn away and villains exposed. He announces that the girl is actually his daughter and that he will strike them with his crutches, even as the clock strikes.

The Mummy tells the Old Man that he has no right to judge others and that he should be exposed as the thief of human souls. She denounces him for having once stolen her with false promises and for having murdered other people. The Milkmaid appears, unseen by all except the Old Man, who shrinks back in horror. The servant Bengtsson appears.

He had been the master while the Old Man was his servant. He says that the old man once was responsible for the drowning of a young girl, apparently the Milkmaid. The Mummy forces the Old Man to kill himself by going into the closet. Bengtsson puts up the death screen. The Girl and the Student are in the Hyacinth Room. The Student recites as the Girl accompanies him on a harp.

Scene three is in the Hyacinth room. The Student and the Girl are falling in love, looking forward to marriage. The Girl says that she is ill, that the Cook takes all the nourishment out of the food she serves the family, but that she cannot be dismissed. All the housekeeping is done badly; nothing stays clean or in order. There is constant labor in trying to keep dirt at a distance. There are many secrets in the house.

The Student tells the Girl about his own family, the secrets that came out when his father exposed the truth. The Girl is frightened, as the Student tells her the truth about the Colonel, who is not a colonel; and about the Mummy who is not a Mummy, and about the Cook who poisons people. He says that everything is false, including that which appears to be beautiful. As he speaks, the Girl fades and calls for the death screen. The Student speaks of a purity that cannot be found on the earth. He prays for comfort beyond that found in the guilt and suffering of mankind. Only the innocent are good. In some productions, the room disappears and music is heard as a painting of the Isle of the Dead is seen. In others, the Student can be seen to grow old and take the place of the dead Hummel, continuing the legacy of guilt and responsibility for murder.

New York Times, January 7, 1924

Strindberg intends in "The Spook Sonata" a phantasmagoria of evil destiny, a symbolic array of the greeds and lusts that rule this wicked world. It is as if someone were to transpose Poe's "Fall of the House of Usher" into terms of the drama, showing the progress of decay and dissolution, not in a mansion and its single lord, but in a group of tangled lives. "The new direction" at the Provincetown Playhouse has done its intelligent best, under the able leadership of Kenneth Macgowan. Robert Edmond Jones had designed a scenic setting of fine simplicity and rare beauty, a symphony of ghostly blues. James Light has furnished masks in which several of the players

© 1924 by The New York Times Company. Reprinted by permission.

take on an aspect of unearthly mystery and cadaverous horror. Edwin Bjorkman has made a workmanlike translation from the Swedish. Eugene O'Neill has press-agented Strindberg as "the precursor of all modernity," exalting him above Ibsen. And the result last Saturday night was hushed awe among the faithful, punctured at times by rude laughter.

In Poe's tale the walls of the house were cracked; in Strindberg's play every brain in the *dramatis personae* shows the same, horrid phenomenon—horrid if also hilarious. The heroine's mother, who is played by Clare Eames, sits all day in a cabinet sealed against the light, which she cannot bear, and from time to time she utters raucous bird calls. The butler opens the door, exhibiting her to a teatime caller and to the audience. "She thinks she's a parrot," he says, "and maybe she is." Whereupon "The Mummy," as the program calls her, gibbers and squawks. The heroine is, to all appearances, a quite normal and wholesome young person, and the hero, who possesses the only uncrumbled intellect in the play, falls in love with her. Very sad is his disillusioning.

It develops that she is the housekeeper and has one overwhelming sorrow. The cook absolutely refuses to give notice. Rude spirits in the audience failed to see tragedy in this. They even suspected that Mr. Macgowan had given this cook a mask to conceal the identity of a unique and coveted treasure. But that wasn't the idea at all. It developed that the cook had a little way of squeezing all the nutriment out of the roast beef, all the stock out of the soup, all the proteins out of the vegetables. So the poor family was starving. As she boasted of this, she waved a bottle of tomato catsup with which she camouflaged the unnourishing product of her kitchen. So sympathy returned to our heroine.

Worse followed. The whole household was shown to be one mess of false titles, abysmal debts and marital infidelities. Our heroine was not the daughter of the man whose name she bore and our hero came eventually to surmise that her own personal conduct had not been of maidenly purity. When he made inquiries on this point, she ordered a white screen to be placed in the front of the couch where she sat. That was always done in this household when someone was about to expire. She expired. Presently the harp on the other side of the couch gave forth a lightly spiritual air played by her ghostly fingers.

These are only a few of many accents of mortal anguish and despair. Old Hummel is the head villain, the arch poisoner of joy. His past in Hamburg (why Hamburg?) is symbolized by "The Milk Girl, an Apparition" who wears a very white mask and draws jugfuls of water from the tap. The meaning of this seems also to be symbolic. Even the milk is adulterated. Old Hummel's evil ways have made him paralytic and he goes on crutches—except when the stage is too crowded, and then he walks very well, tahink you. Here also, doubtless more is meant than meets the ear. For, if "The Spook Sonata" is very phantasmagorical, it is also very allegorical.

It ends by being paregorical. Our disillusioned, our anguished hero apostrophizes Christ to give him courage in so spooky a world. Then, as if to leave no stone unturned, he faces about and delivers a similar apostrophe to an idol of Buddha. It is here that the harp gives out its angel chorus. And with this soothing syrup his infant pain is assuaged.

When Strindberg was quite sane, he was a man of unmistakable, if dark and erratic, genius. When he wore the strait-jacket, as he frequently did, he may have been the precursor of Mr. O'Neill's modernity, but one wonders just a little why our foremost dramatist should make public confession of the fact.

John Corbin

Commentary: A Brief Summary of the Review

The author of the preceding essay did not view the array of symbols in the play as an intentional form of ambiguous expression, but rather as proof of Strindberg's failing logic. More complimentary critiques, unlike the one included here, thought that *The Ghost Sonata* exemplified the idea that a play's structure parallels its meaning.

Objectives

After having studied *THE GHOST SONATA,* you, the student, should be able to do the following:

1. Recognize that the playwright's own inner turmoil and the interest in psychology at the time the play was written contributed greatly to the dream-like, often bizarre quality of *The Ghost Sonata.*
2. View Strindberg's *GHOST SONATA* as a departure from dramatic realism and literal truth. It is, instead, an attempt to explore the depth and ambiguity of "inner man."
3. Identify and describe Strindberg's distortion of dramatic elements and use of symbolism in *The Ghost Sonata.*
4. Understand what conventions in *The Ghost Sonata* caused critiques to categorize it as "expressionistic."

Program Notes

Depicting events from the past, which have festered and poisoned a strange collage of characters presently in a non-compassionate struggle for power, August Strindberg developed his "spook supper" with nightmarish quality. Stripping away illusions and identities, this turbulent and disturbing drama has a powerful impact. Exploration of the play's symbolism, structure, and characterization is included in an accompanying minidocumentary. The program contains the final two of the three scenes, or "movements," of the play, together with three momentary flashbacks to the first "movement."

A List of BBC Actors and Production Coordinators

THE GHOST SONATA

by

August Strindberg

CAST

THE OLD MAN	JOSEPH O'CONNOR
THE MUMMY	BEATRIX LEHMANN
THE STUDENT	DAVID THOUGHTON
THE DAUGHTER	ANNE KIDD
THE COLONEL	FRANK MIDDLEMASS
BENGTSSON	GERALD CROSS
JOHANSSON	PADDY JOYCE
THE COOK	HOPE JACKMAN
THE MILKMAID	SUSIE BLAKE
THE FIANCEE	GRACE ARNOLD
THE NOBLEMAN	BASIL CLARKE

PRODUCTION

SET DESIGN	COLIN BOWLES
MAKE-UP SUPERVISOR	MAGGIE WEBB
COSTUME SUPERVISOR	BRIAN COX
DIRECTOR	RICHARD CALLANAN

(Left to Right) Colonel, Mummy, Fiancee, Nobleman, Hummel

Mummy and Hummel

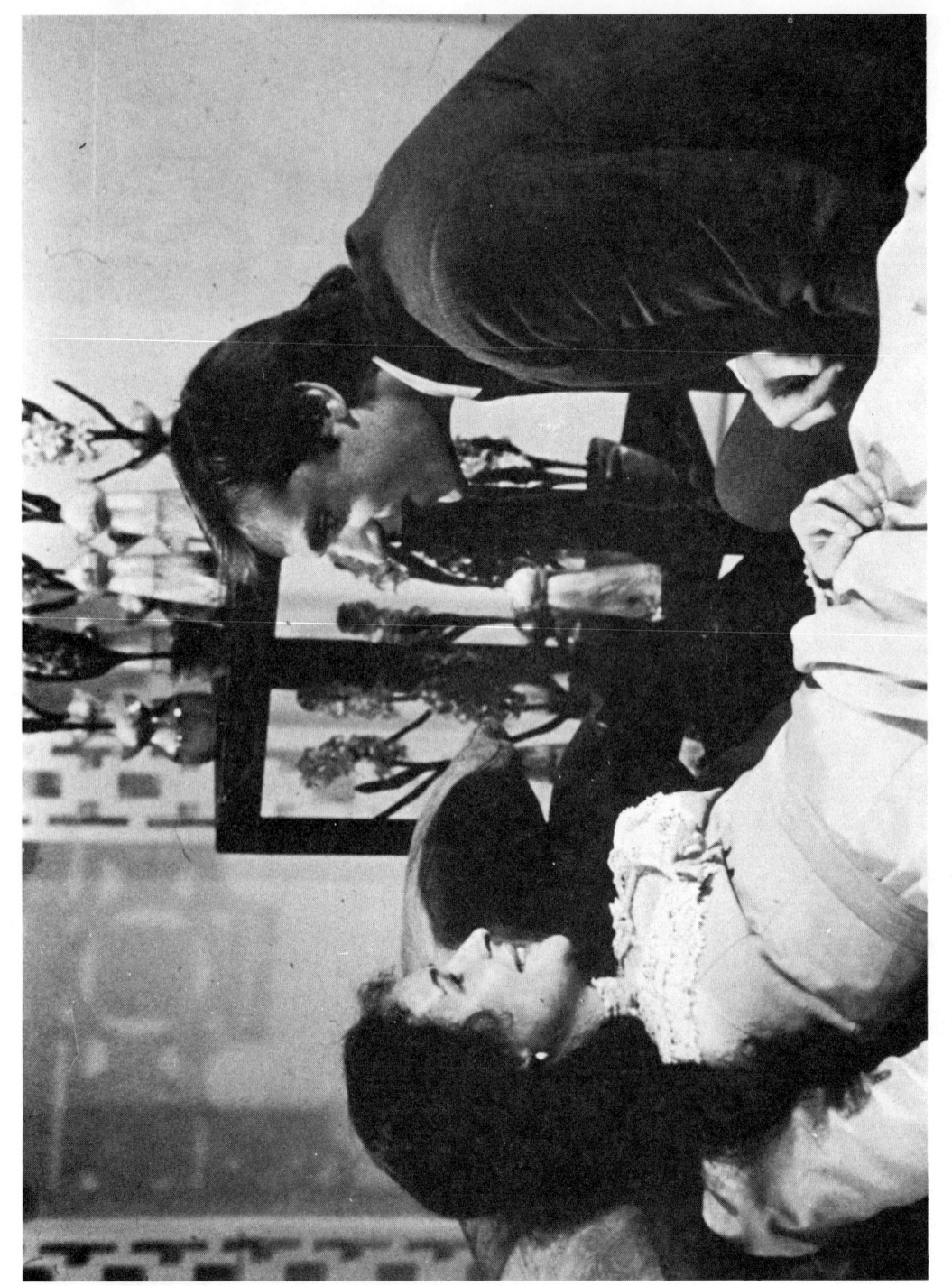

The Daughter and the Student

Commentary on the Director's Notes

The following notes were made by the director of the BBC production of *The Ghost Sonata*. The director follows the common practice of interpreting the author's work in order to stage it more effectively. He pays particular attention to the objects which are featured in the staging and what they symbolize, in an attempt to make the set a compromise between abstraction and naturalism. In some cases, the camera focuses on a statue or a screen having particular significance to the director's concept. He thus emphasizes through visual means his personal interpretation for television of the many ideas to be found in *The Ghost Sonata*.

Director's Notes

The Central Theme and Its Symbols

At the time of writing *The Ghost Sonata* in 1906, Strindberg had three things in his study which help to underline elements in the play. One was a bust of Beethoven whom Strindberg considered to be the supreme artist; another was a figure of Buddha reflecting an increasing obsession with religion and the third was a stuffed owl. Strindberg thought this owl had magical properties and believed that through it he could transmit crippling curses to imagined persecutors.

The owl and Strindberg's paranoid fantasies emphasize the central theme of the play: how people can corrupt and destroy each other even to the point of sucking their blood away. In the central scene of the play ("the spook supper") this theme is very clear, and under the veneer of polite society we discover a tangle of personal and business relations, a series of reversals in the roles of servants and masters; all of which exemplify forms of control which one person can have over another. In the final scene ("the hyacinth room") this theme may not be so absolutely obvious but it has been emphasized in this production. Despite their apparent innocence the young people of the play are corrupted by their elders and then proceed to corrupt each other. Time in this final scene is condensed so that as one critic has noted the action covers the whole range of love from courtsip through disenchanted marriage to death.

The Play as Music

The bust of Beethoven might draw our attention to the "Sonata" element in the title and also that Strindberg called it a "chamber play." The musical analogy helps us to understand the form of the play in three movements, rather than three scenes. The play does not depend on a single narrative line chasing through from beginning to end but, like a sonata, takes quite a different mood for each movement. There are links between the movements, of course, the themes recur sometimes changed or spoken by different people. The most striking of these perhaps is the way the Student takes up ideas spoken earlier by The Old Man. The comparison with music can help too with a barrier many people have when they seek to rationally understand every single element in the play. Although I think it is ultimately a rational play, it cannot be experienced as such. The audience must let it move them along section by section as with a piece of music.

Guilt and Expiation

The Buddha of course is a central piece in the setting of the final scene and much of the play can be seen as a religious debate between the kind of Buddhist belief expressed by The Student when he talks about the hyacinths: "This unhappy earth shall become a heaven" and more pessimistic kind of Christianity where everyone on earth is guilty and may or may not be redeemed. For this production the ideas of guilt and expiation were the ones I emphasized. The Mummy has expiated her guilt as has the Student by the end. These two characters, with of course the Milkmaid, are I think saved. When the Mummy condemns The Old Man to the cupboard she does so in a spirit of justice and not vindictiveness. Her reintroduction in the final scene with the crutches brings out her new saving power, links her to the redeeming image of The Milkmaid and gives us a slight gleam of hope for The Student. The Buddhist element is most evident in the exchange between The Daughter and The Student. The expectation that heaven can exist on earth is not borne out by the rest of the scene but the Buddha, as well as Christ, is the focus for The Student's prayers at the end. The closeness of The Student to the statue as The Daughter dies brings out the complexity, perhaps even the contradiction in the play between human despair and religious hope.

Setting

Strindberg suggests an extremely naturalistic setting for the play but the first really successful production, by Max Reinheardt in 1921, used an abstract expressionist design. For television, totally abstract sets present a real difficulty: they are seen only occasionally in "wide-angle" and the rest of the production is made up, in the main, with close-ups of unabstracted actors. This means that unless you go so far as to abstract the actors' faces by using nonrealistic make-up or masks you get jumps from abstraction to naturalism as you move from wide-angle to close-up. Our solution was to go for two representations of rooms, furnished only with the necessary props for action. It is clear that they are not "real" rooms whose fussiness would detract from the nature of the play. At the same time the props and furniture are real enough to support the naturalistic dialogue and action of the play.

Richard Callanan

Focus in Viewing

Strindberg called his play *The Ghost Sonata* to draw attention to what he believed was its resemblance to a musical structure. He crafted this play not by the mechanics of action and character, but, like a sonata, by statement, development, and resolution. And like a sonata, this play has three movements, each with its own thematic arrangement and characteristics, each related to the other movements. Strindberg presents parallel themes in the play much like the repetition of a musical theme: therefore, take note which characters parallel each other and which attitudes are repeated in the speeches of different characters.

Keep in mind that there is never a single *correct* production of a play, but that imaginative and dramatic logic used by the director and theatre artists should lead to a single consistent interpretation. The BBC production aims were to convey Strindberg's interests and to show how Strindberg's balance between naturalism and expressionism works in practice.

Content Viewing

1. How does this dialogue excerpt explain the play's title?

   > Amelia: If we could die . . .
   > Jacob: Why do you all go on?
   > Amelia: Our crimes bind us. We try to sneak away, but all come back.

2. The daughter complains to the student that they, no matter what, can't get enough maids. Enough maids for what? What do the maids symbolize?
3. Amelia is a parrot at first; then when she tells the truth speaks differently. When Jacob's life of deception is uncovered, he becomes a parrot. What do these reversals say about Strindberg's philosophy on what happens to us when we do not live honestly?
4. The student says, " . . . and yet if we all lived honestly the world would end." If this is the case what alternative is left? (Again your response should relate to the play's title.)
5. The daughter and the student talk about the hyacinth. The student says that the roots symbolize the earth; the stalk, the axis of the earth, and the flowers the stars. He says that the unhappy earth, then, can become a heaven, a heaven in which the brightest star symbolizes Narcissus. Narcissus, because of his faults was made a flower rooted in the ground. So, what is the student actually saying about our destiny?
6. When the student confronts the maid about her taking the family's nourishment, she retorts, "You drain our goodness; we drain yours." Apply this statement to Natasha and the Three Sisters or to Jean and Julie in *Miss Julie*.
7. After Jacob sees his past, Amelia puts her hands over his eyes and says, "Now you see yourself!" After you view Oedipus, compare what happens to Jacob to what happens to Oedipus.

Craft Viewing

1. How does this play distort physical or objective realities of time and space?
2. What is the function of the flashbacks? How do you know in whose minds they exist?
3. Do you think the production was effective? Explain.
4. Is there one moment or scene which stands out in your memory?

Critical Viewing: Overview

1. Jacob laments, "Language is our silence." This paradoxical statement parallels others in the play and suggests what about our lives?
2. Now that this play and its production are part of your experience, what significance does *The Ghost Sonata* hold for you?
3. *Peer Gynt* and *The Ghost Sonata* have both been categorized as expressionistic plays. Why?

Additional Plays That Demonstrate Similar Concepts

A Dream Play—Strindberg
R.U.R.—Karel Capek

The Adding Machine—Elmer Rice
The Great God Brown, The Hairy Ape—Eugene O'Neill

Stage Terms

Expressionism—While "naturalism" suggests attention paid to minute details and "impressionism" suggests attention paid to moods, "expressionism" suggests attention paid to the psychological struggle to find a reason for existence. The dramatic depiction of such a struggle usually includes dream-like scenes like those in *The Ghost Sonata* which are intended to represent the workings of the subconscious.

MODULE 3

Dramatis Personae: Heroes, Heroines, Rogues, Villains

   I. Introduction, The Nature of Character, p. 116
      - A. How the Viewer Learns about Characters, p. 116
      - B. The Tragic Hero of Classical Greece and Elizabethan England, p. 116
      - C. The Modern Tragic Hero, p. 117
      - D. Shaw's Heroine, St. Joan, p. 117
      - E. Commedia Dell'Arte Characters, p. 117
  II. Study materials for *Oedipus Tyrannus*, p. 119
 III. Study materials for *Macbeth*, p. 137
  IV. Study materials for *Woyzeck*, p. 178
   V. Study materials for *St. Joan*, p. 191
  VI. Study materials for *The Venetian Twins*, p. 210

You will find a more detailed outline preceding each of the plays.

THE NATURE OF CHARACTER

How the Viewer Learns about Characters

Characters are the human beings a playwright conceives and creates from his understanding and images of human nature. The playwright's constructed world is revealed through the dialogue and action of the characters. To understand a character in a playscript, a reader must think of the character as a doer or attempter of something, as a seeker of some particular end or goal, rather than as a static collection of personality traits or qualities.

When Aristotle observed that plot was the single most important element in dramatic craft, he also noted that character was closely related to plot. In most plays, there is usually a central character with whom we most often sympathize or empathize. The protagonist (hero/heroine) may strive desperately, nobly, or suffer greatly to make choies and take action. The protagonist is involved in some kind of conflict. The opposing force can be within the central character, another character, or can even be an impersonal, natural, or supernatural force. (society, war, fire, flood, fate). The protagonist's adversary is called the antagonist. A judgment of a play's artistic worth is usually based upon the effectiveness of the central characters, upon our ability to discern in them enduring the universal human qualities, problems, weaknesses, and strengths.

The playwright may introduce a character into a playscript by including a description of the character as a stage direction before the first entrance of the character. The description of one character may also be given by another character, either in the early development of the script or gradually unfolding throughout the script. What others say about a character and how they react to the character are other devices, used by a playwright. More often, the playwright has his characters reveal themselves by their own words and through their actions (*what* they do and *how* they do it). Finally, a playwright may reveal something about the personality of a character through the setting or surroundings in which the character lives and moves.

The introduction of characters is merely a beginning. The playwright must develop the nature of the characters in the playscript. Upon completion of the written guide, the playwright fills in his outline with actors; thus the play script becomes a stage play. The actors combine dialogue and rhythm to bring the characters to life before an audience.

When discussing character, we are concerned generally with the deeper aspects of the nature of the human beings the playwright has created. We are aware that the playwright chose to depict selected, significant moments in the character's existence, and, therefore, we look for significant things about the inmost nature of the character.

The Tragic Hero of Classical Greece and Elizabethan England

Of special concern is the tragic hero, for it is generally believed that tragedy is the noblest and most significant of all the dramatic modes. Playwrights of the past and the present have sought to find the key to greatness in a tragic hero. Most critics agree on one point: the tragic hero's inevitable downfall affects us so that his suffering draws forth our own buried anguish.

Aristotle considered Oedipus to be the perfect example of the tragic hero. Oedipus exemplifies the classical tragic hero because, despite his attempts to control his own life, he cannot. The cards are stacked against him from the start; his fate rests with the gods. The ironic tragedy of Oedipus is that the more determined he is to do right, the closer he comes to destruction.

The Elizabethan dramatists developed a tragic hero who was more the master of his own fate than the classical Greek tragic hero. For example, Othello's life is ruined because he fails to understand, not because his future is predetermined by the gods. In *Macbeth,* we find an interesting combination of the classical Greek and the Elizabethan tragic hero. Macbeth's actions ultimately bring about his demise; yet the witches' prophecies hint that forces beyond Macbeth are responsible for what happens. Macbeth's circumstance and actions suggest that it is in our stars, as well as ourselves, that we determine our lives.

Macbeth is referred to, by certain critics, as a villain-hero. Such critics forgive him while they blame him. They recognize his actions as evil, yet identify with his equivocation and suffering, admiring the poetic magnificence that his wrongdoing produces. So greatly is Macbeth's villainy magnified, so poetic is his evil, that he is hero *and* villain.

The Modern Tragic Hero

Freudian psychology, deterministic philosophy, and behavioral science have caused modern dramatists to reject not only classical heroism but Elizabethan villainy as well. The idea of tragedy in the theatre of our time has moved away from the belief that the hero is the source of tragedy to the belief that man is a battleground of conflicting forces from which tragic meaning or insight may evolve. It is no longer so much the situation of the individual as it is the human condition that is the culprit. If the focal characters in modern tragedy tend to be small people overwhelmed by life, their antagonists tend to be so enormous they often defy labels. Buchner's *Woyzeck* is important for its pioneer efforts to create a tragedy of the *natural man,* whose plight is that of all men caught in a social structure they cannot comprehend or control, and whose weaknesses demand our compassion and understanding.

Shaw's Heroine, St. Joan

The playwright draws not only upon the consciousness of his own society, but of other societies as well. Perhaps he becomes fascinated with the individuals (or an individual) who figure prominently in that society, and this fascination leads to inspiration for a protagonist to be born into the world of dramatic literature.

In *St. Joan,* a play which is set in the past, Shaw does not attempt to become Joan's biographer; rather he dramatizes his interpretation of the Joan story. While Shaw is concerned with aspects of historical development and with the clash of forces (ideological, social, political), which produce an individual destined to become a saint, he is more concerned with bringing to life a young peasant girl who is proud and stubborn and who imposes her ideas on history. Shaw's craft lies not in recreating a lofty heroine as a great historical personage, but in creating a warm human being who once lived and whose spirit continues to live.

Commedia Dell'Arte Characters

Sometimes a playwright will use stereotypes who behave according to a rigid and easily recognizable pattern. These *type* or *stock* characters exaggerate tendencies which are common to many people. Such types are dealt with both seriously and commically by playwrights. Goldoni's *The Venetian Twins* is an example of the theatre art with stock characters called the *commedia dell'arte,* which flourished in Italy from the 16th Century. In the commedia there were no written scripts, only scenarios, and the actors improvised their dialogue and bits of stage business as they performed. They created recognizable types of characters which included mischievous servants, buffoons, young lovers, meddling fathers, braggart soldiers, misers, and bumblers. The influence of the improvisational comedic art form spread throughout Europe, and an entire lineage of "stock characters" wove its heritage into the fabric of character development.

OEDIPUS TYRANNUS

by

Sophocles
(496–406 B.C.)

A. Play Notes: Aristotle on Tragedy, p. 120
B. Stage Terms and Conventions of Greek Theatre, p. 121
C. Story and Plot Summary, p. 122
D. Francis Ferguson on *Oedipus,* p. 124
E. Maxwell Anderson on Tragedy, p. 126
F. Commentary: A Brief Summary of Fergusson's and Anderson's Essays, p. 128
G. Objectives, p. 128
H. Program Notes, p. 128
I. A List of BBC Actors and Production Coordinators, p. 129
J. An Excerpt from *Oedipus Tyrannus,* p. 130
K. Focus in Viewing, p. 135
L. Additional Plays That Demonstrate Similar Concepts, p. 136

Play Notes

Oedipus Tyrannus did not win a first prize for Sophocles, its author, in the contest at which it was first presented, but it was quickly recognized as a masterpiece. Aristotle, the greatest critic of classical times and probably of all time, thought it the perfect example of tragic art. From it, Aristotle derived a set of principles of drama that remained the basis of all writing of tragedy until Shakespeare's day.

Even now, we find it difficult to speak or write of tragedy, and especially of the tragic hero, without reference to what Aristotle said. According to Aristotle, a tragedy is the imitation of an action that is serious, complete in itself, in dramatic form, not narrative, consisting of incidents that arouse pity and terror, and through which a catharsis, or purging of emotions, is achieved.

Action is the end and purpose of tragedy; that is, the living out of a decisive series of events by a significant human being. Tragedy cannot be displayed; it must be enacted. Therefore, plot is the life and soul of tragedy. To understand the tragic hero more clearly, let us take another look at the plot of tragedy.

Plot for tragedy must have three elements: reversal of situation; discovery; and a scene of suffering. Reversal is a change from one state to the opposite. In *Oedipus Tyrannus,* for instance, the opposite state is produced by the messenger who, coming to gladden Oedipus, reveals the tragic secrets of his past.

According to Aristotle, the element of discovery in plot is the change from ignorance to knowledge in the personages marked for good or evil fortune. Discovery is usually the result of reversals, or changes to opposites; thus the discovery is ironic. Again, the perfect example is in *Oedipus*:

SERVANT: *(Falls to his knees.)*
OEDIPUS: *Where did you get the child from? Your own home or someone else's?*
SERVANT: *It wasn't mine. I was given it.*
OEDIPUS: *By one of these citizens? What house did it come from?*
SERVANT: *In God's name, your majesty, don't ask more questions.*
OEDIPUS: *If I have to ask that question again, you will die.*
SERVANT: *It was a child from Laius's house.*
OEDIPUS: *A slave? Or one of his own family?*
SERVANT: *Oh God! I'm on the edge of saying something I'll regret.*
OEDIPUS: *And I of hearing something I'll regret.*
SERVANT: *It was his own child, they said. But your lady within could say how these things are best.*
OEDIPUS: *Was it she who gave you the child?*
SERVANT: *Yes, my lord.*

In the above excerpt from Oedipus, we see how a reversal results in a discovery, which, in turn, produces a situation that is ironic and tragic. Next, we witness the scene of suffering. Aristotle thought that if such a scene were effective it would arouse pity and terror in the audience. To evoke this "pity and terror," Aristotle believes that an on-stage enactment of physical pain was usually necessary. Out of the suffering and torture of the protagonist would come a purity that would convolute the tragedy: the innocent situation that became tragic once again would become innocent.

A study of the meaning of the name "Oedipus" should help us to better understand Aristotle's definition of "the tragic hero." "Oedipus" may be translated as "swollen foot." (This name, of course, alludes to Oedipus' swollen ankles, which were pierced when he was an infant.) But the word also approximates another Greek word that means "I know." (This sentence is constantly on the hero's lips.) Oedipus' insistence on knowing is what makes us admire him; yet it is also what ruins him. It is as if Sophocles were saying that the inquisitive spirit can become dangerous and self-destructive when carried to an extreme. Aristotle recognized the need for a "golden mean"—a balance between the desire to create or to discover and the discipline necessary to temper the creative or discovery process to insure worthwhile results. It is this ability to temper the desire that Oedipus lacks. In a finite world, where only finite knowledge is possible, a relentless drive to know can, of course, cause problems. This drive, this desire which the Greeks called hubris, invited the retribution of the gods. When a man, the toy of the gods, attempted to control his own life by trying to seek his own answers, he invited the wrath of the gods. Upon learning the "truth," Oedipus blinds himself. This intense response to life makes us aware of life's limitations and the human capacity for courage. We lament and are thankful for Oedipus.

Stage Terms and Conventions of Greek Theatre

1. *Masks* were worn by actors in a Greek play. Modern directors modify the masks as they wish, sometimes covering only part of the face. The mask served the purpose of freezing an expression, of making the face partially immobile; it enabled the audience to concentrate on the character, rather than the actor playing the part. The mask changed color to suggest blood and horror.
2. *The chorus,* a group of 12 to 15 men, danced and sang in response to the events affecting the hero of the play. The chorus prayed and speculated on what the gods demanded of mortals. They also filled time between episodes involving the main characters.
3. *Off-stage violence* was reported by a messenger who disclosed what had taken place. Because the plays were performed in large theatres suitable for an audience of at least 14,000, the gestures of strong emotion had to be exaggerated in order for people sitting at some distance to see what was happening.
4. *Male actors* played all roles.
5. *Speaking parts* in the original productions were limited to three actors. In other words, there were never more than 3 people interacting verbally at the same time.
6. *Legends and familiar stories* served as a basis for plot so that characters were rarely introduced in a play but were already well-known to the audience.
7. *Dignified, simple verse* was spoken by principal actors and chorus.
8. *Action* usually took place in a single day and in a single place with no subplots to complicate the playwright's message.
9. *Catharsis* is the act of purging or cleansing, usually in connection with tragedy; Aristotle said that tragedy arouses fear and pity, and that when these emotions are purged away, the audience is left in a state of purification, cleansed and uplifted by the experience.
10. *Deus ex machina* means the "god from the machine," a god who intervened at the end of classical tragedy to resolve the action. It is today the means to a solution that does not grow out of the drama itself, but is imposed by the playwright.

11. *A dithyramb* is a poetic hymn or chant performed by a chorus at the Dionysian festivals; it is a narrative or a lyric.
12. *Discovery* is the revelation of important information about a play's characters, their motivations, feelings, and relationships, often accompanied by recognition (anagnorisis) when a character learns the truth about himself.
13. *Empathy* is a psychological phenomenon in which a spectator through his imagination enters into the being of the character on stage.
14. *Hubris* is as Aristotelian concept, carried over into neoclassical criticism to mean the defiance of divine will by a tragic character.
15. *Orchestra* is the "dancing-floor"; the (usually) circular, flat area occupied by the chorus in 5th Century Greek theatre surrounded on three sides by the audience and tangent to the proscenium.
16. *Pathos* is that part of tragedy dealing with the physical and emotional suffering of the hero.
17. *Periaktos* is a three-sided prism pivoted at each end of the stage-house (skene) to revolve and show different faces in the Hellenistic theatre. Pairs of periaktos were used as changeable scenic units.
18. *Prologue* is the opening portion of a Greek tragedy that orients the audience for what is about to happen.
19. A *protagonist* in the Greek theatre is the principal figure in the principal action.
20. A *skene* was the scene building located across the orchestra from the center point of the audience.
21. *Irony* is an incongruity between the actual result of a sequence of events and the expected result.
22. An *obligatory moment* is at the climax when the protagonist discovers the truth.

Story and Plot Summary

A plague is raging in Thebes. The oracle sends word that the plague will continue until the murderer of the former king has been discovered and punished. Oedipus vows that he will bring the culprit to justice. The audience recognizes his name as that of the legendary figure who had killed his father, the ex-king of Thebes, and who had married his mother, the widowed queen. It knows that Oedipus' investigation will lead him to the discovery of his own guilt.

The Chorus, representing the citizens of Thebes, comments on the action. Oedipus speaks in turn to Creon, his wife's brother; to Tiresias, the blind soothsayer; to the messenger from Corinth, and to the shepherd who had given Oedipus as a baby to the man from Corinth rather than kill Oedipus as instructed by the King and Queen.

When the shepherds from Thebes and Corinth are together, Oedipus is at the point of learning the truth—that the prophecy has been fulfilled and that he is the murderer of Laius, the ex-king of Thebes. At the time of the murder, Oedipus had no idea that Laius was other than a stranger.

The Queen, Jocasta, guesses the truth, that she has been married to her own son and has borne his children. She rushes into the palace and, unknown to Oedipus, kills herself. Oedipus says he supposes the queen is unhappy to learn that he was not the child of the king and queen of Corinth, but instead possibly the child of some unimportant, unfortunate mother.

GREEK THEATER PLAN

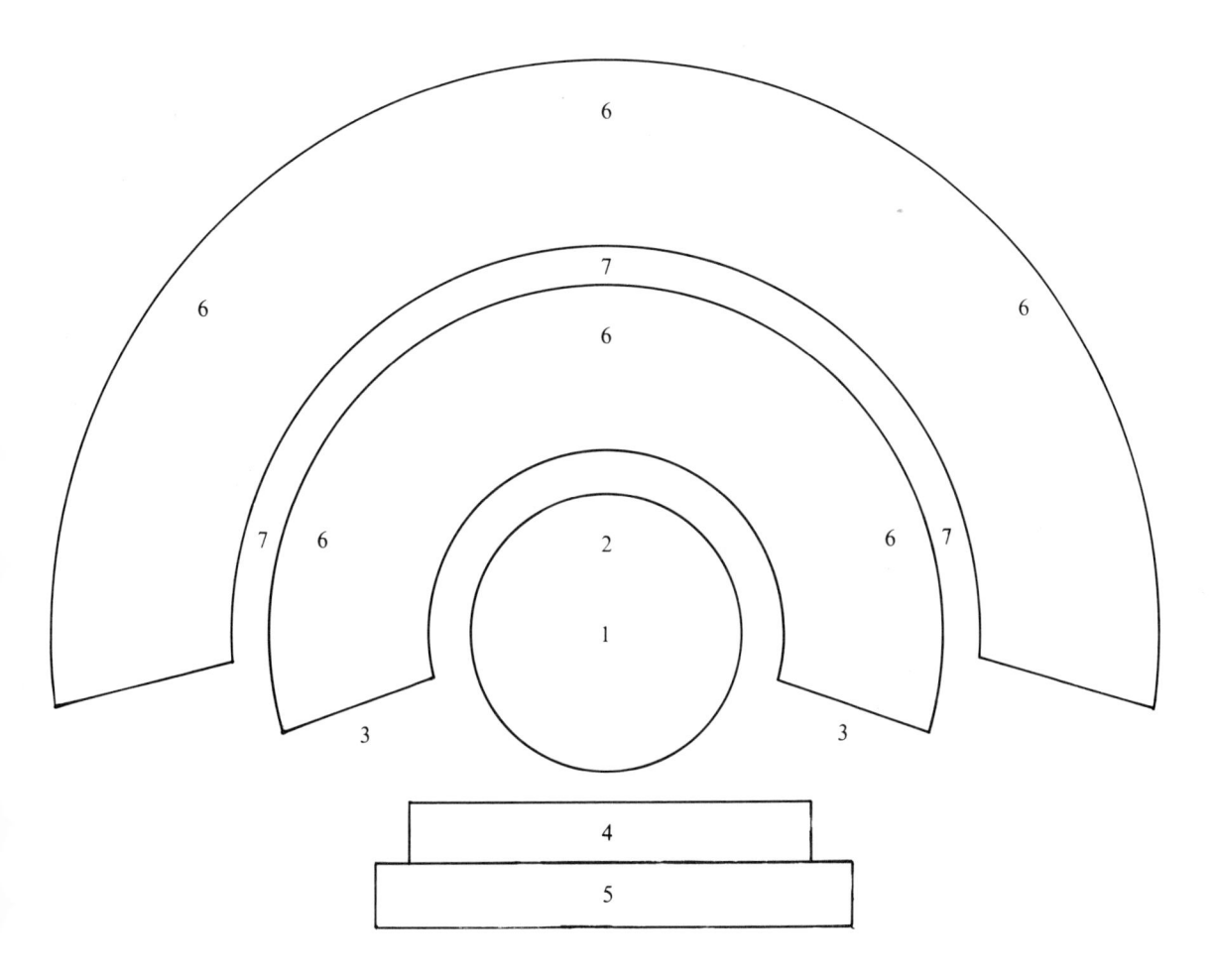

1. Orkestra—Orchestra: Dancing Floor for Chorus
2. Thymele—Altar: For Dionysus
3. Parodos (Parodoi): Entrance/Exit to the Orchestra by the Chorus, Also Used as Entrance by Spectators in Some Theaters
4. Proscenium: Stage Where Actors Performed
5. Skene and Tiring House: Stage Building Which Served as Backdrop for the Action and Retiring Room for Actors
6. Teatron: Viewing Place, Audience Seating
7. Diazoma: Aisle, Audience Walkway

When Oedipus learns his own identity and guilt, he realizes that the prophecy has been fulfilled. He punishes himself by taking pins from the dead queen's gown and plunging them into his eyes. He then requests suitable burial for the dead queen, his wife; the privilege of being with his daughters briefly, and the exile he had proclaimed for the killer of Laius.

He is reminded that he once had mastery but could not keep it, and has no further right to give orders. The Chorus comments on life's changes, saying that no man can be considered happy until his life is over and all is known about his fortune.

From *The Idea of a Theater*
by Francis Fergusson

In the following excerpt from "Oedipus, Myth and Play," Francis Fergusson explains what makes *Oedipus* a tragedy:

When Sophocles came to write his play he had the myth of Oedipus to start with. Laius and Jocasta, King and Queen of Thebes, are told by the oracle that their son will grow up to kill his father and marry his mother. The infant, his feet pierced, is left on Mount Kitharon to die. But a shepherd finds him and takes care of him; at last gives him to another shepherd, who takes him to Corinth, and there the King and Queen bring him up as their own son. But Oedipus—"Clubfoot"—is plagued in his turn by the oracle; he hears that he is fated to kill his father and marry his mother; and to escape that fate he leaves Corinth never to return. On his journey he meets an old man with his servants; gets into a dispute with him, and kills him and all his followers. He comes to Thebes at the time when the Sphinx is preying upon that City; solves the riddle which the Sphinx propounds, and saves the City. He marries the widowed Queen, Jocasta; has several children by her; rules prosperously for many years. But, when Thebes is suffering under a plague and a drought, the oracle reports that the gods are angry because Laius' slayer is unpunished. Oedipus, as King, undertakes to find him; discovers that he is himself the culprit and that Jocasta is his own mother. He blinds himself and goes into exile. From this time forth he becomes a sort of sacred relic, like the bones of a saint; perilous, but "good medicine" for the community that possesses him. He dies, at last, at Athens, in a grove sacred to the Eumenides, female spirits of fertility and night.

• • •

Everyone knows that when Sophocles planned the plot of the play itself, he started almost at the end of the story, when the plague descends upon the City of Thebes which Oedipus and Jocasta had been ruling with great success for a number of years. The action of the play takes less than a day, and consists of Oedipus' quest for Laius' slayer—his consulting the Oracle of Apollo, his examination of the Prophet, Tiresas, and of a series of witnesses, ending with the old Shepherd who gave him to the King and Queen of Corinth. The play ends when Oedipus is unmistakably revealed as the culprit.

At this literal level, the play is intelligible as a murder mystery. Oedipus takes the role of District Attorney; and when he at last convicts himself, we have a twist, a coup de théatre, of

---

From "Oedipus, Myth and Play," in Francis Fergusson, *The Idea of a Theater: A Study of Ten Plays. The Art of Drama in Changing Perspective* (copyright 1949 © 1977 by Princeton University Press; Princeton Paperback, 1968): pp. 14–18. Reprinted by permission of Princeton University Press.

unparalleled excitement. But no one who sees or reads the play can rest content with its literal coherence. Questions as to its meaning arise at once: Is Oedipus really guilty, or simply a victim of the gods, of his famous complex, of fate, of original sin? How much did he know, all along? How much did Jocasta know? The first, and most deeply instinctive effort of the mind, when confronted with this play, is to endeavor to reduce its meanings to some set of rational categories.

• • •

By starting the play at the end of the story, and showing on-stage only the last crucial episode in Oedipus' life, the past and present action of the protagonist are revealed together; and, in each other's light, are at last felt as one. Oedipus' quest for the slayer of Laius becomes a quest for the hidden reality of his own past; and as that slowly comes into focus, like repressed material under psychoanalysis—with sensory and emotional immediacy, yet in the light of acceptance and understanding—his immediate quest also reaches its end: he comes to see himself (the Savior of the City) and the guilty one, the plague of Thebes, at once and at one.

• • •

I have said that the action which Sophocles shows is a quest, the quest for Laius' slayer; and that as Oedipus' past is unrolled before us his whole life is seen as a kind of quest for his true nature and destiny. But since the object of this quest is not clear until the end, the seeking action takes many forms, as its object appears in different lights. The object, indeed, the final perception, the "truth," looks so different at the end from what it did at the beginning that Oedipus' action itself may seem not a quest, but its opposite, a flight. Thus it would be hard to say, simply, that Oedipus either succeeds or fails. He succeeds; but his success is his undoing. He fails to find what, in one way, he sought; yet from another point of view his search is brilliantly successful. The same ambiguities surround his effort to discover who and what he is. He seems to find that he is nothing; yet thereby finds himself. And what of his relation to the gods? His quest may be regarded as a heroic attempt to escape their decrees, or as an attempt, based upon some deep natural faith, to discover what their wishes are, and what true obedience would be. In one sense Oedipus suffers forces he can neither control nor understand, the puppet of fate; yet at the same time he wills and intelligently intends his every move.

The meaning, or spiritual content of the play, is not to be sought by trying to resolve such ambiguities as these. The spiritual content of the play is the tragic action which Sophocles directly presents; and this action is in its essence *zweideutig*: triumph and destruction, darkness and enlightenment, mourning and rejoicing, at any moment we care to consider it. But this action has also a shape; a beginning, middle, and end, in time. It starts with the reasoned purpose of finding Laius' slayer. But this aim meets unforeseen difficulties, evidences which do not fit, and therefore shake the purpose as it was first understood; and so the characters suffer the piteous and terrible sense of the mystery of the human situation. From this suffering or passion, with its shifting visions, a new perception of the situation emerges; and on that basis the purpose of the action is redefined, and a new movement starts. This movement, or tragic rhythm of action, constitutes the shape of the play as a whole; it is also the shape of each episode, each discussion between principals with the chorus following. Mr. Kenneth Burke has studied the tragic rhythm in his *Philosophy of Literary Form,* and also in *A Grammar of Motives,* where he gives the three moments traditional designations which are very suggestive: *Poiema, Pathema, Mathema.* They may also be called, for convenience, Purpose, Passion (or Suffering) and Perception. It is this tragic rhythm of action which is the substance or spiritual content of the play, and the clue to its extraordinarily comprehensive form. . . .

From *Off Broadway*
by Maxwell Anderson

In the following excerpt from "The Essence of Tragedy" Maxwell Anderson, the author, discusses the importance of a recognition scene:

. . . The recognition scene, as Aristotle isolated it in the tragedies of the Greeks, was generally an artificial device, a central scene in which the leading character saw through a disguise, recognized as a friend or as an enemy, perhaps as a lover or a member of his own family, some person whose identity had been hidden. . . . Oedipus, hunting savagely for the criminal who has brought the plague upon Thebes, discovers that he is himself that criminal—and . . . this is a discovery that affects not only the physical well-being and happiness of the hero, but the whole structure of his life. . . .

Now scenes of exactly this sort are rare in the modern drama except in detective stories adapted for the stae. But when I probed a little more deeply into the memorable pieces of Shakespeare's theater and our own I began to see that though modern recognition scenes are subtler and harder to find, they are none the less present in the plays we choose to remember. They seldom have to do with anything so naive as disguise or the unveiling of a personal identity. But the element of discovery is just as important as ever. For the mainspring in the mechanism of a modern play is almost invariably a discovery by the hero of some element in his environment or in his own soul of which he has not been aware—or which he has not taken sufficiently into account. Moreover, nearly every teacher of playwriting has had some inkling of this, though it was not until after I had worked out my own theory that what they said on this point took on accurate meaning for me. I still think that the rule which I formulated for my own guidance is more concise than any other, an so I give it here: A play should lead up to and away from a central crisis, and this crisis should consist in a discovery by the leading character which has an indelible effect on his thought and emotion and completely alters his course of action. The leading character, let me say again, must make the discovery; it must affect him emotionally; and it must alter his direction in the play. . . .

Now this prime rule has a corollary which is just as important as the rule itself. The hero who is to make the central discovery in a play must not be a perfect man. He must have some variation of what Aristotle calls a tragic fault; and the reason he must have it is that when he makes his discovery he must change both in himself and in his action—and he must change for the better. The fault can be a very simple one—a mere unawareness, for example—but if he has no fault he cannot change for the better, but only for the worse, and for a reason which I shall

Reprinted by permission of William Morrow & Company, Inc. From OFF BROADWAY by Maxwell Anderson. Copyright © 1947 by Maxwell Anderson.

discuss later, it is necessary that he must become more admirable, and not less so, at the end of the play. In other words, a hero must pass through an experience which opens his eyes to an error of his own. He must learn through suffering. In a tragedy he suffers death itself as a consequence of his fault or his attempt to correct it, but before he dies he has become a nobler person because of his recognition of his fault and the consequent alteration of his course of action. In a serious play which does not end in death he suffers a lesser punishment, but the pattern remains the same. In both forms he has a fault to begin with, he discovers that fault during the course of the action, and he does what he can to rectify it at the end. . . .

And now at last I come to the point toward which I've been struggling so laboriously. Why does the audience come to the theater to look on while an imaginary hero is put to an imaginary trial and comes out of it with credit to the race and to himself? It was this question that prompted my essay, and unless I've been led astray by my own predilections there is a very possible answer in the rules for playwriting which I have just cited. The theater originated in two complementary religious ceremonies, one celebrating the animal in man and one celebrating the god. Old Greek Comedy was dedicated to the spirits of lust and riot and earth, spirits which are certainly necessary to the health and continuance of the race. Greek tragedy was dedicated to man's aspiration, to his kinship with the gods, to his unending, blind attempt to lift himself above his lusts and his pure animalism into a world where there are other values than pleasure and survival. However unaware of it we may be, our theater has followed the Greek patterns with no change in essence, from Aristophanes and Euripides to our own day. Our more ribald musical comedies are simply our approximation of the Bacchic rites of Old Comedy. In the rest of our theater we sometimes follow Sophocles, whose tragedy is always an exaltation of the human spirit, sometimes Euripides, whose tragicomedy follows the same pattern of an excellence achieved through suffering. The forms of both tragedy and comedy have changed a good deal in nonessentials, but in essentials—and especially in the core of meaning which they must have for audiences—they are in the main the same religious rites which grew up around the altars of Attica long ago.

It is for this reason that when you write for the theater you must choose between your version of a phallic revel and your vision of what mankind may or should become. Your vision may be faulty, or shallow, or sentimental, but it must conform to some aspiration in the audience, or the audience will reject it. Old Comedy, the celebration of the animal in us, still has a place in our theater, as it had in Athens, but here as there, that part of the theater which celebrated man's virtue and his regeneration in hours of crisis is accepted as having the more important function. Our comedy is largely the Greek New Comedy, which grew out of Euripides' tragicomedy, and is separated from tragedy only in that it presents a happier scene and puts its protagonist through an ordeal which is less than lethal.

And since our plays, aside from those which are basically Old Comedy, are exaltations of the human spirit, since that is what an audience expects when it comes to the theater, the playwright gradually discovers, as he puts plays before audiences, that he must follow the ancient Aristotelian rule: he must build his plot around a scene wherein his hero discovers some mortal frailty or stupidity in himself and faces life armed with a new wisdom. He must so arrange his story that it will prove to the audience that men pass through suffering purified, that animal though we are, despicable though we are in many ways, there is in us all some divine, incalculable fire that urges us to be better than we are.

Commentary

In the first critique by Francis Fergusson, an excerpt from *The Idea of a Theater,* Fergusson attempts to characterize the unfolding of events in a tragedy. He finds, as does Maxwell Anderson, that a discovery and a new vision propel the play. Fergusson calls the movement provoked by the revelation "a tragic rhythm of action which is the substance or spiritual content of the play, and the clue to its extraordinarily comprehensive form."

In the second essay, Maxwell Anderson searches for a common denominator for all tragedy. His search leads him to what he believes to be the basis of all theatre. He notes, as does Fergusson, that tragedy occurs when the protagonist discovers something that alters his actions and suffers with the new knowledge. This process of discovery, suffering and awareness makes the protagonist, as well as the audience, aware of a more noble morality. A turn of events, resulting in increased insight, is, so Anderson writes, the basis of all theatre.

Objectives

You the student, after studying *Oedipus* should be able to

1. understand Sophocles' role as a playwright and an innovator in the early development of theatre and dramatic art.
2. recognize dramatic conventions typifying early Greek Theatre.
3. appreciate the significance of *Oedipus Tyrannus* as an example of the tragic mode.
4. explain what makes a classical tragic hero.

Program Notes

Oedipus Tyrannus

This excerpt from Sophocles' classic tragedy begins with the entrance of the Corinthian shepherd who has news of the death of Oedipus' "father." For more than 2,000 years, audiences have been fascinated as they watch the tormented hero come closer to the horrible truth about his origin. This production includes a five-man chorus and stylized masks. This new translation used in the BBC production avoids archaic language, but preserves dignity without sacrificing clarity. Viewers share the horror of the messenger's news as he reports offstage violence. An accompanying documentary shows scenes of Greek theatres, and recounts Aristotle's definition of tragedy. The television program presents the second half of the play.

A Listing of BBC Actors and Production Coordinators

OEDIPUS TYRANNUS

by

Sophocles

CAST

OEDIPUS	PATRICK STEWART
JOCASTA	ROSALIE CRUTCHLEY
FIRST CHORUS	DEREK GODFREY
SECOND CHORUS	JOE MELIA
FIRST MESSENGER	RONALD RADD
SERVANT	JOHN CITROEN
SECOND MESSENGER	ROY MARSDEN
CREON	JOHN FORBES-ROBERTSON
CHORIC DANCERS	(KEN MASON
	(HUGH SPIGHT
	(NICHOLAS CARROLL
	(NICKY BURGE
DAUGHTER I	CAROL WALKER-SMITH
DAUGHTER II	KARIN FOLEY

PRODUCTION

DESIGNER	DACRE PUNT
COSTUMER DESIGNER	BARBARA KIDD
MAKE-UP SUPERVISOR	MAGGIE WEBB
DIRECTOR	RICHARD CALLANAN
CHOREOGRAPHER	JONATHAN TAYLOR

OEDIPUS TYRANNUS

by

Sophocles

Printed here is the scene in which Oedipus discovers his true identity:

FIRST MESSENGER: Corinth, madam. My news in a moment will bring you pleasure, of course. Perhaps some distress too.
JOCASTA: What is it? It's strangely ambivalent.
FIRST MESSENGER: The people of the Isthmus are likely to elect Oedipus as their ruler. That's the general view there.
JOCASTA: How's that? Isn't old Polybus still on the throne?
FIRST MESSENGER: No. He's dead and in the grave.
JOCASTA: What did you say? Is Oedipus's father dead?
FIRST MESSENGER: Polybus is dead, or else may I die!

(Turns to chorus)

JOCASTA *(turns to ATTENDANT)* You, quick, run and tell your master the news.

(ATTENDANT exits)

(She raises her arms) Where are you now, oracles of the gods?
This is the man that Oedipus so long avoided in fear of killing him. And now he's died a natural death, not killed by Oedipus.

(Enter OEDIPUS from the palace)

OEDIPUS: My dearest wife Jocasta why have you sent for me to come out here?
JOCASTA: Listen to this man, and as you listen judge how the proud oracles of the gods turn out.

(OEDIPUS crosses to JOCASTA)

OEDIPUS *(places arm round JOCASTA)* Who is he? What's his news for me?
JOCASTA: He's come from Corinth, with news that your father Polybus is no longer alive but dead.
OEDIPUS *(pause)* What's that sir? Enlighten me yourself. *(crosses toward FIRST MESSENGER)*
FIRST MESSENGER: If you want me to begin with a simple statement of the facts. Polybus is dead and gone. You can be sure of that.
OEDIPUS: Was there treachery or the visitation of some disease?
FIRST MESSENGER: With old age a small weight tips the balance towards sleep.
OEDIPUS: So the poor old man died of some sickness.
FIRST MESSENGER: And of old age. He'd lived a long time.
OEDIPUS: I'm sorry.

(FIRST MESSENGER turns away)

Jocasta, why should one bother with the hearth of Delphic prophecy, or the screams of birds in the sky? On their interpretation I was bound to kill my father. He is dead and buried

---

Translated by John Ferguson, Dean and Director of Studies in Arts, of The Open University, Milton Keynes, England, and reproduced by permission of The Open University.

beneath the soil. I never took up arms against him—unless perhaps he died of longing for me, and then perhaps his death may be laid at my door. But as they stand, Polybus has swept up these oracles, and taken them with him to Hades; they are worthless.

JOCASTA: I told you all that long ago.

OEDIPUS: You did. Fear pulled me the wrong way.

JOCASTA: So don't take them to heart any more.

OEDIPUS: But surely I must fear my mother's bed.

JOCASTA: Why should a man be afraid? Chance rules his life. He has no clear foreknowledge. Better to do what's in your power, and take life as it comes. *(holds out hand to* OEDIPUS*)* And don't you be afraid of marrying your mother. Many men in the past have slept with their mothers in dreams. It's the man who ignores such things who has the easiest life.

OEDIPUS: Fine words all of them—but my mother's alive. And while she is still alive, I can't help being anxious, no matter what you say.

JOCASTA: Well, your father's death is a great shaft of light.

OEDIPUS: Yes, that's true, but the woman's alive, and I am afraid.

FIRST MESSENGER: Who is the woman who stirs you to such fear?

OEDIPUS: Merope, old greybeard, Polybus's partner.

FIRST MESSENGER: But what is there about her to cause you fear?

OEDIPUS: A terrifying divine oracle, sir.

FIRST MESSENGER: Can you reveal it? Or is it unlawful for others to know?

OEDIPUS: Certainly. Apollo once told me that I was doomed to marry with my own mother, and to shed my father's blood with my own hands. That's why I've spent many years so far from Corinth. Years of blessing: though it's a joy to look into one's parent's eyes.

FIRST MESSENGER: And was it in fear of this that you went into exile?

OEDIPUS: Yes, sir, to avoid murdering my father! *(turns to* FIRST MESSENGER*)*

FIRST MESSENGER: Then your majesty, why don't I at once free you from your anxiety? I've come for your good.

OEDIPUS: You'll certainly not find me ungenerous.

FIRST MESSENGER: In fact that was my real reason for coming—something in it for me, when you return home.

OEDIPUS: I shan't go near my parents.

FIRST MESSENGER: My son, clearly you don't know what you're doing—

OEDIPUS: What do you mean, greybeard?

FIRST MESSENGER: If that is why you refrain from coming home.

OEDIPUS: For fear of the fulfillment of Phoebus's oracles.

FIRST MESSENGER: Contamination of guilt through your parents?

OEDIPUS: Yes. That's my fear, and it's continually with me.

FIRST MESSENGER: Don't you realize your fears are quite unjustified?

OEDIPUS: Why, if I'm their son and they my parents?

FIRST MESSENGER: Because Polybus was no relation of yours.

*(*OEDIPUS *steps forward)*

OEDIPUS *(pause)* What?*(steps closer to* MESSENGER*)* Wasn't Polybus my father?

FIRST MESSENGER: As much as any man here, no more.

OEDIPUS: How can one who is nothing to me be equal to my father?
FIRST MESSENGER: I was not your father. He was not either.
OEDIPUS: Then why did he call me son?
FIRST MESSENGER: He took you from my hands as a present.
OEDIPUS: Could he become so attached to a present from another's hand?
FIRST MESSENGER: Yes. He had been so long without a child.
OEDIPUS: You gave me to him: did you buy me? Or find me by chance?
FIRST MESSENGER: I found you in Cithaeron's winding glens.
OEDIPUS: What were you doing in those parts?
FIRST MESSENGER: I was in charge of mountain flocks.
OEDIPUS: You were a hired shepherd?
FIRST MESSENGER: And at that time your preserver, my son.
OEDIPUS: What was the trouble with me when you found me?
FIRST MESSENGER: Your own ankles should be evidence of that.
OEDIPUS: Oh! Why remind me of that pain from the past?
FIRST MESSENGER: There was a pin through your ankles. I released you.
OEDIPUS: Yes, I have carried that mark of shame from my infancy.
FIRST MESSENGER: And it was this that gave you your present name.
OEDIPUS: Was this my mother's doing or my father's? For the god's sake tell me.
FIRST MESSENGER: I don't know. The man who gave you to me would have a better idea of that.
OEDIPUS: You had me from someone else? You didn't find me yourself?
FIRST MESSENGER: No. It was another shepherd who gave you to me. *(steps forward)*
OEDIPUS: Who was he? Can you identify him? Can you tell me?
FIRST MESSENGER: I think he was known as one of Laius's men.
OEDIPUS: The former monarch of this land?
FIRST MESSENGER: Yes. The shepherd was in his service.
OEDIPUS: I want to see him. Is he still alive?
FIRST MESSENGER: You people who live here would best know that.! . . . *(looks at chorus)*
OEDIPUS: Can any of you here identify the man of whom he speaks?

*(Pause—*JOCASTA *turns and goes toward door)*

Have any of you seen him here or in the fields? Tell me. The moment of truth has come.
FIRST CHORUS: I think it is in fact the peasant you've already sent for. But Jocasta is here and could say as well as any.
OEDIPUS *(turns to* JOCASTA*)* Dearest, the shepherd we have asked to come, is this the man in question?
JOCASTA *(turns to face* OEDIPUS*)* Why bother with the man at all? Pay no attention. Forget all that's been said: it's pointless.
OEDIPUS: Impossible. With clues such as these in my possession I can't fail to uncover my birth.
JOCASTA: For the God's sake don't. If you care for your own life at all call off the hunt. I'm plagued enough already.
OEDIPUS: I may be found a triple slave, and my mother a slave of the third generation. But nothing base will attach itself to you.

JOCASTA *(Paces towards* OEDIPUS*)* Please, please listen to me and don't do it.
OEDIPUS: I won't listen. I must find the whole truth.
JOCASTA: I'm speaking in your own best interests.
OEDIPUS: I'm tired of hearing of my own best interests.
JOCASTA: Unhappy man, God save you from knowing who you are!
OEDIPUS *(turns to altar)* Will someone go and bring that shepherd to me? Let the Queen find joy in her noble family.
JOCASTA: Poor lost soul—I have no other word for you—and will never have another.

*(*JOCASTA *exits to the palace)*

(Doors close)

SECOND CHORUS: Oedipus, why has the queen left us in such a passion of wild grief? I fear a storm of disaster will break from her reticence.
OEDIPUS: Let it break if it will. I am determined to see the seed from which I spring, however humble, Jocasta—how like a woman's pride!—is probably ashamed of my low birth. I hold myself a child of Fortune. She is my mother, I her child. The months, my brothers, have marked me out, humble one moment, powerful another. That's my breeding. I could not prove false to it, and fail to discover my birth.
FIRST CHORUS: If I am a prophet and wise in discernment, by Olympus, you, Cithaeron, shall recognize at tomorrow's full moon that Oedipus honors you as his fellow-countryman, his nurse and his mother, that we know you in dance, for you have found favor with our rulers. Apollo, to whom we cry, look kindly on us.

(Choric dance)

SECOND CHORUS: Who was your mother, my son? Which of the long-lived nymphs bore you to mountain-ranging Pan as your father? Or was it some bride of Apollo? He loves all the upland pastures.
Was it Cyllene's lord? Did the Maenads' god, who haunts the mountain-peaks, receive you as a blessing from some nymph of Helicon, with whom he loves to play?

(Choric dance)

*(*SERVANT *enters)*

OEDIPUS: I've never met him, elders, but I think I see the shepherd we have awaited so long. He's an old man; it tallies with our friend here. But you perhaps know better than I do; you've met the man before.

*(*SERVANT *approaches)*

FIRST CHORUS: Yes, I recognize him as reliable a man as Laius ever had in his service as a shepherd.
OEDIPUS: First you, sir, from Corinth, I want to know, is this the man you were talking about?
FIRST MESSENGER *(turns to* OEDIPUS*)* Yes, your majesty. He stands before you.
OEDIPUS: Now you, sir.

*(*SERVANT *comes forward)*

Come here. Look me straight in the eye. Answer my questions. Were you at one time in Laius's service?

SERVANT: Yes, born and bred in the palace, not bought in the slave-market.
OEDIPUS: What was your work? How were you employed?
SERVANT: A shepherd most of my life.
OEDIPUS: In which part of the country did you generally stay?
SERVANT: It would be Cithaeron or thereabouts.
OEDIPUS: Do you remember ever seeing this man there?
SERVANT: In what connection? What man do you mean?
OEDIPUS: Standing in front of you. Have you ever met him?
SERVANT: I can't offhand remember.
FIRST MESSENGER *(steps forward)* There's nothing strange in that, your majesty. I'll soon jog his memory. He knows quite well that part of Cithaeron—he had two flocks, I was neighbor to him with one, for three whole seasons from spring to autumn. Then winter came, and I would drive my sheep to my own fold, he drove his to Laius's estates. Well, am I telling the truth, or making it up?
SERVANT: It's true enough, but it happened a long time ago.
FIRST MESSENGER: Now tell me this, do you remember handing me a baby, to bring up as my own?
SERVANT: Why—why are you asking that?
FIRST MESSENGER *(points at* OEDIPUS*)* My friend, that baby boy is standing here.
SERVANT: Damn you—can't you keep your mouth shut?
OEDIPUS: None of that, sir. Don't speak harshly to him. Your story warrants more harsh words than his.
SERVANT: How have I given offense, your majesty?
OEDIPUS: By not speaking frankly of the child he's talking about.
SERVANT: He's a busybody, he doesn't know what he's talking about.
OEDIPUS: If you won't speak freely, you'll be tortured till you tell.
SERVANT: In God's name, don't hurt me; I'm an old man.
OEDIPUS: Quick, someone, twist his arm behind him.
(FIRST CHORUS *Twists servant's arm round his back*)
SERVANT: Ooooh! What do you want to know?
OEDIPUS: He asked you about a baby. Did you give it to him?
SERVANT: Yes. Oh God! If only I'd died that very day!
OEDIPUS: You'll come to that, if you don't speak the truth.
SERVANT: I'll die a thousand deaths if I do.
OEDIPUS: This fellow's determined to delay us.
SERVANT: I'm not! I've told you I gave it to him.
(SERVANT *falls to his knees*)
OEDIPUS: Where did you get it? Your own home or someone else's?
SERVANT: It wasn't mine. I was given it.
OEDIPUS: By one of these citizens? Which house did it come from?
(SERVANT *rises*)
SERVANT: It was a child from Laius's house.

OEDIPUS: A slave? Or one of his own family?
SERVANT: Oh God! I'm on the edge of saying the dreadful thing.
OEDIPUS: And I of hearing it. But I must.
SERVANT: It was his own child, they said. But your lady within could best say how these things are.
OEDIPUS: Was she the one who gave it to you?
SERVANT: Yes, my lord.
OEDIPUS: For what purpose?
SERVANT: To do away with it.
OEDIPUS: Cruel! Her own child?
SERVANT: She was afraid of oracles of doom.
OEDIPUS: What were they?
SERVANT: He was to kill his father, they said.
OEDIPUS: What made you give it to this old man?
SERVANT: Pity, your majesty. I thought he'd take him off to a foreign country, the one he came from. He saved his life—for a doom of disaster. If you are the man in question, know this, you were born to sorrow.
OEDIPUS: Oh! Oh!

(SERVANT *and* FIRST MESSENGER *turn away*)

All turned out true! Light, may I never look on you again. You have revealed me.

(OEDIPUS *backs away towards palace*)

Cursed in my parents! Cursed in my marriage! Cursed in shedding blood!

(He exits quickly into palace)

Focus in Viewing

Much of what we know about Greek drama has been surmised from clues found within the few extant scripts, from writers (for example, Aristotle) of the Periclean period (495 B.C.–429 B.C.), and from the remains of the amphitheatres. The mini-documentary preceding the play production shows the location of many of these sites in order to recapture the feeling of the natural settings and the conventions of Classical Greek Theatre.

This production of *Oedipus,* of course, was taped in a television studio; the studio set, of an altar and a palace door in a wall set against a light blue cyclorama, however, was designed to imitate the open-air, perhaps hillside, atmosphere. The transparent half-masks, worn by the Chorus, were designed to restrict facial expression and so help to produce a studio equivalent of stylized Greek acting. Expect to hear a formal way of speaking and to see a highly formalized style of movement.

Content Viewing

1. What are three examples of irony in Oedipus?
2. In *The Ghost Sonata* the Daughter tells the student that they keep the cook because they

can't get rid of her. What might the cook symbolize that is represented in another way in *Oedipus*?
3. The Troll-King's motto in *Peer Gynt* is, "To thyself be enough." Could Oedipus have taken this for his motto? Explain.
4. How is the Student's explanation of the hyacinth (refer back to Focus in Viewing for *The Ghost Sonata*) a metaphor for what happens to Oedipus?
5. Tell which two characters in *Oedipus* interest you the most. Why?
6. How would you describe Oedipus' character? Who, or what, is he? What is his philosophy; his view of himself? Does his attitude change? Is Oedipus' character consistent with his philosophy, action, and with the other characters? Is Oedipus's character sympathetic, unsympathetic, or neutral?
7. Is the language (dialogue) natural or poetic? What is the service and function of the language in this play?

Craft Viewing
1. What conventions do you need to know or accept before you can understand or enter into the spirit of this production?
2. Based on your viewing, and reading of the plot summary, do you recognize a plot structure? If so, what is it?
3. What is your reaction to the staging techniques and the director's interpretation of the BBC production? Comment upon the movement upon stage and stylization of sets, costumes, and dialogue.
4. When Oedipus realizes that he has killed his father and married his mother and reacts, what was your opinion of his reaction? (Judge as a critic thinking of both actor and director.) If you have seen a performance of such an emotional scene (in another staging of *Oedipus* or another play), compare it to this one.
5. Do you think the technical design and execution supported the playscript and the stage play? Were the masks effective, or ineffective? In what way?
6. Is there one moment or scene which stands out in your memory? More than one? Which ones, and why?

Critical Viewing: Overview

Now that this play and its production are part of your experience, what significance does *Oedipus Tyrannus* hold for you?

Additional Plays That Demonstrate Similar Concepts

Antigone—Sophocles

Prometheus Bound—Aeschylus

Phaedra—Racine

An Enemy of the People—Ibsen

A Man For All Seasons—Robert Bolt

MACBETH

by

William Shakespeare
(1564–1616)

A. Play Notes: Macbeth and Manhood Variations of a Theme, p. 138
B. The Staging of Shakespeare's Plays, p. 140
C. Story and Plot Summary, p. 140
D. Commentary: A Brief Summary of a Review, p. 141
E. Review, p. 141
F. Objectives, p. 144
G. Program Notes, p. 144
H. Excerpt from Macbeth, p. 145
I. A List of BBC Actors and Production Coordinators, p. 170
J. Director's Notes, p. 175
   1. On Character Interpretation, p. 175
   2. Special Effects and Character Interpretation, p. 175
K. Focus in Viewing, p. 176
L. Additional Plays That Demonstrate Similar Concepts, p. 176
M. Stage Terms, p. 177

Play Notes
Macbeth and Manhood Variations on a Theme

If *Macbeth* were just concerned with a murderer and his murderous wife, Shakespeare's play might be exciting in the way that television's *Columbo* or *Police Story* is exciting, but it would be no more than that. For almost 400 years, *Macbeth,* the story of a political murder, has stirred audiences to the truths and paradoxes of their own existence.

Macbeth is not simply evil, a bad man who says about himself that he has "no spur to prick the sides of my intent, but only vaulting ambition, which o'erleaps itself and falls on th' other side." (Act I, Scene vii) He is a person who wants, above all else, to be king of Scotland because he aspires to greatness, to achieve the position he believes he should have. To realize potential is not, in itself, reprehensible, and Macbeth is not evil because of his ambition. Yet, in addition to Macbeth's obsession with position, his character is marked with flaws that make his actions deplorable.

Macbeth is also a sensitive man whose poetic dialogue is unusually expressive; a man who, at the very outset, recognizes his complicated desires, choices, and the possible consequences. Speaking of his proposed murder of Duncan, Macbeth wishes that ". . . this blow might be the be-all and the end-all here. . . ." But Macbeth knows better than any other character in the play that "bloody instructions . . . return to plague th' inventor."

Therefore, Macbeth fears that he will be punished. Sixteenth century man believed that there was a moral order in the universe. God had created that order out of chaos, and man since the Fall had been disturbing it. Man had a place in that order—above animals but below God. When he tried to disrupt that order in any way, he sinned and would inevitably be punished. It is important to understand this concept of moral order to understand Macbeth's dichotomy. Macbeth had taken matters into his own hands in a way suited only to the Deity, and moral order dictated that man was not God. In short, Macbeth did not know his place; or rather, he knew it and chose to ignore what he knew. Why? Why does a man who knows so much, who is so rational, choose to take such irrational risks?

Macbeth is in conflict. He aspires to kingship, but he knows the consequences of his actions. Like Hamlet, he agonizes over what he really wants to do. As Shakespeare portrays him, he is a good man gone bad, somehow forced to commit murderous deeds. The warrior, especially the warrior king, was an accepted and honored Renaissance man. Political murders were quite commonplace, and men, especially kings, were expected to perform these deeds when necessary.

Where did this evil begin? First within Macbeth. Next, it was reinforced by the witches. And then, by Lady Macbeth. Lady Macbeth is a tremendous influence on her husband. She goads him on, and Macbeth *chooses* to be influenced by her. Despite her influence, he is responsible for his actions. Like the witches, Lady Macbeth gives her husband an excuse for what he really wishes to do.

Macbeth says, "We will proceed no further in this business," but we are uncertain that he is not going through the motions of a change of mind to allow his wife to recharge his will to murder. She does just that, by questioning his manliness: "Art thou afeard to be the same in thine own act and valor as thou art in desire?"

The theme, the question of manliness, is here introduced by Lady Macbeth and becomes an underlying issue in the play. Macbeth wants to be a great man, but he must first, he feels, fulfill the stereotyped role of a "man." Macbeth finally "dares" to murder because he believes it is what a man would do. Throughout the play this idea is repeated: the murderers of Banquo introduce themselves, "We are men, my liege," and Macbeth asks them to "distinguish" themselves by murdering.

When Macbeth sees Banquo's ghost at the banquet table, Lady Macbeth accuses him of being "quite unmann'd in folly," implying that the mad are not manly. Macbeth talks to the ghost:

> What man dare, I dare
> Approach thou like the rugged Russian bear,
> The arm'd rhinoceros, or th' Hyrcan tiger;
> Take any shape but that and my nerves
> Shall never tremble. . . .
>
> (Act III, *Scene iv*)

When the ghost vanishes Macbeth, sane again, says ". . . I am a man again. . . ." Macbeth and his wife appear to believe that to be a man is to act bravely, to dare all, to be unafraid. They thus affirm the traditional "manly" virtues.

Lady Macbeth asks of the spirits: ". . . unsex me here,/And fill me, from the crown to the toe,/top-full Of direst cruelty! (Act I, *Scene v*) When Lady Macbeth is most firm in her resolve to continue the murders, Macbeth, in admiration, says, "Bring forth men-children only/For undaunted mettle should compose/Nothing but males. . . ." (Act I, *Scene viii*) Later on, she chides him further: "When you durst do it then you were a man;/And to be more than what you were, you would/Be so much more the man." (Act I, *Scene vii*)

To be a man, to Macbeth and Lady Macbeth, is to act decisively, bravely, to dare to do what must be done. A warrior definition of manhood such as theirs ignores morality. Their definition of a good king (a strong "man") is not the definition of a good person. Macbeth's dilemma may well be that he desires to be *both* a good person and a strong man and cannot be both. Goodness is important to Macbeth, but a good warrior king and a good person are made of different stuff; the former is not controlled by conscience, as is the latter.

Macbeth struggles to be a king and to be a good person, but he cannot. This inability to reconcile the two ideals is represented in his contradictory reaction to Duncan's murder cited earlier in this essay. The one idea "upsets" the other, as Macbeth recognizes from the beginning:

> My thought, whose murder yet is but fantastical,
> Shakes so my single state of man that function
> Is smother'd in surmise and nothing is
> But what is not.
>
> (Act I, *Scene iv*)

On the other hand, the corollary for woman, throughout the play, is weakness. If manhood is mindless action, womanhood is conscience-ridden weakness leading to inactivity. When Macbeth is most weak, most afraid, most guilty, he is accused of behavior that is like a woman's; when Lady Macbeth is tortured by her guilt and could, like Macbeth, "sleep no more," she recognizes her own reversion to womanliness. Shakespeare characterizes the person who acts ruthlessly as masculine. Which side of their nature, we must ask, undoes Lady Macbeth and Macbeth—the "masculine" or "feminine" side? Or is it their inability to be one or the other that causes them to fail? Perhaps they fail because they lack consistency, the courage to follow the course that they have set for themselves. Their scruples, their "feminine" scruples, undo them when they attempt action with misgiving, and their "masculine" actions provoke in them tremendous guilt.

The irony of Macbeth in the murderous act of becoming "unsexed," is that his "good and virtuous nature (does) recoil in an imperial charge," so that, while he may be both "masculine" and "feminine" in the sense that he and Lady Macbeth understand it, he is never a whole person.

Staging of Shakespeare's Plays

Shakespeare's plays were written for the Elizabethan theater building, which was very different from the modern one. First of all, it was small; the interior of *The Fortune* (built in 1600) was only 55 feet square. This gave an intimacy to the performance which is unattainable now except in arena stagings, and it made asides and soliloquies seem natural. The commercial theaters were open to the sky and the plays were presented by daylight, so that lighting effects were impossible. Costumes were often lavish, but scenery was practically nonexistent. As a result, lighting and scenery were often written into the speeches, in references to the sun, moon, and darkness, to forests, castles, and streams.

The main stage projected out into the theater and could not be concealed by a curtain; therefore a scene had to begin with entrances and close with exits. If bodies were left lying about—as frequently happened—someone had to be instructed to carry them off. This main stage served for open country, city streets and squares, and large rooms, but two other playing areas were also used. At the back of the main stage was a small space which could be closed with curtains. This inner stage was used for small rooms, shops opening on a street, a hovel on the heath (in *King Lear*), the tomb of the Capulets (in *Romeo and Juliet*), and other similar localities. Above it was the upper stage, which served as windows above the street (Juliet's balcony) and as a hilltop overlooking the battlefield (in *Julius Caesar*). Any information about the locale of a scene which the audience needed was worked into the dialogue.

The absence of scenery and the use of several playing areas meant that the action was unbroken. This gave a better illusion of reality and a greater sense of speed and concentration than could be achieved in a production constantly slowed down by installation or removal of elaborate "realistic" scenery. In recent years there has been an increasing tendency to stage Shakespearean plays more like the original productions. Not the least of the advantages of this practice is that the elimination of scene-shifting increases the time available for acting, and there is consequently no need for drastic cutting of the text.

Story and Plot Summary

Act I, Scene ii. Macbeth and Banquo have led the forces of Duncan, King of Scotland, in defeating a group of Scottish rebels under Macdonwald. Macbeth has personally slain the rebel Macdonwald and emerged victorious over a subsequent attack by the invading Norwegian king, who had been assisted by the traitorous Thane (Lord) of Cawdor, captured by Macbeth. Duncan has ordered the immediate execution of Cawdor and granted the Cawdor title to Macbeth.

Act I, Scene iv. When Duncan, the king, and his sons spend a night at Macbeth's castle, Macbeth and Lady Macbeth stab Duncan to death. Fearing that their lives are also in danger, Duncan's sons flee the country. The flight of Duncan's sons has put the suspicion of the murder on them, although Ross claims that their deed seems too unnatural. Macbeth has been named successor and has gone to Scone, the place of coronation of the Scottish kings, to be invested. The body of Duncan is being taken to the royal tombs at Colmekill. Macduff announces that he is not going to be present at the coronation, and he expresses the fear that conditions in Scotland may be worse under the new king.

Act III, Scenes v and vi. Macduff has gone to England where Malcolm has taken refuge with Edward the Confessor. In England, Macduff hopes to enlist the efforts of Siward, the Earl of Northumberland, to restore peace and security to Scotland. Macbeth, having heard of this development, is making some preparations for war.

Act IV, Scenes ii and iii. Macduff's over-impulsive and over-hasty flight has left his loved ones in danger. Before Lady Macduff and her son have time to flee, murderers sent by Macbeth arrive and slay them both. Macbeth's wanton crime causes revolt in Scotland and moves Malcolm and Macduff to immediate revenge.

Act V, Scene ii. Malcolm, Siward, and Macduff have led the English army into Scotland and have reached Birnam Wood. Menteith, Caithness, Angus, and Lennox have gathered their followers and are going to join Malcolm "To give obedience where 'tis truly owed." Meanwhile, Macbeth has taken up his position behind the impregnable walls of Dunsinane Castle. Rumor has him insane while others have called it valiant fury.

Act V, Scene viii. Macduff returns bearing Macbeth's head'upon a spear and hails Malcolm King of Scotland. All join in acclaiming the new king. Malcolm accepts the position, promising rewards for those that helped him and punishment for those who stood by Macbeth. He will recall from exile those who fled from Macbeth and his Queen, who it is said committed suicide. He ends his speech with an invitation to all to see him crowned at Scone.

Commentary on the Critique

In order to achieve his goals of becoming a king and maintaining this status, the hero/villain Macbeth undertakes actions that Matthew N. Proser terms as "manly" in his essay "The Manly Image."

Macbeth's manliness, his conscience, his security, and his physical power are according to Prosen the motivating factors to a destination that he knowingly willed for himself.

From *The Heroic Image In Five Shakespearean Tragedies*
by Matthew N. Proser

The Manly Image

The witches' prophecies, for whatever they are worth as actual prophecies, never suggest a means for obtaining the crown. The weird sisters do not even plant the seed of desire in Macbeth, but rather, their "All hail's," incantatory and enigmatic, act as an objectification of a desire already resident within Macbeth. Thus the guilty start at "things that do sound so fair" which Banquo remarks on the part of his companion.

Excerpts from Matthew N. Proser, THE HEROIC IMAGE IN FIVE SHAKESPEAREAN TRAGEDIES (copyright © 1965 by Princeton University Press): pp. 62–80. Reprinted by permission of Princeton University Press. All quotations from the texts of Shakespeare's plays are taken from Neilson and Hill's THE COMPLETE PLAYS AND POEMS OF WILLIAM SHAKESPEARE. Cambridge, Mass.: The Riverside Press of Houghton Mifflin Co., 1942.

But "manliness" demands action, direct, physical, and executed by soldier-hero himself. Action means everything, verifies everything that Macbeth must have verified. And in order for the seal of "valour" to be set, the necessary action must not only be carried out by Macbeth, it must be fully acknowledged by him. Without acknowledgment of responsibility on Macbeth's part, the act would fail to prove him worthy of the crown. Thus at moments in the play we get the distinct impression that Macbeth instead of being subject to fate is in reality wrenching it into a pattern of his own determination, forcing it to obey *his* will. . . .

After Duncan's murder the tone of *Macbeth* changes. There is a distinct hardening on the part of the hero chiefly attributable to the brutalization of Macbeth's soul caused by murder. But equally important is the suppression of prohibitive conscience which permitted the murder originally. In the succeeding portion of the play conscience ceases to function as an agent capable of preventing further crime; nor does it promote repentance. Instead we begin with a repression of conscience which in fact necessitates further violence. Conscience lives a ghostly life perverted to Macbeth's own uses: ". . . instead of acting directly in the form of remorse," it "comes to act through imaginary terrors, which in turn react on his conscience, as fire is made hotter by the current of air which itself generates." The memory of Duncan's murder, those "terrible dreams" that shake the hero nightly, must be wiped out. Macbeth would be like the dead king, whom "nothing can touch . . . further." But in order to achieve this state he must either die himself or destroy anything that reminds him of Duncan or seems to threaten the static and unfeeling position he seeks to attain.

Furthermore the hero stands in a new relation to time after the king has been dispatched. This new relationship helps intensify the hardening of Macbeth's character. Before the murder Macbeth could look upon his past with satisfaction, while the future, with its promise of kingship, opened out desirably before him. The limitation imposed by the witches—the prediction that Banquo's issue will ultimately reign, no son of Macbeth succeeding—though impressive to Macbeth, had not yet become an obsession. Now, however, the new king has a new future as well as a new past, and both cannot be countenanced. The past, like a "new gorgon" turning Macbeth's heart to stone, is matched by an equally horrifying possibility in the time to come: the accession of Banquo's children.

> Upon my head they plac'd a fruitless crown,
> And put a barren sceptre in my gripe . . . .
> (III.i.)

Thus Macbeth has placed himself in a position where in order to preserve his inner peace and his throne, he must annihilate both the past and the future. He is in a very real way confined by the present moment. He has to prevent his mind from moving backward and time from moving forward; he must prevent the events of the past from determining the future. Working against the natural force of time in this way, he finds himself constrained within his own human limitations, and the hardening process he suffers is the result of his agonizing and futile attempt to push out the walls of time on either side, to make his present state engulf the past and the future, to establish himself as a kind of unreflecting and "memory-less" eternity.

Because of these two factors, conscience and time, Macbeth is led once again to the frontiers of "manly" action as Lady Macbeth has defined it. Once Macbeth wears the crown, the fear of Banquo intensifies. Banquo becomes for Macbeth the frightening symbol of both the threat of the past (he may be suspicious of the circumstances surrounding Duncan's death) and the threat of the future. Action calls to the hero with a new insistence if he is to maintain his present state and throne. "To be thus is nothing,/ But to be safely thus. . . ." (III.i)

In addition, Macbeth's desire for security is related to at least one other matter of significance besides the simple preservation of his throne. His "security" is also connected with the preservation of his sense of himself—of his "manhood." Banquo, says Macbeth, possesses (as Duncan did) "a royalty of nature" and "wisdom that doth guide his valour to act in safety." Those fears of Macbeth which stick deep in Banquo are conceived, then, in terms of "valor," and to a degree Macbeth sees himself in competition with his friend. The threat of the crown is thus established as a threat also to the hero's conception of himself as "valorous" and "dauntless." Macbeth, it would seem, like Marc Antony, must be the "foremost man."

> My genius is rebuk'd, as, it is said,
> Mark Anthony's was by Caesar.
> (III.i.)

Thus the idea of safety is presented in two important ways: once in regard to Macbeth's security and once in connection with the quality of Banquo's wisdom and valor. The conflict between the two kinds of manliness is working here. Brute strength and daring confront once again physical power united with justice: "wisdom" and "a royalty of nature." But in this scene conscience expresses itself merely in Macbeth's attempt to establish a rationale for his projected murder and an "alibi." This effort to prepare an "alibi" is perhaps the more characteristic where the habitual workings of the hero's mind are concerned. Macbeth employs several murderers to kill Banquo, and, in this way, tries to dissociate himself from the deed itself as much as he can, indeed more than he was wont before the murder of Duncan. Once more he attempts to will responsibility for the deed to a force outside himself; yet this time he goes one step further—he assigns the deed to his emissaries instead of using his own hands, and subsequently makes them rather than himself tools of the destroying night. It is a case of murder twice removed:

> Come, seeling night,
> Scarf up the tender eye of pitiful day,
> And with the bloody and invisible hand
> Cancel and tear to pieces that great bond
> Which keeps me pale! Light thickens, and the crow
> Makes wing to th' rooky wood;
> Good things of day begin to droop and drowse,
> Whiles night's black agents to their preys do rouse.
> (III.ii.)

This attempt at dissociation is revealed in Macbeth's almost immediate response to the appearance of Banquo's ghost in the great banquet scene: "Thou canst not say I did it; never shake/Thy gory locks at me." (III.iv.)

Apparently Banquo cannot accuse Macbeth of murdering him because Macbeth was not at the scene of the crime; the king hires the murderers to kill Banquo, as Muir says, "not for money, but out of hatred, so that they can share some part of the guilt, so that he can cry 'thou canst not say I did it,' and Macbeth's absence at the scene of the murder in this light further substantiates his guiltlessness. Once again Macbeth has tried to hide from the world and himself behind an objective force with which he seemingly has no connection. . . .

In the banquet scene in which Banquo's ghost appears, here, for the first time conscience does not manifest itself merely as a horrid image in Macbeth's mind. Although the rest of the company, including Lady Macbeth, does not see the ghost, Macbeth does and so do we. Its objective presence is clearly indicated by Shakespeare's stage directions. This, of course, may be explained as simply an example of the theatrical conventions of the day, i.e., by employing an objective ghost Shakespeare was acquiescing to popular tastes which demanded supernatural sensationalism. Nevertheless, the effect of the ghost's objective reality upon the audience perhaps supercedes theatrical conventions and the fact that others at the banquet do not see it. For the truth is that we do not doubt its reality any more than we do that of Caesar's spirit, or any other spirit in Shakespeare for that matter. And what is important about this ghost is our ability for the first time to see by means of it the results of Macbeth's evil confronting him as a creature disjoined from himself. . . .

With the death of Banquo and the subsequent appearance of his ghost, Macduff's function in the drama begins to assume new proportions. In Macbeth's mind, Macduff's failure to appear at the banquet suddenly connects itself with Banquo's unexpected and revealing (in every sense of the word) attendance. By not appearing at the banquet, Macduff becomes a "substitute" for Banquo. He acts as Macbeth had expected Banquo would. But with Macduff the failure becomes ominous. Macbeth shores up his courage and focuses upon Macduff as a new object of "action"—a surrogate for Banquo. To such an extent has Macbeth bedeviled himself into suppression of memory and conscience that action, resolute and bloody, has become an automatic response to anyone or anything that even appears a threat. It is as if Banquo's ghostly and terrible appearance had revealed too much for Macbeth ever to look back without losing the sense of identity he must preserve in order to retain a crown which has never really been his.

Objectives

After studying Macbeth, you, the student, should be able to do the following:

1. Recognize the relationship between Elizabethan drama and the attitude toward order in 16th Century England.
2. Identify how Shakespeare contributed to theatre craft through the development of conventions in dramatic structure, characterization, language, and staging.
3. Understand why *Macbeth* is an excellent example of Shakespearean tragedy, capturing the conflict between universal forces and the will of man.

Program Notes

Macbeth

The BBC production of the familiar Shakespearean tragedy focuses on the relationship between Macbeth and Lady Macbeth. The viewer follows the choices, the doubts, and the ambitions leading to murder which result in even more crime. The minidocumentary accompanying the BBC production emphasizes the pace of these tragic events and the rich and varied language. All of the scenes between Macbeth and Lady Macbeth are shown, most of them fairly complete; and Act II, Scene 2 has no cuts. The murder of Lady Macduff, the "English" scene, and the various "choric comment" scenes, such as that between Ross and the Old Man, as well as the accession of Malcolm at the end were omitted. Minor characters were cut and the battle scenes were telescoped. The excerpt included here is from the script.

MACBETH

by

William Shakespeare

Act I—Scene i (Three witches—deserted heath)

1ST WITCH When shall we three meet again?
    In thunder, lightning, or in rain?
2ND WITCH When the hurlyburly's done,
    When the battle's lost and won.
3RD WITCH That will be ere the set of sun.
1ST WITCH Where the place?
2ND WITCH Upon the heath.
3RD WITCH There to meet with Macbeth.

    • • •

ALL Fair is foul, and foul is fair:
    Hover through the fog and filthy air.

Act I—Scene iii (A Heath—Enter MACBETH *and* BANQUO*)*

MACBETH So foul and fair a day I have not seen.
BANQUO How far is't call'd to Forres?
    What are these?
    So wither'd, and so wild in their attire,
    That look not like th' inhabitants o' the earth,
    And yet are on't? Live you, or are you aught
    That man can question?
MACBETH . . . Speak, if you can: What are you?
1ST WITCH All hail, Macbeth! hail to thee, thane of Glamis!
2ND WITCH All hail, Macbeth! hail to thee, thane of Cawdor!
3RD WITCH All hail, Macbeth! that shalt be King hereafter.
BANQUO Good Sir, why do you start, and seem to fear

    • • •

Things that do sound so fair? My noble partner

    • • •

You greet with present grace; to me you speak not.

    • • •

1ST WITCH Hail!
2ND WITCH Hail!
3RD WITCH Hail!
1ST WITCH Lesser than Macbeth, and greater.
2ND WITCH Not so happy, yet much happier.
3RD WITCH Thou shalt get kings, though thou be none;
    So all hail, Macbeth and Banquo!

1ST WITCH Banquo and Macbeth, all hail!
MACBETH Stay, you imperfect speakers, tell me more.
   The Thane of Cawdor lives
   A prosperous gentlemen; and to be King
   Stands not within the prospect of belief,
      • • •
   Speak I charge you.
   Witches vanish.
BANQUO The earth hath bubbles, as the water has,
   and these are of them. Whither are they vanish'd?
MACBETH Into the air: and what seem's corporal melted.
   As breath into the wind. Would they had stay'd!
      • • •
   Your children shall be kings.
      • • •
BANQUO You shall be king.
MACBETH And Thane of Cawdor too.
   Went it not so?
BANQUO To the selfsame tune, and words. Who's here?

(Enter ROSS *and* ANGUS*)*

ROSS The King hath happily receiv'd, Macbeth
      • • •
   The news of thy success; As thick as tale
   Came post with post; and every one did bear
   Thy praises in his kingdom's great defense.
      • • •
ANGUS We are sent,
   To give thee, from our royal master, thanks.
ROSS . . . And, for an earnest of a greater honour,
   He bade me, from him, call thee Thane of Cawdor.
BANQUO . . . What! can the devil speak true?
MACBETH The Thane of Cawdor lives: why do you dress me
   In borrow'd robes?
ANGUS Who was the Thane lives yet
      • • •
   But treasons capital, confess'd and prov'd,
   Have overthrown him.
MACBETH *(aside)* Glamis, and Thane of Cawdor.
   The greatest is behind. *(To* ROSS *and* ANGUS*)* Thanks
   for your pains.

  (To BANQUO*)* Do you not hope your children shall be kings,
  When those that gave the Thane of Cawdor to me
  Promis'd no less to them?
BANQUO That, trusted home,
  Might yet enkindle you unto the crown,
  Besides the Thane of Cawdor
   • • •
  Cousins, a word, I pray you.
MACBETH *(aside)* Two truths are told,
  As happy prologues to the swelling act
  Of the imperial theme I thank you, gentlemen
  (aside) This supernatural soliciting
  Cannot be ill, cannot be good if ill,
  Why hath it given me earnest of success.
  Commencing with a truth? I am Thane of Cawdor;
  If good, why do I yield to that suggestion
  Whose horrid image doth unfix my hair,
  And make my seated heart knock at my ribs,
  Against the use of nature? . . .
BANQUO Look, how our partner's rapt.
MACBETH *(aside)* If chance will have me
  King, why, chance may crown me,
  Without my stir.
   • • •
BANQUO Worthy Macbeth, we stay upon your leisure.
MACBETH Give me your favour . . . Let us toward the King.

*Act I—Scene iv (***Forres***—a room in the palace)*

  Present: Duncan, Malcolm, Donalbain, Lennox, Lord and two Ladies
   • • •
DUNCAN O worthiest cousin! . . . Welcome hither:
  I have begun to plant thee, and will labour
  To make thee full of growing. Noble Banquo
  Thou hast no less deserv'd.
   • • •
  Sons, kinsmen, thanes,
   • • •
  We will establish our estate upon
  Our eldest, Malcolm, whom we name hereafter . . .
  The Prince of Cumberland: Now we shall to Inverness
  and bind us further to you.

MACBETH I'll be myself the harbinger, and make joyful
   The hearing of my wife with your approach;
   So, humbly take my leave.
DUNCAN My worthy Cawdor!
MACBETH *(aside)* The Prince of Cumberland! That is a step
   On which I must fall down, or else o'erleap,
   For in my way it lies. Stars, hide your fires!
   Let not light see my black and deep desires. . . .
DUNCAN It is a peerless kinsman.

*Act I—Scene v (***Inverness***—a room in* MACBETH'S *castle)*

*(*LADY MACBETH, *reading a letter from* MACBETH *by window)*

LADY M. ". . . When I burned in desire to question them further, they made themselves air, into which they vanished. Whiles I stood rapt in the wonder of it, came missives from the King, who all hailed me, 'Thane of Cawdor'; by which title, before, these weird sisters saluted me, . . . with 'Hail, King that shalt be.' This have I thought good to deliver thee, my dearest partner of greatness. . . . Lay it to thy heart, and farewell."
   Glamis thou art, and Cawdor, and shalt be
   What thou art promis'd. Yet do I fear they nature:
   It is too full o' the milk of human kindness,
   To catch the nearest way. Thou wouldst be great;
   Art not without ambition, but without
   The illness as should attend it. What thou wouldst highly,
   That wouldst thou holily; wouldst not play false,
   And yet wouldst wrongly win
      • • •

(Enter a MESSENGER*)*
   What is your tidings?
MESSENGER The king comes here tonight.
LADY M. Thou'rt mad to say it.
   Is not thy master with him? who, were't so,
   Would have informed for preparation?
MESSENGER So please you, it is true: our Thane is coming!
   One of my fellows had the speed of him
      • • •

LADY M. Give him tending:
   He brings great news.
(Exit MESSENGER*)*
   The raven himself is hoarse.
   That croaks the fatal entrance of Duncan
   Under my battlements. Come, you spirits
   That tend on mortal thoughts, unsex me here,

And fill me, from the crown to the toe, top-full
Of direst cruelty! make thick my blood,
Stop up th' access and passage to remorse,
That no compunctious visitings of nature
Shake my fell purpose, not keep peace between
Th' effect and it! Come to my woman's breasts,
And take my milk for gall, you murdering ministers,
Wherever in your sightless substances
You wait on nature's mischief! Come, thick night,
And pall thee in th' dunnest smoke of hell,
That my keen knife see not the wound it makes . . .

• • •

(Enter MACBETH*)*

*(*LADY MACBETH *rises)*

Great Glamis! worthy Cawdor!
Greater than both, by the all-hail hereafter!

• • •

MACBETH My dearest love,
Duncan comes here to-night.
LADY M. And when goes hence?
MACBETH To-morrow, as he purposes.
LADY M. O! never
Shall sun that morrow see! . . . He tha's coming
Must be provided for; and you shall put
This night's great business into my dispatch . . .
MACBETH We will speak further.
LADY M. Only look up clear;
To alter favour ever is to fear.
Leave all the rest to me.
(Exit)

Act I—Scene vi (**Inverness**—*courtyard* MACBETH'S *castle*)

(Enter—DUNCAN, MALCOLM, DONALBAIN, BANQUO, LENNOX, MACDUFF, ROSS AND ATTENDANTS*)*

DUNCAN This castle hath a pleasant seat: the air
Nimbly and sweetly recommends itself
Unto our gentle senses

• • •

(Enter LADY MACBETH*)*
See, See! our honour'd hostess.

• • •

LADY M. All our service,
In every point twice done and then done double,

> Were poor and single business to contend
> Against those honours deep and broad wherewith
> Your majesty loads our house . . .
>
> • • •

DUNCAN Give me your hand.
> Conduct me to mine host; we love him highly,
> and shall continue our graces towards him.
> By your leave, hostess.

(Exit)

Act I—Scene vii (Corridor leading from banquet chamber)
> Music and chatter.
> Servants pass carrying food into Banqueting Chamber.

*(*MACBETH *enters from banquet.)*

MACBETH If it were done when 'tis done, then 'twere well
> It were done quickly, If the assassination
> Could trammel up the consequence and catch
> With his surcease success; that but this blow
> Might be the be-all and the end-all here,
> But here, upon this bank and shoal of time,
> We'd jump the life to come. But in these cases,
> We still have judgment here; that we but teach
> Bloody instructions, which, being taught, return
> To plague th' inventor; this even-handed justice doth
> Commend th' ingredients of our poison'd chalice
> To our own lips. He's here in double trust:
> First, as I am his kinsman and his subject,
> Strong both against the deed; then, as his host
> Who should against his murderer shut the door,
> Not bear the knife myself. Besides, this Duncan
> Hath borne his faculties so meek, hath been
> So clear in his great office, that his virtues
> Will plead like angels, trumpet-tongued against
> The deep damnation of his taking-off;
> And pity, like a naked new-born babe,
> Striding the blast, or heaven's cherubin, hors'd
> On the sightless couriers of the air.
> Shall blow the horrid deed in every eye,
> That tears shall drown the wind. I have no spur
> To prick the sides of my intent, but only
> Vaulting ambition, which o'erleaps itself
> And falls on the other.
> (*Enter* LADY MACBETH)
> How now! What news?

LADY M. He has almost supp'd.
   Why have you left the chamber?
MACBETH Hath he sent for me?
LADY M. Know you not, he has?
MACBETH We will proceed no further in this business;
   He hath honour'd me of late, and I have bought
   Golden opinions from all sorts of people,
   Which should be worn now in their newest gloss,
   Not cast aside so soon . . .
LADY M. From this time
   Such I account thy love. Art thou afeard
   To be the same in thine own act and valour
   As thou art in desire? Wouldst thou have that
   Which thou esteem'st the ornament of life,
   And live a coward in thine own esteem?

   • • •

MACBETH Pr'ythee, peace!
   I dare do all that may become a man;
   Who dares do more, is none.
LADY M. What beast was't then,
   That made you break this enterprise to me?
   When you durst do it, then you were a man:
   And to be more than what you were, you would
   Be so much more the man. Nor time, nor place,
   Did then adhere, and yet you would make both:
   They have made themselves, and that their fitness now
   Does unmake you. I have given suck, and know
   How tender 'tis to love the babe that milks me:
   I would, while it was smiling in my face,
   Have pluck'd my nipple from his boneless gums,
   And dash'd the brains out, had I so sworn as you
   Have done to this.
MACBETH If we should fail.
LADY M. We fail!
   But screw your courage to the sticking-place,
   And we'll not fail. When Duncan is asleep—
   Whereto the rather shall his day's hard journey
   Soundly invite him—his two chamberlains
   Will I with wine and wassail so convince,
   That memory, the warder of the brain,
   Shall be a fume, and the receipt of reason
   A limebeck only: when in swinish sleep
   Their drenched natures lie as in a death,

> What cannot you and I perform upon
> Th' unguarded Duncan, What not put upon
> His spongy officers, who shall bear the guilt
> Of our great quell?

(MACBETH *embraces* LADY MACBETH)

MACBETH Bring forth men-children only!
> For thy undaunted mettle should compose

• • •

> Nothing but males I am settled, and bend up
> Each corporal agent to this terrible feat.
> Away, and mock the time with fairest show:
> False face must hide what the false heart doth know.

(Exit) (End of Act I)

Act II—Scene i (a) (*Courtyard within the castle*)

• • •

(Enter BANQUO *with torch through door)*

BANQUO Who's there?

(Enter MACBETH *and* SERVANT *with* FLAMBEAU*)*

MACBETH A friend.
BANQUO What Sir! Not yet at rest? The king's a-bed;

• • •

> This diamond he greets your wife withal,
> By the name of most kind hostess

• • •

> I dreamt last night of the three weird sisters.
> To you they have show'd some truth.

MACBETH I think not of them.

• • •

> Good repose, the while!

BANQUO Thanks, Sir: the like to you. *(Exit* BANQUO*)*
MACBETH Go, bid thy mistress, when my drink is ready,
> She strike upon the bell. Get thee to bed.

(Exit SERVANT*)*

*(*MACBETH *goes through door to castle)*

MACBETH Is this a dagger, which I see before me,
> The handle towards my hand? Come, let me clutch thee.
> I have thee not, and yet I see thee still.
> Art thou not, fatal vision, sensible
> To feeling, as to sight? or art thou but

A dagger of the mind, a false creation,
Proceeding from the heat-oppressed brain?
I see thee yet, in form as palpable
As this which now I draw.

• • •

I see thee still;
And on thy blade and dudgeon, gouts of blood,
Which was not so before. There's no such thing.
It is the bloody business which informs

• • •

Thus to mine eyes Whiles I threat, he lives;
Words to the heat of deeds too cold breath gives.

(A bell rings)

I go, and it is done: the bell invites me.
Hear it not, Duncan: for it is a knell
Which summons thee to heaven, or to hell.

Act II—Scene ii (Corridors outside DUNCAN'S bedchamber)

(Enter LADY MACBETH*)*

LADY M. That which hath made them drunk hath made me bold:
What hath quench'd them hath given me fire. Hark! Peace!
It was the owl that shriek'd, the fatal bellman,
Which gives the stern'st good-night. He is about it.
The doors are open; and the surfeited grooms
Do mock their charge with snores. I have drugg'd their possets.
That death and nature do contend about them,
Whether they live, or die.

MACBETH *(Within)* Who's there? What, ho!

LADY M. Alack! I am afraid they have awak'd,
And 'tis not done! the attempt and not the deed
confounds us.—Hark!—I laid their daggers ready;
He could not miss them. Had he not resembled
My father as he slept, I had done't.

(Enter MACBETH*)*

My husband!

MACBETH I have done the deed. Didst thou not hear a noise?

LADY M. I heard the owl scream, and the crickets cry.
Did not you speak?

MACBETH When?

LADY M. Now.

MACBETH As I descended?

LADY M. Ay.

MACBETH Hark!
       Who lies i' the second chamber?
LADY M. Donalbain.
MACBETH This is a sorry sight.

• • •

LADY M. There's one did laugh in 's sleep, and one cried "Murder!"
       That they did wake each other. I stood and heard them:
       But they did say their prayers, and address'd them
       Again to sleep.
LADY M. There are two lodg'd together.
MACBETH One cried, "God bless us!" and, "Amen," the other,
       As they had seen me with these hangman's hands.
       Listening their fears, I could not say, "Amen,"
       When they did say, "God bless us!"
LADY M. Consider it not so deeply.

(Turning)

MACBETH But wherefore could not I pronounce "Amen?"
       I had most need of blessing, and "Amen"
       Stuck in my throat.
LADY M. These deeds must not be thought
       After these ways; so, it will make us mad.
MACBETH Methought, I heard a voice cry "Sleep no more!"
       Macbeth does murder sleep—the innocent sleep,
       Sleep, that knits up the ravell'd sleave of care,
       The death of each day's life, sore labour's bath,
       Balm of hurt minds, great nature's second course,
       Chief nourisher in life's feast. . . .

(LADY M. *moves close to* MACBETH)

LADY M. What do you mean?
MACBETH Still it cried, "Sleep no more" to all the house.
       "Glamis hath murder'd sleep, and therefore Cawdor
       Shall sleep no more: Macbeth shall sleep no more!"
LADY M. Who was it that thus cried? Why, worthy Thane,
       You do unbend your noble strength, to think
       So brainsickly of things. Go, get some water.
       And wash this filthy witness from your hand.
       Why did you bring these daggers from the place?
       They must lie there. Go carry them, and smear
       The sleepy grooms with blood.
MACBETH I'll go no more.
       I am afraid to think what I have done;
       Look on't again I dare not.

LADY M. Infirm of purpose!
  Give me the daggers. The sleeping and the dead,
  Are but as pictures; 'Tis the eye of childhood
  That fears a painted devil. If he do bleed,
  I'll gild the faces of the grooms withal,
  For it must seem their guilt.

(Exit LADY MACBETH*) (knocking heard)*

MACBETH Whence is that knocking?
  How is't with me, when every noise appalls me?
  What hands are here? Ha! They pluck out mine eyes.
  Will all great Neptune's ocean wash this blood
  Clean from my hand? No, this my hand will rather
  The multitudinous seas incarnadine,
  Making the green one red.

(Re-enter LADY MACBETH*)*

LADY M. My hands are of your colour, but I shame
  To wear a heart so white. *(knock)* I hear a knocking
  At the south entry. Retire we to our chamber
  A little water clears us of this deed:
  How easy is it then! Your constancy
  Hath left you unattended. *(knock)* Hark! more knocking.
  Get on your night-gown, lest occasion call us,
  And show us to be watchers. Be not lost
  So poorly in your thoughts.

(Exit LADY MACBETH*)*

MACBETH To know my deed, 'twere best not know myself.
(KNOCK) Wake Duncan with thy knocking! I would thou couldst!

Act II—Scene iii (a) (Courtyard of castle)

(Enter PORTER—*knocking within)*

PORTER Here's a knocking, indeed! *(*PORTER *comes out of shadow)*
  If a man were porter of hell-gate, he should have old turning
  the key.

(Knocking)
  Knock, knock, knock! Who's there,
  i' the name of Belzebub? Knock, knock. Never at quiet!
  Who's there, i' the other devil's name? But this place is too
  cold for hell. I'll devil-porter it no longer

(Knocking)
  Anon, anon!

• • •

(LENNOX, MACDUFF and PORTER re-enter)

MACDUFF Is thy master stirring?
　　Our knocking has awak'd him: here he comes . . .
LENNOX Good morrow, noble Sir!
MACBETH Good morrow, both!

(Walks forward of group)

MACDUFF Is the king stirring, worthy Thane?
MACBETH Not yet.
MACDUFF He did command me to call timely on him:
　　I have almost slipp'd the hour.

　　• • •

MACBETH *(turns)* I'll bring you to him. This is the door.
MACDUFF I'll make so bold to call,
　　For 'tis my limited service.
(Exit MACDUFF)
LENNOX Goes the king hence today?
MACBETH He does. He did appoint so.
LENNOX The night has been unruly: where we lay,
　　Our chimneys were blown down, and, as they say,
　　Lamentings heard i' the air; strange screams of death,
　　And prophesying with accents terrible
　　Of dire combustion, and confus'd events,
　　New hatch'd to the woeful time.

　　• • •

MACBETH 'Twas a rough night.

　　• • •

(Re-enter MACDUFF)
MACDUFF O horror! horror! horror! Tongue nor heart
　　Cannot conveive nor name thee!
MACBETH, LENNOX What's the matter?

　　• • •

MACDUFF Most sacrilegious murder hath broke open
　　The Lord's anointed temple, and stole thence
　　The life i' the building!
MACBETH What is't you say? The life?
LENNOX Mean you his majesty?

　　• • •

MACDUFF Approach the chamber. Do not bid me speak.

　　• • •

　　Awake! Awake!—

(Exit MACBETH *and* LENNOX*)*
　　Ring the alarum-bell. Murder and treason!
　　Banquo and Donalbain! Malcolm! Awake!
　　Shake off this downy sleep, death's counterfeit,
　　And look on death itself! Up, up, and see
　　The great doom's image! Malcolm! Banquo!
(Bell rings) (Enter LADY MACBETH*)*
LADY M.　What's the business,
　　That such a hideous trumpet calls to parley
　　The sleepers of the house? Speak, speak!
MACDUFF　O gentle lady,
　　'Tis not for you to hear what I can speak.

　　　• • •

(Enter BANQUO*)*
　　O Banquo! Banquo!
　　Our royal master's murder'd.
LADY M.　Woe alas!
　　What! in our house?
BANQUO　Too cruel, anywhere.

　　　• • •

(Re-enter MACBETH, LENNOX, MALCOLM *and* DONALBAIN*)*
DONAL.　What is amiss?
MACBETH　You are, and do not know't.

　　　• • •

MACDUFF　Your royal father's murder'd.
MALCOLM　O! by whom?
LENNOX　Those of his chamber, as it seem'd had done't.
　　Their hands and faces were all badg'd with blood;

　　　• • •

MACBETH　O! yet I do repent me of my fury.
　　That I did kill them.
MACDUFF　Wherefore did you so?
MACBETH　Who can be wise, amaz'd, temperate and furious,
　　Loyal and neutral . . . No man . . . Here lay Duncan,
　　His silver skin lac'd with his golden blood,
　　And his gash'd stabs look'd like a breach in nature
　　For ruin's wasteful entrance. There, the murderers,
　　Steep'd in the colours of their trade, their daggers
　　Unmannerly breech'd with gore. Who could refrain?

　　　• • •

LADY M.　Help me hence, ho!

MACDUFF Let us meet
 And question this most bloody piece of work,
 To know it further.
  • • •
MACBETH Let's briefly put on manly readiness,
 And meet i' the hall together.
ALL Well contented.
(Exit all but MALCOLM *and* DONALBAIN*)*
MALCOLM What will you do? Let's not consort with them;
  • • •
 I'll to England.
DONAL. To Ireland I.
  • • •
MALCOLM Then let us not be dainty of leave-taking,
 But shift away . . .

Act III—Scene i (The throne-room of the palace of Fores)

(MACBETH *and* LADY MACBETH *enter throne room as king and queen*)

BANQUO Thou hast it now, king, Cawdor, Glamis, all
 As the weird women promis'd, and, I fear
 Thou play'dst most foully for't: yet it was said,
 It should not stand in thy posterity,
 But that myself should be the root and father
 Of many kings. If there come truth from them
  • • •
 May they not be my oracles as well
 And set me up in hope? But hush, no more!
MACBETH Here's our chief guest.
  • • •
 Tonight we hold a solemn supper, sir,
 And I'll request your presence.
BANQUO Let your highness command upon me.
  • • •
MACBETH Fail not our feast.
BANQUO My Lord, I will not.
  • • •
(Court dismissed)

MACBETH To be thus is nothing, But to be safely thus.
 Our fears in Banquo stick deep,

And in his royalty of nature reigns that
Which would be fear'd.

• • •

There's none but he
Whose being I do fear . . . He chid the sisters,

• • •

and bade them speak to him; then prophet-like
They hail'd him father to a line of kings.
Upon my head they plac'd a fruitless crown
And put a barren sceptre in my gripe,

• • •

No son of mine succeeding. If't be so,
For Banquo's issue have I fil'd my mind;
For them the gracious Duncan have I murder'd;

• • •

To make them kings, the seeds of Banquo kings!

• • •

(*Enter* MURDERERS)

• • •

Both of you know, Banquo was your enemy.
1ST MURDERER *True, my lord.*

• • •

2ND MURDERER *We shall, my lord,*
Perform what you command us.

• • •

(*Exit* MURDERERS)
MACBETH It is concluded: Banquo thy soul's flight,
If it find heaven, must find it out to-night.

Act III—Scene ii (Bedchamber in the palace)

• • •

(LADY MACBETH *sitting on bed*)
LADY M. Nought's had, all's spent,
Where our desire is got without content.

• • •

(*Enter* MACBETH)
How now, my lord! why do you keep alone

• • •

Things without all remedy
Should be without regard: what's done is done.
MACBETH We have scorch'd the snake, not kill'd it.

• • •

But let the frame of things disjoint, both the worlds suffer.
Ere we will eat our meal in fear, and sleep
In the affliction of these terrible dreams
That shake us nightly: better be with the dead,
Whom we, to gain our peace, have sent to peace,
Than on the torture of the mind to lie
In restless ecstasy.

• • •

LADY M. Come on.
Gentle my lord, sleek o'er your rugged looks;
Be bright and jovial among your guests to-night . . .
MACBETH Be innocent of the knowledge, dearest chuck, . . .
Till thou applaud the deed . . . Light thickens, and the crow
Makes wing to the rocky wood;
Good things of day begin to droop and drowse,
Whiles night's black agents to their preys do rouse.
Thou marvell'st at my words. but hold thee still;
Things bad begun make strong themselves by ill.

• • •

Act III—Scene iii (A Park)
(Enter BANQUO *with torch)*

• • •

BANQUO It will be rain to-night.
1ST MURDERER Let it come down.

(Assaults BANQUO*)*

BANQUO O treachery! . . . O slave!

*(*BANQUO *dies)*

• • •

Act III—Scene iv (A room of state in the palace—banquet provided)

(MACBETH *standing by fire. Servants filling his glass with wine)* *(Present:* LADY MACBETH/ROSS/LENNOX/LORDS/ATTENDANTS*)*

MACBETH You know your own degrees, sit down: at first and last, the hearty welcome.
LORDS Thanks to your majesty.

• • •

MACBETH Both sides are even: here I'll sit i' the midst.

· · ·

(Sees MURDERER. *Goes to him)*

There's blood upon thy face.
MURDERER 'Tis Banquo's then.
MACBETH 'Tis better thee without, than he within
Is he dispatch'd?
MURDERER My lord, his throat is cut; that I did for him.
MACBETH Thou are the best o' the cut-throats.

· · ·

LADY M. My royal lord,
You do not give the cheer:

· · ·

(Exit MURDERER*)* *(*BANQUO *enters . . . sits as ghost)*

Now good digestion wait on appetite.

· · ·

And health on both!

· · ·

ALL Your Majesty
LENNOX May it please your highness sit?

· · ·

MACBETH The table's full.
LENNOX Here my good lord

*(*BANQUO *turns)*

What is't that moves your highness?
MACBETH Which of you have done this?
LORDS What, my good lord?

*(*BANQUO *gets up)*

MACBETH Thou canst not say, I did it; never shake
Thy gory locks at me.
ROSS Gentlemen, rise: his highness is not well.
LADY M. Sit, worthy friends. My lord is often thus,
And hath been from his youth: pray you, keep seat;
He will again be well . . . Are you a man?
MACBETH Ay, and a bold one, that dares look on that
Which might appal the devil.
LADY M. O proper stuff! This is the very painting of your fear.

· · ·

Why do you make such faces? When all's done,
You look but on a stool *(LADY M. crosses)*

MACBETH Pr'ythee, see there! Behold! Look! Lo! How say
you?

• • •

LADY M. What! quite unmann'd in folly?

• • •

MACBETH Avaunt! and quit my sight! let the earth hid thee!
Thy bones are marrowless, thy blood is cold,
Thou hast no speculation in those eyes,
Which thou dost glare with.

LADY M. Think of this, good peers,
But as a thing of custom. . . .

MACBETH Hence, horrible shadow! Unreal mockery, hence! . . .

(Ghost disappears)

LADY M. You have displaced the mirth, broke the good meeting
With most admir'd disorder.

• • •

ROSS My lord.

LADY M. I pray you, speak not: he grows worse and worse.
Question enrages him. At once, good night;
—Stand not upon the order of your going,
But go at once.

LENNOX Good night, and better health
Attend his majesty!

LADY M. A kind good night to all!

(Exit LORDS *and* ATTENDANTS*)*

MACBETH It will have blood, they say: blood will have blood.

• • •

What is the night?

LADY M. Almost at odds with morning, which is which.

• • •

MACBETH I will . . . tomorrow . . . to the weird sisters:
More shall they speak; for now I am bent to know,
By the worst means, the worst . . . I am in blood
Stepp'd in so far that, should I wade no more,
Returning were as tedious as go o'er.

LADY M. You lack the season of all natures, sleep.

MACBETH Come, we'll to sleep.

• • •

We are yet but young in deed.

Act IV—Scene i (Three witches)

   • • •

1ST WITCH Double, double toil and trouble:
  Fire, burn and cauldron bubble.
2ND WITCH Fillet of a fenny snake,
  In the cauldron boil and bake;

   • • •

3RD WITCH Finger of birth-strangled babe,
  Ditch-deliver'd by a drab,
  Make the gruel thick and slab.

   • • •

2ND WITCH Cool it with a baboon's blood;
  Then the charm is firm and good.

   • • •

  By the pricking of my thumbs
  Something wicked this way comes.

   • • •

MACBETH How now, you secret, black and midnight hags!
  What is't you do?
ALL A deed without a name.
MACBETH I conjure you, by that which you profess,
  Howe'er you come to know it, answer me.

   • • •

1ST WITCH Speak.
2ND WITCH Demand.
3RD WITCH We'll answer.

(THUNDER—1ST APPARITION, *an armed head*)

   • • •

1ST APP. Macbeth! Macbeth! beware Macduff; Beware
  the Thane of Fife. Dismiss me. Enough.

   • • •

MACBETH Thou hast harp'd my fear aright—
  But one word more.
1ST WITCH He will not be commanded.

   • • •

(THUNDER—2ND APPARITION, *a bloody child*)

   • • •

2ND APP. Be bloody, bold and resolute: laugh to scorn
  The power of man, for none of woman born
  Shall harm Macbeth.

MACBETH Then live, Macduff: what need I fear of thee?
But yet I'll make assurance double sure,
And take a bond of fate. Thou shalt not live.

• • •

(THUNDER—3RD APPARITION, *statue of child crowned*)
3RD APP. Macbeth shall never vanquish'd be until
Great Birnam wood to high Dunsinane Hill
Shall come against him.
MACBETH That will never be:

• • •

Macbeth shall live the lease of nature, pay his breath
To time, and mortal custom. Yet my heart
Throbs to know one thing. Tell me, if your art
Can tell so much: shall Banquo's issue ever
Reign in this kingdom?
ALL Seek to know no more.

• • •

(Enter LENNOX*)*

MACBETH Infected be the air whereon they ride;
And damned all those that trust them! O, approach!
I did hear the galloping of horse: who was't came by?
LENNOX 'Tis two or three, my lord, that bring you word,
Macduff is fled to England.
MACBETH Fled to England?
LENNOX Ay, my good Lord.
MACBETH (aside) Time, thou anticipat'st my dread exploits:

• • •

The castle of Macduff I will surprise;
Seize upon Fife; give to the edge o' the sword
His wife, his babes, and all unfortunate souls
Who trace him in his line. No boasting like a fool;
This deed I'll do, before this purpose cool.

• • •

Act IV—Scene iii (England)

MACDUFF, ROSS, MALCOLM

• • •

MACDUFF My children too?
ROSS Wife, children, servants.
MACDUFF My wife kill'd too?
ROSS I have said.

• • •

MACDUFF Front to front,
   Bring thou this fiend of Scotland and myself;
   Within my sword's length set him. If he 'scape
   Heaven forgive him too!
MALCOLM Come to the English king. Our power is ready;
   Our lack is nothing but our leave. Macbeth
   Is ripe for shaking.
   . . .

(Exit)

Act V—*Scene i* (Dunsinane—bedchamber)

(Enter DOCTOR *and* GENTLEWOMAN*)*
   . . .

DOCTOR In this slumbery agitation, . . . what at any time, did you
   hear her say?
GENTL. That, Sir, which I will not report after her.
(Enter LADY MACBETH*)*
   . . .
   This is her very guise, and, upon my life, fast asleep!
   . . .

DOCTOR How came she by that light?
GENTL. Why, it stood by her. She has light by her continually.
   'Tis her command.
   . . .

LADY M. Out, damned spot! Out I say. One, two: why, then
   'tis time to do't. Hell is murky. Fie, my lord, fie! A
   soldier, and afeard? What need we fear who knows it, when none
   can call our power to account? Yet who would have thought the
   old man to have so much blood in him?
DOCTOR Do you mark that?
LADY M. The Thane of Fife had a wife. Where is she now? What,
   will these hands ne'er be clean? No more o' that, my lord,
   no more o' that! You mar all with this starting.
DOCTOR Go to, go to! You have known what you should not.
   . . .

LADY M. Here's the smell of the blood still. All the perfumes
   of Arabia will not sweeten this little hand. Oh. oh. oh!
   . . .

DOCTOR This disease is beyond my practice:
   . . .

LADY M. Wash your hands; put on your night-gown; look not so
pale! I tell you yet again, Banquo's buried. He cannot come
out on's grave.
DOCTOR Even so?
LADY M. To bed, to bed! There's knocking at the gate. Come,
come, come, come, give me your hand! What's done cannot be
undone. To bed, to bed, to bed!

(Exit)

• • •

DOCTOR God forgive us all.

• • •

Act V—Scene iii (Dunsinane—banqueting hall)

Enter MACBETH, DOCTOR, SERVANT, *and* ATTENDANTS

• • •

MACBETH The devil damn thee black, thou cream-fac'd loon!

• • •

What soldiers, patch?

• • •

SERVANT The English force, so please you.
MACBETH Take thy face hence.

(Exit SERVANT*)*

• • •

I have liv'd long enough. My way of life
Is fall'n into the sear, the yellow leaf,
And that which should accompany old age,
As honour, love, obedience, troops of friends,
I must not look to have; but, in their stead,
Curses not loud but deep, mouth-honour, breath,

• • •

How does your patient, doctor?
DOCTOR No so sick, my lord,
As she is troubled with thick-coming fancies
That keep her from her rest.
MACBETH Cure her of that:
Cans't thou not minister to a mind diseas'ed,
Pluck from the memory a rooted sorrow,
Raze out the written troubles of the brain,
And with some sweet oblivious antidote
Cleanse the stuff'd bosom of that perilous stuff
Which weighs upon the heart?

DOCTOR   Therein the patient
        Must minister to himself.
MACBETH   Throw physic to the dogs: I'll none of it.
        Come, put mine armour on. Give me my staff.

      • • •

        I will not be afraid of death and bane,
        Till Birnam forest come to Dunsinane.

      • • •

Act V—Scene iv (A wood)

MACDUFF, MALCOLM, ROSS, LENNOX
MALCOLM   What wood is this before us?
ROSS   The wood of Birnam.
MALCOLM   Let every soldier hew him down a bough,
        and bear't before him. Thereby shall we shadow
        The numbers of our host.

      • • •

LENNOX   The confident tyrant keeps still in Dunsinane.

      • • •

MALCOLM   'Tis his main hope,

      • • •

        And none serve with him but constrained things;
        Whose hearts are absent too.
ROSS   Advance the war!

(Exit marching)

Act V—Scene v (Dunsinane, within the castle)

(MACBETH and SOLDIER)

      • • •

MACBETH   Our castle's strength
        Will laugh a siege to scorn . . . (A CRY WITHIN)

      • • •

MACBETH   Wherefore was that cry?
DOCTOR   The Queen, my lord, is dead.
MACBETH   She should have died hereafter;
        There would have been a time for such a word.
        Tomorrow, and tomorrow, and tomorrow,
        Creeps in this petty pace from day to day,
        To the last syllable of recorded time;
        And all our yesterdays have lighted fools
        The way to dusty death. Out, out, brief candle!

> Life's but a walking shadow, a poor player,
> That struts and frets his hour upon the stage,
> And then is heard no more; it is a tale
> Told by an idiot, full of sound and fury
> Signifying nothing.

(Enter a MESSENGER*)*

> Thou com'st to use thy tongue; thy story quickly.

• • •

MESSENGER As I did stand my watch upon the hill,
> I look'd toward Birnam, and anon, methought,
> The wood began to move.

MACBETH Liar and slave!

• • •

MESSENGER Within this three mile may you see it coming;
> I say, a moving grove.

MACBETH If thou speak'st false.
> Upon the next tree shalt thou hang alive.

• • •

> I pull in resolution; and begin
> To doubt the equivocation of the fiend
> That lies like truth: "Fear not, till Birnam Wood
> Do come to Dunsinane!" And now a wood
> Comes toward Dunsinane. Arm, arm, and out!

• • •

> Ring the alarum-bell! Blow wind, come wrack!
> At least we'll die with harness on our back.

Act V—Scene vi (A plain before the castle)

*(*MALCOLM *and* MACDUFF*)*

MALCOLM Now, near enough. Your leavy screens throw down,
> And show like those you are.

• • •

Act V—Scene vii (Interior castle—throne room)

(Enter MACBETH*)*

MACBETH They have tied me to a stake; I cannot fly,
> But bear-like I must fight the course. What's he
> That was not born of woman? Such a one
> Am I to fear, or none.

• • •

(They fight and the lord is slain.)

Act V—Scene viii

(Enter MACDUFF *and* SOLDIERS *in* ARCHES*)*

MACDUFF Turn, hell-hound, turn!

MACBETH Of all men else I have avoided thee;
  But get thee back! My soul is too much charg'd
  With blood of thine already.

MACDUFF I have no words:
  My voice is in my sword, thou bloodier villain
  Than terms can give thee out!

(They fight)

MACBETH Thou losest labour,

  • • •

  Let fall thy blade on vulnerable crests;
  I bear a charmed life, which must not yield
  To one of woman born.

MACDUFF Despair thy charm,
  And let the angel whom thou still hast serv'd
  Tell thee, Macduff was from his mother's womb
  Untimely ripp'd.

MACBETH Accursed be that tongue that tells me so.

  • • •

  I'll not fight with thee.

MACDUFF Then yield thee, coward.

  • • •

MACBETH I will not yield,
  To kiss the ground before young Malcolm's feet,
  And to be baited with rabble's curse,
  Though Birnam Wood be come to Dunsinane,
  And thou oppos'd, being of no woman born,
  Yet I will try the last . . . Lay on Macduff;
  And damn'd be him that first cries: "Hold, enough!"

A Listing of BBC Actors and Production Coordinators

MACBETH

by

William Shakespeare

CAST

MACBETH	CORIN REDGRAVE
LADY MACBETH	ANN BELL
DUNCAN	RICHARD BEALE
BANQUO	JOHN GOLIGHTLY
MACDUFF	MARK PENFOLD
LENNOX	ANTHONY GARDNER
ROSS	JOHN LAWRENCE
WITCHES	AIMEE DELAMAIN
	HOPE JACKMAN
	SUSAN THOMAS
THE PORTER	ERIK CHITTY
THE DOCTOR	ARTHUR HEWLETT
THE GENTLEWOMAN	HOPE JACKMAN
MALCOLM	MICHAEL MUNDELL
DONALBAIN	STUART DOUGHTY
MURDERERS	RICHARD BEALE
	DAVID CORDON
SERVANT/MESSENGER	DAVID CORDON
LORDS/LADIES	BILL WHITEHEAD
ATTENDANTS	LYNNE PRESTON
	CAROL WALKER-SMITH
	STUART DOUGHTY

SOLDIERS .... ALAN SIMMONDS
KEITH SIMMONDS

PRODUCTION

SET DESIGN .... GEORGE WISNER
COSTUME DESIGNER .... BRIAN COX
MAKE-UP SUPERVISOR .... MAGGIE WEBB
DIRECTOR .... PAUL KAFNO

Witches

Macbeth and Lady Macbeth

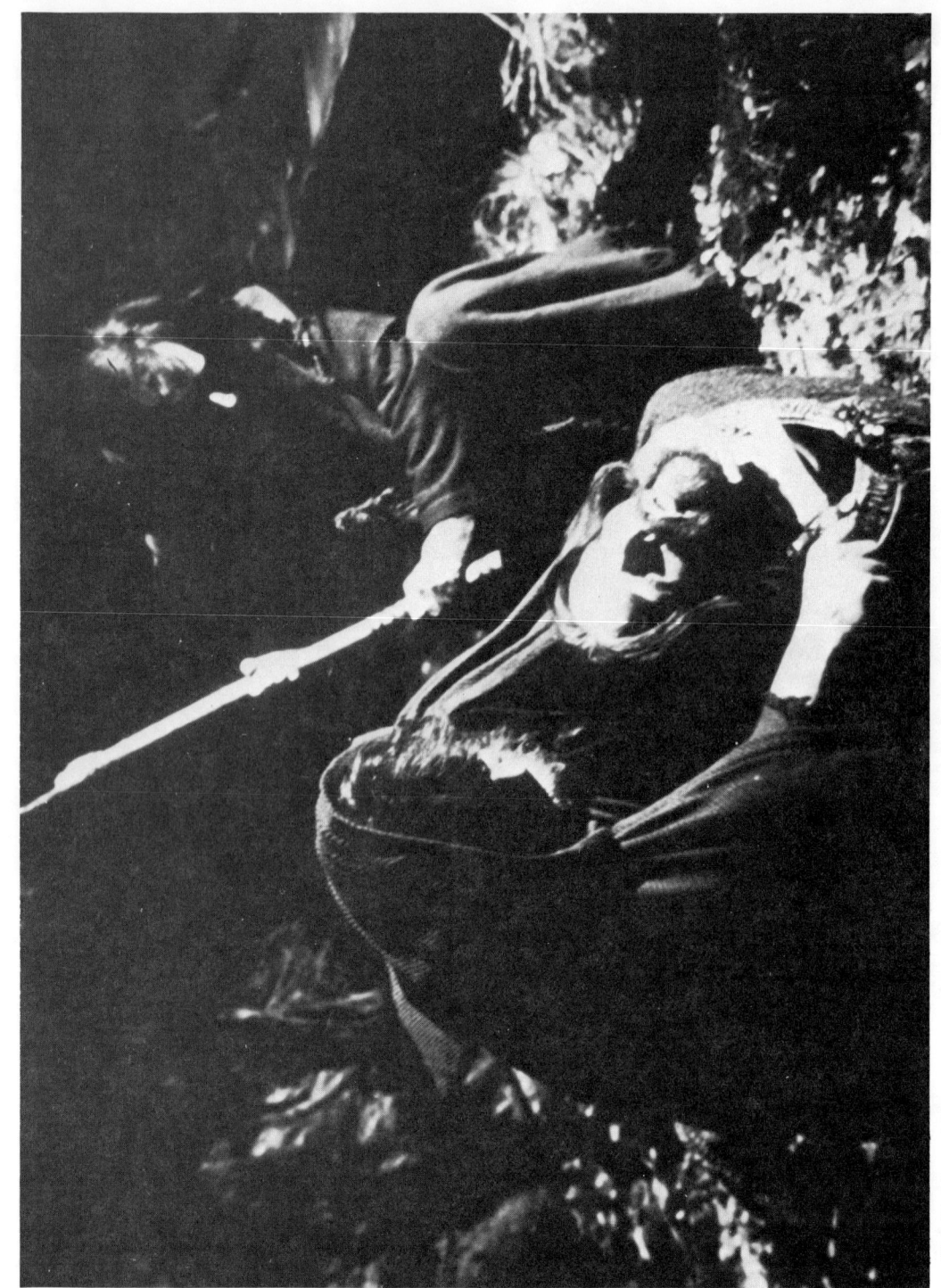

The Murder of Banquo

Director's Notes

On Character Interpretation

Every director recreates a play in his own image. So I should begin by confessing that I find *Macbeth* the most chillingly real of all Shakespeare's tragedies. I have no difficulty in imagining Macbeth and Lady Macbeth inhabiting the same world as myself.

So my starting point was that this is a play about two people. However monstrous their actions might be, they must never be allowed to become monsters. I wanted them to be young people, because I felt that youth highlights the moral dilemmas that confront them. A middle-aged Macbeth is necessarily a more cynical figure, and I felt that this weakens the play.

Faced with the inevitable restraints of time, I decided that our version would concentrate almost entirely on the two main characters. This meant reducing various lords to virtual cyphers. I don't feel especially guilty about this. Shakespeare does not seem to have had much interest in the other characters apart from Banquo. I hoped that condensing the play like this would present the rise and fall of the tragic hero as a developing experience of great intensity.

Special Effects and Character Interpretation

I put great store by the contribution lighting could make. *Macbeth* is a play which takes place almost entirely in cold northern castles from which light is excluded. Much of the action of the play takes place at night, and there are countless references to night and blackness in the text. We tried to recreate this dark night of the soul by using minimum lighting, and employing burning flambeaux to give an authentic effect of flickering flames.

There is, I believe, no area of the play which presents more difficulties than the witches scenes. Modern audiences do not believe in witchcraft, and many directors have strained all intelligibility by finding them new and ever more devious forms of wickedness. I believe myself that the most frightening aspects of the play lie in the characters of Macbeth and Lady Macbeth, and that true impact must lie there. The supernatural scenes are wonderful colour pieces, containing some very fine poetry, but the heart of the play is elsewhere.

Banquo's ghost. To appear or not to appear? A debate of long-standing among directors. I chose to show the ghost because I think the scene makes more sense like that on television. If I were directing the play in the theatre, I might well decide not to. The important thing is to sense Macbeth's terror, and the effect it has on Lady Macbeth.

'Macbeth' has the reputation of being an unlucky play. I am quite sure that this has a great deal to do with the number of special and dangerous effects required. Apart from simulated murders, battles, thunder and lightning, the play culminates in a fight with heavy broad-swords which are very much more dangerous than for example, the epees used at the end of 'Hamlet.' On the last day of rehearsal Corin Redgrave was rehearsing the fight with Mark Penfold. Swords clashed and a broken blade went spinning through the air. Miraculously the blade landed in our midst, missing us by inches. The fates, who play so mischievously with Macbeth were, this once, in our favour.

Paul Kafno
20th February 1976

Focus in Viewing

This production of *Macbeth* concentrates on the language in interpreting the chief parts of the play. Shakespeare's verse dialogue is spoken rapidly without slow, brooding concentration on meaning. Television techniques enhance the imaginative introspection of the characters and provide the close contact between the actor and audience which was a prized quality of the Elizabethan theatre. The audio and visual close-up achieves a focus on the performance and performers so that no subtlety of whispered tone or nuance of even the slightest gesture is missed.

Content Viewing

1. What do you think was Macbeth's most important decision?
2. Compare and contrast Macbeth to Oedipus.
3. How is Macbeth and Lady Macbeth's philosophy different from that of the people in *The Ghost Sonata*?
4. What part does "truth" play in Macbeth's life?

Craft Viewing

1. Compare the actress' portrayal of Lady Macbeth's most distraught moment to that of Oedipus' (actor's) portrayal.
2. Based on your viewing, and your reading of the plot summary, do you recognize a plot structure? If so, what is it?
3. Do you agree, or disagree, with the characterization or interpretation of Macbeth? Was the actor consistent, honest, convincing, clear? Were you sympathetic, unsympathetic, or neutral to him as portrayed?
4. Do you think the technical design and executive supported the playscript and the stageplay? Discuss. (Be sure to mention supernatural effects.)
5. To what extent are the witches emphasized in this production, and do they set the atmosphere for the play?
6. Is there one moment or scene which stands out in your memory? More than one? Which ones? Why?

Critical Viewing: Overview

Now that this play and its production are part of your experience, what significance does *Macbeth* hold for you?

Additional Plays That Demonstrate Similar Concepts

Hamlet, Othello, King Lear—Shakespeare
Medea—Euripides
Agamemnon—Aeschylus
The Visit—Friedrich Duerrenmatt

Stage Terms

Blank Verse—Unrhymed iambic pentameter; the poetic form employed by Shakespeare, as in "Is this a dagger which I see before me?"; it is important to remember that Shakespeare was so much master of the blank verse that an actor's emotional delivery of his lines was not inhibited by the regularity of the rhythm; example is *Macbeth*.

Elizabethan Dialogue—Sets the stage for action by giving the time and place of events.

Soliloquy—A speech delivered by an actor directly to the audience in which he objectifies his thoughts; a convention of the Elizabethan theater, given its greatest treatment by Shakespeare.

WOYZECK

by

Georg Buchner
(1813–1837)

A. Play Notes, p. 179
    1. The Factual Background, p. 179
    2. Interpretations for Staging, p. 179
        (a) *Woyzeck* as a Political Statement, p. 179
        (b) *Woyzeck* as a Psychological Study, p. 179
        (c) Structure in *Woyzeck*, p. 180
        (d) *Woyzeck* as a Hero, p. 180

B. Story and Plot Summary, p. 180
C. Commentary: A Brief Summary of a Review, p. 181
D. Review of *Woyzeck*, p. 182
E. Objectives, p. 182
F. Program Notes, p. 183
G. A List of BBC Actors and Production Coordinators, p. 184
H. Director's Notes, p. 188
    1. Information on the Playwright, p. 188
    2. Performances of Buchner's Work, p. 188
    3. Discussion of Various Interpretations of *Woyzeck*, p. 188
    4. BBC Director's Interpretation, p. 188
I. Focus in Viewing, p. 189
J. Additional Plays That Demonstrate Similar Concepts, p. 190
K. Stage Terms, p. 190

Play Notes

The Factual Background

Woyzeck is a play based on an actual incident. In 1821, an ex-soldier, working as a barber, murdered his mistress. The man's name was Johann Christian Woyzeck, 41. His mistress was a widow who had other lovers during the two years she and Woyzeck were together. In a jealous rage, Woyzeck stabbed her with a knife he had bought that day. He then made no effort to escape sentencing; rather, he seemed to welcome execution. His lawyer, however, insisted that Woyzeck should not be convicted of murder, by reason of insanity. At the trial it was brought out that the accused had suffered from hallucinations and a persecution complex. The judge remained unconvinced, and Woyzeck was executed in 1824. Controversy over the execution continued, reflecting the public's increasing interest in the nature of the human mind.

A Marxist revolutionary student, Georg Buchner, was interested in Woyzeck's case because Woyzeck represented the oppressed man. Buchner's father, a physician, had medical records on Woyzeck which further stimulated Buchner's interest in him. However, before Buchner could begin a play on Woyzeck, he was forced to free his native land, Germany, because of his political activism. (He had distributed a tract similar to the *Communist Manifesto*.)

Buchner wrote three plays, two in exile: *Woyzeck* and *Danton's Death*. Both plays are considered "naturalistic works" by critics and deal with the problems that result from class differences. Some critics see *Danton's Death,* a play about a disillusioned activist, as Buchner's greatest work. Others (Jose Ferrer, included) see *Woyzeck,* a play about a downtrodden man who's manipulated by everyone around him, as Buchner's masterpiece, because Buchner died before completing *Woyzeck,* it is difficult to say what the playwright's main intent was. Directors, therefore, are somewhat free to interpret the play as they choose, emphasizing a viewpoint that most closely parallels their interest.

Interpretations for Staging

Woyzeck as a Political Statement

If *Woyzeck* were given a political interpretation by a director sympathetic to revolutionary causes, the production would stress the oppression of Woyzeck by those in more powerful social positions. The actor interpreting the main role would appear as the victim of his exploiters; by the same token, those making demands on him—the Captain, the Doctor, the Drum Major—would be shown as villains, mocking their prey. This melodramatic technique would cause the audience to side with Woyzeck, the underdog, and whatever cause he represents.

Standard revolutionary drama suggests that social conditions can improve. As written, *Woyzeck,* however, does not offer earthly hope. There is in the script talk of the Bible, but not of political action. In the written play the only hint of a desire for social reform occurs when Woyzeck tells the Captain that morality is a luxury for the truly poor. For the play to become a political statement, actors, costumes, props, and lighting would have to be directed to this end.

Woyzeck as a Psychological Study

Through a different interpretation, *Woyzeck* could become the study of the psychological aberrations of a twisted mind attempting to comprehend a healthy society. The burden of communicating such an interpretation would be placed upon the actor playing the title role. To convince the audience of the character's insanity and prepare it for irrational responses, the actor, playing Woyzeck, might effect a fixed stare, slurred speech, jerky movements, and an inability to focus on anything. Emphasis would be placed on Woyzeck's reactions rather than social conditions that might provoke them.

Structure in Woyzeck

Because of its unusual structure, *Woyzeck* does not require innovative interpretations to give it character. The structure—a series of vignettes—marks a break with the conventional method for telling a story in the theatre. The play, a mosaic, allows for little development of character, but instead provides a forum for philosophical questions that are not provoked when one reads a plot summary. One such question the fragmented scenes prod us to ask, is "What is the definition of humanity?" (Who is human in the play—the uniformed Captain, the Drum Major, the Doctor Scientist, the unnatural animals, or Woyzeck?) This question raises another question about heroes. How can Woyzeck be viewed as a hero?

Woyzeck as a Hero

The answer to the preceding question may be found in Herbert Lindenberger's work, *Georg Buchner*. Lindenberger writes:

> Buchner does not idealize their [that is, the low class characters'] naturalness in any conventionally Rousseauistic way. . . . His (Woyzeck's) strains of insanity, though Buchner attempts no direct diagnosis, could almost be interpreted as an involuntary immersion in a private world in response to the "unnatural oppression from without."

Lindenberger suggests that Woyzeck's reactions are normally abnormal when one views him as the product of an abnormal environment. In other words, Buchner suggests that Woyzeck is what is to be expected; he is natural, and being natural in an unnatural environment is as close as one can get to heroism.

Story and Plot Summary

The use of the narrator's voice to announce time and place not only sets the stage for the opening action and introduces other scenes, it also deliberately "distances" the spectator from the action by reminding us that this is a story. It was a device used by other playwrights, particularly Bertolt Brecht, in order to prevent audiences from being lulled into the illusion that they were watching a replay of reality. The playwright must have audiences that remain aware of historical perspective and do not identify with any one character so that an overview is lost. The viewer who forgets this reminder and "cannot see the forest for the trees" is apt to reject a play for the wrong reasons, seeing the characters as presented as "correct" spokespeople for all ages. Through the distancing technique of a narrator, it is possible to see Woyzeck as the product of an age rather than as a role model. Similarly, Marie's behavior is spontaneous and "true" for someone in her situation, rather than an indictment of women as weak and unable to control their passions. Nor is the presentation of superstitions and prejudices (the pawnbroker, for instance) meant to be accepted uncritically as an endorsement of such beliefs for our own time. Being alert to the placement of characters within an historical context is vital to prevent misunderstanding. It is difficult for most viewers to see the larger picture, far more tempting to applaud one character and thus justify all his actions. For example, Woyzeck's speech about the difficulty of being poor might well enlist an audience's sympathy thus blurring its ability to distinguish between what is caused by social pressures and what is the individual's fault.

Woyzeck's fears were whispered to his friend Andres as they cut wood for the Captain. He believes in the special power of "Freemasons," and anti-church faction of which the playwright's father was a member. He tells Marie of his fear that something terrible will happen. Marie remarks on his strange behavior.

At the fair, during a display of "unnatural" animals able to do human things, Marie attracts the attention of a Drum Major. Later, she looks in the mirror at a shiny pair of earrings, wondering if they are gold. She sings a lullaby to her baby. Woyzeck, seeing the earrings, accuses her of being a whore. Marie tells him she found the earrings. After he leaves, she admits to herself that Woyzeck was right. She has been unfaithful to him.

As Woyzeck shaves the Captain, he works nervously and too fast. The Captain teases him, reminding him that the time saved won't matter. The Captain speaks of eternity, the weather, and decency—all matters of no concern to Woyzeck, who is working to survive. For him, abstractions are unnecessary.

In a scene on the street the Drum Major boasts that his uniform adds to his qualities as a man. He tells Marie that she is a real woman, a possible breeder for other drum majors. They wrestle briefly, then Marie gives in. The doctor, trusting science, urges Woyzeck to give a urine sample for his research project. Woyzeck replies that he cannot always control this. The doctor says he does not believe in anger and, therefore, is in control of his emotions. As a man who tries to be rational, he does not understand Woyzeck's ravings. The Doctor then diagnoses The Captain as being seriously ill, but assures him that his case is "interesting." The Captain insults the Doctor and then suggests to Woyzeck that he has been cuckolded by Marie. Woyzeck reacts with emotion at the thought of his wife's betrayal, and the Doctor takes his pulse. Both men insult Woyzeck who does not defend himself. Rushing away without the pay he would receive as a subject for research, Woyzeck confronts Marie. He is determined to stab Marie. His friend Andres urges him to try to get some sleep. The Doctor continues to be interested in Woyzeck as a physical phenomenon, from whose body the effects of eating peas may be determined.

Marie, feeling guilty, recalls Mary Magdelene and tries to pray. Woyzeck, unable to afford a gun, purchases a knife from a pawnbroker. Back at the barracks, he gives his few possessions to Andres. He announces his name, rank, and age, as written on an Army document. It is as if he is summing up his life for his epitaph. Then he takes Marie out on a pier over the river, and stabs her. Woyzeck goes to the tavern, where the blood on his hands is incriminating. He runs back to the pier, looks for the knife, and talks to the dead Marie.

In the last scene of this production Woyzeck kneels behind his sleeping child. Other versions include Woyzeck's arrest for murder.

Commentary

In the critique that follows, Edith Oliver points out that the dramatic irony of *Woyzeck* has been reduced to muddled experimentation. She recognizes the talent of Joseph Chaikin but finds little else in the play worthy of comment.

New Yorker April 5, 1976

Off Broadway—Woyzeck, Sort of

The production of Georg Buchner's "Woyzeck," at the Public, is, if little else, the occasion for the re-emergence of that extraordinary actor Joseph Chaikin in a role peculiarly suited to his talent. Woyzeck is a poor soldier in the early-nineteenth-century German Army who is used and put upon by everybody except one fellow-soldier and is finally betrayed by the wanton woman he loves, the mother of his illegitimate son. He is tragic, rather than just pathetic, because he is passionate and shrewd as well as inarticulate, and the passion finally explodes into murder. He stabs the woman to death, and the play ends with a hangman preparing the noose for his execution. Mr. Chaikin plays the part with eloquence, most of that eloquence being physical. He walks with an odd, shambling gait, like a puppet. His face, most of the time, is numb and expressionless and his eyes nearly unfocussed; suddenly they blaze with overwhelming feeling—hurt or anger. He shuffles along and then abruptly stops, sensing a movement in the earth beneath him or seeing a vision of blazing light in the sky. All of the character is in every muscle of his body, and when he speaks, he speaks to a purpose. None of his lines go to waste.

The play, which was found among Buchner's papers in 1837, after his death, at the age of twenty-three, is a series of disconnected scenes, each of them as simple and clear as a pane of glass. Their cumulative effect should be devastating. But this performance is elaborate and glum and muddled and entirely lacking in the dramatist's irony; it is also poorly acted by almost everyone in the company. Woyzeck's only moments of overt physical passion are his embraces with his soldier comrade, for which there is no justification in the script. The poor soul is in enough trouble without homosexual implications. The production, under Leonardo Shapiro's direction, is experimental, and I'm all for experiments, win or lose, but after seeing Mr. Shapiro's "Ghosts" I wish he'd lay off literature for a bit. "Woyzeck," as we have been somewhat overtold, is the precursor of any number of current theatrical movements—Brechtian alienation, existentialism, Beckethan pessimism, the theatre of the absurd, social realism, expressionism, and other college-seminar categories. (I use the word "current" with little conviction, since all these dramatic elements have been around for well over two thousand years; it is just the terminology that is current.) By the way, Mr. Chaikin's Woyzeck reminded me of a smoldering Petrouchka, and in an early scene when he explains to his captain that virtue and morality are privileges of the rich, denied to the poor, we could be, in a sense, listening to Alfred Doolittle talking to Professor Higgins, but without Shaw's humor or relish or high spirits. So it goes.

Edith Oliver

Objectives

You, the student, should have a better understanding of Georg Buchner's craft and creativity in the context of 19th Century playwrighting by learning to

1. recognize Buchner's distinction as a playwright who was vastly ahead of his time and who utilized a surprisingly innovative style.

Reprinted by permission; © 1976 The New Yorker Magazine, Inc.

2. identify several of Buchner's significant contributions to content and craft in theatre.
3. describe the elements of plot, characterization, and language that typify Buchner's "natural hero."
4. view *Woyzeck* as a tragedy that also offers humor and compassion in its treatment of the natural man.
5. recognize how *Woyzeck* lends itself to a number of directorial interpretations.

Program Notes

Woyzeck

When Georg Buchner wrote *Woyzeck,* in 1837, he included a number of innovations: the nature of his "hero," a poor, untutored worker; the structure of his play, deliberately episodic; the victimizers, a captain, a physician, a carnival barker, sketched as occupations rather than well-developed characters; songs and soliloquies, and an ambiguous ending.

In the television production, the log-gathering scene is placed first, where Buchner put it in all the versions of the manuscript. The play has been shortened for television by the omission of the first barracks scene, the second tavern scene (between the Drum Major and Woyzeck), and the story-telling scene. Other detailed changes have been made in the performance version, notably the use of the Showman/Barker (the two characters are combined) as Narrator throughout the play, and the replacement and alteration of many of the songs.

Dramatis Personae

A Listing of BBC Actors and Productions Coordinators

WOYZECK

by

Georg Buchner

CAST

NARRATOR/SHOWMAN	DAVID WOOD
ANDRES	COLIN FARRELL
FRANZ WOYZECK	DAVID COLLINGS
MARIE	CYD HAYMAN
MARGRET	OLWEN GRIFFITHS
OLD MAN/2ND MAN	SYDNEY ARNOLD
DRUM MAJOR	DAVID CALDER
SERGEANT/JFW	MICHAEL DA COSTA
CAPTAIN	JOHN BRYANS
DOCTOR	PETER COPELY
1ST MAN	ALLAN MCCLELLAND
GRANNY	BETTY HARDY
KATHE	SUSIE BLAKE
LANDLORD	CYRIL TAWNEY

PRODUCTION

COSTUME DESIGNER	BRIAN COX
MAKE-UP SUPERVISOR	MONICA LUDKIN
SET DESIGN	DAVID HITCHCOCK
DIRECTOR	JOHN SELWYN GILBERT

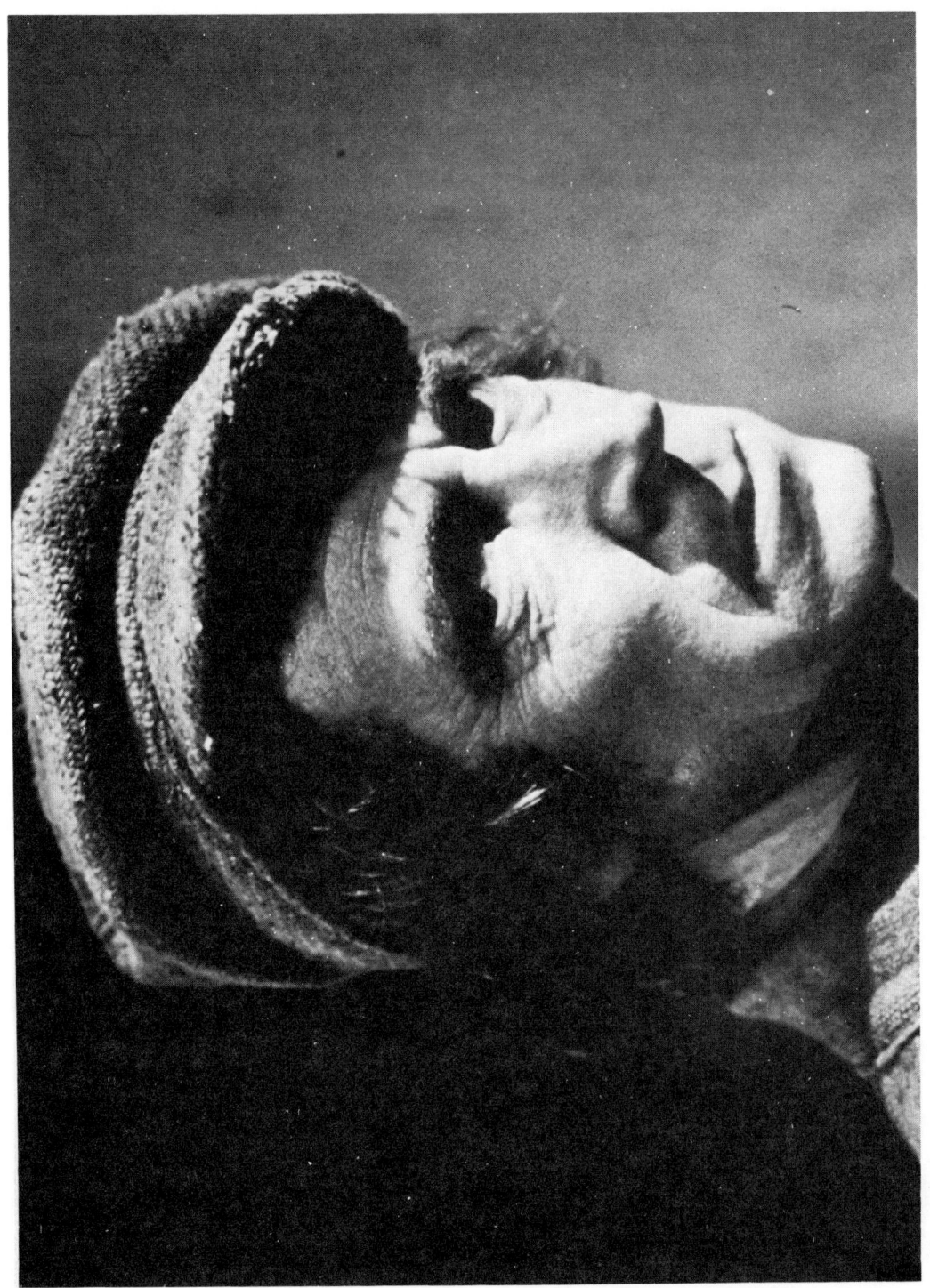

Woyzeck

Woyzek and Marie

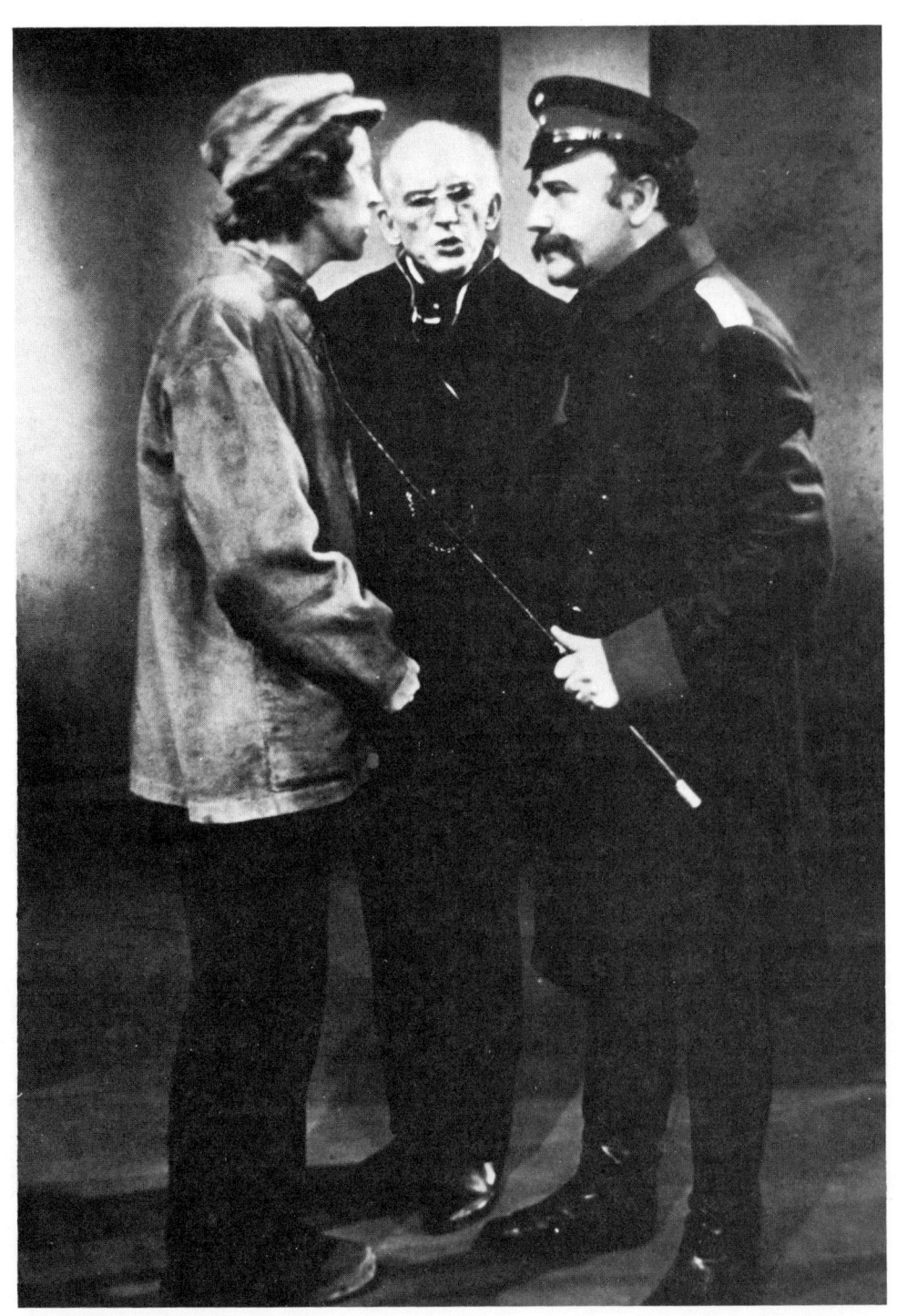

Woyzeck, Doctor and Captain

Director's Notes

Information on the Playwright

Georg Buchner was not principally a dramatist. He never saw or heard a scene that he wrote performed by an actor, and there seems to be no concrete evidence that he was ever able to visit a theatre. His three plays ('Danton's Death,' Leonce and Lena,' and 'Woyzeck') are the product of an enormous natural talent which was given almost no chance to develop in a normal way. Buchner was only 23 when he died of typhus in February 1837 and he left 'Woyzeck' apparently unfinished—in fragments.

Performances of Buchner's Work

Sixty years after Buchner's death, his works began to be performed. Karl Emil Franzos published a complete edition of the plays and pamphlets in 1879 and, despite its substantial inaccuracies, this pioneering critical study gave Frank Wadekind's generation the opportunity to recognise Buchner as a forerunner and admit him as an influence.

At the beginning of the twentieth century, after productions by Leopold Jessner and Max Reinhardt, Buchner also became an influence on Bertolt Brecht and his contemporaries. In 1925, Alban Berg created an opera based on the narrative of Buchner's play.

Discussion of Varying Interpretations of *Woyzeck*

Because Buchner was a political activist (and also because of the dramatists and directors who have taken an interest in him), the social and political content of his plays is generally emphasized. 'Woyzeck' has been described as "the first working class tragedy," and Ingmar Bergman, who produced it for the theatre in Stockholm in 1969, presented it in just this light. "Aiming at a complete 'democratisation' of the theatre," writes Victor Price, "Bergman closed the dress circle and gallery and turned the stalls into an arena, the actors coming and going through a passage, as in a circus. All the seats were cheap, and none was reserved. A chorus of soldiers . . . served to link actors and public, and the fact that they wore Swedish uniforms of the pre-war period emphasised the contemporary nature of the play."

The social elements in 'Woyzeck,' although powerful, are not the only important features of the play. As well as being a political activist, Buchner was a doctor and a teacher of anatomy and philosophy. He specialised in the anatomy of the nervous system of a common fish.

BBC Director's Interpretation

He was also, we must remember, a relatively untutored and inexperienced playwright, and this, of all his plays, is the only one left in an incomplete and fragmentary form. If there are several distinct strands in the text of 'Woyzeck,' this should not surprise us. Perhaps Buchner himself had not finally decided on the emphasis which he desired the play to have.

Buchner's information about the historical Woyzeck (a real soldier/barber executed for the murder of his common law wife in 1824) came from an account in a journal by the medical examiner who had certified the man as sane enough to stand trial.

There was, at the time, a great deal of disagreement about whether the medical examiner had been right, but in the play, it is quite clear that Woyzeck is not to be blamed for his actions, he is to be pitied. Woyzeck's actions and delusions are the product of insanity. Buchner shows in him all the symptoms of schizophrenia, in broadly accurate clinical terms.

So Woyzeck is not simply persecuted into mania by the grotesque representatives of an exploitative society who oppresses and bullies him. From the first moments of the first scene that Buchner wrote, Woyzeck is a sick man.

This does not necessarily increase our sympathy for him. It is much easier to sympathise with the needlessly oppressed than with the mad. It is, in fact, society's failure to recognise Woyzeck's insanity that Buchner is criticising, and he is also, several generations before Freud, both describing and analysing the world in terms which relate to Freud's symbolism. "Woyzeck, you are always in such a hurry," says the Captain, "You'd think that you were going to shave a regiment of geldings, and they were going to hang you with the last hair."

Buchner's play is a play in embryo, perhaps a masterpiece in embryo rather than a complete blueprint for a successful performance. Politics, nervous disorders, social life, an element of the sort of melodramas which Buchner might have seen—there are too many elements, and they are too schematically manipulated for any text or performance of this play to be regarded as final. In this television production, setting the play with a narrator in a simple Brechtian set, we have tried only to do justice to its possibilities and resonances. But there are always alternative views.

John Selwyn Gilbert

Focus in Viewing

Woyzeck is often called the first modern tragedy because its hero was of the working class. The play attains an even greater dimension when the principal character, Woyzeck, is seen as natural man. It should be borne in mind that this was one of the first dramas to break with the tradition of theatre dialogue as poetry. Buchner wrote the play in the dialect (almost a prosepoetry) of his native Hess-Darmstadt. Certainly the playwright's poetic vision of human interaction is pervasive in this play.

Content Viewing

1. The Doctor in *Woyzeck* says that "man is the transfiguration of the urge for freedom." Do Woyzeck, Maria, the Doctor and the Captain personify this urge? Explain.
2. Is Woyzeck mad? Discuss.
3. Is this a play about an adulteress, a jealous lover, and a murderer? Or is it about a society that oppresses certain individuals and forces them to commit extreme acts? Is this a play about madness and despair? Or is it about man's need to exist with a belief in moral freedom? Discuss.
4. What might Woyzeck have in common with the Mummy in *The Ghost Sonata,* Olga ("3 years later") in *The Three Sisters* and Oedipus?
5. Certain modern critics have called *Woyzeck* a "hero." How does his heroism differ from that of Macbeth's and Oedipus'?

Craft Viewing

1. How is the plot structure of Woyzeck like an apple?
2. Do the vignettes of *Woyzeck* lend themselves to a television production?
3. Was there one moment or scene that stands out in your memory? More than one? Which ones, and why?

Critical Viewing: Overview

1. Now that this play and its production are part of your experience, what significance does *Woyzeck* hold for you?

Additional Plays That Demonstrate Similar Concepts

Danton's Death—Buchner
Doctor Faustus, Tamburlaine—Christopher Marlowe
Mother Courage—Bertolt Brecht
The Plough and the Stars—Sean O'Casey
Death of a Salesman—Arthur Miller

Stage Terms

Brechtian Alienation—Using devices such as a narrator to distance the spectator from the action. This keeps him aware that the play is not real.
Social Realism—Using the arts to develop a social consciousness.

ST. JOAN

by

Bernard Shaw
(1856–1950)

A. Play Notes, p. 192
   1. The Play and History, p. 192
   2. Shaw's Interpretation, p. 193
   3. Plot Structure in *St. Joan,* 193
   4. The Epilogue, p. 194
B. Story and Plot Summary, p. 194
C. Commentary: A Brief Summary of Reviews, p. 195
D. Reviews, p. 195
E. Objectives, p. 199
F. Program Notes, p. 199
G. An Excerpt from the Play, p. 200
H. A List of BBC Actors and Production Coordinators, p. 205
I. Focus in Viewing, p. 209
J. Additional Plays That Demonstrate Similar Concepts, p. 209

Play Notes
Legacy of a Legend: *Saint Joan*

The Play and History

Historians know that there is no one version of an historical event which continues to satisfy the fresh perspectives of succeeding generations. The audiences who saw Sophocles' play about the legendary Oedipus were seeing selected incidents, told in an order devised by a creative artist with some points to make about the Athens of his day.

When George Bernard Shaw wrote *Caesar and Cleopatra,* in 1898, he devised a sophisticated Caesar instructing an emotional girl just as the playwright attempted to instruct audiences in the foolishness of irrational ways. In *Saint Joan* (1923–24), Shaw commented not only on institutions and people of Joan's 15th Century, but of his own 20th Century as well. In discussing the persecution in Joan's time and his own, he wrote, "We must face the fact that society is founded on intolerance."

The viewer watching an historical play must be aware of the playwright's purpose in mixing fact and imagination. Rarely does the playwright consider himself to be a biographer in the sense that the script reflects accurate reporting of the facts. Shaw, for instance, in an opening paragraph of notes on the first London production of *Saint Joan,* stated ". . . I had better point out how far the play this evening will depart from historical facts."

After commenting that he had not departed from historical facts "in any essential particular," Shaw makes an important observation about the theatrical condition: ". . . historical facts cannot be put on the stage exactly as they occurred, because they will not fit into its limits of time and space." Therefore, Shaw, like any other playwright who chronicles the past, must choose events and people, then arrange them into action which supports his dramatic purpose and fits the confinements imposed by the theatrical condition.

Joan of Arc (Jeanne d'Arc) had a natural and powerful appeal to Shaw because her life provided an abundant resource for imagination. The facts can be briefly told. Joan was a village girl, born in the early 1400s in Domremy, France. As she reached her teen-age years, she had become devoutly religious and deeply concerned over her native country, which had been battling with the English and their ally, the Duke of Burgundy, for almost a century. The confrontation is now called The Hundred Years' War.

Joan began to hear heavenly voices and to see visions of the angel Michael, patron saint of the soldiers, and of Saint Catherine and Saint Margaret. They instructed Joan to go to the Dauphin (the young prince of France, Charles VII, called the Dauphin because he had not yet been crowned king at Reims), lead his troops to victory, and free France of the invaders. Overcoming the opposition of her family, the village priest, officials, bishops, and nobles, Joan reached the Dauphin himself, and won his belief in her mission. She acquired a horse, soldier's clothing with armor, and an army. With the golden-lilied banner of France waving above her, Joan led the army of France to the besieged walled city of Orleans, cut through the enemy, and entered the city. Four days later, after sallies and attacks, she sent the English flying. This was in May, 1429, when Joan was not yet 17. By July, Joan conducted the Dauphin in triumph to Reims Cathedral for his coronation at the altar where the kings of France were always crowned.

Although Joan regarded her mission completed, the king persuaded her to march against the Burgundians, who were besieging Compiègne. She was defeated, taken prisoner, and sold as a prize of war to the English. For months she was kept in a prison in the Norman city of Rouen, and was subjected to indignities and a long trial before an ecclesiastical court where the king left her to defend herself. She was accused of heresy and witchcraft because she would not deny her visions and voices. She was convicted and burned at the stake in May, 1431. Almost 500 years later, Joan was declared innocent by the Pope, and on May 16, 1920, she was formally enrolled as a saint of the Catholic Church.

Shaw's Interpretation

Shaw is primarily interested in Joan as someone who imposes her ideas on history. He is less concerned with her martyrdom or with making Joan a romantic heroine and the medieval church a villain. Shaw, in fact, stated that there were no villains involved in Joan's death. He felt that those who had tried and condemned Joan did so in good faith, and they believed with just cause. To Shaw, the conflict was between the individual and society. He believed that like Caesar, Socrates, and Jesus, Joan was one of those extraordinary individuals who, from time to time, rise from the ranks of the human race, challenge it to rethink its beliefs, and cause it to change its concept of man and the world.

Joan, a girl from nowhere in particular, talked with feudal lords, church officials, and nobility, and helped to get a king crowned. She took an army, bogged down from too many years of warring, gave it inspiration, and led it to victory. One woman, with a mission, advanced the spirit and the conscience which rekindled the hopes of a people and a nation. For Shaw, Joan was the first great protagonist of the national spirit, who not only led the troops to drive the English out of France, but also heralded the fall of the feudal structure of the Middle Ages.

Joan's actions were based on her faith in her voices and visions. The messages that came to her from her saints were direct communication between the human and divine. Joan needed no intermediary, for she spoke to and heard from God directly. For Shaw, this was the spirit which pointed the way to Protestantism, and Joan was the first great protagonist to represent the Protestant spirit.

Shaw approaches Joan historically but develops the character mainly in terms of ideological clashes. The leaders of human institutions—church, state, and feudal lords—tolerate her independence, but protest the revolutionary idea of recognizing no authority but God. She undermines their authority and their security by listening to her voices. Therefore, the leaders sincerely believe they must exert their power and take action against the potential danger of anarchy which Joan represents.

Plot Structure in St. Joan

Shaw's method of telling the Joan story requires that an audience allow itself to be carried along with Joan's experiences as selected and arranged by Shaw. In the first scenes, Shaw sets up a momentum which he calls "the romance of her rise" which catches us up in Joan's cause. By the fourth scene, when the forces behind the story are treated as issues to be revealed and discussed, a different tone is established. The fifth and sixth scenes blend the romance and the issue, as Shaw develops an impressive case against Joan. We see her unconsciously confess to heresy, then recant and receive her judgment. The Epilogue gives the play the historical perspective that Shaw wished.

The Epilogue

Much has been written on the reactions of viewers to the Epilogue. Some have felt that it is anticlimactic, even impertinent; Shaw, however, felt that it was necessary. Pointing out that it obviously was not intended as a representation of an actual event, but that it was nonetheless "historical," in his program notes, he explained that without the Epilogue, "the play would be only a sensational story of a girl who was burnt. . . ." Shaw maintained that "the true tale of St. Joan is a tale with a glorious ending; and any play that did not make this clear would be an insult to her memory."

In writing about the Epilogue in a review in 1951, Brooks Atkinson changes his mind about his earlier opinion, of 1923:

> I remember that as a private theatergoer in those days, I regarded the conclusion as willful iconoclasm. But today there is not the slightest doubt that the Epilogue is essential to the thought of the play. Despite the sardonicism of some of the lines, it provides the sorrowful perspective that gives 'St. Joan' its greatness.

In the Epilogue, Shaw, the playwright, makes his point about the legacy of Joan. He seems to say that individual greatness found in any era will always challenge social mediocrity. He suggests that society will continue to persecute and execute its saints until it rises to their level and accepts their challenge.

Story and Plot Summary

Scene I. Joan, a young peasant girl guided by divinely inspired voices, requests horses and soldiers from Captain Robert de Baudricourt to aid the Dauphin in fighting the English at Orleans. Bertrand de Poulengey, who has already been "enlisted" by Joan, tells de Baudricourt that she is, in fact, unique and that there may be something here worthwhile. De Baudricourt, not sure he hasn't been made a fool, accedes to Joan's inspired demands.

Scene II. Charles, the Dauphin, after conferring with his Lord Chamberlain and the Archbishop, anticipates meeting Joan, who is seeking his audience. He arranges for an aide named Bluebeard to stand in for him in hopes that Joan would be able to detect true royalty. Joan quickly sees through the masquerade and goes directly to the (real) Dauphin, who is pleased that his legitimacy has been verified. The Archbishop, recognizing the manipulative power of faith, no matter how contrived, welcomes Joan and proclaims her exalted presence. Joan then persuades the Dauphin to fight for France: he turns the command of the army over to her.

Scene III. Joan confers with Dunois, the Bastard of Orleans, on the banks of the Loire. Their troops must cross the river and capture the English fort on the other side. Dunois' troops are downstream and a change of wind direction is necessary for the rafts to be able to cross the river at the appropriate location. As Dunois and Joan prepare to leave for church to pray for God's assistance, the wind direction changes, as if by special providence.

Scene IV. Cauchon, the Bishop of Beauvais, meets with de Beauchamp, who is Earl of Warwick, and the Chaplain de Stogumber to discuss the threat that Joan poses. Cauchon views Joan as a heretic who must be saved; Warwick and the chaplain are more concerned with eliminating her as a military and political threat to English power and the system of nobility in general. They agree that they are facing a common enemy in Joan; whether as a Protestant or a Nationalist, she is a danger to both the church and the course of nature.

Scene V. Joan finds herself in conflict with the court; it is no longer willing to cooperate with her in driving the English from France. The Archbishop and the Dauphin accuse her of self-deluded excesses; Dunois insists that their military successes against the English will soon come to an abrupt halt. But Joan remains adamant in pursuing what she knows is God's design—driving the English from France.

Scene VI. Having been captured by the Burgundians and then turned over to the English, Joan faces a trial. The Inquisitor establishes that she should be tried for heresy. She is questioned thoroughly but she refuses to acknowledge any wrongdoing on her part. When she is told that she will be burnt at the stake she succumbs, for her voices had promised her that this would not happen. She signs a recantation of her heresy but when she is subsequently sentenced to life imprisonment, she tears up the document and declares that God has been on her side. The Church quickly excommunicates her and turns her over to the secular powers, who burn her at the stake.

Epilogue. Twenty-five years after Joan's martyrdom, Charles is now officially king of France—Joan's sentence has been annulled and the judges have been discredited. The ghost of Joan appears and a "reunion" takes place. A gentleman dressed in 1920s fashion appears and announces that Joan has been canonized as a saint. Each of the figures involved in her trial praises her, and she asks them if she should come back to them. Each departs and Joan wonders when the Earth will be ready to receive its saints.

Commentary

Saint Joan has been a popular play, performed many times by a variety of celebrated artists since its premiere production in 1923.

The following articles review two productions thirty-three years apart. Both critics seem more interested in reviewing Shaw and his ideas in the play, than in giving a critique of the actual performance. Over the years, Shaw's ideas seem less daring, as time has caught up with some and rejected others as impossibly idealistic.

New York Times, March 15, 1936

Joan of G.B.S.
Katherine Cornell's Revival
of a Major Chronicle Drama

"O God that madest this beautiful earth, when will it be ready to receive thy saints? How long, O Lord, how long?"

No, those lines of spiritual anxiety do not come from a church calendar. They come from George Bernard Shaw's "Saint Joan," which Katherine Cornell has just revived at the Martin Beck Theatre. They come, in fact, from the least Shavian play of the lot and by common consent the best and the one that most nearly approaches greatness. For the story of the Maid of Orleans almost persuaded the devil's cleverest disciple to drop his scalpel and identify himself with the human race. There are many passages in "Saint Joan" that are laden with passion. There are

© 1936 by The New York Times Company. Reprinted by permission.

characters of integrity and eminence. It is a witty play, sprinkled with cheap-jack gibes, and it has a shrewd knowledge of the political cant Joan's career brought to the forefront in church and State activities. But it is full of evidence that Shaw knew he was in contact with something bigger than himself when he was writing these pages thirteen years ago. If you have come to think of Shaw as destitute of pity, consider his play about the country girl whose peasant faith concluded the Hundred Years' War.

It is difficult to be fair about Bernard Shaw. If the renegade jeers and sneers of a giddy world start closing in around him now in his eightieth year, he has only himself to blame. He has founded his career on heartless egotism; he has invited the world's resentment and now that he is humorless, mentally diffuse and, after a fashion, defenseless, those who cheered are restlessly defaming. Sycophancy is the only kind of loyalty a career like his can inspire. How deep the resentment against him is I never realized until his name came up in the officers' mess of a cargo ship in which I was a passenger three years ago. The Empress of Britain was on the opposite course; and although she was never closer than a hundred miles her position was regularly plotted on our chart for about two days. At dinner I remarked that Shaw was one of the Empress passengers and that he proposed to speak in New York. The violence with which the assembled officers attacked him was a little surprising. These British mariners were not precisely intellectuals and in the course of things did not see many plays. But they were familiar with a good many of Shaw's cold-blooded jests about questions that had wounded the hearts of ordinary men, and in their opinion, none of his achievements was grand enough to make them forgive him. If he had had a streak of humility in the face of the tragedy of human life, Shaw might at one time have been not only a brilliant man but a great one. His soul has been nearly crushed between the upper and nether millstones of intellect and body.

Saint Joan is the legend, pretty thoroughly corroborated by history, of a bourgeois girl whose religious faith revived a sullen army, led them to the crucial victory of Orleans and more and more aroused the animosity of the learned prelates, whom she appeared to be superseding, and of the enemy army, whom she had very nearly routed. After she was burned at the stake for heresy her soul went marching on, and ultimately the English had to abandon the Hundred Years' War. Although the legend is basically true according to the facts of history, it requires interpretation—either the interpretation of religion, which acknowledges the superhuman power of faith, or the interpretation of the intellect, which explains everything in terms of natural circumstances. The remarkable thing about "Saint Joan" is this: although Shaw is an intellectual and an instinctive skeptic, he humbly acknowledges the power of Joan's faith. In conflict with the profound wisdom and high-mindedness of the Inquisitor and the clever brutishness of the Earl of Warwick the unlettered faith of the country maid is invulnerable; and, although Shaw does not light her head under a halo and intimates that Joan's miraculous victory at Orleans had also a sound military basis, he does not underestimate the triumph of her faith. If "Saint Joan" has a moral for us today, as well as for the post-war world to whom it was dedicated, it is that faith moves the world as well as mountains. The scholarship and dogma of the church, the authority of the State cannot hold in check an expression of simple faith. All the man-made defenses, including most of those of George Bernard Shaw, topple in the presence of a believer. And more than that, the church and State cannot countenance a genuine believer; they have no machinery for dealing with valiant innocence of spirit.

Since "Saint Joan" was written Shaw has given other indications of distrust in reason and of faith in the natural destiny of the human race.[1] That last despairing speech in "Too True to be Good" was a flight from man-made logic, and "The Simpleton of the Unexpected Isles" concluded with an expression of cosmic evangelism. The disaster of the war and since then the disintegration of civilization have apparently shaken the confidence Shaw once had in intellectual enlightenment; and although it is too late for him to turn apostle he has been man enough to confess a change of mind. In his declining years he does begin to identify himself with mankind. If you are looking for the finest lines he has ever written you will find them in this medieval chronicle play—the Inquisitor's long, clear, devout, pitying speech, which is less lyric but more sincere than Portia's appeal to the court; and finally, Joan's ode to the sweetness of life under the open sky—"if only I could still hear the wind in the trees, the larks in the sunshine, the lambs crying through the healthy frost, and the blessed church bells that send my angel voices floating to me on the wind." Shaw has always been a keen writer, but only a man with a compassionate imagination could at the age of 67 put phrases as delicate and willowy as these into the mouth of an artless country girl. "Saint Joan" is not all of a piece; Sean O'Casey, Maxwell Anderson and T.S. Eliot could turn Shaw's coin metal into the pure gold of poetry, which is what the theme deserves. But it towers so high above the rest of the Shaw library and it casts so grand a shadow down the aisle of modern drama that let's have done with petty equivocation. Shaw borrowed the tongue of an angel for the best speeches in this play.

In the current revival he has a few angel tongues to speak them. Miss Cornell's suppliant voice for the maid and Arthur Byron's kindly voice for the Inquisitor evoke the glories of the two grandest characters. But Miss Cornell and her husband, Guthrie McClintic, are too high principled to use "Saint Joan" as a vehicle. Under Mr. McClintic's thorough and discerning direction it has become an exalted testimony to faith. Whenever Miss Cornell appears in a play the star system dominates the theatrical firmament, for she is one of the theatre's luminaries. But, as in the instance of Helen Hayes in "Victoria Regina," the modern star system guarantees a performance as radiant, in all quarters, as the resources of the theatre permit. Miss Cornell is surrounded with actors who can match her scene by scene; one of the scenes in which she does not appear, laid in the Earl of Warwick's tent, is as vibrant as any episode in the play. The basic quality of the Cornell and McClintic productions is their high-mindedness about the theatre. "Saint Joan" responds to high-mindedness. Shaw wrote it on that plane.

Brooks Atkinson

New York Times, January 14, 1968

How Did the Old Boy Bring It Off

. . . Shaw's "St. Joan," even in revival at this late date, still hopes to persuade us of something not altogether obvious: that a girl with scarcely a revolutionary thought in her head did in fact create the Protestantism, the nationalism, and the insistence upon the primacy of independent judgment that continue to serve as the scaffolding for the world we live in. An argument is

---

1. Atkinson is saying that *St. Joan* is evidence that the playwright is trusting less in reason and more in faith than he had previously.

© 1968 by The New York Times Company. Reprinted by permission.

marshaled; spokesmen in bronzed armor, in black-and-white clerical gowns, in coronation robes that resemble Byzantine playing cards, hurry to support it, one way or another, listening, we are going to be impressed or indifferent.

It is Shaw who is persuasive, now as before, even in a production that is only a pretty good production. (John Hirsch's staging is thoroughly efficient, and at no point inspired; Diana Sands' Joan is smoothly pleasing and somehow depersonalized). That Shaw had a way with him cannot really come as news; he has the unfair advantage of having been around long enough by this time for his message to have sunk in; and it would be a silly game to try to turn all later men into lesser men simply because they came later or weren't born witty in Dublin.

But there's a real purpose to be served in asking, once more, how the old boy brought it off; what is learned can be used, and it may help the next man's play ram its point home all the harder. Basically, Shaw flirted with fire the whole time. He didn't know how to keep a safe distance.

Certainly he was eager to make his case. He'd have used a club, or a knobbed walking stick if he had to. No one in the auditorium was to escape collaring, go home free of the stubborn impress of his mind. But he knew that real persuasion was very much a matter of brinkmanship, of walking one's victim to the very edge of disbelief in the proposition to be proved, of *almost* making him believe in the opposite. You've got to tease a possible opponent into thinking that he may just see the truth better than you do before hitting him with your last shaft of light. You've got to honor his obstinacy and even his damn fool arguments.

And so in the celebrated tent scene—as well as in the everlastingly startling self-justification of the Inquisitor—Shaw walks boldly, brazenly, into the enemy camp, giving unheard-of aid and comfort to the enemy. As Warwick, Cauchon, and de Stogumber settle down to the business of closing every loophole through which Joan might escape, Shaw at once sets to work with his very deft fingers prying open escape hatches faster than his conspirators can tie knots. His scoundrels won't stand still as scoundrels, they keep turning into intelligences. Instead of villains and asses hopelessly blinded by their respective interests (there are no villains in the play, Shaw tells us), they become seers, restless men, who will do what they are going to do, but not without confessing to themselves all the conceivable consequences. Protestantism may be a mixed blessing; nationalism may be no blessing at all; the loosing upon the world of a chaos of independent minds may, we faintly sense, make even a Shaw shudder. We are permitted to think these things, though the thought of the play moves vigorously in another direction. We are even, at one point, alarmed for the author: Has he finally played Devil's Advocate for so long that he has ceased believing in his own case, moved so close to the fire that it is too late to turn back?

But that is how he turns *us* back. He has given us enough rope, permitted us to exercise our convictions and our prejudices, said to us that there is indeed another sort of truth to pursue and freely given us his permission to pursue it, if we wish to. Now we no longer wish to. Having heard ourselves, having heard every shade of opinion that might be tossed into the cauldron, we are at last eager only to hear him. He has been brave enough to chance a singeing by exposing himself to other men's heat, and he has won his victory.

Walter Kerr

Objectives

You, the student, after studying St. Joan, should be able to

1. understand that *St. Joan* is an important step in legitimatizing the female protagonist.
2. recognize Shaw's preoccupation with the contributions made by heroic characters such as Joan.
3. appreciate Shaw's ability to present important issues through witty debate in crucial episodes.
4. identify the implication and irony as stimulating attributes of modern theatre.

Program Notes

Saint Joan

George Bernard Shaw's heroic girl soldier is in conflict with the establishment of her day—military, royal, ecclesiastic. There are clever twists of logic by a playwright who is often called the wittiest in English theatre history. The television version begins at the point of Joan's imprisonment. It proceeds through trial, recantation, and decision to face execution rather than surrender her beliefs. Guest artist Julie Harris discusses her role as Joan in *The Lark,* and reenacts a stirring speech of *Sain Joan's* from an earlier episode. Scenes, V, VI, and the Epilogue are in the video production.

ST. JOAN

From *Scene VI*

TWO SCRIBES ENTER. JOAN IS BROUGHT IN BY TWO SOLDIERS, WHO TAKE OFF HER CHAINS. THE MEMBERS OF THE COURT TAKE THEIR PLACES.

THE INQUISITOR *(kindly)* Sit Down, Joan.

(She sits.)

You look very pale today. Are you not well?

JOAN Thank you kindly: I am well enough. But the Bishop sent me some carp; and it made me ill.

CAUCHON I am sorry. I told them to see that it was fresh.

JOAN You meant to be kind to me, I know, but it is a fish that does not agree with me. . . . The English Chaplin here thought you were trying to poison me.

THE CHAPLAIN My lord, I must protest.

JOAN *(continuing)* He sent a doctor to cure me. The English are determined to see that I am burnt as a witch. Why must I be left in their hands? I should be in the hands of the Church. And why must I be chained by the feet to a log of wood? Are you afraid I will fly away?

D'ESTIVET *(harshly)* Woman:

*(*JOAN *turns)*

It is not for you to question the court: it is for us to question you.

COURCELLES When you were left unchained, did you not try to escape by jumping from a tower sixty feet high? If you cannot fly like a witch, how is it you are still alive?

JOAN I suppose because the tower was not so high then. It has grown a little higher every day since you first began asking me questions about it.

D'ESTIVET Why did you jump from the tower?

JOAN How do you know I jumped?

D'ESTIVET You were found lying in the moat. Why did you leave the tower?

JOAN Why would anybody leave a prison if they could get out?

D'ESTIVET You tried to escape?

JOAN Of course I did; and not for the first time either. If you leave the door of the cage open the bird will fly out.

D'ESTIVET This is a confession of heresy. I call the attention of the court to it.

JOAN Heresy, he calls it? Am I a heretic because I try to escape from prison?

D'ESTIVET Assuredly, if you're in the hands of the Church, and you willfully take yourself out of its hands, you are deserting the Church; and that is heresy.

JOAN It is great nonsense. Nobody could be such a fool as to think that.

D'ESTIVET You hear, my lord, how I am reviled in the execution of my duty by this woman.

THE INQUISITOR . . . Let us not be moved by the rough side of a shepherd lass's tongue.

JOAN Nay: I am no shepherd lass, though I have helped with the sheep like anyone else. I will do a lady's work in the house—spin or weave—against any woman in Rouen.

Excerpt from SAINT JOAN by Bernard Shaw. Reprinted by permission of The Society of Authors on behalf of the Bernard Shaw Estate.

THE CHAPLAIN If you are so clever at woman's work why do you not stay at home and do it?
JOAN There are plenty of other women to do it; there is nobody to do my work.
CAUCHON Come! We are wasting time over trifles. Joan: I am going to put a most solemn question to you. Now take care how you answer; for your life and salvation are at stake on it. Will you for all that you have said and done, be it good or bad, accept the judgement of God's Church on earth? . . .
JOAN I am a faithful child of the Church. I will obey the Church—
CAUCHON *(hopefully leaning forward)* You will?
JOAN Provided it does not command anything impossible.
D'ESTIVET She imputes to the Church the error and folly of commanding the impossible.
JOAN If you command me to declare that all that I have said and done, and all the visions and revelations that I have had, were not from God, then that is impossible: I will not declare it for anything in the world . . . And in case the Church should bid me do anything contrary to the command that I have from God, I will not consent to it, no matter what it may be. . . .

(The assembly reacts in shock.)

D'ESTIVET My lord: do you need anything more than this? . . .
LADVENU *(pleading with her urgently)* You do not know what you are saying, child. Do you want to kill yourself? Listen. Do you not believe that you are subject to the Church of God on earth?
JOAN Why yes. When have I ever denied it?
LADVENU Good. That means, does it not, that you are subject to our Lord the Pope, to the cardinals, the archbishops, and the bishops for whom his lordship stands here today?
JOAN God must be served first.
D'ESTIVET Then your voices command you not to submit yourself to the Church Militant?
JOAN My voices do not tell me to disobey the Church; but God must be served first.
CAUCHON And you, and not the Church, is to be the judge?
JOAN What other judgement can I judge by but my own?
THE ASSESSORS *(scandalized)* Oh!

(They cannot find words)

CAUCHON Out of your own mouth you have condemned yourself. We have striven for your salvation to the verge of sinning ourselves: we have opened the door to you again and again; and you have shut it in our faces and in the face of God. Dare you pretend, after what you have said, that you are in a state of grace?
JOAN If I am not, may God bring me to it: if I am, may God keep me in it!
LADVENU This is a very good reply, my lord.
COURCELLES *(rising)* Were you in a state of grace when you stole the Archbishop's horse?
CAUCHON *(rising in a fury)* Oh, devil take the Archbishop's horse and you too! We are here to try a case of heresy; and no sooner do we come to the root of the matter than we are thrown back by idiots who understand nothing but horses.

(COURCELLES sits and CAUCHON, trembling with rage, forces himself to sit down)

THE INQUISITOR Gentlemen, gentlemen: in clinging to these small issues you are The Maid's best advocates. I am not surprised his lordship has lost patience with you. What does the Promoter say? Does he press these trumpery matters?

D'ESTIVET I am bound by my office to press everything: . . . but I share the impatience of his lordship as to these minor charges. Only, with great respect, I must emphasize the gravity of two very horrible and blasphemous crimes which she does not deny. First, she communicates with evil spirits, and is therefore a sorceress. Second, she wears men's clothes, which is indecent, unnatural, and abominable; and in spite of our most earnest remonstrances and entreaties, she will not change them even to receive the sacrament.

JOAN Is the blessed St. Catherine an evil spirit? Is St. Margaret? Is Michael the Archangel?

COURCELLES How do you know that the spirit which appears to you is an archangel? Does he not appear to you as a naked man?

JOAN *(turns)* Do you think God cannot afford clothes for him?

LADVENU Well answered, Joan.

THE INQUISITOR It is, in effect, well answered. But no evil spirit would be so simple as to appear to a young girl in a guise that would scandalize her when he meant her to take him for a messenger from the Most High. Joan: the Church instructs you that these apparitions are demons seeking your soul's perdition. Do you accept the instruction of the Church?

JOAN I accept the messenger of God. How could any faithful believer in the Church refuse him?

CAUCHON Wretched woman: again I ask you, do you know what you are saying?

THE INQUISITOR You wrestle in vain with the devil for her soul, my lord: she will not be saved. Now touching the matter of this man's dress. For the last time, will you put off that impudent attire, and dress as becomes your sex?

JOAN I will not.

D'ESTIVET *(pouncing)* The sin of disobedience, my lord.

JOAN *(distressed)* But my voices tell me that I must dress as a soldier.

LADVENU Joan, Joan: does that not prove to you that the voices are the voices of evil spirits? Can you suggest to us one good reason why an angel of God should give you such shameful advice?

JOAN Why, yes: what could be plainer commonsense? I was a soldier living among soldiers. I am a prisoner guarded by soldiers. If I dress as a woman they would think of me as a woman; and then what would become of me? If I dress as a soldier they think of me as a soldier, and I can live with them as I do at home with my brothers. That is why St. Catherine tells me I must not dress as a woman until she gives me leave.

COURCELLES When will she give you leave?

JOAN When you take me out of the hands of the English soldiers. I have told you that I should be in the hands of the Church, and not left night and day with four soldiers of the Earl of Warwick. Do you want me to live with them in petticoats?

LADVENU My lord: what she says is, God knows, very wrong and shocking; but there is a grain of worldly sense in it such as might impose on a simple village maiden.

JOAN If we were as simple in the villages as you are in your courts and palaces, there would soon be no wheat to make bread for you. . . .

LADVENU Try to resist the temptation to make pert replies to us. Do you see that man who stands behind you?

JOAN *(turning and looking at the man)* Your torturer? But the Bishop said I was not to be tortured.

LADVENU You are not to be tortured because you have confessed everything that is necessary to your condemnation. That man is not only the torturer: he is also the Executioner. Executioner:

let The Maid hear your answers to my questions. Are you prepared for the burning of a heretic this day?

THE EXECUTIONER Yes, Master.

LADVENU Is the stake ready?

THE EXECUTIONER It is. In the market-place. The English have built it too high for me to get near her and make it easier. It will be a cruel death.

JOAN *(horrified)* But you are not going to burn me now?

THE INQUISITOR You realize it at last.

LADVENU There are eight hundred English soldiers waiting to take you to the market-place the moment the sentence of excommunication has passed the lips of your judges. You are within a few short moments of that doom.

(Silence)

JOAN *(looking round desperately for rescue)* Oh God!

LADVENU Do not despair, Joan. The Church is merciful. You can save yourself.

JOAN *(hopefully)* Yes, my voices promised me I should not be burnt. St. Catherine bade me be bold.

CAUCHON Woman: are you quite mad? Do you not yet see that your voices have deceived you?

JOAN Oh no: that is impossible.

CAUCHON Impossible! They have led you straight to your excommunication, and to the stake which is there waiting for you.

LADVENU *(pressing the point hard)* Have they kept a single promise to you since you were taken at Compiègne? The devil has betrayed you. The Church holds out its arms to you.

JOAN *(despairing)* It is true: it is true: my voices have deceived me. I have been mocked by devils: my faith is broken. I have dared and dared; but only a fool would walk into a fire; God, who gave me my commonsense, cannot will me to do that.

LADVENU Now God be praised that He has saved you at the eleventh hour!

CAUCHON Amen!

(LADVENU goes and sits)

JOAN *(pause)* What must I do?

CAUCHON You must sign a solemn recantation of your heresy.

JOAN Sign? That means write my name. I—I cannot write.

CAUCHON You have signed many letters before.

JOAN Yes; but somebody held my hand and guided the pen. I can—I can make my mark.

THE CHAPLAIN *(who has been listening with growing alarm and indignation)* My lord: do you mean that you are going to allow this woman to escape us?

THE INQUISITOR The law must be respected Master de Stogumber, even by the English. And you know the law.

THE CHAPLAIN *(rising)* I know that there is no faith in a Frenchman.

(Tumult)

I know what my lord the Cardinal of Winchester will say when he hears of this. I know what the Earl of Warwick will do when he learns that you intend to betray him. There are eight hundred men at the gate who will see that this abominable witch is burnt in spite of your teeth. . . .

(The assembly reacts)

THE INQUISITOR *(rising)* Silence. Gentlemen: pray silence! Master Chaplain: bethink you of your holy office: of what you are, and where you are. I direct you to sit down.

THE CHAPLAIN *(folding his arms doggedly, his face working convulsively)* I will NOT sit down.

CAUCHON Master Inquisitor: this man has called me a traitor to my face before now.

THE CHAPLAIN So you are a traitor. You are all traitors. You've been doing nothing but begging this damnable witch on your knees to recant all through this trial.

THE INQUISITOR *(placidly resuming his seat)* If you will not sit, then you must stand: that is all.

THE CHAPLAIN I will NOT stand. *(He flings himself back into his chair)*

LADVENU *(rising with the paper in his hand)* My lord: here is the form of recantation for The Maid to sign.

CAUCHON Read it to her.

JOAN Do not trouble. I will sign it.

THE INQUISITOR Woman: you must know what you are putting your hand to. Read it to her, Brother Martin. And let all be silent.

LADVENU *(reading quietly)* "I, Joan, commonly called The Maid, a miserable sinner, do confess that I have most grievously sinned in the following articles. I have pretended to have revelations from God and the angels and the blessed saints, and perversely rejected the Church's warnings that these were temptations by demons. I have blasphemed abominably by wearing an immodest dress, contrary to the Holy Scripture and the canons of the Church. Also I have clipped my hair in the style of a man, and, against all the duties which have made my sex specially acceptable in heaven, have taken up the sword, even to the shedding of human blood, and inciting men to slay each other. . . . All of which sins I renounce and abjure and depart from, humbly thanking you Doctors and Masters who have brought me back to the truth and into the grace of our Lord. And I will never return to my errors, but will remain in communion with our Holy Church and in obedience to our Holy Father the Pope of Rome. All this I swear by God Almighty and the Holy Gospels, in witness whereto I sign my name to this recantation."

THE INQUISITOR Do you understand this, Joan?

JOAN *(listless)* It is plain enough.

THE INQUISITOR And is it true?

JOAN It may be true. If it were not true, the fire would not be ready for me in the market-place.

LADVENU Come child: let me guide your mark. Take the pen.

(She does so)

So, Now make your mark by yourself.

(She writes)

JOAN There!

LADVENU Praise be to God, my brothers, the lamb has returned to the flock; and the Church rejoices in her more than in ninety and nine just persons.

(Hands the recantation to CAUCHON *with reverence)*

THE INQUISITOR We declare thee by this act set free from the danger of excommunication in which thou stoodest.

JOAN I thank you.

A Listing of BBC Actors and Production Coordinators

SAINT JOAN

by

George Bernard Shaw

CAST

JOAN	ANGELA PLEASENCE
DUNOIS	BRUCE PURCHASE
CHARLES VII (THE DAUPHIN)	DAVID FIRTH
THE ARCHBISHOP	RAY SMITH
LA HIRE	MICHAEL CADMAN
THE INQUISITOR	MARK DIGNAM
PETER COUCHON (BISHOP OF BEAUVAIS)	FRANK MIDDLEMASS
CHAPLAIN DE STOGUMBER	JOHN BRYANS
D'ESTIVET	DAVID STRONG
COURCELLES	PATRICK MARLEY
LADVENU	JOHN MORENO
EXECUTIONER	ERIC MASON
EARL OF WARWICK	JOHN WESTBROOK
GENTLEMAN (FROM THE VATICAN)	DON FELLOWS
SOLDIER	RICHARD BEALE

PRODUCTION

SET DESIGN	STEVE SCOTT
COSTUME DESIGNER	ROGER REECE
MAKE-UP SUPERVISOR	MAGGIE WEBB
DIRECTOR	RICHARD CALLANAN

Joan

(Left to Right) Dunois, Dauphin, La Hire, Archbishop

(Left to Right) The Inquisitor, Gentleman from the Vatican, Soldiers, Joan

Focus in Viewing

This production centers on the trial part of the play as representative of the action and emotion of the whole play. Among his many references to Joan, Shaw used the words *original* and *presumptuous*; the program that you have viewed emphasized the natural and powerful appeal of its heroine, the village girl who becomes a saint. While a certain romantic quality is inherent, this production attempts to strike a medium between idealism and pragmatism by concentrating on Joan as an individualist.

Content Viewing

1. Give an example of how Shaw presents important issues through witty debate.
2. *Oedipus* like *St. Joan* is about a trial of sorts—the proving of guilt. Of the two trials which involves your emotions the most? Explain. Of the two "defendants" with whom do you identify the most? Explain.
3. How would you describe Joan's character? Who, or what, is she? What is her philosophy; her view of herself? Does her attitude change? Is Joan's character consistent with her philosophy and action?
4. Is the language (dialogue) natural? Is there a particular flavor or tone inherent in Shaw's use of language? If so, what is it?

Craft Viewing

1. Can you determine a directorial concept or interpretation? Are you in agreement, or disagreement? What or how would you have directed differently?
2. Do you agree, or disagree, with the actors' characterizations and interpretations? Choose two and discuss.
3. In the characterization of Joan, what qualities do you think are essential to the part and what ones would you most like to avoid?
4. Is there one moment or scene which stands out in your memory? More than one? Which ones, and why?

Critical Viewing: Overview

1. Would you describe Shaw as a playwright who carries on the legacy of naturalism, realism, expressionism, tragedy, or one who begins a new "school?" Explain.
2. Now that this play and its production are part of your experience, what significance does *Saint Joan* hold for you?

Additional Plays That Demonstrate Similar Concepts

Candida—George Bernard Shaw
The Lark, Antigone, Becket—Jean Anouilh
Galileo—Bertolt Brecht
Luther—John Osborne
J.B.—Archibald Macleish
The Crucible—Arthur Miller

THE VENETIAN TWINS

by

Carlo Goldoni
(1707–1793)

A. Play Notes: The Commedia Dell'arte, p. 211
    1. Background, p. 211
    2. Characters, p. 211
    3. The Influence, p. 213
B. Story and Plot Summary, p. 213
C. Commentary: A Brief Summary of a Review, p. 216
D. Review, p. 217
E. Objectives, p. 218
F. Program Notes, p. 218
G. Excerpt from *The Venetian Twins,* p. 219
H. A List of BBC Actors and Production Coordinators, p. 224
I. Focus in Viewing, p. 225
J. Additional Plays That Demonstrate Similar Concepts, p. 226
K. Stage Terms, p. 226

Play Notes

Background of Commedia Dell'arte

Commedia dell'arte was a combination of dramatic traditions. The term means "comedy of the guild." The guild was a group of actors who performed essentially improvisational comedy. This improvisation, certain scholars believe, came from the extemporaneous verbal duels common to Italian academicians of the Renaissance, who often sacrificed truth for the "bon mot." Because such verbal sparring was more of an opportunity for one-upmanship than a forum for ideas, it lent itself to a tongue-in-cheek imitation—the commedia dell'arte.

Some of the scenarios and plots have been traced to early Italian folklore. This folklore became the subject of the carnival plays that preceded the commedia dell'arte. Other scenarios have been traced to the Roman comedy writer, Plautus, who wrote about 200 B.C.

Characters of Commedia Dell'arte

When Goldoni wrote *The Venetian Twins,* he chose character prototypes from Plautus and the carnival plays. These roles became the stock characters of the commedia dell'arte. Some of them are the following: an arlecchino, a clever jester; a pantalone, an elderly parent or guardian; a dottore, a foolish and gullible old man; the amorosi, young lovers; a braggart, who turns out to be a coward; the maid of the young heroine who helps the lovers outwit their elders; the zannis, clever servants or buffoons (from which the English word "zany" comes), and the jealous suitor.

The characters of the commedia dell'arte wore masks (except for the protagonists), but could be identified by their costumes, which also were prototypes. For example, the arlecchino (jester) wore a costume with a harlequin pattern. This pattern, a diamond-shaped design, indicated that the character wearing it was a "joker." The pantalone (elderly father) always sported a white goatee to insure that he was properly identified by the audience, and the zannis (servants or buffoons) wore baggy clothes to suggest that they would be involved in some sort of foolishness.

An actor would not change roles from play to play but would, instead, specialize in one stock character, repeating movements and dialogue that eventually became his trademark. The characters also adopted the dialogues of different cities. In *The Venetian Twins,* the pantalone was from Venice, the dottore from Bologna, and the arlecchino from Bergamo. The various dialects not only served to stereotype the roles; they also increased the silliness of the play.

Because the plays were improvisational comedy, the actors had to be especially skilled. It was up to them to take skeletal plots and develop characterizations and situations that their audiences would understand and enjoy. The differences in improvisation were dependent upon differences in audience. The traveling companies would perform before peasants one day and aristocrats the next, adjusting the level of humor accordingly.

Of all the commedia dell'arte characters, the one that is most widely known is the arlecchino, the jester, who is frequently called the harlequin. This character is paradoxical—a dimwit of sorts, who shows a native cleverness. He is naive and gullible and, at the same time, cunning enough to steal purses and watches. He is something of an idealist and yet a cynic. Constantly in love, and yet something of a woman hater, he would typically say, "Oh, if I could deserve the honour of deserving some small portion of your desserts how I would love you, how I would caress you, how I would flatter you, how I would—beat you, madame!" The harlequin, of all the actors, had to be the most versatile because of the complexities and demands of the role.

Harlequin

The Influence of the Commedia Dell'arte Play upon Seventeenth and Eighteenth Century Theatre

Between 1571 and 1750 commedia dell'arte companies played before royalty and the general public throughout Europe, affecting all the countries in which they appeared. In France, the influence is most apparent in the plays of Molière. Some of Molière's earliest productions were little more than adoptions of commedia dell'arte. Later, familiar stock characters appeared in his plays, *The School for Wives, The Would-be Gentleman, The Doctor in Spite of Himself,* and *The Imaginary Invalid.*

Elizabethan dramatists, such as Shakespeare, Marlowe, Beaumont, and Fletcher, also borrowed character types from the commedia. Shakespeare's clowns are extensions of the zanni tradition. Polonius in Hamlet comes from the pantalone; the twin brother-sister situation in *Twelfth Night* reflects the relationship present in so many Italian plots of the period. Ariel in *The Tempest* is an arlecchino, Falstaff a zanni, and Shylock a pantalone. *A Midsummer Night's Dream,* of all of Shakespeare's plays, comes closest in theme, plot, setting, and characterization to commedia dell'arte. Punch and Judy, too are the progeny of this art form.

Commedia dell'arte influenced the drama of its native Italian playwrights. By the mid-1700's writers were bringing to the genre innovations and reforms of their own devising. One of these playwrights, Carlo Goldoni, began his career by writing scenarios for a company famous for its actors' interpretations of the pantalone and the arlecchino. Goldoni wrote the dialogue for these two roles and sketched the action of the other stock characters. By fixing the dialogue of his characters Pantalone and Arlecchino, Goldoni began modification of what had been, for two centuries, a purely improvisational genre. In later plays, Goldoni fixed the dialogue of the young lovers, and still later reduced the size of the cast to four characters from the usual twelve.

Goldoni, for the first time, made the lovers the center of the story, as they are in *The Venetian Twins.* In *The Woman of Grace* (1743), for the first time, all the dialogue was written down. Eventually, masks were discarded and *commedia dell'arte,* as a particular form of comedy, disappeared, giving way to a new form of Italian comic theatre.

Story and Plot Summary

All the action in *The Venetian Twins* is built around this simple situation:

Identical twin, young men have separately visited the same city. Neither is aware that his brother is there. Their looks and clothing are so similar that there are frequent comic situations based on mistaken identity. One twin, Zanetto, is foolish and impressionable. His fiancee, Rosaura, is a naive young woman whom he has never met. The other twin, Tonio, is brave and resourceful. His fiancee is Beatrice, who was temporarily separated from him as he and Beatrice were fleeing her family because of objections to their marriage. The complications arise because a number of other men are also suitors of Rosaura and Beatrice. Pancrazio wants Rosaura. Lelio and Florindo want Beatrice. The action takes place in and near the house of Rosaura's father.

Since the situation is the basis for the comedy, there is no emphasis on character development. Each character broadly represents a commedia dell'arte type. The language is simple and straightforward, without subtlety.

Audiences usually like the play for the following reasons: (1) The audience is aware of the mix-ups that confuse the characters. (2) A seemingly simple situation becomes amazingly complicated. (3) The actor who plays both twins shows much acting talent in being able to assume two contrasting roles. (4) From the beginning, the audience can be certain that there will be many surprises and a happy ending for almost everyone.

Scene i. The play opens in Rosaura's room in Verona. Rosaura, the daughter of a lawyer, is combing her hair, preparing to meet her fiance for the first time. She is to marry Zanetto. Her maid, Colombina, is to marry someone she has never met, Zanetto's servant Arlecchino.

Rosaura's father, called the Doctor (he is a Doctor of Laws) shares a secret with Colombina. When he attempts to reprimand Colombina, she reminds him that she knows "everything," but is keeping quiet.

Zanetto's arrival at Rosaura's home is announced. According to Dr. Balanzoni's male servant, Brighella, the groom-to-be is not bad looking but rather simple in his behavior, not so polished and elegant as his twin brother Tonino. Arlecchino, Zanetto's servant, is expected later, with the luggage.

When Zanetto and Rosaura are left alone, Zanetto seems interested in making love even before the wedding ceremony. Rosaura slaps him, and he leaves.

Rosaura is confronted by the family guest Pancrazio, who urges her to shun all young men as unworthy of her love. (He would like to have her for himself, but knows that he lacks youth, good looks, and money.)

Scene ii. A street outside the Doctor's house, across from an Inn. Zanetto's twin brother Tonino and the young lady he loves, Beatrice, have arranged to meet in Verona. Beatrice is waiting for him to join her. Meanwhile, she is being protected by Tonino's friend Florindo, who would like to have her for himself. Beatrice is afraid some accident has prevented Tonino from joining her. Florindo pretends to help her, but would actually like to keep the two lovers from eloping. Meanwhile, another would-be suitor of Beatrice's arrives. He is Lelio, a nobleman. Lelio and Florindo begin to argue over the girl, and start to fight. Beatrice runs into the inn. Just as Lelio is about to defeat Florindo in a duel, Tonino arrives, fights Lelio, and disarms him. Lelio vows revenge. Florindo lies to Tonino, says that he has not seen Beatrice. Tonino decides that he has been foolish to trust her. He had wanted to marry her, but her father objected, preferring for a son-in-law a foreign gentleman with whom Tonino had fought. He left home without money or a change of clothes, expecting to meet Beatrice in Verona. Now, disappointed in Beatrice and afraid of further fights with his enemies, he asks Florindo not to call him by his own name but rather by the name of his twin brother Zanetto. He does not realize that his brother is also in Verona. Florindo agrees. When Tonino leaves to go to the inn, Florindo announces in an aside to the audience that he intends to keep Tonino separate from Beatrice in order to win her for himself.

Zanetto and Lelio meet. Lelio, believing Zanetto to be the brave swordsman Tonino is eager for a rematch. Zanetto is surprised to be hit by a man so soon after he has been slapped by Rosaura. Florindo rescues Zanetto, but is surprised to see the difference in the behavior of the man he believes to be Tonino. Zanetto is confused, too, in one of many cases of mistaken identity occurring throughout the play.

Zanetto is joined by Pancrazio, who persuades him to stay away from women. Then Beatrice arrives, believing she is speaking to Tonino. Zanetto, hurt because he believes she has rejected him, rejects her in return. Beatrice, believing her beloved Tonino has gone mad, is miserable and determined to learn the truth.

Act II. *Scene i.* Arlecchino, Zanetto's servant, arrives with a porter carrying a large trunk. He doesn't know where his master is staying. When he sees Tonino he teases him, but is alarmed when Tonino draws his sword and claims not to recognize him. In an effort to jog the memory of the man he believes to be Zanetto, the servant gives Tonino money and jewels belonging to his master. Then he goes into the inn. Tonino retains the valuables, determined to find their rightful owner.

Colombina comes out of the house and, thinking she is speaking to Zanetto, invites Tonino to come inside and see her mistress. Tonino, thinking she is a prostitute, asks how much it will cost to visit the strange lady who seems to be selling her favors. Rosaura's father persuades Tonino to go inside and to visit his daughter at any time. He is pleased to see the jewels.

Arlecchino and Colombina meet, delighted to learn that they will wed. Each is impressed by the charms of the other. When Zanetto finds Arlecchino, he is alarmed to learn that his money and jewels have been given away. Arlecchino thinks that his master is a lunatic for not remembering that he has already received them.

Scene ii. Tonino visits the doctor's house, thinking it is a brothel. While he waits for Rosaura, he meets the servant Brighella, who says he had once worked in Venice for the family of the twins. There seems to be a family secret, but he leaves, and Rosaura comes in. The conversation between Tonino and Rosaura is at cross-purposes, with Tonino offering jewels as payment for lovemaking and Rosaura believing that Zanetto has returned as a more articulate and sophisticated suitor—but still very strange and impudent. When she mentions the slap in the face, referring to the one she gave him, he believes she refers to the slap he gave her rival for Beatrice in Venice. The jewels are interpreted as a wedding gift, but talk of a wedding and of favors before the wedding is upsetting to each of them, for different reasons. Tonino leaves a confused Rosaura, and continues to wonder why Beatrice has apparently broken her vow to meet him.

Brighella begins to speak again about his knowledge of Tonino's family, but Pancrazio sends him away and then tells Tonio that the Doctor's family is wicked. He repeats his warnings against marriage, which had so impressed Zanetto earlier that day. This time, though, the other brother protests that marriage depends on the worth of the people involved. Pancrazio believes that Zanetto is less foolish than he appeared to be. He agrees to take care of the jewels Tonino says were given to him by mistake; only he intends to use them to impress Rosaura.

Scene iii. On the street, Arlecchino insists that he gave the jewels and money to Zanetto, who believes he has been robbed. He denounces Arlecchino, who is taken off to prison.

Beatrice comes by, sees Zanetto, and speaks to him of the love they share. Zanetto is bewildered but delighted. Florindo, still desiring Beatrice, tries to break up the wedding. He takes Zanetto inside and reminds him that it would be illegal to marry Beatrice when he is already pledged to Rosaura, whose house he has just visited. Alarmed, Zanetto agrees he doesn't want to go to prison. He leaves Florindo and tells Beatrice that Tonino has fallen in love with another woman. Lelio enters. He and Florindo compete for Beatrice. Tonino watches in amazement, hearing them speak of Beatrice as having been abandoned. Tonino leads Beatrice off, as the other two men vow revenge by sword.

Act III *Scene i.* Pancrazio attempts to sell the jewels, but the chief constable recognizes them as ones reported stolen and accuses him of theft. Zanetto comes by, claims them, but denies having given them to Pancrazio. The constable decides to bring the case to court; meanwhile, he orders the release of Arlecchino. Zanetto is afraid of the fees involved, when he learns about lawyers and court costs. He decides to return to the country, where living is simpler.

Pancrazio needs evidence that he has honestly obtained the jewels. He begs Tonino to swear to the story. Tonino agrees. Arlecchino comes along and is outraged when Tonino points to him as the original source of the jewels. Arlecchino believes that Zanetto, his master, has gone mad, saying that he received the jewels that he previously claimed he never saw.

Zanetto decides to visit Rosaura, who tells him her father no longer wants him as a son-in-law, now that Zanetto believes she is a prostitute.

Zanetto declares true love for her. Rosaura accuses him of seeming stupid at times and witty at other times, constantly changing. Beatrice arrives; overhearing declarations of love for Rosaura from a man who seems to be Tonino, she believes herself to be deceived once more. She denounces him and promises to return with the letter in which he declared his love. Rosaura is outraged, despising him as a hypocrite. She, too, goes for the letter in which Zanetto asked for her hand in marriage. Zanetto, alone, decides women are jealous and that he can never marry. He leaves; when Rosaura sees that he has run away, she tears up her letter.

Tonino arrives, and picks up the pieces of Rosaura's letter. Then Beatrice arrives, sees Tonino and tears up the letter he has sent her. Tonino looks at both letters, and finally realizes that the letter signed by Zanetto may explain all the strange happenings. He asks the servant Brighella to explain what he knows about the family of twins. Brighella tells him of Zanetto's courtship of Rosaura and of the twins' lost sister. Tonino decides to search for his twin. Colombina complains to Tonino that Rosaura behaves like a fine lady but that she is actually not the Doctor's daughter. Originally, she was an orphan of unknown origin. She turns out to be the lost sister of Tonino and Zanetto.

The Doctor is determined on the immediate marriage of Rosaura and Zanetto. Zanetto, not knowing about either the marriage or the identity of Rosaura, swallows a powder which Pancrazio claims will make him indifferent to women. It is actually a poisonous cleanser for jewelry. Zanetto falls to the ground later dying in the inn. The others mourn his loss, though some believe him to be Tonino. When Tonino arrives on the scene, they think he is a ghost. The errors are straightened out. Tonino is to inherit Zanetto's money, marry Beatrice, and be reunited with his sister Rosaura. The Doctor confesses his trick in bringing up the orphan girl as his own in order to continue receiving an inheritance from his nephew Lelio. It is arranged for Lelio and Rosaura to marry. Pancrazio is accused of murdering Zanetto. He kills himself. The remaining couples rejoice.

Commentary

Brendan Gill of the *New Yorker* was pleasantly surprised with the Teatro Stabile de Genova's production of *The Venetian Twins*. Expecting to find slap-stick humor, weak characterization, and foreign-tongued dialect, Gill was delighted to find, instead, a play written in the 1700's that, in the hands of skillful actors, restored *the commedia* to its intended purpose: to make the audience laugh at the complications and twists that disrupt our lives.

New Yorker, June 8, 1968

The Theater—Imbroglios

The funniest play I have seen this season is the handiwork of a racy young Venetian lawyer-turned-author, and it was written something over two hundred and twenty years ago. The name of the play is "The Venetian Twins," and its author is Carlo Goldoni, who lived a life splendid in variety and duration (1707–93), and who found composition so light a burden that he was able to write a total of about a hundred and fifty plays, no fewer than sixteen of them in the course of a single *annus mirabilis.* "The Venetian Twins" has been brought to Henry Miller's Theatre in a handsome production by the Teatro Stabile di Genova; this is a repertory group that, though based in Genoa, emulates that sea city's Renaissance great captains by frequently sallying forth to such far corners of the earth as La Plata, Minsk, Edinburgh, and—here be dragons—Philadelphia. It is not only an exceptionally well-orchestrated company but an exceptionally comely one, and I am not surprised that its suavity and grace win the admiration of natives normally skeptical of foreign tongues and tales; on opening night here, it was given so many curtain calls that I quickly lost count of them, and since it will be in residence only until June 23rd, the sooner you hurl yourself with Pantalonelike guile upon the Miller box office the better.

I confess to having approached "The Venetian Twins" uneasily. The garrulous fops and yokels that people seventeenth and eighteenth-century English comedies have wrung few laughs from me, so what was I to expect of an eighteenth-century comedy in an unfamiliar language? Moreover, I am especially wary of that snobbism which sees in any lingering manifestation of the commedia dell'arte tradition a natural occasion for praise, on the ground that because it is a tradition that flourished among the anonymous fold it is close to some preliterate autochthonous "real thing" that the folk are assumed to possess (an assumption as ill-founded as that circus clowns are funny because they have funny faces, or, still more falsely, are tragic because they have funny faces; in my experience they have never been either.) What gives "The Venetian Twins" its peculiar nervous vitality is the fact that Goldoni is simultaneously exploiting the conventions of commedia dell'arte and abandoning them, and in his wry, mocking, and often self-mocking text we encounter a dramatist working his way toward notions of personality and identity that remain a matter of concern to many writers today. It would be patronizing to congratulate Goldoni on being a premature Pirandello; the truth is that he drops hints that the theatre at large still pursues and is nourished by. The merry, morbid climax of "The Venetian Twins," which makes a jest of death and resurrection (eastward-looking Venice has always taken its religion with a pinch of pagan salt), throws a bright shadow athwart "Finnegans Wake" and as far forward as Behan's "The Hostage" and even Bellow's "The Last Analysis."

The plot of "The Venetian Twins" being preposterously labyrinthine, we can give thanks that I am incapable of recounting it. Let me just mention that one of the twins is brave and sensible and the other craven and foolish, that nobody can tell which twin is which, and that each of the twins is unaware of the other's presence. The complications that flow out of this highly unlikely state of affairs suffice to fill the evening with continuous confusion. The twins are played by Alberto Lionello, a youngish man of formidable charm and immense skill. By a miracle of energetic

Reprinted by permission; © 1968 The New Yorker Magazine, Inc.

miming and speedy footwork, at one point he makes it appear that the two brothers are actually onstage at the same moment; by a further ingenuity of prestidigitation, at the end of the play he manages to take one bow as the brave twin and a second as the craven one, and I could swear that I saw them passing each other. Camillo Milli steals several scenes as a lecherous old humbug, and the two girls with whom the twins fall in love are attractively embodied by Silvia Monelli and Lucilla Morlacchi. The play was directed by Luigi Squazini with a breezy directness that does much to make us forget that the words we hear, and soon come unselfconsciously to laugh at, are not in English. The simple scenery and piebald period costumes are by Gianfranco Padovani. Still, it is the company as a whole that deserves our bravos, and I offer mine here a second time, *di tutto cuore.*[1]

Brendan Gill

Objectives

You, the student, after viewing *The Venetian Twins*, should be able to do the following:

1. Recognize comic conventions in *The Venetian Twins* and their influence on subsequent comic writers.
2. Define commedia dell'arte including in your definition an explanation of how it developed.
3. Recognize the stock characters of *The Venetian Twins* and the acting skills they require.
4. Appreciate Carlo Goldoni's talent as a comic playwright.

Program Notes

The Venetian Twins

Carlo Goldoni's wild, fast-paced farce of mistaken identity, with mixed pairs of lovers, blustering soldiers, clever servants, windy pedants, etc., is based on *commedia dell'arte* types. Broad and obvious, *The Venetian Twins* is the forerunner of a modern situation comedy. Deliberately artificial-looking, painted scenery is the backdrop for swordplay, eavesdropping, and slapstick. Scenes of Venice and a discussion of this type of drama provide an exposition of historical background and theater craft. This excerpt from the BBC production is a shortened version of the original, omitting the subplot concerning the jewels, and telescoping the physical action surrounding Zanetto's death.

1. With all my heart

THE VENETIAN TWINS

This excerpt begins in the middle of Scene I, when Zanetto is suggesting to Rosaura that they make love before they marry:

ZANETTO Of course I want to amuse myself.
ROSAURA Well, in due time you can.
ZANETTO The proverb says, there's no time like the present. Don't keep me in suspense. *(He approaches)*
ROSAURA I've warned you, take your time.
ZANETTO Exactly! I'll take my time. Now!

(He embraces her passionately and she slaps his face)

ROSAURA Presumption!
ZANETTO Oh!
ROSAURA Oh!

(ZANETTO stands astonished then runs silently out of room)

ZANETTO Oh! . . . Oh!
ROSAURA Heavens, what an improper young man! We women should never be left alone with men. There's always some danger to be faced.

(PANCRAZIO enters—peering around door)

PANCRAZIO Heaven keep you, my child! But what's the matter?
ROSAURA Oh, Signor Pancrazio, if you knew what had just happened to me? *(ROSAURA sits)*
PANCRAZIO Reveal all to me freely. Naturally, you can trust me completely.
ROSAURA I will tell you, Signore. You knew, of course, that my father has decided that I am to marry a Venetian. What you do not know is the man's a fool, a presumptuous fool.

(PANCRAZIO sits down)

PANCRAZIO Presumption is only to be expected from foolish people.
ROSAURA My father insisted on my speaking with him.
PANCRAZIO Bad!
ROSAURA He actually left me all alone with him.
PANCRAZIO Still worse!
ROSAURA And then this fellow . . .
PANCRAZIO Yes, yes, I can imagine!
ROSAURA . . . in the most indecent words.
PANCRAZIO Smooth and glib, no doubt?
ROSAURA Yes, Signore.
PANCRAZIO Then—he attempted some immodesty?
ROSAURA Exactly.
PANCRAZIO Continue! What took place?

A slight adaptation edited from *The Venetian Twins* from Carlo Goldoni: FOUR COMEDIES, translated and introduced by Frederick Davies (Penguin Classics, 1968), pp. 29–38, © Frederick Davies, 1968. Reprinted by permission of Penguin Books, Ltd.

ROSAURA He offended me so much that I slapped his face.
PANCRAZIO Oh . . . Oh, what a good, what a wise, what an exemplary girl you are! Oh, heroic hand! Oh, illustrious and glorious hand! On this hand, allow me with reverence and admiration to imprint, a kiss. *(He takes her hand and kisses it with smooth tenderness)*
ROSAURA It uh . . . it merits your approval, then? The way I showed my resentment?
PANCRAZIO Oh, you must continue. You must go on slapping them in the face. You must accustom yourself to despising these young scoundrels. And if ever your heart decides to love, look for an object worthy of your love.
ROSAURA You are right, Signor Pancrazio. Forgive my weakness. I will go tell my father I do not want such a man. *(ROSAURA goes)*
PANCRAZIO Bravo. If I don't obtain Rosaura by false virtue and pretended prudence, I can't hope to, that's certain. I haven't got youth, good looks or money. But I've found a way.

(Exit)

Act I, Scene ii (A Street, On one side the DOCTOR'S house, on the other is an Inn with the sign "The Two Towers.")

(BEATRICE enters with FLORINDO)

BEATRICE Signor Florindo. I must return to Venice!
FLORINDO But—why this sudden decision?
BEATRICE For six days I've been waiting for Signor Tonino. Some accident has kept him in Venice. I simply must go and find out for myself.
FLORINDO To return to Venice whence you've just fled on Signor Tonino's advice?
BEATRICE No one will recognize me.
FLORINDO No, Signorina Beatrice. Signor Tonino entrusted you to my protection. It's my duty to restrain you. My friendship for Signor Tonino demands nothing less. *(to himself)* As does my love for you.
BEATRICE I am determined to go. My heart tells me that I have lost my Tonino. What good will there be in staying in Verona?
FLORINDO Here, perhaps, you may find somebody who is convinced of your worth, somebody who would take the place of your dear Tonino.
BEATRICE I am Tonino's or no one's.
FLORINDO *(to himself)* Still, if she stays here and if her fiance doesn't turn up, little by little I could hope to win her.
BEATRICE *(to herself)* When he least expects it, I will flee from his protection.

(LELIO enters)

FLORINDO Oh, here comes that affected dandy, Lelio. Forever running after you. Heaven knows what would happen if I were not with you.
LELIO *(to BEATRICE)* Most beautiful Venetian. I have just heard from the post driver that you are yearning to return to Venice. Make use of me! I will give you a coach, horses, grooms, servants, as much money as you like, if you will give me the pleasure of accompanying you.
BEATRICE *(to herself)* What presumption!

(FLORINDO moves between BEATRICE and LELIO)

FLORINDO Signore, permit me to ask by what right you offer the Signoria Beatrice such things when you see she is in my company?
LELIO Who are you? Her brother? A relative? Or some fortune-hunter?
FLORINDO Sir, I am a gentleman. I am, moreover, under obligation to look after this lady.
LELIO Well, then, friend, you're in a difficult situation.
FLORINDO And why?
LELIO Because it takes more of a man than you are to look after a lady. Signorina Beatrice, give me your hand and let me be of service to you. Come, let us go.

(He tries to take her hand)

FLORINDO *(giving him a slap)* I told you to remember your manners.
LELIO This to me? To me, whom nobody has ever dared give an insolent glance? D'you not know who I am? I am the Marquis Lelio, Lord of Monte Fresco, Count of Fonte Chiara, Magistrate of Selva Ombrosa. I have more estates than you've hairs in that badly combed wig. And more money than you'll ever see in your life.
FLORINDO *(to himself)* As if everybody didn't know him. Calls himself Count Marquis, when he's only the nephew of Doctor Balanzoni.
LELIO Either the lady comes with me, or you will fall victim of my anger.
FLORINDO This lady is in my protection, and in a minute I will reply with my sword.
LELIO Poor young man! I feel sorry for you. You want to die? Is that it?
BEATRICE *(softly to* FLORINDO*)* Signor Florindo! Do not endanger yourself with such a fellow.
FLORINDO *(to* BEATRICE*)* Do not worry. I'll bring him down a peg or two.
LELIO Hold on to life! You are young. Hold on to life. Leave this lady to me. The world is full of women. You've only one life.
FLORINDO I value honor more than life. Now are you going or do you prefer the sword? *(he draws his sword)*
LELIO You're not of the nobility. I do not fight with such as you. *(turns)*
FLORINDO Nobility or no, this is the way to treat cowards like you. *(gives him a blow with the flat of his sword)*
LELIO This to me! Gods of my ancient house assist me in the contest to the death! *(draws sword and attacks)*
BEATRICE Oh, dear! This is no place for me.

*(*LELIO *and* FLORINDO *fight,* LELIO *attacks,* LELIO *parries,* FLORINDO *attacks,* LELIO *trips* FLORINDO, FLORINDO *falls.)*

FLORINDO Oh! I fell! I slipped!
LELIO *(holding his sword to his chest)* Now you are vanquished!
FLORINDO No. It was an accident.
LELIO No! My nobility defeats you! Die!

*(*TONINO *enters, sword in hand in defence of* FLORINDO*)*

TONINO *(to* LELIO*)* Stop! Stop! When an adversary is on the ground you should lower your sword.
LELIO What concern is this of yours?
TONINO Because I am a man of honor.
FLORINDO It can't be . . . Signor Tonino . . . Dear friend . . .

TONINO *(aside to* FLORINDO*)* Ssh! Do not mention my name. *(to* LELIO *who no longer looks so confident)* Come, Signor Bully, and apply yourself to me.

LELIO But I've no quarrel with you! Why d'you want to fight me?

TONINO Because you have insulted my friend. You threaten a man on the ground? You tell me he is to die! Raise your sword!

FLORINDO *(to* TONINO*)* No, dear friend, don't endanger yourself for me.

TONINO Please! It's a trifle.

LELIO Impertinence. You have questioned my honor. Shamed the honor of my ancestors.

TONINO That's true. What will grandmamma say? Rock-a-bye baby? What will daddy say about his great big cowardly son?

LELIO Here I am! *(puts himself on guard opposite* TONINO*)*

TONINO Bravo! Take courage!

(They fight)

LELIO LUNGES. TONINO PARRIES. 3 BLOWS AT POSITIONS 9 O'CLOCK AND 12 O'CLOCK. LELIO LUNGES FORWARD. TONINO STEPS ASIDE, LELIO ATTACKS AND TONINO PARRIES. LELIO HACKS AT TONINO. TONINO LOCKS SWORDS, THEY REVOLVE SWORDS LOCKED. TONINO BREAKS LOCK. LELIO LUNGES ONCE AGAIN. TONINO LOCKS LELIO'S SWORD AND DISARMS HIM.

LELIO Augh! I'm unarmed!

TONINO You're *dis*armed, and that's enough for me. I don't kill you. I don't say "die." It's enough for my honor to have beaten you.

LELIO I'll have my revenge! (TONINO HANDS SWORD BACK)

TONINO Any time. Whenever you wish.

LELIO You will see! You will see!

(Exit LELIO*)*

FLORINDO Dear friend, how very much I'm obliged to you.

TONINO Think nothing of it. Now. Beatrice! Where is she?

FLORINDO Beatrice *(aside)* I'd best dissemble *(to* TONINO*)* Who is this Beatrice?

TONINO Why, the girl I helped to escape from Venice. The girl I asked you to look after until I arrived.

FLORINDO Friend, I've seen no one.

TONINO What?

FLORINDO I mean it. I've not seen this woman you speak of.

TONINO I see. Ah, well. And I thought I had found a faithful woman at last. But it appears she has made a fool of me. So that's that. One word more, friend: don't call me Tonino. I don't want to be recognized.

FLORINDO Ah!

TONINO Call me Zanetto.

FLORINDO Why Zanetto?

TONINO Because I have a twin brother who lives in Bergamo who's called that and he's very like me in looks. People will think I am he, and in that way I will avoid any danger.

FLORINDO And this brother of yours, does he still live in Bergamo?

TONINO I believe so. We've never been on friendly terms. I've heard he's getting married, though I don't know where or to whom. He's the world's biggest ass.
FLORINDO My house is at your disposal, friend, if you care to honor it.
TONINO My dear fellow!
FLORINDO Although, to tell the truth, my father doesn't like seeing people.
TONINO Oh, I see. Well, think nothing of it, my dear friend, I'll put up here at this Inn.
(Exit)

A Listing of BBC Actors and Productions Coordinators

THE VENETIAN TWINS

by

Carlo Goldoni

CAST

THE TWINS (Zanetto and Tonino)	DONAL DONNELY
ROSAURA	AMANDA BARRIE
FLORINDO	JONATHAN CECIL
BEATRICE	JACQUELINE PEARCE
LELIO	NEIL CUNNINGHAM
PANCRAZIO	MILTON JOHNS
DOCTOR BALANZONI	JOHN EVITTS
ARLECCHINO	DAVID WOOD
COLOMBINA	JUDITH FIELDING
BRIGHELLA	CHRIS SULLIVAN
PORTER	KENNETH WALLER

PRODUCTION

SET DESIGN	DAVID HITCHCOCK
COSTUME DESIGNER	BARBARA KIDD
MAKE-UP SUPERVISOR	MAGGIE WEBB
DIRECTOR/PRODUCER	PAUL KAFNO

Focus in Viewing

The shortened BBC version of the play shows the intricacies of plot and the development of character types inherited from the commedia dell'arte. Goldoni uses the highly artificial convention of the aside to signpost the characters' thought. Most of the characters find themselves in a constant state of bewilderment because they believe they are talking to the double of the person with whom they are actually speaking; therefore, the aside is a device to keep us precisely informed as to what their real thoughts and reactions are.

Goldoni's intention was to preserve the commedia tradition; however, he discarded the use of the masks to identify the character types, but maintained the traditional costumes. This production retains an element of the mask by using very stylized make-up; it bases the costumes on those which would have been worn by the commedia characters. In addition, the artificiality of the play is underlined by the avoidance of a natural-looking set. Expect to see a deliberately theatrical setting which has a cardboard quality.

Content Viewing

1. Describe 4 stock characters in *The Venetian Twins*.
2. Why do we not take the death of Zanetto more seriously?
3. How does Goldoni use language (dialogue) in this play? Comment on the use of the aside.

Craft Viewing

1. What conventions do you need to know or accept before you can understand or enter into the spirit of this production? Can you trace the characters of the play back to their commedia dell'arte originals?
2. Based on your viewing of the BBC production and reading of the plot summary, do you recognize a plot structure? If so, what is it? How, within the play's conventions, do the contrivances of the plot work and with what effect?
3. Can you determine a directorial concept or interpretation? Are you in agreement or disagreement? In what way, if at all, would you have directed the production differently?
4. Choose an actor and tell if you agree, or disagree, with the characterization in the production. Explain.
5. Do you think the technical design and execution supported the playscript? (Include comments on the costumes, make-up, and music.)
6. Is there one moment or scene which stands out in your memory? Why?

Critical Viewing: Overview

1. Now that this play and its production are part of your experience, what significance does *The Venetian Twins* hold for you?

Additional Plays That Demonstrate Similar Concepts

A Servant of Two Masters—Goldoni
The Menaechmi, Miles Gloriosus—Plautus
Twelfth Night, The Comedy of Errors—Shakespeare
Volpone—Ben Jonson
The Would-be Gentleman, The Miser—Moliere
A Funny Thing Happened on the Way to the Forum
Book by Burt Shevelove and Larry Gelbart, Lyrics by Stephen Sondheim

Stage Terms

Aside—Something that an actor tells an audience while other characters are on stage. The other characters are not aware of the message.

Stock Characters—An overdone character whose role is evidenced by time-honored attributes; for example, the villain wears a black cape.

MODULE

4

The Conventions of Theatre

I. Introduction: The Theatre and Conventions, p. 228
   A. Adjusting to Theatre Conventions, p. 228
   B. *The Way of the World*, p. 229
   C. *Ubu Roi*, p. 229
   D. Black Theatre, p. 229
   E. *Six Characters*, p. 230
II. Study materials for *The Way of the World*, p. 231
III. Study materials for *Ubu Roi*, p. 259
IV. Study materials for *Sizwe Bansi Is Dead*, p. 275
V. Study materials for *Six Characters in Search of an Author*, p. 283

You will find a more detailed outline preceding the introduction and each of the plays.

"THE THEATRE: THE MOST REAL UNREAL PLACE THERE IS"

Adjusting to Theatre Conventions

Theatre art always has functioned at its best when its audience has fully accepted the theatre condition, which allows the imagination to be transported beyond surface reality. The BBC television productions for this course have been filmed to capture the theatre-like quality of the settings rather than the realism of a true-to-life environment. Viewers, realizing that this effect was intended, must see the productions as an attempt to maintain the atmosphere of the stage. It is unfortunate that most viewers have become so accustomed to the pervasive convention of realism, especially in movies and on television, that it becomes difficult for them to adjust their viewing sensibilities to cope with the theatre's more varied repertoire of conventions. Not only evaluation, but also pleasure in the theatre experience, is dependent upon a viewer's recognition of an adjustment to the conventions which have influenced any production.

A convention is a method of staging which creates the illusion of the theatre. Conventions remind us that we are watching a deliberate attempt to imitate life. When a playwright tries to move a play beyond convention to life, itself, he soon finds that his innovation is in itself, a convention. Pirandello, for example, placed his characters on a bare stage. Before other playwrights imitated this effect, it was an innovation, but as more and more plays began this way, the true-to-life beginning became instead a well-known theatrical device or convention.

Conventions are the result of earlier innovations that are familiar to and therefore accepted by audiences. While many sources can influence the creative artist to change—to violate—a convention or set of conventions, audiences rarely seek such a change. As a matter of theatre historical fact, many audiences, experiencing the production of a new dramatic work, have revolted against it by hissing, booing, tossing objects (juicy and otherwise), and even stopping the actors' performances with physical and vocal objections. Often, these audiences were unwilling or unprepared to expect the unexpected, so they were confounded and confused by the creative artists' needs not only to use the taken-for-granted conventions but to extend the theatre beyond convention as well.

Herein lies one of the paradoxes found in drama and theatre art. Although conventions are considered as "ground-rules" or common, unwritten agreements between spectator and performers, which allow the pretense on the stage and the illusion of actuality to exist, playwrights and theatre artists often expand, delete, or experiment (changing the "ground-rules") as they creatively respond to their world. The Coleridge phrase "willing suspension of disbelief" implies that a spectator enters a theatre situation as a partner to those known conventions and to those in the making in order that the drama can take place.

Conventions vary from time to time, from country to country, from genre to genre, from theatre to theatre. This fluid nature of conventions is dependent on the changing perceptions of the world and of the theatre as a representation of it. Theatre artists shape and reshape theatre possibilities to either express new viewpoints, insights, and aspirations that they would like to see become a reality or to reflect viewpoints that they believe already are part of reality.

The Way of the World

The conventions of theatre are influenced by such factors as the historical period of the play's writing, the social and cultural setting in which the playwright lived, the stage or physical theatre setting in which the play was produced, and even the playwright's and performers' desired audience response.

Social mores of Europe's 17th Century elite provided comic material and conventions for playwrights such as Molière and Congreve. Characteristically, comedy is time-bound to its period, time, and locale. Heightened consciousness of the social context in which the play appeared is necessary for a full viewing enjoyment. Congreve's *The Way of the World* offers us a rare opportunity to see the kind of stylization of character, movement, and dialogue which glittered on the London and Paris stages of the 17th Century.

Influenced by Molière, Congreve drew from society's elite his subject matter as he depicted his vision of the manners and cutoms in high society. He populated the stage with characters who are self-deceived, or who are busy deceiving others with wit, grace, and ceremony. The plot of *The Way of the World* is highly complicated, the language extremely elaborate and polished, the costumes and stage settings richly elegant and decorous—all indications of the period's revolt against or restoration from Puritan rule with its emphasis on moral restrictions, plainness in dress, and simplicity or purity of language. Congreve's social context was that of the minuet and the masquerade ball, of a society less concerned with *what* it did than with *how* it did it, and of man seen as the representative or product of a specific social order rather than as an individual. Through an understanding of Congreve's conventions, a viewer can capture the spirit of the play, reacting as Congreve intended to the repartee of his characters who speak as elegantly as they dress.

Ubu Roi

Those playwrights who lead the way for changes in the theatre by continually violating established conventions are often called the front guard. One of the foremost examples of avantgardism is the Theatre of the Absurd. This dramatic form represents a revolt against naturalistic and realistic styles. Alfred Jarry's *Ubu Roi* is frequently credited as the forerunner for this type of drama, which takes to task elaborate settings, contrived plots, order, language, and meaning of any kind. Reducing and presenting the universe and existence as something inherently absurd, Jarry makes an assault on language as a symbolic representative of man's communication system. Thus, he relies on the techniques of nonsense, irrationality, and broad verbal and physical humor. Emphasis is placed on discovering the condition of man as meaningless (on situation rather than on plot), as man weaves his web of emotional confusion. This playwright's view of life ushered in innovations that today are conventions.

Black Theatre

The establishment of black theatre is an example of drama and of theatre artists' response to their world and their need. Black theatre reflects and promotes black culture. The history, the social, political, and economical organization, the creative motif, and the ethos of most black people are expressed in black theatre. It attempts to voice the ideas, hopes, fears, images, and actions of black people. Poetry, music, dance, and church may often provide a vehicle for black theatre.

Black dramatists throughout the 20th Century have used drama to recreate the ritual celebrations of their heritage and to make society more conscious of black experience. Conventions emerging from this drama reflect its ethnic origin. The contributions of black theatre are significant, not only to theatre art but to the facilitation of social change as well. *Sizwe Bansi Is Dead* provides a powerful viewing example of a contemporary issue of burning concern to the public—the passbook laws in the Republic of South Africa and their effect upon the black population. With integrity and dignity, despite his humiliating predicament, Sizwe Bansi must decide whether or not to take on the identity of a ghost to survive. Survival depends upon the mask one wears; a smile conceals the inner struggle for pride and dignity against the degradation wrought by the system. The photograph of the dead man becomes a living symbol, poignant and painful, of a current human reality: those victimized by society are bereft of that which defines human life—freedom of choice.

Six Characters

Realism in the theatre depends on what the audience is willing to pretend is real. Dramatic literature and its subsequent stage depiction are illusion. A dramatist must make choices and selections. These choices represent the playwright's, directors, and performers viewpoints, and perhaps suggest accuracy or verisimilitude. The artists portray or represent reality, not necessarily with a mirror reflection but possibly with a prismatic impression. Realism, then, is only one convention of drama and theatre art which is used to persuade us that a play is dealing with reality.

Pirandello's *Six Characters in Search of an Author* depicts various kinds of reality: (1) the world of art as it exists in the artist's imagination, (2) the concrete world as it exists in the disciplined state of creating an artistic work, and (3) the artist's manipulation between the two worlds. *Six Characters* illustrates the theatre-life paradox of illusion/art vs. reality, of man's inherent sense of role-playing and drama-making, indeed, of all people seeking to dramatize their lives by playing out a role as a character of theatrical significance.

It may well be that people in everyday life live and create some sort of drama for themselves, not unlike Pirandello's characters; however, it is of utmost importance for us to recognize that when this drama is transferred to the theatre stage it is no longer reality but a *representation* of reality or rearranged reality. The theatre condition always is limited by a viewer's judgment criterion which assesses the effectiveness of drama and its production by asking, "How real to life is this play?" The work of creative artists is real, but the product of that work is an interpretation of reality. Explorations of the levels of reality are possible only in the specialized environment within the true theatre condition: the most real unreal place there is.

THE WAY OF THE WORLD

by

William Congreve
(1670–1729)

A. Play Notes: Customs and Comedy, p. 232
B. Story and Plot Summary, p. 234
C. Commentary: A Brief Summary of a Review by Walter Kerr, p. 235
D. Walter Kerr's Review, p. 235
E. Objectives, p. 237
F. Program Notes, p. 237
G. Play Excerpt, p. 238
H. A List of BBC Actors and Production Coordinators, p. 252
I. Director's Notes, p. 256
J. Focus in Viewing, p. 257
K. Additional Plays that Demonstrate Similar Concepts, p. 258
L. Stage Terms, p. 258

Play Notes

Customs and Comedy

Customs

Much of the action in *The Way of the World* depends on assumptions about class, rights, and the privileges of the sexes. Knowing about how property is controlled according to the play, is part of the ability to cope in sophisticated society. Those who don't know about property are rustics, uncomfortable in London society. These rustics dare to disobey the unwritten laws that forbid marrying outside their class. Also, females grant dowries, turning over property to males, in the belief that they, the women, cannot understand matters of investment. (Indeed, if there had been true equality of the sexes the play would have been quite different.) Millamant talks of giving up her liberty when she marries. To an extent she is being coy, but in a real sense she would have to abide by her husband's decisions, just as Mrs. Fainall did. Those characters in *The Way of the World,* who challenged accepted customs, provoked laughter among Restoration audiences; however, modern audiences, for the most part, laugh at those characters who are slaves to custom, applauding, instead, the characters who challenge tradition.

A reversal in customs often is a subject for humor because we often see as funny a situation that is an exaggerated departure from what we believe to be "right." For example, a reversal of sex roles in the early 18th century evoked laughter from the audience, but today such a reversal is not considered by most audiences as an "exaggerated departure," but rather a representation of what should be accepted.

Even twenty years ago it was possible to make jokes about too-long hair on a man, or about a woman who "wore the pants" in the family. Today, however, the struggle for female/male equality and increased sexual liberation has made the cartoons and jokes of a few years past no longer amusing. Customs have changed, and so has that comedy which depends on customs.

Comedy

Comedy in *The Way of the World* depends in part on period customs and in part on the continuing characteristics which seem to exist in all ages, which we call "human nature." The contemporary viewer will find it necessary to concentrate on what the actors say, because there is little physical action of the sort we have come to expect in a funny play, except for Lady Wishfort's antics prior to Sir Rowland's arrival.

We are grateful for the clumsy efforts of Lady Wishfort, as she anxiously rehearses her "spontaneous" response to the visit of her supposed suitor, Sir Rowland. Watching her try out different poses—sitting, walking, turning coyly, or lying down is still funny to most people. She doesn't know how awkward, pretentious, and unattractive she is. The only barrier to enjoying that scene would be the effort to feel what she is feeling—to take on an attitude of so much sympathy that the strong identity would interfere with the ability to laugh. Pretense in minor matters is still a good subject for comedy. Carried to extremes, an old woman convinced of her beauty might be a serious problem if she spent the family fortune running to spas, hairdressers, and theatrical agents, insisting on her eligibility for roles others knew were unsuitable. It might be possible nowadays to make Lady Wishfort the subject of a serious psychological study of self-delusion.

But such an approach would violate the whole spirit of Restoration comedy. To enjoy *The Way of the World,* it is better simply to laugh at Lady Wishfort's futile efforts at beauty, and thus join Foible, Mrs. Marwood, and the other characters who agree on her foolish affectations.

Less comical to the modern viewer would be talk of cruelty toward others—of marrying someone in order to get revenge, of cuckoldry, of deliberate trading of affection in return for money. We may recognize that these matters were considered funny to aristocratic audiences of the time. We, however, do not ourselves share their amusement.

The most notable and enduring moment is the marriage contract scene with Mirabell and Millamant. Though the vocabulary for such an exchange has since changed, the feelings have not. In setting forth conditions that would make her "dwindle into a wife," Millamant holds out for genuine affection, affection that would avoid public display of endearments. She prefers, instead, love. She mentions her misgivings about surrendering the pleasures of independence in her demand that her future husband promise not to take her for granted. He must pursue her after marriage just as before, and he must also ask permission to attend the tea table over which she is sovereign. Mirabell's amusement over some of the conditions shows his own control. He is the one who mentions sex and breeding. It is he who makes the sly remark about "pleasures" before marriage. Millamant, for all her efforts to be cool, detached and sophisticated, reveals her own inexperience. In our own age, though the game is played differently (the marriage contract having more to do with disposition of the joint salaries of husband and wife), we can still enjoy the spirited exchange of Millamant and Mirabell.

The contract of Mirabell and Millamant has to do with their expectations of how the other should behave rather than how to arrange their finances. Their manners toward each other dictate that they avoid open talk of love. They seem to be sparring, but their crisp dialogue can be understood as an affectionate exchange by any couple preferring understated feelings to open emphasis on words of love. Theirs is the indirect communication of the drawing room.

Language and Wit

The language in the play is neither poetic nor an imitation of everyday speech. Instead it is highly verbal and clever. The dialogue is so rich and full that it seems sometimes the characters talk too much. Unlike the relaxed, pause-filled movie dialogue, the language of Restoration comedy is quick, stylized, and pretentious. The characters of Restoration theatre conceal their true feelings, in attempts to make clever pronouncements about love, infidelity, money, and betrayal. They speak generally, rather than personally. Our speech, today, as represented in the movies, is filled with direct statements about our preferences and plans ("I like . . . think . . . I wish . . . What I hate is. . . ."). *The Way of the World* dialogue consists of epigrams which presumably will apply to society in general. For example Mirabell says " . . . a man may as soon make a friend by his wit, or a fortune by his honesty, as win a woman with plain-dealing and sincerity." (Act II, Scene 2) In *The Way of the World* the characters want money and social position, but they don't come out and say it because to do so would be embarrassing. Instead, all the characters take for granted these goals, and the talk is about what mistresses and cuckolds (husbands with unfaithful wives) do. These characters feel love, but would almost rather die than confess to strong feelings of affection. They pretend to be cool and unattainable. They conceal emotions and flirtatiously talk about their need for solitude.

The lover knows—or suspects—that his attentions are wanted more than the lady will admit, and he is willing to play a game which seems to modern viewers unnecessarily complicated and wordy. For those who were conditioned to play the game, though, the words became the ball hit across the net, and both players took pleasure in hitting and scoring points. Mirabell and Millamant would have been appalled by a modern day encounter group, with its emphasis on revelation of honest feelings. For the 17th–18th Century couple, there was more pleasure in dressing up an expression of love with the language of wit than admitting it openly.

When witnessing the repartee of two restoration characters, the viewer would do best to detach himself from their problems. Usually such period comedy is exaggerated to emphasize the foolishness of how certain characters think. When the viewer laughs at their folly, he is accepting the playwright's idea of what is ridiculous. In effect, the playwright is warning others about mistakes to avoid. The reason the viewer should "stand back" is so that he will not make the mistake of accepting and making excuses for the foolishness of a character's speech or actions, as he might accept and make excuses for his own behavior.

When one reads or looks at a traditional comedy, he should pretend that he is at some distance from the characters—on a mountain top looking down. He should be "close" enough to hear what is said, but not so close that the character's problems evoke empathy rather than amusement. If one is oblivious to pain, is one then being cruel? According to a culture brought up on compassion as an ideal, such an attitude may seem to be cruel, but the comic writer would argue that he is like a doctor, observing, describing, and attempting to cure a sickness. To do so requires that the doctor and his student have an overview of the problem instead of an emotional reaction to the pain it causes.

Story and Plot Summary

Mirabell and Millamant are in love. Opposition of Millamant's aunt and guardian, Lady Wishfort, however, prevents their marriage because she is seeking revenge against Mirabell for having pretended to be in love with her. Mirabell devises a plot to embarrass Lady Wishfort, who is eager for a suitor.

Mirabell persuades his servant, Waitwell, to dress as a possible suitor for Lay Wishfort. The servant has been married that day to Lady Wishfort's waiting woman, Foible. It is hoped that when Lady Wishfort realizes how foolish she has been in allowing herself to be courted by this false suitor, she will give permission for the marriage of Mirabell and Millamant—and also part with the fortune she controls. This is the main plot. There are other characters and incidents involving marriage and money. One concerns Lady Wishfort's daughter, Mrs. Fainall, whose husband has been having an affair with Mrs. Marwood.

Also involved is the prospective husband for Millamant, whom Lady Wishfort has selected for her. He is Sir Wilfull Witwoud. There are other admirers of both Mirabell and Millamant. Possibly the least sympathetic character is Mr. Fainall, son-in-law of Lady Wishfort and lover of Mrs. Marwood. Though all characters know the importance of money, Fainall seems most cynically opportunistic and least aware of love. The viewer seeing the play for the first time should be concerned with the main plot—the courtship of two attractive, witty people, the foolishness of a vain lady, and the common sense of the bright, loyal servants.

Commentary

Language is, of course, an integral part of drama; however, Congreve's *The Way of the World* is based almost solely on dialogue, and fast-paced at that. Therefore line readings are most important and need to be handled with the utmost of care. Walter Kerr's critical review of *The Way of the World* holds Maggie Smith in the highest regard. To him, she conveys the lines as though she herself had written them. With the bat of an eyelash, the uppity Millamant spatting out a marriage contract becomes a low-keyed, touching woman requesting privacy. Notice the way in which Kerr appraises the characters portrayed.

New York Times, July 4, 1976

Maggie Smith Has Her 'Way' at Stratford

Congreve's "The Way of the World" is both the most successful and the most curious of the three main-stage productions that have begun this season's Stratford Festival in Canada, and Maggie Smith is the most successful and most curious creature in it. That figures, Miss Smith has more or less taken over the snake-charmer concession in that continuing sideshow we call the theatre, and has, in the past 10 years or so, laid waste more living-rooms, chaises lounges, leading men, ottomans, vanity tables and handy bric-a-brac than any other enchantress in the business. She coils herself around things, and they disappear in small puffs of smoke, leaving only her violent red hair and her small contrite mouth behind as a memento of the holocaust. Usually it's a comic holocaust; Miss Smith makes annihilation funny.

• • •

What didn't figure in the least was the way she'd choose to play "The Way of the World." She's Millamant, of course, haughtiest of the naughty, witty even before breakfast, so swift and lethal of tongue that one of the fops-about-town who appears early in Congreve's elaborate conceit announces that he wouldn't go near her "were she as Cleopatra." (Inasmuch as we can also see her as Cleopatra in Shakespeare's "Anthony and Cleopatra" the very next night or so, we are in a position to appreciate the gentleman's apprehension.)

But let the chaps talk. When Miss Smith comes on as Millamant, in the palest of pale blues to let that hair set the world afire, she does indeed prattle on until someone must point out that she doesn't give echo fair play. (Echo must wait till she's stopped before it dare begin, and what echo could ever remember all that?) She prattles about the papers she uses as haircurlers ("I never pin up my hair with prose"), she prattles about suitors ("I love to give pain"), she prattles about landscapes and lying and the unreliability of love. If everyone else talks in periods, coming to rounded, thumping stops, she lets one line breed another indiscriminately, until you think language must have overpopulated the globe.

And yet, if there is one thing she is not, it is too mighty, too overwhelming, too bright. She almost hinted, right from the beginning, that she talks to keep her composure, that language is her last line of defense, that she's secretly more vulnerable than anyone on stage. Surrender syntax and all is lost, and there is a constant danger that syntax may flounder. Without slowing her pace,

© 1976 by The New York Times Company. Reprinted by permission.

she manages to break sentences, retrace words, let lines trail to diminuendo (she is magnificent, and gets a laugh that must be heard all the way to Toronto, as she refers to a bumpkin as "this flower of knighthood," each word issuing more limply dismayed than the one just before).

From the celebrated "marriage contract" scene, in which she and her lover Mirabell state the conditions under which they will agree to domesticate themselves, she's got a base to do something utterly unexpected. She is every bit as funny as she ought to be for the most of it, enjoying herself enormously in a tragedy-queen near-faint as she reacts in shock ("Oh, name it not!") to her prospective husband's monstrous mention of childbearing. But, without a flick of those heavy-lidded eyes of hers, she alters tone utterly with one seemingly unremarkable request. Mirabell is always to "knock at the door before you come in." With that—who'd have counted on it?—she is totally touching. During all of the imperiously outrageous terms this early apostle of freedom (1700) has been setting, terms bolder and in spots saner than those demanded today, she's been most deeply concerned about one small, ordinary, unmistakably human need: the barest minimum of privacy.

I don't suppose many Millamants have made this line the heart of the entire, brilliantly epigrammatic passage. But then I don't suppose many Millamants have laid such an odd foundation: a woman who can become so flustered that, in a flurry of self-consciousness, she assiduously fans someone else rather than herself. (She also knows that this bit of business is funny; but you see, she must do something to cover for herself.) An original, affecting, altogether superb reading of the role.

With Jessica Tandy shoring up the sidelines, Miss Tandy, scowling at a servant for bringing her cherry brandy in a container the size of an "acorn," plays an aging, heavily enameled dowager ("I look like an old peeled wall") who controls the purse-strings of the plot. With her great frilled bonnet rising vertically from her head as though it were standing at attention, she raps her dependents to order with a stout tongue and a sometimes candid, sometimes self-deluding appraisal of her own chances for coaxing a bit of romance back into her life. . . .

The play has always given producers trouble; too many minor characters, too many major characters, too many scenes described that might have been played, too many scenes played for a nice architectural balance. Director Robin Phillips hasn't cut any of this overload, which means that we drift off here and there, being in left field so often. But putting a first-rate company to the task of setting it all out firmly—from the opening tableau, which looks as though a high wind had hurled an entire bewigged century through a church door and up against the organ, to the final demure, candlelit dance—does finally show us the play's subterranean complexity. There is a canker at its core. Though I don't know if a concordance has ever been provided for *The Way of the World,* it would surely show the word "hate" recurring at least as often as any other. . . .

These worldly-wise, verbally felicitous tools ("One must have a wife to be untrue to and a mistress to blame") aren't happy with their wisdom or their felicity. Manner is a mask; behind it, energy, real delight, is running down. Perhaps that is why Miss Smith can be so irresistible and so right as she says "I could laugh inordinately" in tones that actually suggest ennui. The way of the world, so glittering, is wicked, as we learn. A production that can make us laugh at the glitter while taking note of the dour truth is one that demands to be seen. . . .

Walter Kerr

Objectives

You the student after studying *The Way of the World* should be able to

1. recognize Restoration comedy as a humorous but insightful commentary on its time.
2. identify William Congreve's craftsmanship and stylization in characterization and language that is as complex and elegant as the society it represented.
3. appreciate the lavish costumes and sets created by theatre craftsmen as conventions which convey the spirit of Restoration comedies, exemplified in *The Way of the World*.

Program Notes

The Way of the World

The most elegant comedy of the Restoration era is presented in a version which eliminates confusing subplots and concentrates on the main characters. Lady Wishfort foolishly attempts to disguise her age with cosmetics as she prepares to greet her purported suitor, who is actually the servant of the play's hero. Mirabell is plotting to win permission to marry the conquettish Millamant. Comic episodes from William Congreve's play include a portrayal of the artifices of Lady Wishfort and the marriage contract of the hero and the heroine. Fortune hunting, man-hating, and flirtation are discussed in witty epigrams delineating what was once for high society "the way of the world."

The video version has an accompanying guest performance by parodist Anna Russell, making fun in her inimitable way of the pretenses of this artificial, yet human, group.

The production begins with the opening of Act II and consists of a shortened version of that act, the first and last sections of Act III, and curtailed versions of Acts IV and V, parts which concern the major relationships of the play: the lovers, the liaisons, and Lady Wishfort's intrigues.

THE WAY OF THE WORLD

by

William Congreve

Act II

(Enter MRS. FAINALL *and* MRS. MARWOOD*)*

MRS. FAINALL Aye, dear Marwood, if we will be happy, we must find the means. Men are ever extremes, either doting or averse. While they are lovers, their jealousies are insupportable. And when they cease to love, they loathe.

MRS. MARWOOD But say what you will, 'tis better to be left than never to have been loved. To refuse the sweets of life because they once must leave us, is as preposterous as to wish to have been born old. For my part, my youth may wear and waste, but it shall never rust in my possession.

MRS. FAINALL Then it seems you but dissemble an aversion to mankind.

MRS. MARWOOD Certainly.

MRS. FAINALL Bless me, how have I been deceived! Why you profess a libertine!

MRS. MARWOOD Come, be as sincere, acknowledge that your sentiments agree with mine.

MRS. FAINALL Never!

MRS. MARWOOD You hate mankind?

MRS. FAINALL Heartily, inveterately.

MRS. MARWOOD Your husband?

MRS. FAINALL Most transcendently; aye, though I said meritoriously.

MRS. MARWOOD Give me your hand upon it.

MRS. FAINALL There.

MRS. MARWOOD I join with you; what I have said has been to try you.

MRS. FAINALL It is possible? Dost thou hate those vipers, men?

MRS. MARWOOD I have done hating 'em, and am now come to despise 'em. The next thing I have to do is eternally to forget 'em.

MRS. FAINALL There spoke the spirit of an Amazon.

MRS. MARWOOD Though I'm sometimes thinking to carry my aversion further.

MRS. FAINALL How?

MRS. MARWOOD Faith, by marrying; if I could but find one that loved me very well and would be thoroughly sensible of ill usage, I sometimes think I should do myself the violence of undergoing the ceremony.

MRS. FAINALL You would not make him a cuckold?

MRS. MARWOOD No, but I'd make him believe I did, and that's as bad.

MRS. FAINALL Why had not you as good do it?

MRS. MARWOOD Oh, if he should ever discover it, he would then know the worst, and be out of his pain; I would have him ever to continue on the rack of fear and jealousy.

MRS. FAINALL Ingenious mischief!

(Enter MR. FAINALL *and* MR. MIRABELL*)*

FAINALL My dear!
MRS. FAINALL My soul!
FAINALL You don't look well today, child.
MRS. FAINALL D'ye think so?
MIRABELL He is the only man that does, madam.
MRS. FAINALL The only man that would tell me so at least.
FAINALL Oh my dear, I am satisfied of your tenderness, I know you cannot resent anything from me.

(MRS. FAINALL Stands)

MRS. FAINALL Mr. Mirabell, my mother interrupted you last night. I would fain hear you out.

(Exit MRS. FAINALL and MIRABELL)

FAINALL Excellent creature! I'm sure if I should live to be rid of my wife, I were a miserable man.
MRS. MARWOOD Aye!
FAINALL For having only that one hope, the accomplishment of it must, of consequence, end all my hopes. What a wretch is he who must survive his hopes!

(Exit FAINALL and MRS. MARWOOD)

(Enter MIRABELL and MRS. FAINALL)

MRS. FAINALL While I only hated my husband, I could bear to see him; but since I have despised him, he's too offensive.
MIRABELL Oh, you should hate with prudence.
MRS. FAINALL Yes, for I have loved with indiscretion.
MIRABELL You should have just so much disgust for your husband as may be sufficient to make you relish your lover.
MRS. FAINALL Why did you make me marry this man?
MIRABELL Why do we daily commit dangerous and disagreeable actions? To save that idol, reputation. If the familiarities of our loves had produced that consequence of which you were apprehensive, where would you have fixed a father's name with credit, but on a husband? When you are weary of him, you know your remedy.
MRS. FAINALL I ought to stand in some degree of credit with you, Mirabell.
MIRABELL In justice to you, I have made you privy to my whole design, and put it in your power to ruin or advance my fortune.
MRS. FAINALL Whom have you instructed to represent your pretended uncle, Sir Rowland?
MIRABELL Waitwell, my servant.
MRS. FAINALL He is a humble servant to Foible, my mother's woman, and may win her to your interest.
MIRABELL Care is taken for that. She is won and worn by this time. Foible and Waitwell were married this morning.
MRS. FAINALL So, if my poor mother is caught in a contract, you will discover the imposture and release her by producing a certificate of her gallant's former marriage.
MIRABELL Yes, on the condition that she consent to my marriage with Millamant and surrender the moiety of Millamant's fortune in her possession.

MRS. FAINALL Well, I have an opinion of your success, for I believe my Lady Wishfort will do anything to get a husband.
MIRABELL Yes, I think the good lady would marry anything that resembled a man, though 'twere no more than what a butler could pinch out of a napkin.
MRS. FAINALL Female frailty! We must all come to it, if we live to be old. Here comes your mistress!
MIRABELL Here she come, i'faith. Full sail, with fans spread and streamers out!

(She approaches)

You seem to be unattended, madam. You used to have the beau monde throng after you.
MILLAMANT Oh, I have denied myself airs today. I have walked fast through the crowd.
MRS. FAINALL But, dear Millamant, why were you so long?
MILLAMANT Long! Lord, have I not made violent haste? I have asked every living thing I met for you; I have inquired after you, as after a new fashion.
MRS. FAINALL You were dressed before I came abroad.
MILLAMANT Aye, that's true. Oh, but then I had—Mincing, what had I? Why was I so long?
MINCING O, mam, your la'ship stayed to peruse a pacquet of letters.
MILLAMANT Oh, aye, letters; I had letters. I am persecuted with letters. I hate letters. Nobody knows how to write letters; yet one has 'em, and one does not know why. They serve only to pin up one's hair.
MIRABELL Is that the way? Pray, madam, do you pin up your hair with all your letters? I find that I must keep copies.
MILLAMANT Only with those in verse, Mr. Mirabell. I never pin up my hair with prose. I fancy one's hair would not curl if it were pinned up with prose. I think I tried once, Mincing.
MINCING O, mam, I shall never forget.
MILLAMANT Mirabell, did not you take exceptions last night? O, aye, and went away. Now I think on't, I'm angry. No, now I think on't, I'm pleased; for I believe I gave you some pain.
MIRABELL Does that please you?
MILLAMANT Infinitely.
MIRABELL You will not affect a cruelty that is not in your nature.
MILLAMANT One's cruelty is one's power; and when one has parted with that I fancy one's old and ugly.
MIRABELL Suffer one's cruelty to destroy one's lover, and then how vain, how lost a thing you'll be! For beauty is the lover's gift: 'tis he betstows your charms, your glass is all a cheat.
MILLAMANT Oh, the vanity of men! Beauty, the lover's gift! Lord, what is a lover, that it can give? Why, one makes lovers as fast as one pleases, and they live as long as one pleases, and they die as soon as one pleases; and then, if one pleases, one makes more.
MIRABELL Very pretty.
MILLAMANT Fainall, let us leave this man.
MIRABELL I would beg a little private audience, madam. You had the tyranny to deny me last night.
MILLAMANT You saw I was engaged.
MIRABELL Unkind! You had the leisure to entertain a herd of fools. How do you find delight in such society?
MILLAMANT I please myself. Besides, sometimes to converse with fools is for my health.

MIRABELL For your health! Is there a worse disease than the conversation of fools?
MILLAMANT Mirabell, if you persist in this offensive freedom, you'll displease me. I think I must resolve, after all, not to have you; we shan't agree. I shan't endure to be reprimanded nor instructed; 'tis so dull to act always by advice, and so tedious to be told of one's faults—I can't bear it. Well, I won't have you, Mirabell—I'm resolved—I think—you may go. Ha! Ha! Ha! What would you give that you could help loving me?
MIRABELL I would give something that you did not *know* I could not help it.
MILLAMANT Come, don't look grave then. Well, what do you say to me?
MIRABELL I say that a man may as soon make a friend by his wit, or a fortune by his honesty, as win a woman with plain dealing and sincerity.
MILLAMANT Sententious Mirabell!
MIRABELL You are merry madam, but I would persuade you for one moment to be serious.
MILLAMANT What, with that face? No, if you keep your countenance, 'tis impossible I should hold mine. Well, after all, there is something very moving in a love-sick face. Ha! Ha! Ha! Well, I won't laugh, then, don't be peevish—Heigh ho! Now I'll be melancholy, as melancholy as a watch-light. Well, Mirabell, if ever you will win me, woo me now. Nay, if you are so tedious, then, fare you well.
MIRABELL Can you not find in the variety of your disposition for one moment. . . .
MILLAMANT To hear you tell me Foible's married, and of your plot? No.
MIRABELL But how came you to know it?
MILLAMANT I shall leave you to consider; and when you have done thinking of that, think of me.
MIRABELL Gone! Think of you! To think of a whirlwind, though 'twere in a whirlwind, were a case of more steady contemplation; a very tranquility of mind and mansion. A fellow who lives in a windmill has not a more whimsical dwelling than the heart of a man that's lodged in a woman.

ACT III

(Her ladyship at her toilet)

(Enter)

MRS. MARWOOD I'm surprised to find your ladyship in dishabille at this time of day.
LADY WISHFORT Mistress Foible's a lost thing; she has been abroad since morning, and never heard of since.
MRS. MARWOOD I saw her but now, in conference with Mirabell.
LADY WISHFORT With Mirabell! You call the blood into my face with mentioning that creature. I sent her to negotiate an affair in which, if I'm detected, I'm undone.
MRS. MARWOOD O madam, you cannot suspect Mistress Foible's integrity.
LADY WISHFORT Oh, he carries poison in his tongue that would corrupt integrity itself! Hark! I hear her!

(Enter FOIBLE)

Dear friend, dear Marwood, retire into my closet, that I may dress with more freedom. You'll pardon me, dear friend; I can make bold with you.

(Exit MRS. MARWOOD)

Where hast thou been, Foible? What hast thou been doing?

FOIBLE Madam, I have seen Sir Rowland.

LADY WISHFORT But what hast thou done?

FOIBLE Nay, 'tis your ladyship has done; and are to do; I have only promised. A man so enamoured, so transported! Well, here it is. *(shows miniature)* All that is left; all that is not kissed away.

LADY WISHFORT But hast thou not betrayed me, Foible? Hast thou not detected me to that faithless Mirabell?

FOIBLE *(aside)* So that devil has been beforehand with me. What shall I say? Alas, madam, could I help it if I met that confident thing? Oh, if you had heard how he used me, and all upon your ladyship's account. Aye, he had a fling at your ladyship too.

LADY WISHFORT Me? What did the filthy fellow say?

FOIBLE O madam! 'Tis a shame to say what he said, with his taunts and jeers and tossing up his nose.

LADY WISHFORT My life! I'll have him murdered. I'll have him poisoned. Where does he eat?

FOIBLE Poison him? Poisoning's too good for him. Starve him, madam, starve him; marry Sir Rowland and get him disinherited. Humph! (says he). I hear you are laying designs against me (says he) and Mistress Millamant is to marry my uncle (oh, he does not suspect a word of your ladyship); but (says he) I'll hamper you for that (says he), you and your superannuated old frippery too (says he). I'll handle you. . . .

LADY WISHFORT Audacious villain! Handle me! Would he durst! Frippery? Old frippery! I'll be married to Sir Rowland tomorrow; I'll be contracted tonight.

FOIBLE The sooner the better, madam.

LADY WISHFORT Frippery? Superannuated frippery! I'll frippery the villain; I'll reduce him to frippery and rags! A tatterdemalion! A slander-mouthed railer! I shall never recompose my features to receive Sir Rowland with any economy of face. That wretch has fretted me that I am absolutely decayed. Look, Foible.

FOIBLE Your ladyship has frowned a little too rashly, indeed, madam. There are some cracks discernible in the white varnish.

LADY WISHFORT Let me see the glass. Cracks, say'st thou? Why I am arrantly flayed; I look like an old peeled wall. Thou must repair me, Foible, before Sir Rowland comes, or I shall never keep up to my picture.

FOIBLE I warrant you, madam, a little art once made your picture like you; and now a little of the same art must make you like your picture.

LADY WISHFORT You see this picture has a sort of a-ha, Foible? A swimmingness in the eyes. Yes, I'll dress above. Is he handsome? Is Sir Rowland handsome? Don't answer me. I won't know. I'll be surprised, I'll be taken by surprise.

FOIBLE By storm, madam. Sir Rowland's a brisk man, I'll vow.

LADY WISHFORT Is he? Oh, then he'll importune, if he's a brisk man. I shall save decorums if Sir Rowland importunes. Oh, I'm glad he's a brisk man. Let my things be removed, good Foible.

(She exits and FOIBLE *crosses to ring the bell. Enter* MRS. FAINALL*)*

MRS. FAINALL O Foible, I have been in a fright, lest I should come too late! That devil Marwood saw you with Mirabell, and I'm afraid will discover it to my lady.

FOIBLE Discover what, madam?

MRS. FAINALL Nay, put not on that strange face with me. I am privy to the whole design, and know that Waitwell to whom thou wert this morning married, is to impersonate Mirabell's uncle.

FOIBLE I beg your pardon, madam. I thought the former good correspondence between your ladyship and Mr. Mirabell might have hindered his communicating this secret.

MRS. FAINALL Dear Foible, forget that.

FOIBLE Dear madam. Mistress Marwood had told my lady Wishfort, but I warrant you I turned it all for the better. I thold her that Mr. Mirabell railed at her. And now my lady is so incensed that she'll be contracted with Sir Rowland tonight, she says. I warrant you I worked her up, so that he may have her for asking for, as they say of a Welsh maidenhead.

MRS. FAINALL O rare Foible!

FOIBLE I beg your ladyship, acquaint Mr. Mirabell of his success. I would be seen as little as possible to speak with him, besides, I believe Madam Marwood watches me. She has a month's mind—but I know Mr. Mirabell can't abide her.

(Enter FOOTMAN)

John, remove my lady's toilet. Madam, your servant, I fear my lady is so impatient, that fear she'll come for me, if I stay.

MRS. FAINALL I'll go with you up the backstairs, lest I should meet her.

(They exit and MRS. MARWOOD enters)

MRS. MARWOOD Indeed, Mistress Engine, is it thus with you? Are you become a go-between of this importance? Why this wench Foible is the pass-partout, the very master key to everybody's strongbox. My friend, Mistress Fainall! I thought there was something in it with Mirabell but it seems 'tis over with you. "Madam Marwood has a month's mind, but Mr. Mirabell can't abide her." 'Twere better for Mirabell she had not been his confessor in that affair, without she could have kept his counsel closer. I shall not prove a pattern of generosity and stalk for him. He has not obliged me to that. And now I'll have none of him!

FAINALL Why, then, Foible's a bawd, an arrant, rank, match-making bawd, and I, it seems, am a husband, a rank husband; and my wife a very arrant, rank wife, all in the way of the world. "Sdeath, to be out-witted, to be out-jilted, to be out-matrimonied! If I had kept my speed like a stag, 'twere somewhat; but to crawl after, with my horns like a snail, to be outstripped by my wife, 'tis scurvy wedlock!

MRS. MARWOOD Then shake it off. You have often wished for an opportunity to part; and now you have it. But first prevent their plot; the half of Millamant's fortune is too considerable to be parted with, to a foe, to Mirabell.

FAINALL Damn him! That had been forfeited, had they been married. My wife had added luster to my horns with that increase of fortune.

MRS. MARWOOD They may prove a cap of maintenance to you still, if you can away with your wife.

FAINALL The means, the means.

MRS. MARWOOD Discover to my Lady Wishfort your wife' conduct with Mirabell; threaten to part with her. My lady loves her and will come to any composition to save her reputation. And if she should flag in her part I will not fail to prompt her.

FAINALL Faith, this has an appearance.

MRS. MARWOOD Well, how do you stand affected towards your lady?

FAINALL Why, faith, I'm thinking of it. Let me see. I am married already, so that's over. My wife has played the jade with me; so that's over too. I never loved her, or if I had, why that would be over too by this time. Jealous of her I cannot be, for I am certain. Weary of her I am, and shall be. No, there's no end of that. No, no, that were too much to hope. So much for my repose; now to my reputation. As to my own, well, I married not for it; so that's out of the question. And as to my part in my wife's, well she had parted with hers before; so bringing none to me, she can take none from me. 'Tis against all rule of play that I should lose to one who has not where-withall to stake.

MRS. MARWOOD Besides, you forget, marriage is honourable.

FAINALL Hum! Faith, and that's well said. Marriage is, as you say, honourable; and being so, wherefore should cuckoldom be a discredit, being derived from so honourable a root? If the worst come to the worst, I'll turn my wife to grass. I have already a deed of settlement of the best part of her estate, which I have wheedled out of her; and that you shall partake at least.

MRS. MARWOOD I hope you are convinced that I hate Mirabell now. You'll be no longer jealous.

FAINALL Jealous! No, by this kiss. Let husbands be jealous; but let the lover still believe. Or, if he doubt, let it be only to endear his pleasure, and to prepare the joy that follows, when he proves his mistress true. But let husbands' doubts convert to endless jealousy; or, if they have belief, let it corrupt to superstition and blind credulity. I'm single, I'll herd no more with 'em. True, I wear the badge, but I disown the order. And since I am to leave 'em I care not if I leave 'em a common motto to their common crest.

    All husbands must or pain or shame endure;
    The wise too jealous are, fools to secure.

Act IV

(Enter LADY WISHFORT *and* FOIBLE*)*

LADY WISHFORT Is Sir Rowland coming, say'st thou, Foible? And is all in order?

FOIBLE Yes, madam, I put wax lights in the sconces, and placed the footmen in a row in the hall.

LADY WISHFORT And are the dancers and the music ready?

FOIBLE All is ready, madam.

LADY WISHFORT And—well-and how do I look?

FOIBLE Most killing well, madam.

LADY WISHFORT Well, and how shall I receive him? In what figure shall I give his heart the first impression? There is a great deal in the first impression. Shall I sit? No, I won't sit—I'll walk—aye, I'll walk from the door upon his entrance; and then turn full upon him. No, that will be too sudden. I'll lie—aye, I'll lie down—I'll make the first impression on a couch. I won't lie, neither, I'll loll and lean upon one elbow, with one foot a little dangling off and jogging in a thoughtful way—as soon as he appears, I'll start, and be surprised, and rise to meet him in some disorder—yes—oh, nothing is more alluring than a levee from a couch in some confusion. It shows the foot to advantage, and furnishes with blushes, and recomposing airs beyond comparison.

FOIBLE Yes, Madame.

LADY WISHFORT Hark! There's a coach!

FOIBLE 'Tis he, madam.

LADY WISHFORT Oh dear, has Sir Wilfull made his addresses to Millamant? I ordered him.

FOIBLE Sir Wilfull is set in to drinking, madam, in the parlor.

LADY WISHFORT My life! I'll send him to her, and when they are together, then come to me that I may not be too long alone with Sir Rowland.

(Exit)

FOIBLE Madam, Mr. Mirabell has been waiting this half-hour for an opportunity to speak with you, though my lady's orders were to leave you and Sir Wilful together.

MILLAMANT I am thoughtful and would amuse myself—bid him come another time.

FOIBLE Shall I tell Mr. Mirabell to go away?

MILLAMANT Aye, if you please, Foible, send him away—or send him hither—just as you will, dear Foible—I think I'll see him—shall I? Aye, let the wretch come.

(She looks at her book, repeating verses out loud)

"There never yet was woman made
Nor shall but to be cursed." (That's hard!)

(She turns on)

"Like Phoebus sung the no less amorous boy . . .

(Enter MIRABELL*)*

MIRABELL Like Daphne she, as lovely and as coy."

Do you shut yourself up from me, to make my search more curious? Or is this artifice contrived, to signify that here the chase must end and my pursuit be crowned, for you can fly no further?

MILLAMANT Vanity! I'll fly and be followed to the last moment. I'll be solicited to the very last, nay and afterwards.

MIRABELL What, after the last?

MILLAMANT Oh, there is not so impudent a thing in nature as the saucy look of an assured man, confident of success. Ah! I'll never marry, unless I am first made sure of my will and pleasure.

MIRABELL Would you have 'em both before marriage? Or will you be contented with the first now, and stay for the other till after grace?

MILLAMANT Ah! My dear liberty, shall I leave thee? My faithful solitude, my darling contemplation, must I bid you then adieu? I can't do't, 'tis more than impossible, Positively, Mirabell, I'll lie abed in a morning as long as I please.

MIRABELL Then I'll get up in a morning as early as I please.

MILLAMANT Ah! Idle creature, get up when you will. And d'ye here, I won't be called names.

MIRABELL Names?

MILLAMANT Aye, as wife, spouse, my dear, joy, jewel, love, sweetheart, and the rest of that nauseous cant. I shall never bear that. Good Mirabell, don't let us be familiar or fond, or kiss before folks, or go to Hyde Park together the first Sunday in a new chariot, to provoke eyes and whispers; and then never to be seen there together again; as if we were proud of one another the first week, and ashamed of one another ever after. Let us never go to a play together or visit together. But let us be very strange and well-bred; let us be as strange as if we had been married a great while, and as well-bred as if we were not married at all.

MIRABELL Have you any more conditions to offer? Hitherto your demands are pretty reasonable.

MILLAMANT Trifles! As liberty to pay and receive visits to and from whom I please; to wear what I please; to have no obligation upon me to converse with that I don't like, because they are your acquaintances or to be intimate with fools, because they may be your relations; to have my closet inviolate; and to be sole empress of my tea table which you must never approach without first asking leave. And lastly, wherever I am you shall always knock at the door before you come in. These articles subscribed, if I continue to endure you a little longer, I may by degrees dwindle into a wife.

MIRABELL Well, have I liberty to offer conditions—that when you are dwindled into a wife, I shall not be beyond measure enlarged into a husband?

MILLAMANT Speak and spare not.

MIRABELL I thank you, Imprimis then, I covenant that your acquaintance be general, that you admit no sworn confidante, no intimate of your own sex; no she-friend to screen her affairs under your countenance. . . .

MILLAMANT Oh, detestable imprimis!

MIRABELL Item, I article that you continue to like your own face as long as I shall; and that while it passes current with me, that you endeavour not to new-coin it. To which end, together with all vizards of the day, I prohibit all masks of the night, made of oiled skins and I know not what—hog's bones, hare's gall, pig-water, and the marrow of a roasted cat. Item, when you shall be breeding. . . .

MILLAMANT Ah! Name it not.

MIRABELL Which may be presumed, with a blessing on our endeavors. . . .

MILLAMANT Odious endeavours!

MIRABELL I denounce against all straitlacing, and the squeezing for a shape, till you mold my boy's head into a sugar loaf, and instead of a man-child, make me the father to a crooked billet. Lastly, to the dominion of the tea table I submit, but with proviso, that you exceed not your province, but restrain yourself to genuine and authorized tea table talk—such as mending of fashions, and spoiling of reputation, railing at absent friends, and so forth; but that on no account you encroach upon the men's prerogative, and presume to drink healths, and toast fellows.

MILLAMANT I toast fellows, odious men! I hate your odious provisos.

MIRABELL Then we're agreed. Shall I kiss your hand upon the contract? And here comes one to be a witness to the sealing of the deed.

(Enter MRS. FAINALL*)*

MILLAMANT Fainall, what shall I do? Shall I have him? I think I must have him.

MRS. FAINALL Take him, take him, what should you do?

MILLAMANT Well then—I'll take my death I'm in a horrid fright—Fainall, I shall never say it—well—I think—I'll endure you.

MRS. FAINALL Have him, have him, and tell him so in plain terms for I am sure you have a mind to him.

MILLAMANT Are you? I think I have—and the horrid man looks as if he thought so too. Well, you ridiculous thing you, I'll have you—I won't be kissed, nor I won't be thanked—here, kiss my hand, though. So, hold your tongue now, and don't say a word now.

MRS. FAINALL Mirabell, you have neither time to talk nor stay. My mother is coming; and should she see you, would fall into fits. Therefore, spare your ecstasies for another occasion and slip down the backstairs, where Foible waits to consult you.

MILLAMANT Aye, go, go. And in the meantime I suppose you have said something to please me.

MIRABELL I am all obedience.

(He exits)

MRS. FAINALL Yonder Sir Wilfull is drunk, and so noisy that my mother has been forced to leave Sir Rowland to appease him; and he answers her with nothing but singing and drinking. What they have done by now I know not.

MILLAMANT Well, if Mirabell should not make a good husband, I am a lost thing—for I find I love him violently.

MRS. FAINALL So it seems, when you mind not what is said to you. Well, if you doubt him, you had best take up with Sir Wilfull Witwoud.

MILLAMANT How can you name that superannuated lubber? Foh!

(Enter LADY WISHFORT *and* FOIBLE)

LADY WISHFORT Out of my house, out of my house, thou viper! Thou serpent, that I have fostered! Thou bosom traitress that I raised from nothing! Go! Go! Starve again, do, do!

FOIBLE Dear madam, I'll beg pardon on my knees.

LADY WISHFORT Away! Out! Out! Go set up for yourself again! With your three-pennyworth of small ware . . . an old gnawed mask, two rows of pins, and a child's fiddle; a glass necklace with the beads broken, and a quilted nightcap with one ear. Go, drive a trade, do! These were your commodities, your treacherous trull! This was the merchandise you dealt in, when I took you into my house, and placed you next to myself, and made you governante of my whole family.

FOIBLE Dear madam. Do but hear me. Mr. Mirabell seduced me. If you knew but what he promised and how he assured me your ladyship should come to no damage.

LADY WISHFORT No damage? What, to betray me, to marry me to a cast servingman? O thou frontless impudence, more than a big-bellied actress.

FOIBLE Oh, dear madam, do but hear me; he could not have married your ladyship, for he was married to me first. He could not have bedded your ladyship.

LADY WISHFORT What, then I have been your property, have I? What have you made a passive bawd of me? I'll couple you! Your turtle is in custody already, and you shall coo in the same cage, if there be constable or warrant in the parish.

(Exits)

FOIBLE That ever I was born! That I was ever married! A bride! Aye, I shall be a Bridewell-bride. Oh!

(Enter LADY WISHFORT*)*

LADY WISHFORT O my dear friend, how can I enumerate the benefits I have received from your goodness? To you I own the detection of that imposter Sir Rowland. And now you are become an intercessor with Mr. Fainall, to save the honour of my house, and compound for the frailities of my daughter. Well, friend, you are enough to reconcile me to the bad world.

(Enter MRS. FAINALL)

LADY WISHFORT O daughter, daughter, is it possible thou shouldst be my child, bone of my bone, flesh of my flesh, and, as I may say, another me, and yet transgress the most minute particle of severe virtue?

MRS. FAINALL I don't understand your ladyship.

LADY WISHFORT Not understand? Why, have you not been naught? Have you not been sophisticated? Not understand? And here I am ruined to compound for your caprices and cuckoldoms.

MRS. FAINALL I am abused and wronged, and so are you. 'Tis a false accusation, as false as hell, as false as your friend there, aye, or your friend's friend, my false husband.

MRS. MARWOOD My friend, Mistress Fainall? Your husband my friend? What do you mean?

MRS. FAINALL I know what I mean, madam, and so do you; and so shall the world at a time convenient.

LADY WISHFORT Why, if she should be innocent, if she should be wronged after all. O my dear friend, I don't believe it, no, no! As she says, let him prove it, let him prove it.

MRS. MARWOOD Prove it, madam? And have your name prostituted in the public courts! Yours and your daughter's reputation worried at the bar by a pack of bawling lawyers!

LADY WISHFORT Oh, 'tis insupportable!

MRS. MARWOOD Nay, madam, I advise you nothing; here comes Mr. Fainall. If he shall be satisfied to huddle up all in silence, I shall be glad.

FAINALL Well, madam, I have suffered myself to be overcome by the importunities of this lady, your friend, and I am content that you shall enjoy your own estate during life, upon condition that you oblige yourself never to marry.

LADY WISHFORT Never to marry?

FAINALL No more Sir Rowlands.

LADY WISHFORT Never to marry. But in case of necessity, as of health, or some such emergency.

FAINALL Oh, if you are prescribed marriage you shall be considered. I will reserve to myself only the power to choose your physic. Next, my wife shall settle upon me the remainder of her fortune, and for her maintenance be dependent entirely on my discretion.

LADY WISHFORT This is most inhumanly savage.

FAINALL And lastly, I will be endowed, with that six thousand pounds, which is the moiety of Mrs. Millamant's fortune in your possession; and which she has forfeited by her disobedience in contracting herself with Mirabell, against your knowledge or consent.

LADY WISHFORT This is insolence beyond all precedent, all parallel. Must I be subject to this merciless villain?

MRS. MARWOOD 'Tis severe indeed, madam, that you should smart for your daughter's wantonness.

LADY WISHFORT 'Twas against my consent that she married this barbarian, but she would have him. You will grant time to consider?

FAINALL Yes, while the instrument is drawing, to which you must set your hand.

(Exit FAINALL*)*

LADY WISHFORT Oh my dear friend, is there no comfort for me? Must I live to be confiscated at this rebel rate?

(Enter MILLAMANT *and* SIR WILFULL*)*

SIR WILFULL WITWOUD Aunt, your servant.

LADY WISHFORT Out, caterpillar, call me not aunt! I know thee not!

SIR WILFULL I confess I have been a little in disguise, as they say. 'Sheart! And I'm sorry for't. What would you have? For what's to come, to pleasure you I'm willing to marry my cousin.

LADY WISHFORT How's this, dear niece?

MILLAMANT I am content to be a sacrifice to your repose, madam; and to convince you that I had no hand in this plot, I have laid my commands on Mirabell to be a witness that I give my hand to this flower of knighthood, Sir Wilfull Witwoud.

LADY WISHFORT But I cannot admit that traitor Mirabell. He is as terrible to me as a Gorgon.

MRS. MARWOOD This is precious fooling, but I'll know the bottom of it.

MIRABELL Ah, madam, there was a time! But let it be forgotten. Nay, kill me not by turning from me in disdain. Let me be pitied first, and afterwards forgotten—I ask no more.

SIR WILFULL S'heart. The gentleman's a civil gentleman. We are sworn brothers and fellow travelers. Oh, come, come, aunt, forget and forgive; you must or you be a Christian.

LADY WISHFORT Well, nephew, upon your account. Well, sir, I will endeavour to forget, but on proviso that you resign your contract with my niece, immediately.

MIRABELL It is in writing, madam, and with papers of concern.

LADY WISHFORT Oh, there's witchcraft in his eyes and tongue! When I did not see him, I could have bribed a villain to his assassination; but his appearance rakes the embers that have so long lain smothered in my breast.

(Enter FAINALL *and* MRS. MARWOOD*)*

FAINALL Madam, here is the instrument; are you prepared to sign?

LADY WISHFORT If I were prepared, I am not empowered. My niece exerts a lawful claim, having matched herself by my direction to Sir Wilfull.

FAINALL This sham is too gross to pass upon me, though 'tis imposed on you, madam.

MILLAMANT Sir, I have given my consent.

MIRABELL And I, sir, have resigned my pretensions.

SIR WILFULL And, sir, I assert my right.

FAINALL Indeed? But I insist upon my first proposal. You, madam, shall submit your own estate to my management and make over absolutely my wife's fortune to my sole use. Now I suspect, madam, that your consent is not requisite in this case, nor Mr. Mirabell, your resignation, nor Sir Wilfull, your right. This my Lady Wishfort, must be subscribed or your darling daughter's turned adrift like a leaky hulk, to sink or swim, as she and the currents of this lewd town can agree.

LADY WISHFORT Is there no means, no remedy to stop my ruin? Ungrateful wretch! Dost thou not own thy being, thy subsistence to my daughter's fortune?

FAINALL I'll answer that when I have the rest of it in my possession.

MIRABELL But that you would not accept a remedy from my hands—or else perhaps I could advise. . . .

LADY WISHFORT What? Oh, what? To save me and my child from ruin, from want, I'll forgive everything that's past; nay, I'll consent to anything to come.

MIRABELL Aye, madam, but it is too late. You have disposed of her who only could have made me a compensation for all my services. But be that as it may, I am resolved, I'll serve you.

LADY WISHFORT How! Oh dear Mr. Mirabell, can you be so generous at last? Harkee, I'll break my nephew's match; you shall have my niece yet, and all her fortune.

MIRABELL I ask no more. I must have leave for two criminals to appear.

LADY WISHFORT Aye, aye! Anybody, anybody!

MIRABELL Foible is one, and a penitent.

(Enter FOIBLE *and* MINCING *and confer with* LADY WISHFORT*)*

MRS. MARWOOD (To FAINALL) These two corrupt things are bought and brought hither to expose me.

FAINALL Well, let it all come out, and let 'em know it. I will insist the more.

LADY WISHFORT O Marwood, Marwood, art thou false? Hast thou been a wicked accomplice with that profligate man?

MRS. MARWOOD Have you so much ingratitude and injustice, to give credit against your friend to the aspersions of two such mercenary trulls?

MINCING Mercenary, mem? I scorn your words. 'Tis true we found you and Mr. Fainall in the blue garret. No, if we would have been mercenary, we should have held our tongues; you would have bribed us sufficiently.

FAINALL Go, you are an insignificant thing! Well, what are you the better for this? Is this Mr. Mirabell's expedient? I shall stand off no longer. You thing, that was a wife, shall smart for this! I'll not leave thee wherewithal to hide thy shame; your body shall be as naked as your reputation.

MRS. FAINALL I despise you, and defy your malice! Go you and your treacherous—I shall not name it, but starve together, perish!

FAINALL Not while you are worth a groat indeed, my dear.

LADY WISHFORT Ah, Mr. Mirabell, there is small comfort, in the detection of this affair.

MIRABELL Mr. Fainall, it's now time that you should know that your lady, while still at her own disposal, and before you had your insinuations wheedled her out of a pretended settlement of the greatest part of her fortune. . . .

FAINALL Sir! Pretended!

MIRABELL Yes, sir. I say that this lady, while still a widow, did deliver this as her act and deed in trust to me. You may read, sir, if you wish. *(Holding out the parchment)*

FAINALL What's here? Damnation!

(Reads)

"A deed of conveyance of the whole estate of Arabella Languish, widow, in trust to Edward Mirabell." Confusion!

MIRABELL Even so, sir; 'tis the way of the world, sir, of the widows of the world. I suppose this deed may bear an elder date than what you have obtained from your lady.

FAINALL You perfidious fiend! Then thus I'll be revenged.

(Offers to run at MRS. FAINALL*)*

MIRABELL Hold, sir! Now you may make your bear-garden flourish somewhere else, sir.

FAINALL You shall hear of this, sir; be sure you shall. Let me pass, oaf!

(Exit, followed by MRS. MARWOOD*)*

LADY WISHFORT O daughter, daughter, 'tis plain thou hast inherited thy mother's prudence.

MRS. FAINALL Thank Mr. Mirabell, a cautious friend, to whom all is owing.

LADY WISHFORT Well, sir, you have kept your promise, and I must perform mine. The next thing is to break the matter to my nephew, and how to do that. . . .

MIRABELL For that, madam, give yourself no trouble. Sir Wilfull is my friend and has had compassion upon lovers.

SIR WILFULL 'Sheart, aunt, I have no mind to marry. My cousin is a fine lady, this gentleman loves her, and she loves him, and they deserve one another; my resolve is to see foreign parts. I am set on't, and when I'm set on't I will do't.'
LADY WISHFORT Well, sir, take her and with her all the joy I can give you.
MILLAMANT Why does the man not take me? Would you have me give myself to you over again?
MIRABELL Aye, and over and over again; for I would have you as often as I possibly can. *(kisses her hand)* Well, heaven grant I love you not too well; that's all my fear.
LADY WISHFORT As I am a person, I can hold out no longer. I swear I have spent my spirits so today already that I am ready to sink under the fatigue; and I cannot but have some fears upon me yet that my son Fainall will pursue some desperate course.
MIRABELL Madam, disquiet not yourself on that account for my part, I will contribute all that in me lies to a reunion. In the meantime, madam,

(To MRS. FAINALL*)*

let me before these witnesses restore to you this deed of trust; it may be a means, well-managed, to make you live easily together with your husband.

> From hence let those be warned, who mean to wed,
> Lest mutual falsehood stain the bridal bed;
> For each deceiver to his cost may find,
> That marriage frauds too oft are paid in kind.

(They all exit)

A Listing of BBC Actors and Production Coordinators

THE WAY OF THE WORLD

by

William Congreve

CAST

MRS. FAINALL	PETRA DAVIES
MRS. MARWOOD	ANN BELL
MR. FAINALL	NEIL STACY
MR. MIRABELL	ANTHONY AINLEY
MRS. MILLAMANT	FRANCESCA ANNIS
MINCING	MARGO COOPER
LADY WISHFORT	MARY WIMBUSH
FOIBLE	JO KENDALL
SIR WILFULL WITWOUD	JOHN SAVIDENT
FOOTMAN	EDWARD HALSTED

PRODUCTION

SET DESIGN	DACRE PUNT
COSTUME DESIGNER	BRIAN COX
MAKE-UP ARTIST	JO YOUNG
DIRECTOR	JOHN SELWYN GILBERT

(Left to Right) Mr. Mirabell, Lady Wishfort, Foible, Mincing, Mrs. Fainall, Mr. Fainall, Mrs. Marwood, Sir Wilfull Witwoud, Mrs. Millament

(Left to Right) Mrs. Fainall, Mrs. Millamant, Mr. Mirabell, Mincing

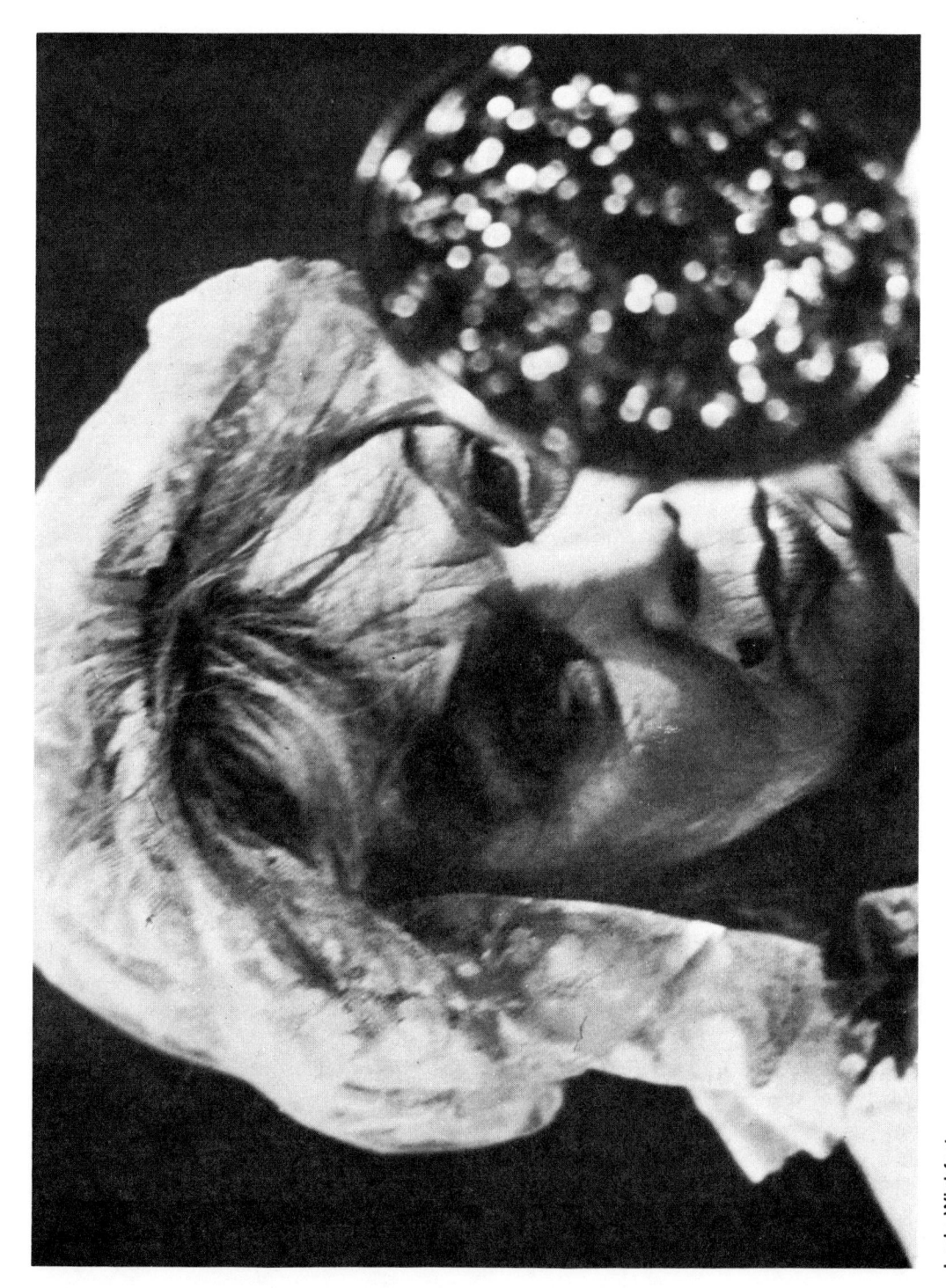

Lady Wishfort

Director's Notes

Nobody has ever accused *The Way of the World* of an excess of narrative drive. Even after its first performance, in 1700, the play's critics dismissed the plot as lamentably weak and yet took fierce exception to the strength of Congreve's satire. The portraits of the characters in the play are sharply, almost spitefully, etched into a text whose language is as beautiful and potent as anything written in English. But what the characters do is always improbable and occasionally impossible. *The Way of the World* is not a realistic comedy, more an act of ceremonial display.

The text of *The Way of the World* was printed in Congreve's lifetime. There are no essential problems or disputes about the words. However, Restoration comedy in general, *The Way of the World,* in particular, taken on a very special quality because of two extremely successful productions during the 20th Century. *The Way of the World* was relatively neglected from 1777 until 1924. When it was revived in 1924 (and again in 1958, with Edith Evans and John Gielgud), these were productions in which manner and style, the glittering surfaces of an idealised picture of Congreve's world, were emphasized, perhaps at the expense of content.

The original critics of Congreve's play resented it (and rejected it) because it was both unbelievable and all too real for them. They went to the theatre (a cultured, distinguished and exclusive audience) to laugh at the outsider, the stranger, the country bumpkin or at stereotypes of themselves which were so gross and schematic that the satire was easy to accept. Congreve's failure, in the eyes of his first audiences, was to invest his caricatures with a burden of serious comment which transcended wit or comedy as they were familiar to his contemporaries. It is this purposeful thread, an element of sadness, which it is all too easy to lose sight of in modern productions of Congreve's work.

At the centre of this play, rounded and realised even when the play is substantially abbreviated, Lady Wishfort, Mrs. Fainall, Mistress Marwood, Millamant, Mirabell and Mr. Fainall impress, interest (and amuse) us as human beings, despite the complications of Congreve's plot, enormous gulf between his period and ours and the need, in this production, to omit several of the minor characters and sub-plots with which Congreve intended to surround the principals.

The characters are inextricably, and sometimes hatefully, intertwined with each other (and will remain so after the play is over—Congreve does not attempt to *solve* their problems). They are caught in an elaborate web, of mutual jealousies, financial relationships and social and personal suspicions. It is their efforts to break free, to assert their individuality, at which Congreve invites us to laugh.

Society— "the currents of this lewd town"—dominates and corrupts what the characters in *The Way of the World* are and must be. There is no escape for them and, apart from Congreve's wit, nothing very entertaining will happen to them. At the end of this long play, Lady Wishfort still has no lover; Mrs. Fainall's marriage is more than ever hateful to her; Mirabell and Millamant supposedly blissful, are privately counting the cost and risks of their successful rapprochement. Only Sir Wilful Witwoud, determined to see foreign parts, has a future life to which he can look forward without reservation.

Within the form of Restoration comedy, Congreve gives us a tart commentary upon his characters and the society in which they have to live. In the full text, the dark side of the play is amply relieved by the frolics and foolishness of Petulant and Witwoud, the by-play with Peg the maid servant and Lady Wishfort's dalliance with 'Sir Rowland.' But in this production, the director and the cast have tried to point a way into the play, to suggest, for those who have not already detected it for themselves, that there is meat and substance in the play, that it is not only (as its recently acquired performing reputation would suggest) a confection of cream and sugar, puff pastry and rich decoration.

The Way of the World is a comedy, but not a slight or silly work. Like all good comedy, it needs to be taken seriously. Perhaps a simple and straightforward plot (if Congreve had been capable of writing one) would not altogether have served the author's purpose. The confusions and the complications of the narrative of *The Way of the World* may be there to decorate and to disguise the depth of the author's feelings.

John Selwyn Gilbert
20th February 1976

Focus in Viewing

The set designed for this production establishes the tone and spirit for this play. It fosters a certain icy feeling within its pastry pink colors set against a rather flat, mirror-like background. The characters parade and pose within this setting, which reflects their artificial facades and fancies. The real set/stage decoration in this production are the characters themselves, their language, and how they use it.

Content Viewing

1. What are the main interests of the society depicted in this play? Its values? Its criteria for excellence?
2. What are the prevailing attitudes toward love and marriage? Is the expression of these attitudes by the characters disreputable, cynical, or realistic?
3. How much emphasis do the characters give to emotion?
4. How does Millamant compare with Mrs. Marwood and Mrs. Fainall? Do you consider her to be self-centered, superficial, hard-hearted? Does she give any indication of more tender sentiments?
5. Do the characters express a philosophy? Explain. Does anything differentiate Mirabell from Fainall in their relations with the ladies? Would you expect Lady Wishfort to react differently to the deception worked upon her?
6. Is this a play of language and wit, customs manners, and character or is this a play in which wit cannot be distinguished from language, nor language from character, nor action from plot? Explain.

Craft Viewing

1. Is *The Way of the World* so much about the plottings of its characters that it seems plotless?
2. Do the costumes and sets add to the play or detract from it? Choose an actor. Do you agree, or disagree, with his/her characterization or interpretation?
3. Is there one moment or scene which stands out in your memory? More than one? Which one(s), and why?

Critical Viewing: Overview

1. Now that this play and its production are part of your experience, what significance does *The Way of the World* hold for you?

Additional Plays that Demonstrate Similar Concepts

Love for Love—Congreve
The Country Wife—Wycherley
She Stoops to Conquer—Goldsmith
School for Scandal—Sheridan
The Importance of Being Earnest—Oscar Wilde
Arms and the Man—George Bernard Shaw
Private Lives—Noel Coward

Stage Terms

Comedy of Manners—Comedy, popular during the 17th Century, which holds up for admiration the behavior of upper class people and for ridicule those who do not measure up to aristocratic standards. This type of play specializes in witty dialogue.

Context—The historical period in which a work was written. The prevailing values of this process are inevitably reflected, even if the subject of the play is an earlier period: Examples: *Macbeth, St. Joan.*

Convention—Any artificial element of a play or film.

Cuckold—A man with an unfaithful wife. Usually, those who know him comment on his "horns," which are the physical sign, so they say, of a poor, deluded gent.

Incongruity—Often the basis of theatre comedy; a situation or line that startles the viewer with its ridiculousness. For example, Lady Wishfort's obsession with maintaing beauty and youth.

The Restoration—The period in English history that coincides with the reign of Charles II (beginning 1660).

Wit—Remarks showing verbal dexterity, ingenuity, and quick perception that often evoke laughter. Wit is the product of reasoning power and astute judgment.

UBU ROI

by

Alfred Jarry
(1873–1907)

A. Play Notes: From the Sublime to the Pedestrian, p. 260
B. Story and Plot Summary, p. 261
C. Objectives, p. 262
D. Program Notes, p. 262
E. Play Excerpt, p. 263
F. A List of BBC Actors and Production Coordinators, p. 268
G. Focus in Viewing, p. 273
H. Plays that Demonstrate Similar Concepts, p. 274
I. Stage Terms, p. 274

Play Notes

From the Sublime to the Pedestrian

Perhaps the major changes in drama from classical to avant garde are most obvious through a study of characterization. For example, in Sophocles' play *Oedipus* the emphasis is on Oedipus, a superman of sorts, and his struggle with the gods, who are, of course, even greater than he. In *Macbeth,* Shakespeare pitted kings against one another so that the actions of the characters affect great numbers of people. The characters in both works are of epic proportion: larger-than-life heroes fulfilling the promise of their awesome potential. We identify with aspects of Macbeth's and Oedipus' character; yet, we are also awed by them. The schism in our view of them allows us to step back and study them in a more detached way than we can today's "hero." The modern "hero" does not make decisions of great magnitude, nor does he even commit the clear-cut folly of a Moliere, Congreve, or Goldoni character. To characterize the modern "hero" is difficult because of his obtuseness. In fact, it is this very lack of definition that sets him apart from his more definable progenitors. With the dissolution of the clear-cut character, comes an end also to plot structure. The order and logic so important to earlier dramatists becomes the subject of satire. The 20th Century avant-garde playwright reflects the collective doubts of the age which in turn reflect the aware individual's suspicion that his fate, whether in the stars or himself, is inconsequential.

Modern philosophy, literature, and drama suggest that our only greatness is in the recognition that there is no longer any way to be great. Alfred Jarry's play *King Ubu* mocks the "great hero" that was an integral part of characterization for centuries and explores what can happen when one accepts that greatness is only a delusion.

Influence of Artuad

When in 1938 Antonin Artaud published a selection of his essays entitled "The Theatre and its Double," he crystallized into text theatrical implications which had arisen as early as the 1896 premier of *King Ubu*. Indeed, the close relationship Artaud felt to Alfred Jarry is signified by the name he and Roger Vitrac gave to the experimental theatre they founded at Paris in 1927: Theatre Alfred Jarry.

Describing the program of the Theatre Alfred Jarry at its inception, Artaud stated that it proposed ". . . to contribute by strictly theatrical means to the ruin of the theatre as it exists today in France." He elaborated: "The Theatre Alfred Jarry has been created to . . . return to the theatre that total liberty which exists in music, poetry, or painting, and of which it has been curiously bereft up to now."

In "The Theatre and its Double" Artaud placed the blame for the poverty of the conventional French theatre on "culture." By culture, Artaud meant the patterns of artificiality which civilization—especially Western civilization—had imposed upon human nature, and, indeed, Artaud's concept of the theatre obviously stemmed from an intense desire to do justice to what he considered the essentials of the human personality, as well as from purely artistic considerations. Artaud, who yearned for a theatrical innocence reminiscent of Rousseau, believed that the human soul was crushed by the restraints imposed upon it by a corrupting civilization. For Artaud, the hidden core of art was pure emotion; only human desires (anger, hate, longing, and the most intense physical desires) were worthy of consideration by the artist. The theatre, he believed, should resist the artificial hierarchy of values imposed by "culture" and be consistently uninhibited to demonstrate the true reality of the human soul and the mercilessly savage conditions under which the soul operates. An expression of this oppression is what Artaud called "Theatre of Cruelty."

Cruelty in the theatre does not mean, Artaud was careful to point out, the mere dramatization of the techniques of physical laceration. Artaud thought that, above all, there had to be theatrical expression of an impersonal, implacable cruelty, lying essentially outside of man: the cruelty of the universe itself, in all its natural, violent force. "Everything that acts is a cruelty," Artaud wrote. "It is upon this idea of extreme action, pushed to its limits, that the theatre must be built."

Artaud realized that in order to express best his idea of primordial theatre, a state would be necessary that would completely overwhelm its audience. He therefore recommended the abolition of all physical barriers between theatre goer and actor. "We abolish the stage and the auditorium and replace them by a single site," he wrote. "Without partition or barrier of any kind . . . a direct communication will be reestablished. . . . The spectator, placed in the middle of the action, is engulfed and physically affected by it." He also recommended the intensification of the theatrical means itself and utilized the full theatre, drawing upon dance, song, and pantomime.

The Balinese theatre, which used words in a ritualistic, incantatory sense only and presented a perfect antidote to ". . . purely verbal theatre, unaware of everything that makes theatre," inspired Artaud. Emphasizing special vocal intonations, spectacle, ritual, actors' masks, as well as fresh concepts of lighting, scenery, and costuming—in short, as many techniques specifically at the disposal of the theatre as possible—Artaud outlined a system of almost totally antirealistic drama. Even today, Artaud's dramatic prescriptions are among the most technically and philosophically revolutionary in existence; and there are few avant-garde playwrights today who have not been influenced by Artaud's comprehensive and esthetic crystallizations.

Story and Plot Summary

All the following events have a wild, extremely undignified quality; they are a deliberate burlesque of the dignity usually associated with established society.

Ma Ubu urges Pa Ubu to go after the crown of Poland, rather than remain a mere captain of dragoons. She tempts him by reminding him that as king he could wear better clothes and eat whatever he liked. In a scene filled with oaths and insults, Ma plants the idea of assassinating the present king.

Guests arrive for dinner—Captain MacNure and his companions. Ma names what she has prepared for a magnificent meal. Pau Ubu throws food around, calls names, exhibits a toilet brush. Eventually, he evicts all guests except MacNure, whom he promises the dukedom of Lithuania in return for help in killing the king. MacNure agrees.

Pa Ubu is summoned by the King in honor of past services. He is asked to be present the next day for a great reveiw. Ubu presents the King with a toy musical instrument. The conspiracy goes forward. The King is to be murdered, after a not-so-solemn oath in which Ma Ubu stands in for a priest.

The next day, the Queen urges the King not to go out. She has had a dream foretelling Pa Ubu's treachery.

The King is murdered in a deliberately ribald manner, at odds with the "dignified" murders of leaders in Shakespearean plays. (In this sense, Jarry's play raises consciousness, challenging assumptions about the nobility of characters in *Macbeth* and *Julius Caesar* in which stately deportment and blank verse lend serious meaning to horrible events.) Jarry's characters perform in the manner of children shouting "Bang bang, you're dead," which is no more *un*real than the lofty speeches that Macbeth and his lady deliver when they murder Duncan. (Perhaps such adolescent behavior is a more fitting depiction of the aftermath of a violent murder.)

Pa Ubu, as King, enjoys the wealth of the royal treasury and ignores Ma Ubu's warnings about possible enemies. He puts to death nobles, financiers, and judges, sending them down a chute. He intends to run the country without help. The widow and son of the dead king have fled to the mountains. Massacres are widespread, and Ubu has doubled taxes. He intends to make his fortune and continue the killing.

Opposition arises: Captain M'Nure, who was denied the promised appointment, raises an army to help re-establish the young prince as ruler and he receives aid from the Russian Army, thus beginning the downfall of the lusty, crude monarch.

Objectives

After studying *Ubu Roi,* you, the student should be able to

1. recognize avant-gardism as a revolution in theatre that reflects a break from conventions as epitomized by the spirit of social revolution in the 1960's.
2. identify the changes in dramatic conventions created by Artaud's "Theatre of Cruelty."
3. appreciate avant-gardism as an experimental form of theatre that continually violates conventions in order to maintain the responsive, ever-changing nature of theatre.

Program Notes

Ubu Roi

This anarchic travesty makes fun of revered traditions when *Macbeth* is parodied by the earthy Pa and Ma Ubu. Not for the squeamish, the play has a parade of pin-striped gangsters, a grotesque "heroine," a king who plays the kazoo, the execution of national leaders ("Down the chute!" cries the new King Ubu.) and such nonrealistic theatrical conventions as the paper sign "Russian army" carried by a bedraggled actor.

Alfred Jarry wrote the play in the last decade of the 19th Century. It was outrageous at the time. Events in our own century have made it ominous as well, as reality has caught up with mockery. A minidocumentary explains how the play is tied to modern expressionistic drama. Jarry, in his preliminary address at the first performance of *Ubu Roi,* said, "We are going to make do with three complete acts, followed by two acts incorporating some cuts." The BBC production omitted the scenes involving Tsar Alexis and most of the battle scenes.

Reprinted by permission of Grove Press, Inc. UBU REX: this translation copyright © 1968 by Cyril Connolly and Simon Walson Taylor.

Act I, Scene vii

Ubu's house, smoke-filled and beer can littered (GYRON, HEADS, TAILS, PA UBU, MA UBU, MACNURE)

PA UBU Well, my good friends, it's high time we planned our little conspiracy. Let each give his counsel. With your permission, we will begin with mine.

CAPTAIN MACNURE Speak, Mister Ubu.

(UBU sits down)

PA UBU Very good, my friends. I am of the opinion that we should simply poison the King by stuffing his lunch with arsenic. The moment he starts the browsing and scoffing, he'll drop dead and I shall be king.

GYRON O, you wicked old thing, you!

PA UBU What, you don't like that idea? All right then, let's hear from M'Nure.

CAPTAIN MACNURE My suggestion is that I fetch him a good wallop with my sword and cleave him from top to toe.

ALL Ah yes! That's noble and gallant.

PA UBU But . . . but supposing he kicks out at you? I've just remembered; for his Grand Parades he wears iron boots which can be jolly painful. If I had half a chance, I'd snitch on the lot of you. That way, I'd be rid of the whole beastly business, and very likely pick up a reward in the bargain.

MA UBU Oh, the traitor, the coward, the rotten, mean skunk!

ALL Down with Old Ubu!

PA UBU Shut your traps, gentlemen, or I'll turn you all in. Very well, I'll take on the risks on your behalf. Uh, Captain M'Nure, is it agreed that your job is to split the king down the middle?

CAPTAIN MACNURE Wouldn't it be better if we all jumped on him at once, shouting and yelling? That way, we'd have a better chance of winning over the troops.

PA UBU No, look, I'll tell you what. I'll try to tread on his toe, he'll kick out at me, I'll yell "PSCHITT," and that will be the signal for you all to hurl yourselves upon him.

MA UBU And then the moment he's dead, you'll pinch his crown and sceptre.

CAPTAIN MACNURE And I and my men will go in pursuit of the royal family.

PA UBU Keep a sharp lookout for young Boggerlas.

(They start to go)

One moment, gentlemen, we are forgetting an indispensable ceremony. We must all take an oath to quit ourselves like men.

CAPTAIN MACNURE How can we? We haven't got a priest.

PA UBU My old woman will be the priest.

ALL All right, so be it.

PA UBU Do you all swear on the head of Madam Ubu to kill the King good and proper?

ALL We swear it. Long live Old Ubu!

(UBU group gives thumbs up salute and chants "UBU")

Act II, Scene i

The Palace: WENCESLAS, QUEEN ROSAMUND, DOLESLAS, LADISLAS, BOGGERLAS, GYRON.

THE QUEEN Really, Sire, are you quite determined to attend this parade?

THE KING And, pray, madam, why not?

THE QUEEN I'll tell you once more. I saw him in a dream, smiting you with mass weapons and throwing you into the Vistula, and an eagle like that which figures in the Arms of Poland placing the crown on his head.
THE KING On whose head?
THE QUEEN Old Ubu's.
THE KING Oh, ridiculous! Master Ubu is a most worthy gentleman who would let himself be dragged apart by wild horses rather than betray my interests.
THE QUEEN AND BOGGERLAS How wrong you are.

(KING *slaps* BOGGERLAS' *face*)

THE KING Silence, young rascal. And as for you, madam, to show you what complete faith I have in Master Ubu, I shall attend the Grand Parade, dressed as I am, without sword or breastplate.
THE QUEEN Oh, what fatal rashness! I shall never see you again alive. Oh!
THE KING Come Ladislas. Come, Doleslas. *(They go out. The* QUEEN *and* BOGGERLAS *Go to the window)*
THE QUEEN AND BOGGERLAS May God and the great Saint Nicholas protect you!

Act II, Scene ii

The parade Ground—POLISH ARMY, THE KING, DOLESLAS, LADISLAS, PA UBU, CAPTAIN MACNURE AND HIS MERRY MEN, GYRON, HEADS, TAILS.

THE KING Ah, noble Master Ubu, enter the royal enclosure with your followers, and we will review the march together.

(UBU *motions his men forward*)

PA UBU *(to his henchmen)* Look sharp, you clots. *(To the* KING*)* Coming, Sire.

(UBU'S *men get onto platform pushing* LADISLAW/BOLESLAS *aside*)

THE KING Ah, there's my regiment of Danziger Horseguards. Oh, what a magnificent spectacle!
PA UBU You really think so? Looks like something the cat brought in. Look at that one! *(pointing to a soldier)* You, there! When did you last have a shave, you lousy slob?
THE KING But this fellow is very well turned out. What on earth is the matter with you, Old Ubu?
PA UBU This! *(He stamps on the* KING'S *foot)*
THE KING Treason! *(*KING *stamps on* UBU'S *Toe. There's a delay as* UBU *remembers the word)*
PA UBU Pschitt.
CAPTAIN MACNURE At him! Hurrah! *(all strike the* KING*)*
THE KING Help, help! Holy Virgin, I'm dying.

(UBU *removes the* KING'S *crown and puts his own hat on the* KING'S *head*)

PA UBU Ha! I have the crown.
CAPTAIN MACNURE Death to the traitors!

(The KING'S *sons flee. All pursue them)*

Act II, Scenes iii and iv

The Palace

THE QUEEN Help, help! Those maniacs have forced their way into the palace. They're coming up the stairs.

(The din grows louder)

THE QUEEN AND BOGGERLAS *(on their knees)* May God protect us.
BOGGERLAS Oh, that vile UBU, wretch, rascal, I'd just like to get my hands on him. . . .
PA UBU Oh, you would, would you? And what, pray, BOGGERLAS, would you do to me?
BOGGERLAS By God's will, I shall defend my mother to the death. The first man to take a step forward is as good as dead.
PA UBU M'Nure, get me out of here. I'm scared.
A SOLDIER *(advances)* BOGGERLAS, surrender.
BOGGERLAS Here's one for you, you dog.

(He slits his skull) (SOLDIER *falls to earth*)
THE QUEEN That's the spirit, Boggerlas, keep it up!

(HEADS, TAILS, GYRON *pick up* SOLDIER *and throw him into combat again)*
SEVERAL *(advancing)* We promise to save your life.
BOGGERLAS Blackguards, wine-bladders, mercenary scum. *(He flourishes his sword)*
PA UBU Oh, bother, but I'll still win in the end.
BOGGERLAS Mother, escape by the secret staircase.
THE QUEEN And you, my son, what about you?
BOGGERLAS I'll follow you.

(QUEEN *tiptoes away)*
PA UBU Capture the Queen. Drat, she's got away. As for you, you little worm! . . . *(He advances on* BOGGERLAS *)*
BOGGERLAS By God's will, here's my vengeance.

(BOGGERLAS *wraps mace round* UBU's *brolly as he rips open* PA UBU's *boodle with a sword thrust.)*
BOGGERLAS Mother, I follow you!

Act III, Scene i

The palace, PA UBU, MA UBU (PA *is on the throne eating dates.)*

PA UBU Behold me, monarch of this fair land. I've already got the guts-ache with overeating, and soon they are going to bring in my great bonnet.
MA UBU We owe a great debt of gratitude to the Duke of Lithuania.
PA UBU Who's that?
MA UBU Why, Captain M'Nure.
PA UBU *(getting down from throne)* For god's sake, woman, don't ever mention that slob to me. So far as I'm concerned he can whistle for his dukedom, but he's not going to get it.

(MA UBU *switches off throne lights)*
MA UBU You're making a great mistake, Pa Ubu. He'll turn against you.
PA UBU I should worry! So far as I'm concerned he and Boggerlas can go and jump in a lake.(UBU *switches throne lights back on.)*

Act III, Scene ii

The great hall of the palace—PA UBU, MA UBU, OFFICERS, GYRON, HEADS, TAILS, NOBLES, FINANCIERS, JUDGES, REGISTRARS.

PA UBU Bring out the chest for Nobles, and the slasher for Nobles, and the boat hook for Nobles, and the account book for Nobles, and then bring in the Nobles.

(The NOBLES *are brutally shoved in)*

MA UBU For pity's sake restrain yourself, Pa Ubu.

PA UBU Gentlemen, I have the honour to inform you that, as a gesture to the economic welfare of my country, I have decided to liquidate the nobility and confiscate their goods.

NOBLES Horror of horrors! Soldiers and citizens, defend us.

PA UBU Bring on the first Noble and pass me the boat hook. Those who are condemned to death, I shall push through this door here where they will fall down into the bleed-pig chambers, and then proceed to the cash-room, where they will be debrained. *(To the* NOBLE*)* What's your name, you slob?

NOBLE Count of Vitebsk.

PA UBU What's your income?

NOBLE Three million rix-dollars.

PA UBU Guilty. *(He grabs him with the hook and pushes him through the door. Doors open and* TAILS *pushes* COUNT *through. Doors close.)*

MA UBU This is base brutality!

PA UBU You, there, what's your name?

(The NOBLE *doesn't answer.)*

Come on, answer, you slob.

NOBLE Grand Duke of Posen.

PA UBU Excellent! Excellent! I couldn't ask for a better. Down the hatch. You, there. What's your name, ugly mug?

NOBLE Duke of Courland, and of the Cities of Riga, Revel, and Mitau.

PA UBU Oh, very good. Are you sure that's the lot?

NOBLE That's all.

PA UBU Get down the hatch. What's your name, number four?

NOBLE Prince of Podolia.

PA UBU What's your income?

NOBLE I'm bankrupt.

PA UBU Take that for disobedience. *(Hits him with hook)* Now get down the hatch. Number five, what's your name?

NOBLE Margrave of Thorn, Count Palatine of Polock.

PA UBU That's not very much. Are you sure that's all you are?

NOBLE It's been good enough for me.

PA UBU Well, it's better than nothing, I suppose. Get down the hatch. What's eating you, Ma Ubu?

MA UBU You're too bloodthirsty, Pa Ubu.

PA UBU I'm getting rich. Now I'm going to have them read out the list of what I've got. Registrar, read out my list of my titles and possessions.

GYRON Count of Sandomir . . . Count . . .

PA UBU The princedoms first, stupid bugger!

GYRON Princedom of Podolia, Grand Duchy of Posen, Duchy of Courland, Count of Sandomir, Count of Vitebsk, Palatinate of Polock, Margravate of Thorn.
PA UBU Go on.
GYRON That's the lot.
PA UBU What do you mean, that's the lot! Oh, well, I'm going to make some laws next.
GYRON That'll be worth watching.
PA UBU I shall begin by reforming the judicial code and then turn my attention to financial matters.

(Enter JUDGES*)*

SEVERAL JUDGES We are strongly opposed to any change.
PA UBU So, pschitt. In the first place, judges will no longer receive a salary.
JUDGES And what shall we live on? We are all poor men.
PA UBU You keep the fines you impose and the possessions of those you condemn to death.
FIRST JUDGE It's unthinkable.
SECOND JUDGE Infamous.
THIRD JUDGE Scandalous.
FOURTH JUDGE Contemptible.
ALL We refuse to judge under such conditions.
PA UBU Down the hatch with the judges. *(They struggle in vain)*
MA UBU Oh, what have you done, Pa Ubu? Who will administer justice now?
PA UBU Why, I will. You'll see how well it will work out.
MA UBU Yes, it'll be a right old mess.
PA UBU Aw, shut your gob, clownish female, I am now going to turn my attention to financial matters.

(Enter FINANCIERS*)*

PA UBU In the first place, I intend to pocket half the tax receipts.
FIRST FINANCIER But that's ridiculous.
SECOND FINANCIER Quite absurd.
THIRD FINANCIER It doesn't make sense.
PA UBU Are you making fun of me? Get down the hatch, all of you.

(The FINANCIERS *are pushed through the door)*

A Listing of BBC Actors and Productions Coordinators

UBU ROI

by

Alfred Jarry

CAST

UBU ROI (PA UBU)	DONALD PLEASANCE
MA UBU	BRENDA BRUCE
CAPTAIN MACNURE	NEIL CUNNINGHAM
KING WENCESLAS	JOHN EVITTS
BOGGERLAS	OENGUS MACNAMARA
GYRON	CHRISTOPHER ASANTE
HEADS	BUNNY REED
TAILS	PAUL TOOTHILL
QUEEN ROSAMUND	JACQUELINE DELHAYE
BOLESLAS BEAR COUNT OF VITEBSK JUDGE 1 FINANCIER 1 HORSE	GLEN CUNNINGHAM
LADISLAS DUKE OF POSEN JUDGE 2 FINANCIER 2 COUNSELLOR 1	ROGER NEIL
YOUNG PEASANT DUKE OF COURLAND JUDGE 3 FINANCIER 3 COUNSELLOR 2 HORSE	MICHAEL CULLEN

STANISLAS LECZINSKI
PRINCE OF PADOLIA
COUNSELLOR 3 . . . . BASIL CLARKE
SOLDIER
MARGRAVE OF THORN
JUDGE 4
COUNSELLOR 4
CAPTAIN . . . . GERALD MOON

PRODUCTION

SET DESIGN	DACRE PUNT
COSTUME DESIGNER	ROMAYNE WOOD
MAKE-UP SUPERVISOR	MAGGIE WEBB
DIRECTOR/PRODUCER	PAUL KAFNO

Pa Ubu

King Ubu, Gyron and Ma Ubu

Pa Ubu, Ma Ubu, Officer and Captain MacNure

272

Focus in Viewing

Viewers of this production should be prepared for an out-and-out assault on their senses and sensibilities. Of all the productions in this series, this program contains the most outrageous humor. The director has interpreted his mock heroic extravaganza in a most contemporary way and uses some of the techniques which have been developed in movies and television for presenting cariacature and farce. The production includes elements found in a *Punch and Judy* puppet show and a *Tom and Jerry* cartoon. Comic routines are reminiscent of those of Laurel and Hardy, the Marx Brothers, and even Monty Python. The viewer should surrender to the absurdity, rather than attempt to analyze it.

Content Viewing

1. Does *Ubu Roi* have an overall message or theme? What, if any, is it?
2. How is this play a presentation of bourgeois grossness? Does it reflect a political position or attitude?
3. What emphasis does Jarry place on violence in the play?
4. Which characters intrigue you? Why? In what way?
5. The characters in the play, most often Pa Ubu, use words which are inventions of Jarry's. What effect do these words have in the play? What meaning do they convey?

Craft Viewing

1. What are some conventions you need to know or accept before you can understand how this play satirizes tradition? How would you describe the portrayal of violence in this production?
2. Based on your viewing, the reading of the plot summary, do you recognize a plot structure? If so, what is it? Does Jarry seem to capture the spirit of the traditional commedia dell'arte? Explain.
3. Can you determine a directoral concept or interpretation? Did the director emphasize the general lampooning of heroic attitudes and the order they glorify? Explain. In what way, if at all, would you have directed the production differently? (For instance, what might have been other deliberate anachronisms?)
4. Do you agree, or disagree, with the characterizations and interpretations? Select a character and discuss.
5. Do you think the costumes and props supported the stageplay?
6. Is there one moment or scene which stands out in your memory? More than one? Which ones, and why?

Critical Viewing: Overview

1. Compare Pa Ubu to Oedipus or Macbeth. Can you think of another tragedy that *Ubu* might parody?
2. Now that this play and its production are part of your experience, what significance does *Ubu Roi* hold for you?

Additional Plays That Demonstrate Similar Concepts

Waiting for Godot—Samuel Beckett

Rhinoceros, The Bald Soprano—Eugene Ionesco

The Blacks, The Balcony—Jean Genet

The Zoo Story, The American Dream—Edward Albee

Films:

Duck Soup with the Marx Brothers

Stage Terms

Anachronism—A person or thing that is chronologically out of place.

Avant Garde—The development of (or those who develop) experimental concepts in the arts based upon an intellectual eye for the "new."

Episodic Plot—A casual, illogical arrangement of incidents; the opposite of the pyramidal plot structure.

Parody—An art, literary, musical, or dramatic work that imitates the style of a related work in order to make fun of it.

Theatre of the Absurd—Refuses to employ verisimilitude or definite symbolism and is generally predicated on the existential view that we exist with little or no meaning. This meaninglessness is represented in dialogues and situations that seem to be nonsensical and ridiculous.

SIZWE BANSI IS DEAD

by

Athol Fugard, John Kani, and Winston Ntshona
(1932–)

A. Play Notes, p. 276
B. How Sizwe Bansi and Mr. Buntu Complement Each Other, p. 277
C. Commentary on Clive Barnes' Review, p. 278
D. Review, p. 278
E. Objectives, p. 279
F. Program Notes, p. 279
G. A List of BBC Actors and Production Coordinators, p. 280
H. Focus in Viewing, p. 281
I. Additional Plays that Demonstrate Similar Concepts, p. 282
J. Glossary, p. 282

Play Notes

The Thesis

Sizwe Bansi Is Dead, "devised" by Athol Fugard, John Kani, and Winston Ntshoma and first produced in 1972, makes a strong statement about an injustice in society with the intent of effecting change. Quite different from Ibsen's plays, the improvisational techniques cause the action to advance quickly and impressionistically as the two actors portray varied characters. The play is a strong social statement in opposition to the repressive practices and attitudes of the South African government. In particular, by focusing on the plight of a poor illiterate black man who needs a valid permit to work in Port Elizabeth, the play opposes the restrictive laws requiring Blacks to carry identity cards; but in general, the play goes far beyond suggesting a change in the police procedures or laws governing employment. It denounces racism and exploitation, without regard to place or situation, and examines the larger question of what constitutes a human being.

The Title

The play title has more than one meaning. Sizwe Bansi is the native man who has left his family to find employment in the city, with the hope of eventually sending for them. When, through ill luck, he is arrested in a police search, his "dum book," vital to any business or travel arrangements, is stamped in a way which makes him unable to live or work in the city. In the exchange of his identity card for that of a dead man, Sizwe Bansi loses his name. To the world at large, he takes on the identity of Robert Zuwelzima, the dead man. When he protests to his knowledgeable mentor Buntu that he has lost his name and that of his family, Buntu points out that so long as a policeman or a white child can call any black man by any name including "John" or "Boy," there can be no pride or dignity in a name which merely allows degradation at the whim of the powerful. Sizwe is better off with the anonymity of the new name and identity number. He is dead to the bureaucracy which keeps files on the blacks. But he was already dead in the sense of human dignity before he agreed to make the change, Buntu explains.

Characterization and Set

In this play, there was only two actors but many characters. The inarticulate Sizwe—or Zuwelzima—seems comical as he poses for the photographer in Styles' studio. But as Styles and the other characters he portrays, he denounces repression, and as the audience sees flashbacks of the events leading up to the opening scene, the mood changes. The man posing for the picture is not just a country bumpkin foolishly smiling as he crosses his legs and holds a pipe; instead he becomes a man to be treated seriously and to be remembered.

Because of the improvisational technique, the sparsely furnished stage becomes any setting required by the dialogue: government office, sidewalk, church, clothing store, the home of a proud man on Sunday, the payroll office of Feltex, and the small town of Sizwe's origin on the day a letter is delivered. Changes in costume are not necessary. Through flashback and through the convention of Sizwe's voice in the letter addressed to his wife, as black-and-white still photographs replace color film, the story is told.

How Sizwe Bansi and Mr. Buntu Complement Each Other

Sizwe Bansi Is Dead is intense and painful. Through one of the central characters, Mr. Buntu, there is revealed the hopeless and bitter reality of trying to exist in a country that refuses to recognize his humanity and dignity because he is black. Through the other main character, Sizwe Bansi, a glimmer of hope is shown. It is not that everything ends up rosy and wonderful for Sizwe and Mr. Buntu at the close of the play; on the contrary, it is evident that the system which oppresses both men is still in effect. The hope seems to spring, instead, from a faith in the individual.

Although regarded as a mere number and treated either as a child or a criminal by the society he lives in, Sizwe Bansi still holds on to a deeply-rooted, basic pride. He is shown as a loving husband and father. He is also capable of finer human feeling, as demonstrated by his informing the dead Robert Zuwelinzima's family of his death, despite the risk to Sizwe.

This goodness could be taken as simple stupidity if it were not for the fact that he is presented in the play respectfully, even lovingly. He is portrayed as a simple man, uncontaminated by cynicism. This seems to point out that whereas people are often oppressed and imprisoned by complex and difficult-to-understand systems and societies' they are, generally, simple folk like Sizwe. They do not comprehend the involved politics and psychology that robs them of security and dreams. If they are not permitted a future to plan for, then they live from day to day.

Contrasted with this simplicity is Mr. Buntu, who understands very well where his oppression originates. He is clever and witty in his bitterness and has a strong survival instinct. Sizwe has a thicker skull; Mr. Buntu has a thicker skin. Mr. Buntu's hide was acquired through necessity. He tells Sizwe, at one point in the play, "If I could keep my pride (support his wife and children), I would keep my name. To hell with your bloody name! Take my pride and give me bread for my children."

Mr. Buntu's acute awareness set against Sizwe's painful bewilderment and confusion becomes more than a mere cataloging of the daily indignities to which a black man is subjected. It is a cry for the restoration of his pride. It seems to be a plea for Sizwe's sake. Mr. Buntu does not somehow appear to be wholly human, as Sizwe does. He is like a defense lawyer, arguing a case for Sizwe, the common man. He intervenes, he protects, he advises, he explains. He explains life and its realities to Sizwe and, in so doing, explains Sizwe to us.

We can see the effects of injustice in Sizwe's perplexed expression and his simple, hurt question: Am I not a man?

Mr. Buntu, then, gathers up the feelings of outrage, which Sizwe's threatened self-respect has evoked, and directs them against the source of the injustice: the white, segregationist establishment.

The message that it is wrong to strip a person of his or her self-esteem and human rights transcends the specific dilemma presented in the play, which is the plight of the South African Blacks. The need for self-respect, the striving for happiness, are not peculiar to Sizwe and Mr. Buntu. They are common to all of humankind, just as the capability to be inhuman and cruel in order to maintain a social system is common to all of us. It is not an easy problem to overcome, and the play suggests no solutions. Its purpose is to make us realize how wrong this reality is.

Commentary

Clive Barnes of the *New York Times* describes the impact of *Sizwe Bansi Is Dead* in this critical review of the Royal Court's production. He compares movement in the play to a "train gathering speed." Like a train, the play moves slowly at first, bogged down by the weight of its cargo; yet as it converts its burden to the energy of a burning message, a cumbersome vehicle becomes a "thunderbolt of pain."

New York Times, November 14, 1974

"Sizwe Bansi" Is A Message from Africa

Theatrical power is a curious thing. It can start small, like a murmur in a chimney, and then build up to a hurricane. It can slide into you as stealthily as a knife. It can make you wonder, make you think. The South African play "Sizwe Bansi Is Dead" starts almost slower than slow. A black South African photographer from Port Elizabeth wandered onto the stage at Edison Theater last night and started chatting to the audience, talking nonchalantly about Ford, Kissinger, Nixon and the like.

It was beautifully acted, mildly amusing, but I must admit that I thought this improvisatory and, I now believe, deliberately, low-key introduction boded a strange evening. I realized that this play, when at London's Royal Court Theater, had been triumphantly received by audiences and critics alike, but there was a moment there when I thought that this was just a tribute to liberal Britain's guilt over South Africa. But slowly it happened, like a train gathering speed. The play, the theme, the performances, gradually took over, and the sheer dramatic force of the piece bounced around the theater like angry thunderbolts of pain. From this slow, kidding beginning there comes a climax that hits and hurts. You will not forget "Sizwe Bansi" easily.

The play comes from South Africa, was performed in South Africa, and apparently following its fantastic international success, official South Africa—by which, of course, I mean white South Africa—is rather proud of it. Which is fantastic, for this is a terrible and moving indictment against the South African government and the horrifying way it treats its black majority. Interestingly, a government that can let a play like this be shown and even exported, doesn't know its behind from its elbow, or perhaps doesn't even have the miserable courage of its own evil convictions.

The play, like "The Island," which joins "Sizwe Bansi" in repertory next week, has been devised by the white South African actors, John Kani and Winston Ntshona. Mr. Fugard has directed the play and presumably acted as some kind of umpire to its creation.

Styles, the jokingly ironic photographer, gets a customer and takes his picture, which is to be sent to the man's wife. They get into conversation, and the man tells him that he is staying with Buntu, a textile worker. And so the story of Sizwe Bansi and his death is told in flashback.

"The world and its laws leave us nothing but ourselves." This is the awful message of the play. Buntu and Sizwe are what South Africans call Buntus. As recently as 1969, the South African Deputy Minister of Justice referred to these 15 million black South Africans as "appen-

© 1974 by The New York Times Company. Reprinted by permission.

dages." They are forced to carry a passbook, which has stamps on it saying where these "appendages" can or cannot work.

Sizwe's passbook is wrong. Coming to Port Elizabeth for work, he will have to go back to the country or face arrest. Already he is overdue, but without getting a job in the city he has no way of supporting his wife and four children. Sadly, he and Buntu go to a bar and get drunk. Coming home, they find the dead body of a stabbed man. Buntu removes the dead man's passbook. All they have to do is change around the photographs—and Sizwe Bansi is dead, and Sizwe himself, under a new identity, is free to live and work. After all, to South African officials a black man is not a man but a boy, not a creature but a worker.

A stirring moral message is one thing; a good play is another. And in its strange way "Sizwe Bansi Is Dead" is an astonishingly good play. From its satirically sly opening—with its corrosive remarks on the Ford factory in Port Elizabeth—to its slashing climax, where, echoing Shylock, Buntu and Sizwe insist on their human dignity, the play has a style, manner and grace of its own.

You can hardly talk about the play without talking about the two actors and its staging, because it is all of one piece. John Kani, sleek and flashing, is dynamite as both the cynical Styles and the embittered Buntu, while Winston Ntshona has just the right puzzled dignity and despair as Sizwe. Mr. Fugard's staging is inseparable from them and the play.

There is a great deal of fun here as well as tragedy. It is human nature to fight disaster with laughter, and this play is a joyous hymn to human nature.

Clive Barnes

Objectives

After studying *Sizwe Bansi Is Dead,* you, the student should be able to

1. recognize that theatre art is a live, immediate form of communication, directly influenced by the response of the audience.
2. identify the significance of dramatic conventions used as expressive tools by the playwright, actor, and director in *Sizwe Bansi Is Dead.*
3. appreciate the significant contributions of black theatre, not only to theatre art but also for the facilitation of social change.

Program Notes

Sizwe Bansi Is Dead

Filmed as it was staged at the Royal Court in 1974, the play is a two-man *tour de force* on repressive laws in the Republic of South Africa. Athol Fugard's play is humorous, ironic, and angry, as it explores the plight of a black man whose identification card prevents him from living or working at Port Elizabeth. The television drama begins after the first long monologue and continues to the play's end.

Innovative theatrical conventions include one actor's playing several parts, pantomime, changes from color to black and white, and from moving pictures to still photography. There is commentary by Ossie Davis and Ruby Dee, reading from the works of black American writers. The original television performance (recorded in January, 1974, and first broadcast in March, 1974) is cut, with the deletion of the section about Ciskeian independence.

A Listing of BBC Actors and Production Coordinators

SIZWE BANSI IS DEAD

by

Athol Fugard, John Kani, and Winston Ntshona

CAST

SIZWE BANSI	WINSTON NTSHONA
STYLES AND BUNTU	JOHN KANI

PRODUCTION

SET DESIGN	MICHAEL EDWARDS
MAKE-UP SUPERVISOR	MAGGIE WEBB
DIRECTOR	JOHN DAVIES
STAGE DIRECTOR	ATHOL FUGARD

Focus in Viewing

It is important to recall that all the productions we have seen so far have been interpretations of playscripts. Here the playscript is in fact an interpretation of a stageplay performance; that is, the performance came before the script since the actors and Fugard devised the play through improvisation. It, therefore, follows that this production is one version of this continuously changing play. The viewer must allow a few minutes for adjustment to the South African dialect, which is not a familiar sound to us.

Content Viewing

1. Compare Robert/Sizwe to Woyzeck.
2. What is the main theme of the play? Why would it have meaning for you?
3. Which character most intrigued you? Why?
4. What philosophy does this character represent?
5. Do you agree with Sizwe's decision to be "dead?"
6. How does Robert change? When do you first notice the change?

Craft Viewing

1. Of these plays, which was easiest to follow? *Woyzeck, Ubu Roi, Sizwe Bansi Is Dead.* Explain your response.
2. In what way, if at all, would you have directed the production of *Sizwe* differently? What in the direction and production did you find effective?
3. What was your opinion of the actors' portrayals?
4. Is there one moment or scene that stands out in your memory? Why?
5. Do you think the technical design and execution supported the stageplay? Some elements were only suggested. How did you respond to the suggestions?
6. Is there one moment or scene which stands out in your memory? More than one? Which ones, and why?

Critical Viewing: Overview

1. Now that this play and its production are part of your experience, what significance does *Sizwe Bansi Is Dead* hold for you?

Additional Plays That Demonstrate Similar Concepts

The Island—devised by Athol Fugard, John Kani, and Winston Ntshona
Statements After an Arrest under the Immorality Act—Athol, Fugard
The Escape, or a Leap to Freedom—William Wells Brown
Nat Turner—Randolph Edmonds
The Amen Corner—James Baldwin
Ceremonies in Dark Old Men—Lonnie Elder
A Medal For Willie—William Branch

Idabelle's Fortune—Ted Shine
Rosalee Pritchett—Carlton and Barbara Molette
Purlie Victorious—Ossie Davis

Glossary

ag voetsek—GO TO HELL
bioscope—CINEMA
broer—BROTHER
Ciskei—ONE OF THE BLACK SEPARATIST "HOMELANDS"
dankie— THANK YOU
hai—EXCLAMATION OF SURPRISE
hier is ek—HERE I AM
kieries—FIGHTING STICKS
lap; lappie—RAG
makulu—GRANDMOTHER
moer—LITERALLY, WOMB (USED AS A SWEAR WORD)
nyana we sizwe—BROTHER OF THE LAND
tshotsholoza kulezondawo, yabaleka—OPENING PHRASE OF AFRICAN WORK CHANT; LITERALLY, "WORK STEADY, THE TRAIN IS COMING."
tsotsis—BLACK HOOLIGANS

SIX CHARACTERS IN SEARCH OF AN AUTHOR

by

Luigi Pirandello
(1867–1936)

A. Play Notes, p. 284

B. Story and Plot Summary, p. 285

C. Commentary on Stark Young's Review, 287

D. Stark Young's Review, p. 287

E. Commentary on Richard Gilman's and Richard Haye's Reviews, p. 290

F. Richard Gilman's Review, p. 291

G. Richard Hayes' Review, p. 293

H. Objectives, p. 293

I. Program Notes, p. 293

J. A Listing of BBC Actors and Production Coordinators, p. 294

K. Focus in Viewing, p. 296

L. Additional Plays that Demonstrate Similar Concepts, p. 297

M. Stage Terms, p. 297

Play Notes
In Search of Reality: Theatrical Conventions

Relativism in Six Characters

Drama usually reflects the philosophical dilemmas of its time, not just in subjects chosen but in the structure of the play itself and the manner of stage presentation. The world of Pirandello is in flux, the only absolute being the experience of each individual. By 1921, when *Six Characters* was written, world events no longer seemed to warrant continued hope for improvement or even belief in eventual stability. Pirandello reflects this historical climate by showing a world in which one can be certain only of what he feels the moment he feels it. This fleeting realization becomes the only truth; the next moment, there is another truth. To present this kind of philosophical relativism, the belief that there is no lasting truth, is a part of Pirandello's purpose. His fragmented method of presentation also is a means of expressing the many truths of the play. At its extreme, relativism leads to nihilism—the belief that life has no meaning at all.

Conventions in Six Characters

Theatrical conventions vary from age to age and drama to drama. Audiences have accepted masks, soliloquies, an all-male cast, chorus, scenery and no scenery, verse dialogue, prose dialogue, and a host of other ways of presenting a play. In *Six Characters* audiences were challenged to accept unfamiliar twists that eventually became conventions of theatre. For example, in *Six Characters,* Pirandello makes some ironic comments about theatre language. He has the actors who are involved in a make-believe play, *Mixing It Up* (there is such a play, written by Pirandello in 1918), speak "realistically" as in real life, and the characters who tell a "real" story speak a kind of unrealistic interior language that leaves no room for small talk, their language expressing their intense suffering and passion.

At the end of *Six Characters in Search of an Author,* the Manager says: "Pretense? Reality? To hell with it all! Never in my life has such a thing happened to me. I've lost a whole day over these people, a whole day." It is ironic that Pirandello mentions time, "a whole day," in a play that feels out of time, is unrelated to any recognizable time, as if the action of the play is happening in the disoriented timeless world of the rehearsal hall. Time is a theatrical convention, a device the author uses in any way he wishes. Time can pass as slowly or as rapidly as the writer requires. An actor may say, "You've been talking for twenty minutes," when, in fact only three minutes have lapsed. The second act can begin two years after the first act. A seasoned audience goes along with this convention. Time can go backward or forward. Pirandello's handling of time however, was not one with which audiences could feel comfortable.

Still another theatrical convention of more traditional theatre is that, when the audience enters the theatre, the curtain is up. Pirandello made dramatic history by directing that the audience enter the auditorium with the curtain up and the stage bare—no set, no wings. This technique, which permits the audience to feel that it is a part of the play, has been copied many times since Pirandello introduced it.

The Influence of Six Characters

Six Characters in Search of an Author has been an important influence on modern dramatic form. Naturalistic, well-made plays have given way to the more expressionistic plays of Eugene O'Neill (*The Great God Brown, Marco's Millions, Strange Interlude*), Tennessee Williams (*The Glass Menagerie*), Thornton Wilder (*Our Town*), and Peter Schaffer (*Equus*). As serious playwrights have experimented with the conventions showing reality, serious audiences have responded by being willing to play the game.

Story and Plot Summary

Act I. A stage manager and a group of actors are starting to rehearse a Luigi Pirandello play, *Mixing It Up*. The stage manager is giving directions to the actors, the prompter, and the property man when the Six Characters enter from the back of the stage: The Father, a man of about 50; the Mother, dressed in black; the Stepdaughter; a Son of 22; a boy of 14; and a little girl. The father explains that they have come in search of an author for their drama. The Father adds that because life takes many forms and many shapes, he has been born into life as a character in a play and because the author who created the Six Characters is no longer willing or able to put them in a work of art, they are offering themselves to the Manager, so that he may put their drama on stage. The Manager asks that the Father explain his relationship with the woman in black and the story of the Six Characters unfolds in a long speech (which takes up most of the first act).

The Father says that he once had in his service a poor man, a Secretary, who became a friend of his Wife's. Eventually he sent the Secretary away, and, according to the Father, his Wife then moped about the house. He sent their Son to a wet nurse in the country because he felt his Wife was not strong enough to take care of him, and he later sent his Wife to the Secretary. He admits that this act was liberating for him, but that he sent his Wife away more for her sake than his. After the Son was educated he returned, but he seemed not to belong to the Father. He began to think of his Wife and her life with the Secretary and then took to following their child, the Stepdaughter, in school. The Secretary died and the Mother and children returned. Destitute, the Mother went to work as a seamstress in Madame Pace's dress shop, which concealed a bordello. The Father did not know of the family's return and, visiting Madame Pace's establishment, was provided with a prostitute, his Stepdaughter, whom he did not recognize. The Father explains that, fortunately, he did recognize her in time. He then took home the Mother and her three illegitimate children: the Stepdaughter and the two younger children. The Stepdaughter adds bitterly that the Son treated the Mother's children as intruders and that she owes her life on the streets to him.

The Father, Stepdaughter, and Son argue over versions of their story. The Son asks to be excluded from the drama; the Manager wishes to cut the small children out of the story, and the Stepfather assures him this is possible and that, in fact, the Stepdaughter will also disappear, leaving only the Father, the Mother and the Son. When the young boy and the girl leave, the original three members of the family live together, according to the Father, as strangers.

The Manager is intrigued and, again, the Father tells him that he must be the author. At first the Manager refuses, but he is tempted. Finally, he gives the actors a 20-minute break, and they can be heard commenting on the madness of the characters and the vanity of the Manager who thinks he is an author.

The curtain remains up and the action of the play is suspended for 20 minutes.

Act. II. The Stepdaughter emerges from the Manager's office, angry at the way things are going. She tries to calm her frightened sister and notices a revolver her brother is hiding in his pocket. The Manager goes about ordering the props for the play and asks the prompter to outline the scenes act by act and to take down in shorthand the important points. He asks the actors to watch and listen as the characters play the scene that they, the actors, will later have to play. At this point the Father interrupts and explains that this play is not for the actors but that it belongs to the characters themselves, and there is no need for actors.

After some discussion about the difference between the actors and the characters, the Manager consents to using the characters for the rehearsal. He wonders where Madam Pace is and if they are going to do the scene in the dress shop. The Father sets the scene, taking some hats and cloaks from the actresses to put on a rack. The scene is now set for Madame Pace, and at the back of the stage Madame Pace enters. She is a fat, oldish woman with dyed hair. She is rouged and powdered and dressed in black silk. The Stepdaughter and Madame Pace begin their scene quietly, ignoring the convention of raising their voices for the stage. The Mother screams at Madame Pace, and Madame Pace, offended, leaves the stage.

The rehearsal continues with the Mother watching and listening. From time to time she hides her face in her hands and sobs at the reenactment of the scene in which her husband plans to purchase the favors of the girl he did not recognize as his Stepdaughter. The action is stopped and the scene which the characters just did is repeated by the actors. The Stepdaughter laughs. The Father says that although the actors want to be the Characters, they simply are not. The Manager tells the actors that they will rehearse later, and he asks the Father and Stepdaughter to resume their scene. As the Stepdaughter is about to undress behind a screen the Manager stops the action, crying that this cannot be permitted on stage. There is discussion about what is possible for the stage and, finally, the scene is resumed as the Stepdaughter leans her head on her father's breast. This time the scene is stopped by the Mother, who pulls the girl away from her husband as she screams that he is with her daughter. The Manager, delighted, notes that at this point the curtain should fall. The stagehand, misunderstanding, drops the curtain.

Act III. On the stage are some trees and a portion of a fountain. The characters are on one side of the stage, the actors on the other, the Stage Manager in the middle. The Father talks of the difference between reality and the illusion of reality found in conventional stage representations and in life itself. The Manager admonishes the Father to stop philosophizing and return to the action. He calls the stagehand to set up the garden scene. He asks the young boy to hide behind the trees and peek out occasionally, as if looking for someone. The boy goes through the action. The Son wants to leave, but the Father reminds him that he must act the scene in the garden. First, says the Stepdaughter, the young girl must go to the fountain, and she leads the child to it. The actors study the Mother and the Son. The Son explains that this is his scene and that what actually happened was that his Mother came into his room rather than the garden to talk and he refused and left. The Mother had nothing to do with the garden. The Manager tells him that for theatrical effect the scenes must be grouped together. The Father screams at the Son to play the scene and begins to shake him. The Son tells the Manager that the Father has not only told him things that have happened but things that have not happened at all. The Manager asks the Son to tell *his* version of what happened. Reluctantly, the Son talks of walking into the garden. When the Manager asks what happens next, the Son says that it is too horrible. The Mother, crying, looks toward the fountain, and the Father explains that she has been following behind her Son. Then the Son tells that he found the body of the little girl in the fountain pool and the young boy staring insanely at it. At that moment a revolver shot sounds behind the stage trees where the boy has been hiding. There is confusion, and the Manager asks if the boy is wounded. The actors disagree as to whether he is dead or merely pretending to be. The Father cries that it is not pretense but reality.

Exasperated, the Manager gives up on the Play, claiming he has wasted a whole day on these Six Characters.

Commentary

"Brains," Stark Young's critical review of Pirandello's *Six Characters in Search of an Author,* is appropriately titled. A complete picture is offered to the reader in a thorough review. Not only is the play summarized (a feature offered by most critics), but comments on the playscript, production, and interpretation are included as well. Young explains his reaction to both the production and Pirandello's ideas.

The New Republic October 30, 1922

Brains

Six Characters in Search of an Author, by Luigi Pirandello.
Translated from the Italian by Edward Storer. Princess Theatre.
October 30, 1922.

We can judge the excellence of a man's legs by how well he can run or jump or dance, and can see easily enough how much eye for color he has. And we can judge his ear for music. We know how strong his muscles are by what he can lift, move or endure. Happily by some kind fortune this does not hold true of the mind. We have no reason to believe that there is any higher average of mental endowment of its kind than there is of the eyes for color or of muscles or musical ears. But there is no straight-off way of judging these hidden gifts; and any man is free to think his invisible powers as good as the best. No matter what outward signs and fruits there be, he can go on consoling himself with his unseen depths. For Pirandello's play at the Princess this is a fine thing; otherwise many of our theatre audiences when they run into such subtlety of analysis, originality of invention and brilliant and poignant stress of mentality, would be overwhelmingly put in their places. And without this secure and unseen certainty of their own powers many of our citizens might be upset to hear that these metaphysical, tragic, accurately fantastic and laughable plays by Pirandello are to no small extent mouthpieces of much of young Italy; that on the streets of Rome a year or two ago there was a mob with six hundred persons in it over one of these dramas; and that when one of these works is performed, in the intervals between the

Reprinted by permission of *The New Republic.* © 1922, The New Republic, Inc.

acts the aisles and the foyers of an Italian theatre are crowded with discussion like a hot debating academy. However—

The rehearsal of a Pirandello play, ill thought of by the director, is about to begin when six characters from the author's brain appear. They wish to be allowed to react themselves and to set forth the event that is part of what they are. There are the father and his son, the son's mother and three other children by a man with whom the husband, driven by a demon of experiment, has let the wife elope. One of these children is the daughter who has run away and gone to the dogs; the other two are dead but are present on the scene because they have been given a reality and are therefore unchanging. The director at last consents to see their story. They create great parts of scenes; the actors are assigned roles and try them to the great amusement of the realities for whom they create the illusion. The father argues metaphysics with the director. The play is halted. It goes on again. The father, repulsed by the son, is more and more attracted to the young woman, who gives way to him. The mother intervenes. The life of these six characters emerges somehow, real and unreal at once. The theatre is mocked for the absurdity of its medium and its inadequacy for any revelation of truth. In the end the little girl is drowned in the fountain and the boy shoots himself. The agony of the mother is terrible and overpowering. Nobody on the stage knows any longer which is reality and which is illusion. The mother goes out with the dead boy in her arms. Is he wounded? the director asks, Is he really wounded? He is dead, some of the actors cry. No, other actors say, it is fiction, don't believe it. The father cries that it is not fiction, it is reality, and runs out. Fiction, reality, the director says. He has never seen anything like it. And they have made him lose a morning.

The play is transplanted from Italy without any great sense of loss and with a very wise omission of any attempt at Italian production or method of acting. Italian dramatists instinctively write for the actors, and this play of Pirandello's is easily accessible to acting and full of possibilities. And this, together with Mr. Pemberton's plausible casting of the characters and his excellent directing, partly accounts for the high level that we get throughout the performance.

As the father Mr. Moffat Johnston was admirable. He got remarkably well into the reading of his many long speeches their essential quality, which was a strange mixture of analytical and physical passion and of boldness and fear, candor and shame. Mr. Dwight Frye brought a convincing imaginative insight to the part of the son, whose life had been outraged by contrast between his idea of parents and his actual instance of them, and whose place in the whole situation was violently against his will and at the same time an inner necessity. Mr. Frye is a beginner with something very much beyond what the New York stage expects of its young men; he has talent and intelligence; though he should get his r's rightly placed—his "father" and "mirror" and "horror" come off with great travail so far—he should work on his English as Miss Woodruff must have done, whose whole tone and accent is better than last year. And Miss Florence Eldridge needs to cherish her speech now and then; she has a way of speaking too fast and of slurring her consonants till they are lost. But as the daughter her work was astonishingly good; it was impetuous, flickering, sometimes crude, sometimes leaping up, sometimes darkened from within. She achieved the ebullience and tragedy of the character, the necessity for living and for speaking out, the tears and animation and mind. Against the more stolid and upright bodies of the director's own company of actors, Miss Eldridge created something strangely real and unreal and irrepressible. There were moments when she seemed to be a flame; behind her eyes and brow there seemed to shine the light of some youthful and urgent and eternally fixed reality, and about her movement the force of some haunting fatality and enthusiasm. The part of the mother it would be hard to imagine done with more rightness than Miss Wycherly gave to it. As the woman who had loved this man but who had been blind to him and misjudged him, and who had borne four children only to have them dashed from her by death and shame and pride, her suffering was the deepest of all the six; the deep degree of it pushed her grief beyond the actual and gave to it a kind of eternity. Miss Wycherly got this effect. Her eyelids, her brow, her hands, the line of her figure, her cries, had about them that last and final tragic reality of the eternal type.

The translation of Pirandello's play is not a bad one. The philosophic speeches fare best; as a matter of fact they come over very straight into the English. There are vulgarities now and then that fall below the original— "sopporto la sua vista," for example, is hardly "stand for this face." And to tag on at the very last the bit where the director turns to the actors and says to get on with The Bride's Revenge seems uselessly silly. It is the wrong sort of humor. And what's worse, it is quite out of the key of Pirandello, who ends on reality and unreality and a hint of satire in the director's notion of losing a morning's time. This addition at the very last is a perfect example— more obvious than any Pirandello allows himself to use in the play—of exactly what he satirizes in the theatre, the catering, and fear of not making a go of it, and thick instrusiveness. I hope Mr. Pemberton will risk lopping it off.

In Six Characters in Search of an Author Pirandello first of all manages to contrive a fine theatrical piece. It exhibits everywhere one of his most noticeable gifts—something that may have been seen already even in so early a work as his *Sicilian Limes,* translated in the last number of the *Theatre Arts Magazine*—the ability to set forth quite well enough what needs to be known and at the same time to clear it out shortly and make ready for what he really wishes to stay on and emphasize. *Six Characters in Search of an Author* shows a brilliant originality and invention in the situation. The machinery is highly expert with which the double line of incident is established. The transitions, which are so frequent and so varied in event and ideas, are facile and profound. Pirandello's play is thought to become theatric. And his thought is subtle, and subtle not through the sense of any vagueness but through luminous combinations of precise ideas and suggestions. This drama of his is satirical about the theatre but also in the same way about life. The blind and unending and unconcluded shifting of life is portrayed as it struggles against the accidents and illusion of society. No philosophy is pure, no theory gets a chance to exist in its clear reality, exactly as nothing that one of these characters thinks or feels or intends ever means to another character what it means to him.

Six Characters in Search of an Author has a plot suspense and a thought suspense. You are keen to see what happening will come next; your mind is excited by the play of thought till your head seems to hold a kind of cerebral melodrama. But the greatest achievement in Pirandello's play is that the sum of it is moving. It gives the sense of spiritual solitude. Under this fantasy and comedy and brilliant mockery and pity, it releases a poignant vitality, a pressure of life. It moves you with the tragic sense of a passionate hunger for reality and pause amid the flux of things.

Stark Young

Commentary

Richard Hayes in the first review severely criticizes Tyrone Guthrie, the director of a 1956 production of *Six Characters,* for turning a delicate expression of metaphysics and emotion into a circus. Richard Gilman in the second critique compliments William Ball, the director of a 1963 production of *Six Characters,* for his subtle interpretation of the passion and mystery that is the core of Pirandello's play.

Commonweal, April 19, 1963

The Stage
Pirandello to Perfection

In his preface to *Six Characters in Search of an Author* Pirandello tells us that he has the "misfortune" to be a philosophic writer. The complaint is for the most part a disingenuous one, since he acknowledges that it is just the philosophic or metaphysical impulse in his work that gives it its force and special nature, that it is what distinguishes him from those writers who simply describe or narrate. Yet Pirandello was not being wholly disingenuous; in the light of the artificial and crippling distinctions that are made between philosophy and art, between thought and drama, to be considered a philosophic playwright can indeed be a source of real misfortune.

The evil can show itself in several ways. You can regard Pirandello as so abstract, so immersed in a purely intellectual game that you miss entirely the deep passion of his work, a passion set apart from its traditional treatment in drama by its fusion with intellect, its being made to rise out of intellect and especially from the clash of mind with itself and with the enigmas of existence. Or can you deliberately play down the metaphysical aspects in order to release the sheer theatricality, turning the work into physical farce, the way Tyrone Guthrie did a few years ago in his rambunctious and soul-killing production of *Six Characters* at the Phoenix. Only when you understand that to see Pirandello whole means to see ideas and actions in the most thoroughgoing fusion can you do his work justice in the mind and in production.

William Ball is a director who does see Pirandello whole and who has the taste, wit, mind and inventiveness to mount what he sees with nearly flawless beauty. His production of "Six Characters" is by far the finest I have ever seen nor have I any hesitation in saying that I cannot imagine there ever having been a better one in this country.

He has used a new translation by Paul Avila Mayer, which gets him off to a flying start, since the English version that has most frequently been used up to now, the one by Edward Storer, is stiff and in many places archaic and is, moreover, based on a text which does not incorporate the changes, especially those affecting the final scenes, which Pirandello continued to make. Mayer's rendering is based on one of the late texts; its English is immensely lively and accurate, colloquial where that is called for and grave, lyrical or declamatory when those qualities are required.

On this floor Ball has constructed a miracle of subtle staging. The key to *Six Characters* is of course in the relationships and interplay between the troupe of actors and the family that has come to get its "story" performed. Ball handles this interplay with brilliant craftsmanship, creating

Reprinted from THE STAGE, PIRANDELLO TO PERFECTION, Richard Gilman, pp. 105–106, April 19, 1963. © 1963 Commonweal Publishing Co., Inc.

an extraordinary rhythm of speech, gesture and movement, maintaining through the most imaginative and finely paced groupings the tensions and ambiguities that hold the two "casts" in equilibrium with one another, just as illusion and reality, the play's subjects, are held in the richest balance.

In a production so beautifully of a piece as this one is, it seems superfluous to single out individual scenes for praise. But two retain a special resonance in my memory. One is the first appearance of the family, who after a momentary failure of the lights on the stage where the company is rehearsing, are revealed in a compact group at the rear, swaying silently from side to side and bathed in a thin light; it is a shattering moment. The other scene is that in which the stepdaughter pleads with the absent author to "write our play!" and his presence is overwhelmingly evoked.

The performances are on a level with the direction, and indeed in some cases seem to have been elicited by the direction like a genie from a bottle. Jacqueline Brooks, for example, has never been noted for more than routine capacity in the classical roles she has been assaying, but she plays the stepdaughter with truly splendid verve and ferocity. As the director of the acting company Michael O'Sullivan is superbly the figure of Pirandello's intention: vigorous yet whimsical, put upon, diplomatic and long-suffering, a hard-headed man of the theatre who is nevertheless swept up into a new dimension of experience. Among others I might mention are David Margulies and Anne Lynn of the acting troupe and Richard A. Dysart as the father. But with the exception of James Valentine's somewhat strident and oratorical conception of the son, the performances are deserving of nothing but admiration.

In case I have failed to make it clear enough, I will say again that this *Six Characters* is not to be missed. You are not likely ever to see Pirandello presented with greater imagination and vivacity or with greater fidelity to his complex vision of the relationship between levels of truth and his passionate inquiry into the nature of reality. You are not likely, for that matter, to see any play this season which comes close to matching the pleasures and excitements of this one. (*At the Martinique*)

Richard Gilman

Commonweal, February 10, 1956

THE STAGE
Pirandello

Of the four great dramatists who have given us the most profound versions of modern life in histrionic terms—Ibsen and Shaw, Pirandello, Chekhov—Pirandello alone has been denied, in our time, the fullness of stage life. Shaw is adequately served by our theatre: if not always with excellence, then at the very least with a certain status and currency and continuing interest—respect too, though perhaps not for the proper things. Ibsen indeed demands some reconstitution—one might say we have never known the essential Ibsen—yet the flinty austere beauty of his drama is variously recognized, and the rich theatrical occasions his plays offer not infrequently seized.

Reprinted from THE STAGE, PIRANDELLO, Richard Hayes, pp. 483–484, February 10, 1956. © 1956 Commonweal Publishing Co., Inc.

And a ritual piety dictates the occasional Chekhov revival, though we have had to wait for Mr. David Ross and his company at the Fourth Street Theatre to give us a full and pure account of this one great scale in contemporary drama. But Pirandello languishes, wanting insistently—like one of the hooded black presences in *Six Characters*—the total life of the imagination. Prior to the mounting of this same play, currently at the Phoenix, I recall no representations of Pirandello on our stage beyond the usual intermittent experimental skirmishes (the Living Theatre Group will revive this spring what I understand to be an excellent version of "Tonight We Improvise"), and Mr. Eric Bentley's production of the masterly "Right You Are" some summers ago at the Brattle Theatre, Cambridge.

A prodigal indifference, this—scandalous—when one considers that *Six Characters, Right You Are, Henry IV* (to instance but three) are among the most absolute plays in the contemporary repertoire: works which sustain powerfully the weight and intense pressure of the modern sensibility: existential drama, if you will—lucid with daylight disillusion and terror yet dense with the flood and torment of being. No longer need one claim for theatre: the passionate dilemmas—dualities—of his drama, their metaphysical agonies, are the same nightmare shapes and two-backed beasts that haunt the private dreams of our age. For to explore so obsessively, as Pirandello has ". . . the deceit of mutual understanding irremediably founded on the empty abstraction of words, the multiple personality of everyone (corresponding to the possibilities of being to be found in each of us), and finally the inherent tragic conflict between life (which is always moving and changing) and form (which fixes it, immutable) . . ." is to dissolve a visionary acid that veils of appearance and reality and confront something naked, ultimate. At one point in his autobiography, Mr. Stephen Spender quotes Yeats on Shakespeare: "In the end, Shakespeare's mind is terrible . . . the final reality of existence in his poetry is of a terrible kind." One could not more potently express the nature of Pirandello's particular domination—what Stark Young calls his "high and violent world of concepts and living."

It is only in the perspective of this metaphysical grandeur—yet nothing alien or remote about it: always quick, intimate, bourgeois, and hence the more awful—and the neglect that our theatre has imposed on him, that one can judge how bitter an insult to Pirandello is the production of *Six Characters In Search of an Author* at the Phoenix. I have not seen, at this theatre which promised so much and yet has scored such a lamentable record, quite so wanton an act of dramatic mutilation. It would be possible, I suppose, to claim for Mr. Tyrone Guthrie's production theatrical life within some plausible context: certainly, however, it is not Pirandello's—either the context or the life—and nowhere has new value been created or disclosed: the context is ever so much poorer, duller, less significant, and the life thin, flippant, common. Mr. Guthrie, elsewhere so distinguished and responsible a man of the theatre, is here the sportive fawn: he has come up, vulgarly, with what he takes to be the "real truth" about Pirandello—that he was a *farceur* and a metaphysical playboy, that the stain of agony which colors his work can be lightened, not with wit (it can, and is—by Pirandello), but with impertinence.

Hence Mr. Guthrie's useless pedantry in staging so timeless a drama in the bizarre costumes of 1922, the year of its first American production—a gesture, one suspects, adopted only to evoke another "Boy Friend" *frisson,* all baubles, bangles, beads and boas. Hence the outrageous parody in which the "real" actors indulge when they are attempting to reproduce the domestic tragedy of the six characters. Hence, too, the blunting of some of Pirandello's most suggestive motifs—the disposition of the sinister Madame Pace, for example, in a cheaply effective flash of Houdini smoke. This last instance is wholly characteristic of Mr. Guthrie's abrasive manipulation of the play, which begins by coarsening, and ends by corrupting it: for nothing could expose more patently his total misreading of *Six Characters* than the new ending he has fashioned and imposed on it. The profound terror which has been gathering through the play—the awareness that imagination has preempted reality, has indeed created its own reality—and which is brought finally to a violent and terrible birth, is here reduced to the dimensions of fraud, while a mocking off-stage voice ("Laugh, Clown, Laugh," shall we say?) is heard announcing a banal epistemological cliché which the philosopher in Pirandello would austerely have scorned.

In accordance with the economic law which rigidly governs the fortunes of minority drama in our theatre, we shall probably have no professional representation of Pirandello in this city for at least another decade, and thanks to Mr. Guthrie and the directors of the Phoenix, we may shore against that loss only these grotesque memories.

Richard Hayes

Objectives

You, the student after studying *Six Characters* should be able to

1. recognize that stage reality is the condition in which theatre professionals confront reality.
2. understand the plot and innovation in Luigi Pirandello's *Six Characters in Search of an Author* and how they relate to life experiences.
3. appreciate theatre professionals as artists and craftsmen who meet collaboratively to create a theatrical event.

Program Notes

Six Characters in Search of an Author

Luigi Pirandello questions the nature of reality in scenes played by both Actors and Characters; yet his drama is far from metaphysical. Instead, it is a lively and thoughtful presentation of a play in rehearsal, with conflict among a director, his cast, and intruders demanding time to put on their version of actual events involving a family, a seduction, and violent death. In an accompanying guest appearance, Ossie Davis discusses the work of the creator in the theatre. The television program consists of the whole of the central section of the play, prefaced by a condensed version of the opening.

A Listing of BBC Actors and Production Coordinators

SIX CHARACTERS IN SEARCH OF AN AUTHOR

by

Luigi Pirandello

CAST

THE CHARACTERS

THE FATHER	NIGEL STOCK
THE MOTHER	MARY WIMBUSH
THE STEPDAUGHTER	LISA HARROW
THE SON	ANTHONY CHAMBERS
THE BOY	ASHLEY KNIGHT
THE CHILD	JANE MULDOON
MADAME PACE	CLAIRE DAVENPORT

THE ACTORS AND COMPANY

THE PRODUCER	CHARLES GRAY
LEADING LADY	DIANA FAIRFAX
LEADING MAN	JOHN WESTBROOK
SECOND ACTRESS	RICHENDA CAREY
THIRD ACTRESS	JENNIFER GUY
JUVENILE LEAD	MICHAEL COCHRANE
STAGE MANAGER	JO ROWBOTTOM
PROPERTY MAN	ERIC MASON
PROPERTY ASSISTANT	SIDNEY KEAN

PRODUCTION

DESIGNER	DACRE PUNT
COSTUME DESIGNER	BARBARA KIDD
MAKE-UP SUPERVISOR	MAGGIE WEBB
DIRECTOR	JOHN SELWYN GLIBERT

Focus in Viewing

Some fifty years ago, the beginning and setting for *Six Characters in Search of an Author* were revolutionary convention changes. Prepared to see a curtain which opened onto a set designed for a production, the audience, instead, was met with an already opened curtain revealing a stage which looked as though it were waiting for a rehearsal to begin. In preparing *Six Characters* for television, the director and designer must decide how to establish the theatre setting of the play in television studio terms. In this production, the studio is set up as a studio for rehearsal without its appearing as a set of any kind. The atmosphere and activity are those found in the backstage work of theatre artists. Notice that the Actors are made up naturalistically, but the Characters all have a somewhat waxen pallor. Also notice that while the actors are informally dressed in clothing of bright colors and flashy styles, the Characters are formally dressed in dark clothes of the 1920s.

Content Viewing

1. Compare the plot structure of *Six Characters* to *Woyzeck*, *Ubu Roi* and *Sizwe Bansi*.
2. What is this play's overall theme?
3. How does Pirandello depict "Reality?" Does his attitude seem bitter, pessimistic, depressing?
4. Describe and identify two characters in this play. How does the playwright reveal and develop them? What is their function and relationship?
5. How has the playwright emphasized *entrances?*
6. What is the relationship of the Actors to each other, to the Characters? What is the relationship of the Characters to each other?
7. Do the Characters express a philosophy? How does each Character's behavior compare with the character, philosophy, and actions of the other Characters? Which of the Characters has the playwright made sympathetic?
8. Is this a play of language and thought? Does the language convey the psychological attitude of the playwright? What does the language (dialogue) reveal about the theatre condition?

Craft Viewing

1. What conventions do you need to know or accept before you can enter into the spirit of this production? Pirandello is considered a creator of conventions; in what way did he alter established conventions?
2. What significance do you see in Pirandello's having placed the action of this play on a theatre stage? How is *Six Characters* a play-within-a-play?
3. Did the director effectively, or ineffectively, adapt this play which was written for a theatre setting to a television studio setting? What or how would you have directed differently?
4. Do you agree, or disagree, with the actors' interpretations and characterizations? Explain.
5. Did the lighting, costumes, and make-up clarify and support the production? Explain.
6. Is there one moment or scene which stands out in your memory? More than one? Which ones, and why?

Critical Viewing

1. How is *Six Characters* a reflection of the philosophy of the time (1920's) when it was written?
2. Now that this play and its production are part of your experience, what significance does *Six Characters in Search of an Author* hold for you?

Additional Plays That Demonstrate Similar Concepts

Right You are, If You Think You are—Luigi Pirandello
Our Town, The Skin of Our Teeth—Thornton Wilder
Camino Real—Tennessee Williams
Man and Superman ("Don Juan in Hell")—George Bernard Shaw
Who's Afraid of Virginia Woolf?—Edward Albee
The Caretaker—Harold Pinter
The Real Inspector Hound—Tom Stoppard
The Roar of the Greasepaint, The Smell of the Crowd and *Stop the World, I Want to Get Off*—both by Anthony Newley and Leslie Bricuse

Stage Terms

Relativism—Knowledge is relative to the conditions of knowing limited to the nature of the mind.
Satire—A work that holds up human vices and follies to scorn.